iPod® & iTunes® FOR DUMMIES®

4TH EDITION

by Tony Bove and Cheryl Rhodes

WILEY

Wiley Publishing, Inc.

iPod® & iTunes® For Dummies,® 4th Edition

Published by
Wiley Publishing, Inc.
111 River Street
Hoboken, NJ 07030-5774
www.wiley.com

WILEY

About the Authors

Tony Bove (www.tonybove.com) has written more than two dozen books on computing, desktop publishing, and multimedia, including *iLife '04 All-in-One Desk Reference For Dummies* (Wiley), *The GarageBand Book* (Wiley), *The Art of Desktop Publishing* (Bantam), and a series of books about Macromedia Director, Adobe Illustrator, and PageMaker. Tony also founded *Publish* magazine and the *Inside Report on New Media* newsletter, and he wrote the weekly Macintosh column for *Computer Currents* for a decade, as well as articles for *NeXTWORLD*, the *Chicago Tribune* Sunday Technology Section, and *NewMedia*. Tracing the personal computer revolution back to the 1960s counterculture, Tony produced a CD-ROM interactive documentary in 1996, *Haight-Ashbury in the Sixties* (featuring music from the Grateful Dead, Janis Joplin, and the Jefferson Airplane). He also developed the Rockument music site, www.rockument.com, with commentary and radio programs focused on rock music history. As a founding member of the Flying Other Brothers (www.flyingotherbros.com), which tours professionally and has released two commercial CDs (*52-Week High* and *San Francisco Sounds*), Tony has performed with Hall-of-Fame rock musicians and uses his iPod to store extensive concert recordings. Tony has also worked as a director of enterprise marketing for a large software company, and as a communications director and technical publications manager.

Cheryl Rhodes has co-authored more than a dozen books on computing, desktop publishing, and multimedia, including *iLife '04 All-in-One Desk Reference For Dummies* (Wlley), *The Art of Desktop Publishing* (Bantam), and a series of books about Macromedia Director, Adobe Illustrator, and PageMaker. Cheryl contributed to the influential *Inside Report on New Media* newsletter and wrote articles for *NeXTWORLD*, *Computer Currents*, the *Chicago Tribune* Sunday Technology Section, and *NewMedia*. Cheryl also co-founded and edited *Desktop Publishing/Publish* magazine. Cheryl recently founded and served as director of a charter school and has worked as a professional courseware designer and an instructor in computer courses at elementary and high schools.

Dedication

This book is dedicated to John Paul Bove and James Eric Bove, both of whom contributed tips and spent considerable time testing iPods.

Authors' Acknowledgments

We want to thank John Paul and Jimi for providing technical expertise and performing valuable testing. We also want to thank Rich Tennant for his wonderful cartoons. And let's not forget our Wiley editors Rebecca Senninger and Virginia Sanders for ongoing assistance that made our job so much easier. A book this timely places a considerable burden on a publisher's production team, and we thank the production crew at Wiley for diligence beyond the call of reason.

We owe thanks and a happy hour or three to Carole McLendon at Waterside, our agent. And we have acquisitions editor Bob Woerner at Wiley to thank for coming up with the idea for this book and helping us to become professional dummies — that is, dummy authors.

Finally, our heartfelt thanks to members of the Flying Other Brothers (Pete Sears, Barry Sless, Jimmy Sanchez, Bill Bennett, Bert Keely, TBone, Roger and Ann McNamee, and G.E. Smith) for the music that inspired us while writing this book.

Publisher's Acknowledgments

We're proud of this book; please send us your comments through our online registration form located at www.dummies.com/register/.

Some of the people who helped bring this book to market include the following:

Acquisitions, Editorial, and Media Development

Project Editor: Rebecca Senninger

(Previous Edition: Tonya Maddox Cupp)

Acquisitions Editor: Bob Woerner

Copy Editor: Virginia Sanders

Technical Editor: Dennis Cohen

Editorial Manager: Leah Cameron

Media Development Specialists: Angela Denny, Kate Jenkins, Steven Kudirka, Kit Malone

Media Development Coordinator: Laura Atkinson

Media Project Supervisor: Laura Moss

Media Development Manager: Laura VanWinkle

Editorial Assistant: Amanda Foxworth

Sr. Editorial Assistant: Cherie Case

Cartoons: Rich Tennant (www.the5thwave.com)

Composition Services

Project Coordinator: Ryan Steffen

Layout and Graphics: Claudia Bell, Lauren Goddard, Denny Hager, Joyce Haughey, Barbara Moore, Alicia B. South, Ronald Terry

Proofreaders: Jessica Kramer, Christy Pingleton, Techbooks

Indexer: Techbooks

Special Help

Teresa Artman, Jennifer Riggs

Publishing and Editorial for Technology Dummies

    Richard Swadley, Vice President and Executive Group Publisher

    Andy Cummings, Vice President and Publisher

    Mary Bednarek, Executive Acquisitions Director

    Mary C. Corder, Editorial Director

Publishing for Consumer Dummies

    Diane Graves Steele, Vice President and Publisher

    Joyce Pepple, Acquisitions Director

Composition Services

    Gerry Fahey, Vice President of Production Services

    Debbie Stailey, Director of Composition Services

Table of Contents

Introduction

You don't need much imagination to see why we're so happy with our iPods.

Imagine no longer needing CDs. We take road trips that last for weeks, and we never hear the same song twice. We leave our music library safe at home and grab an iPod for a hike or jog and always listen to something different.

Imagine no longer needing DVDs (or, heaven forbid, ancient VHS cassettes). We can take our favorite videos with us on the road and watch them on our iPods or connect our iPods to televisions to see them on larger screens. The iPod is a convenient video player that holds over 100 hours of video. That represents far more DVDs than you would normally carry with you on the road.

Imagine not waiting for hot new music or a hot TV show. You can purchase the content and load it onto your iPod within minutes of discovering it on the Internet. Be the first in your circle of friends to experience the exclusive new music and videos available from the iTunes Music Store.

Imagine not having to buy music and videos more than once. You can purchase a CD or downloadable music and import the music into a digital library that lasts forever. You can purchase a video or convert your favorite videos and add them to your everlasting library. Imagine never again having to replace an unplayable CD or DVD.

Imagine a musician going backstage after a performance and meeting a promoter who says that he can get him ten more gigs if he can confirm the dates *right now*. This musician calmly scrolls through his calendar for the entire year (conveniently stored on his iPod), finding all the details that he needs about gigs and recording sessions, right down to the minute, including travel directions to each gig. "No problem," he says. And of course, he gets the gigs.

Okay, maybe you're not a rock star whose career depends on the information on your iPod. But if rock stars can use them, so can average music lovers.

When we first encountered the iPod, it came very close to fulfilling our dreams as road warriors — in particular, the dream of filling up our cars with music as easily as filling it up with fuel. Tony uses an iPod with the Alpine KCA-420i, an in-vehicle interface adapter, which lets him plug any iPod with a dock connection into a compatible 2004 Alpine Ai-NET head unit. That unit can be installed in just about any car. (It works great in a Volkswagen Passat.) Another car integration is available for BMW cars — you can control an iPod or iPod mini through the BMW audio system and multifunction steering wheel. Whether you want to be *On the Road* with Jack Kerouac (in audio book form) or "Drivin' South" with Jimi Hendrix, just fill up your iPod and go!

About This Book

We designed *iPod & iTunes For Dummies,* 4th Edition, as a reference. You can easily find the information you need when you need it. We organized the information so that you can read from beginning to end to find out how to use iTunes and your iPod from scratch. But this book is also designed so that you can dive in anywhere and begin reading the info you need to know for each task.

We don't cover every detail of every function of the software, and we intentionally leave out some detail so that we don't befuddle you with techno-speak when it's not necessary. (Really, engineers can sometimes provide too many obscure choices that no one ever uses.) We write brief but comprehensive descriptions and include lots of cool tips on how to get the best results from using iTunes and your iPod.

If your PC is on the trailing edge rather than the leading edge, don't worry — you won't miss out on the iPod revolution. True, if you don't use Windows 2000 or Windows XP on your PC, you can't use iTunes for Windows. However, if you use Windows Me (Millennium Edition), you can use Musicmatch Jukebox. Please note that if you're using Musicmatch, you can find that content online. A companion Web site is available for you at `www.dummies.com/go/ipod4e`.

At the time we wrote this book, we covered every iPod available and the latest version of iTunes. Although we do our best to keep up, Apple occasionally slips a new iPod model or new version of iTunes in between book editions. If you've bought a new iPod that's not covered in the book or your version of iTunes looks a little different, be sure to check out the companion Web site (`www.dummies.com/go/ipod4e`) for updates on the latest releases from Apple.

Conventions Used in This Book

Like any book that covers computers and information technology, this book uses certain conventions:

✔ **Choosing from a menu:** In iTunes, when you see "Choose iTunes⇨ Preferences in iTunes," you click iTunes on the toolbar and then click Preferences on the iTunes menu.

With the iPod, when you see "Choose Extras⇨Calendars from the iPod main menu," you highlight Extras in the main menu with the scroll wheel, press the Select button to select Extras, and then highlight and select Calendars from the Extras menu.

✔ **Clicking and dragging:** When you see "Drag the song over the name of the playlist," we mean click the song name, hold the mouse button down, and drag the song with the mouse over to the name of the playlist before lifting your finger off the mouse button.

✔ **Keyboard shortcuts:** When you see ⌘-I, press the ⌘ key on a Mac keyboard, along with the appropriate shortcut key. (In this case, press I, which opens the Song Information window in iTunes.) In Windows, the same keyboard shortcut is Ctrl-I (which means press the Ctrl key along with the I key).

✔ **Step lists:** When you come across steps you need to do in iTunes or on the iPod, the action is in bold, and the explanatory part is underneath. If you know what to do, read the action and skip the explanation. But if you need a little help along the way, check out the explanation.

And Just Who Are You?

You don't need to know anything about music or audio technology to discover how to make the most of your iPod and the iTunes software that comes with it. Although a course in music appreciation can't hurt, the iPod is designed to be useful even for air-guitar players who barely know the difference between downloadable music and System of a Down. You don't need any specialized knowledge to have a lot of fun with your iPod and the iTunes software while building up your digital music library.

However, we do make some honest assumptions about your computer skills:

✔ **You know how to use the Mac Finder or Windows Explorer:** We assume that you already know how to locate files and folders and that you can copy files and folders from one hard drive to another on the computer of your choice: a Mac or a Windows PC.

✔ **You know how to select menus and applications on a Mac or a Windows PC:** We assume that you already know how to choose an option from a menu; how to find the Dock on a Mac to launch a Dock application (or use the Start menu in Windows to launch an application); and how to launch an application directly by double-clicking its icon.

For more information on these topics, see that excellent book by Mark L. Chambers, *Mac OS X All-in-One Desk Reference For Dummies,* or the massive tome *Windows XP GigaBook For Dummies,* by Peter Weverka and company (both from Wiley).

A Quick Peek Ahead

This book is organized into six parts, and each part covers a different aspect of using your iPod. Here's a quick preview of what you can find in each part.

Part I: Setting Up and Acquiring Media Content

This part gets you started with your iPod, powering it up, recharging its battery, using its menus, and connecting it to your computer. You install and set up the iPod and iTunes software on your Mac or Windows PC. We show you what you can do with iTunes. To acquire music, you can buy music from the iTunes Music Store or rip audio CDs. You can also find podcasts, audio books, and videos in the iTunes Music Store or import them into iTunes from other sources. You can even play Web radio stations.

Part II: Managing Your Media Content

This part shows you how to sort the content in your iTunes library by artist, album, duration, date, and other items. You can add and edit iTunes song information. You discover how to arrange songs and albums into iTunes playlists that you can transfer to your iPod. When you have your music, audio books, podcasts, photos, and videos organized efficiently, transfer them to the iPod. For your peace of mind, we also cover backing up your content library, burning CDs, and printing CD jewel case inserts with the song information.

Part III: Playing Your iPod

We show you how to locate and play all types of content — music, audio books, podcasts, and videos — on your iPod. We also describe how to connect your iPod to your home stereo or speakers, and to a television for a larger video picture. You then discover how to fine-tune the sound playback with the iTunes equalizer and on your iPod with the iPod equalizer.

Part IV: Using Advanced Techniques

In this part, you discover digital music encoding and how to change your importing preferences. We describe what you need to record sound and music into your computer from old records and tapes, and you find out how to modify songs in iTunes for playback on your iPod.

Part V: Have iPod, Will Travel

This part covers how to use your iPod on the road with car stereos and portable speakers. You find out all the techniques of an iPod road warrior: setting your alarm clock, sorting your contacts, recording voice memos, entering personal information into your computer (such as calendar appointments, To-Do lists, and contacts), and synchronizing your iPod with all your personal information. We also provide troubleshooting first steps and details about updating and restoring your iPod.

Part VI: The Part of Tens

In this book's Part of Tens chapters, we outline common problems and solutions for most iPods and provide tips about the iPod equalizer.

Bonus Chapters

This book includes bonus chapters about using Musicmatch Jukebox on a Windows PC to manage your iPod music library. You can find these chapters on the companion Web site at www.dummies.com/go/ipod4e.

Icons Used in This Book

The icons in this book are important visual cues for information you need.

Remember icons highlight important things you need to remember.

Technical Stuff icons highlight technical details you can skip unless you want to bring out the technical geek in you.

Tip icons highlight tips and techniques that save you time and energy, and maybe money.

Warning icons save your butt by preventing disasters. Don't bypass a Warning without reading it. This is your only warning!

On the Web icons let you know when a topic is covered further online at www.dummies.com/go/ipod4e, this book's companion Web site.

Part I
Setting Up and Acquiring Media Content

The 5th Wave   By Rich Tennant

"I wish you'd take the theme from 'Rocky' off your workout playlist."

In this part . . .

*P*art I shows you how to do all the essential tasks with your iPod and iTunes.

- ✔ Chapter 1 gets you started with your iPod. Here you find out how to get the most from your battery, use the menus and buttons, connect your iPod to your Mac or PC, and reset your iPod.

- ✔ Chapter 2 describes how to install the iPod software and iTunes on a Mac or on a Windows PC.

- ✔ Chapter 3 gets you started with iTunes on a Mac or a Windows PC.

- ✔ Chapter 4 covers purchasing content online from the iTunes Music Store.

- ✔ Chapter 5 describes how to get music, audio books, videos, and podcasts into your iTunes library.

- ✔ Chapter 6 describes how to play the music, audio books, videos, radio shows, and podcasts in your iTunes library.

- ✔ Chapter 7 shows how you can share content (legally) with other iTunes users on your network and copy items to other computers (even songs, audio books, and videos purchased online).

Chapter 1

Firing Up Your iPod

● ●

In This Chapter

▶ Comparing iPod models

▶ Powering up your iPod

▶ Using and recharging your battery

▶ Scrolling through the iPod main menu

▶ Resetting the iPod

● ●

The B-52s sing "Roam if you want to, roam around the world" through your headphones as you take off. The flight is just long enough to watch the "Mr. Monk and the Airplane" episode from the first series of the *Monk* TV show and catch up on the latest episodes of *The Daily Show with Jon Stewart* and *The Colbert Report* — it's so easy to hold and watch your iPod that you don't have to put it away when your flight dinner arrives. You even have time to listen to the "NFL Rants and Raves" podcast to catch up on American football. As the plane lands, you momentarily forget where it is you're going — so you read your destination information on your iPod without even pausing the podcast, and you queue up a playlist of songs to get you through the terminal. If Chicago is your kind of town, you might choose Frank Sinatra. If San Francisco, you might choose anything from Tony Bennett to the Grateful Dead. You have so much content on your iPod, and you can select and play it so easily, that you probably could land anywhere in the world with appropriate music in your ear and convenient eye candy in your hand.

First the iPod changed the way people play music on-the-run, and now it's changing the way people play TV shows and videos. A full-size video iPod holds so much music that no matter how large your music collection is, you will seriously consider putting all your music into digital format on your computer, transferring portions of it to the iPod, and playing music from both your computer and your iPod from now on. And why wait for the best episodes of your favorite TV shows to be broadcast, when you can download the shows anytime you want and play them on a video iPod anywhere you want? Albums, music videos, TV shows, and movies — you might never stop buying CDs and DVDs, but you won't have to buy *all* your content that way. And you'll never again need to replace the content that you already own.

As an iPod owner, you're on the cutting edge of entertainment technology. This chapter introduces the iPod and tells you what to expect when you open the box. We describe how to power up your iPod and connect it to your computer, both of which are essential tasks that you need to know how to do — your iPod needs power, and it needs audio and video, which it gets from your computer.

Introducing the iPod

The iPod is, essentially, a hard drive or flash memory drive, and a digital music and video player in one device. But that device is such a thing of beauty and style and so highly recognizable by now that all Apple needs to do in an advertisement is show it all by itself.

The convenience of carrying music on an iPod is phenomenal. For example, the 80GB iPod model can hold around 20,000 songs. That's about a month of nonstop music played around the clock — or about one new song a day for the next 54 years. And with the iPod's built-in skip protection in every model, you don't miss a beat as you jog through the park or when your car hits a pothole.

Although Apple has every right to continue to promote its Macintosh computers, the company saw the wisdom of making the iPod compatible with Windows PCs. Every iPod now comes with the software that you need to make it work with Windows systems as well as Macintosh OS X.

A common misconception is that your iPod becomes your music and video library. Actually, your iPod is simply another *player* for your content library, which is safely stored on your computer. One considerable benefit of using your *computer* to organize your content is that you can make perfect-quality copies of music, videos, podcasts, and audio books. You can then copy as much of the content as you want, in a more compressed format, onto your iPod and take it on the road. Meanwhile, your perfect copies are stored safely on your computer. Your favorite albums, TV shows, videos, and podcast episodes can be copied over and over forever, just like the rest of your information, and they never lose their quality. If you save your content in digital format, you will never see your songs or videos degrade, and you'll never have to buy the content again.

The iPod experience includes iTunes (or, in older-generation Windows models, Musicmatch Jukebox), which lets you organize your content in digital form, make copies, burn CDs, and play disc jockey without discs. Without iTunes (or Musicmatch Jukebox), your iPod is merely an external hard drive. As a result of using iTunes (or Musicmatch Jukebox), your content library is essentially permanent because you can make backup copies that are absolutely the same in quality. We introduce iTunes in Chapter 2.

If you're using Musicmatch, visit the companion Web site at `www.dummies.com/go/ipod4e` to find out how to use Musicmatch.

The iPod is also a *data player,* perhaps the first of its kind. As an external hard drive, the iPod serves as a portable backup device for important data files. You can transfer your calendar and address book to help manage your affairs on the road, and you can even use calendar event alarms to supplement your iPod's alarm and sleep timer. Although the iPod isn't as fully functional as a personal digital assistant (PDA) — for example, you can't add information directly to the device — you can view the information. You can keep your calendar and address book automatically synchronized to your computer, where you normally add and edit information. We cover using the iPod as a data player in detail in Chapter 22 and as a general-purpose hard drive in Chapter 23.

Comparing iPod Models

Introduced way back in the Stone Age of digital music (2001), the iPod family has grown by five generations as of this writing, and it has spawned more than 20 different models, including a private-label version (the HPod from Hewlett-Packard), a custom version (iPod U2 Special Edition, featuring all of U2's songs), and offshoots such as the popular iPod nano, iPod mini, and iPod shuffle. Even from the beginning, iPod models were truly innovative for their times. With the MP3 music players of 2001, you could carry about 20 typical songs (or a single live Phish set) with you, but the first iPod could hold more than 1,000 typical songs (or a 50-hour Phish concert).

Today's iPod works with iTunes on either Windows computers or Macs, but that wasn't always the case. The first-generation iPods worked only with Macs. In 2002, Apple introduced the second generation — one version for Windows and another for the Mac, using the same design for both. For the third generation (2003), Apple changed the design once again.

Third-, fourth-, and fifth-generation iPods, and offshoots such as iPod mini, iPod nano, and iPod shuffle, work with either Windows or Mac and come in a variety of hard-drive or flash-memory sizes. One way to tell what kind of iPod you have is by its navigational controls. By design, you can hold an iPod in your hand while you thumb the *scroll wheel* (our generic term for scroll wheel, scroll pad, touch wheel, or click wheel). The LCD screen on full-size models offers backlighting so that you can see it in the dark.

For a nifty chart that shows the differences between iPod models, see the Identifying Different iPod Models page on the Apple iPod Web site (`http://docs.info.apple.com/article.html?artnum=61688`).

First-generation iPods

Apple doesn't sell first-generation iPods anymore, but you might see a few on eBay. More likely, their proud owners are Mac users who still find them useful. Despite its high price tag ($399) compared with other MP3 players, the first 5GB iPod (with 5GB of storage space) was an unqualified success when it was introduced in October 2001. Apple sold more than 125,000 units within 60 days. "Listening to music will never be the same again," Apple CEO Steve Jobs told the press at the introduction of the first iPod, and he was right. Months later, Apple introduced the 10GB model.

First-generation iPods work only with Macs, connecting to a Mac with a standard FireWire cable. The first generation offers a distinctive scroll wheel that physically turns with your finger as you use it. These early iPods are hefty at 6.5 ounces and have a stainless-steel back and dual-plastic top casing.

FireWire is called *IEEE 1394* by the engineers who designed it and *DV terminal* by camcorder manufacturers that use it, except Sony, which calls it *i.Link*.

These models don't offer all the features of newer generations and can't be used with accessories that are designed for newer generations. For example, you can't expect these older models to use extensions such as voice recorders and memory card readers. First-generation models can't be updated to version 2 or newer versions of the iPod software, so they also lack support for features such as adding notes to the iPod and setting up an on-the-go playlist. However, battery life is comparable to newer models, offering up to eight hours before requiring a recharge. (For more about battery life, see "Facing Charges of Battery," later in this chapter.)

Second-generation iPods

Apple introduced a second-generation design in the form of two models: the 20GB iPod for the Mac and the 10GB for Windows. The Windows model of the second generation shipped with Musicmatch Jukebox. Apple doesn't sell these anymore either, but you might find one on eBay.

Second-generation models use an innovative solid-state touch wheel that doesn't physically turn as you use it but instead responds to finger pressure. These models use a standard FireWire connection to connect to the computer with a six-pin FireWire cable.

Second-generation models can't be updated to version 2 or 3 of the iPod software, so they don't offer all the features of the third, fourth, and fifth generation and can't be used with dock-connector and voice recorder accessories designed for newer models. Although standard FireWire accessories (such as power adapters for automobiles) are available for these models, digital camera accessories such as memory card readers are not (as of this writing).

Third-generation iPods

The third-generation models include the 10GB, 15GB, and 30GB models introduced in 2003, and the 20GB and 40GB models introduced later in that same year. All have been discontinued, but you can find them on eBay. All third-generation models share the same basic features and work with Mac or Windows, and Apple continually provides software updates for these models.

Models of the third generation are thinner than the second generation and use touch-sensitive buttons with audible feedback (replacing the pressure-sensitive buttons of the second generation that offer tactile feedback). Third-generation models also use a *dock connector* to connect to a computer or power supply; see Figure 1-1. The dock keeps your iPod in an upright position while connected and lets you connect a home stereo or headphones, which makes the dock convenient as a base station when you're not traveling with your iPod — you can slip the iPod into the dock without connecting cables.

The dock didn't come standard with the 15GB model, but you can order it as an extra from the Apple Store.

The supplied cables connect to the dock on one end (or to the iPod itself if you don't use a dock) and connect to a computer or power supply on the other end, using standard FireWire or USB 2.0. Some models did not include the USB cable, but you can order it from the Apple Store for about $20. (PC users crave choice. You can read about USB in the sidebar "USB or FireWire: That is the question" in this chapter.)

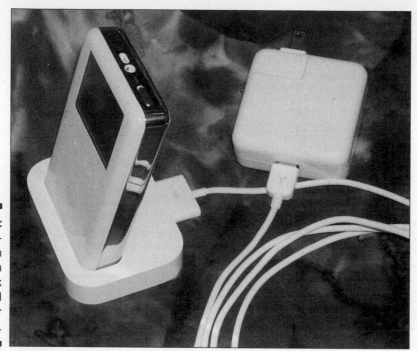

Figure 1-1:
The third-
generation
iPod in
its dock
connected
to the power
adapter.

iPod mini

iPod mini, an offshoot of the third generation, is small enough to fit in a
shirt pocket; see Figure 1-2. Its smooth, ultra-thin, anodized aluminum case
came in five different colors. Apple has since phased out iPod mini (replaced
essentially by iPod nano), but you can find one on eBay. The original model
houses a 4GB drive that can hold about 1,000 songs — as much as the original 5GB model. Newer models sport a 6GB drive that holds about 1,500 songs.
(iPod mini can fit more songs in the same amount of space because Apple
introduced a better compression format called AAC in second-generation
models. The AAC format can also be used in older models, so when Apple
introduced AAC, the capacity of all models increased.)

Besides its smaller size (and therefore, smaller dock), another of iPod mini's
distinguishing characteristic is the click wheel, which offers the same functions as the third-generation iPod touch wheel but is more suitable for such
a small device. The click wheel combines the scroll wheel and buttons, with
pressure-sensitive buttons underneath the top, bottom, left, and right areas
of the circular pad of the wheel.

Figure 1-2:
iPod mini
fits in a shirt
pocket.

iPod mini has the same features as full-size third-generation iPods except that it uses a different set of accessories because of its size, and it offers up to 18 hours of battery time between charges. We describe both types of iPods and their accessories throughout this book.

Fourth-generation and color-display iPods

In 2004, Apple introduced a fourth-generation iPod that uses the same click wheel and buttons that iPod mini uses. Fourth-generation iPod software includes the ability to randomly shuffle song playback with the press of a button, and to charge up the iPod through the USB connection to your computer. The fourth-generation iPods were at first available in 40GB and 20GB models with black-and-white displays. Later in 2004, Apple offered 30GB and 60GB models with color displays that can store photos and display slideshows. The fifth-generation models have replaced the fourth generation, but you can find these in some stores and on eBay.

The fourth-generation units with black-and-white displays offer up to 12 hours of battery time between charges. You can play up to 15 hours of continuous music on a color-display iPod between charges or up to five hours of continuous slideshows with music. The battery is the same type as used in other models — the improvement is in how the software manages power in the iPod. Like third-generation iPods, the fourth generation also uses a dock connector to connect the iPod to a computer or power supply, and the dock itself is available separately from the Apple Store. The fourth-generation iPods connect to computers by using either FireWire or USB connections.

The fourth-generation iPod models differ from earlier models by offering a top-level Music choice on the main menu and the ability to create multiple on-the-go playlists. You can also play audio books at slower or faster speeds while maintaining natural-sounding pitch.

The iPod color-display models of the fourth generation, including the earliest model known as *iPod photo,* let you store and view color digital photos as well as store and play sound. These models also do everything a fourth-generation iPod can do and use the same accessories. Apple offered a 20GB model and a whopping 60GB model that can hold up to 15,000 songs and full-color album cover art — or as many as 25,000 photos.

The 60GB iPod with color display uses the same click wheel and buttons iPod mini uses. The color display provides crisp definition for the iPod's menus, making them easier to read, even in sunlight.

The iPod color display, at 220-x-176 pixel resolution and over 65,000 colors, offers excellent viewing with built-in backlighting. With the optional AV cable, you can connect the iPod to a television monitor or video projector for a video-quality slideshow. It even optimizes your photos to fit on a standard (4:3 ratio) or widescreen (16:9 ratio) TV.

Fifth-generation iPods with video

Apple shook the world once again in late 2005 by introducing a new generation of iPod that plays video along with music and photos. The fifth-generation iPod is a bit slimmer than the previous generation while adding a generous 2.5-inch color display that offers remarkable picture clarity for video content.

As of this writing, Apple provides a 30GB model that holds about 7,500 songs or about 40 hours of video, and its battery offers up to 14 hours of music playback, 4 hours of slideshows with music, or 3.5 hours of video playback.

The 80GB fifth-generation iPod (shown in Figure 1-3), holds about 20,000 songs or about 100 hours of video, and its battery offers up to 20 hours of music playback, 6 hours of slideshows with music, or 6.5 hours of video playback. Both fifth-generation iPods use the same click wheel and buttons as the fourth-generation models.

You can put videos on your fifth-generation iPod by using iTunes. You can even get some of your favorite TV shows, plus music videos, movie trailers, and short films, directly from the iTunes online store. The color display provides crisp definition for the iPod's menus, making them easier to read, even in sunlight. The iPod color display, at 320-x-240-pixel resolution and over 65,000 colors, offers excellent viewing with built-in backlighting. With the optional AV cable, you can connect the iPod to a television monitor or video projector to show videos and slideshows. It even optimizes your photos to fit on a standard (4:3 ratio) or widescreen (16:9 ratio) TV.

Like fourth-generation iPods, the fifth generation also uses a dock connector to connect the iPod to a computer or power supply, and the dock itself is available separately from the Apple Store. The fifth-generation iPods connect to computers by using USB connections.

Figure 1-3:
Fifth-generation iPods with color displays let you play not only music, but also videos and photo slideshows.

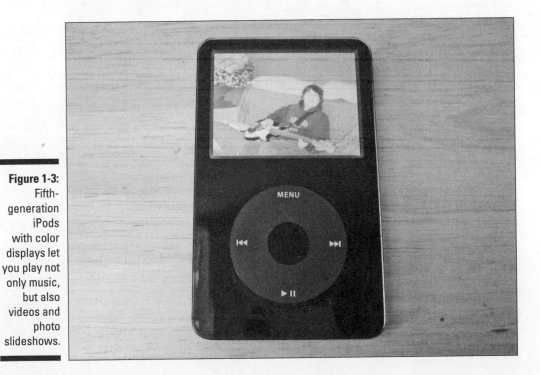

Mano a mano with iPod nano

Honey, Apple shrunk the iPod. The pencil-thin iPod nano is only 3.5 x 1.6 inches and weighs only 1.4 ounces — and packed into this mini marvel is a 1.5-inch color LCD display that crisply displays the iPod menus and album artwork. Apple offers a 2GB model that holds about 500 songs; a 4GB model that holds about 1,000 songs; and an 8GB model, shown in Figure 1-4, that holds 2,000 songs. Each model offers a battery that can play up to 24 hours of music or 5 hours of slideshows with music.

Figure 1-4: iPod nano is the smallest iPod that can display photos as well as menus, calendars, and contacts in color.

You read that right — the little wonder can also display photos just like full-size color-display iPods. It is also the smallest iPod that can serve up your personal calendar and contacts. Unlike the smaller iPod shuffle, iPod nano is a full-featured iPod with loads of accessories tailored specifically for it.

iPod nano uses the same style of click wheel and buttons as the fifth-generation models. Like fifth-generation iPods, iPod nano also uses a dock connector to connect to a computer or power supply. iPod nano connects to computers by using USB connections.

Doing the iPod shuffle

If the regular iPod models are not small enough to fit into your lifestyle, try iPod shuffle. iPod shuffle, shown in Figure 1-5, is 1.07 inches long, 1.62 inches wide, and 0.41 inches thick (including the built-in clip). It weighs about half an ounce, which is little more than a car key or pack of gum. With its ultra-compact design and built-in clip, the iPod shuffle is the most wearable iPod.

The 1GB iPod shuffle can hold 240 songs — assuming an average of 4 minutes per song, using the AAC format at the High Quality setting (as described in Chapter 18). Remember, iPod shuffle is not for storing music permanently — you use it just to play selections from your iTunes library on your computer. It has no display, but that's actually a good thing because it keeps the size and weight down to a minimum — and you don't need a display to play a couple hundred songs in random or sequential order. You can also use your iPod shuffle to hold data files, just like an external flash memory drive.

Figure 1-5: An iPod shuffle weighs about half an ounce and offers skip-free playback.

With skip-free playback, lightweight design, and no need for a display, you can easily use it while skiing, snowboarding, or even skydiving. That's because it uses flash memory rather than a hard drive — you can shake it as hard as you want without a glitch. iPod shuffle's battery offers up to 12 hours of power between charges.

Unlike other iPods, iPod shuffle can't play tunes in the Apple Lossless format, which consumes a lot of storage space but is higher in sonic quality. You can play songs in the AAC format (including songs from the online iTunes Music Store) or the MP3 format. These formats compress the music to use much less space. You can also use the Audible book format and the uncompressed AIFF or WAV format. On Windows PCs, you can use the free WMV format but not the copyright-protected WMV format. See Chapter 18 for more details on encoding formats.

The headphone jack on your iPod shuffle does double-duty as a dock connector. Flip iPod shuffle upside-down and drop it into the dock that was included with your iPod shuffle and then connect the dock to your computer via USB for a quick sync and to recharge its battery. iPod shuffle charges its battery from your computer, so you don't need the optional power supply. You can also get the optional $29 iPod power adapter to charge your iPod at home, on the road, or whenever your iPod is not connected to a computer.

Thinking Inside the Box

Don't destroy the elegantly designed box while opening it; you might want to place it prominently in your collection of Technology That Ushered in the 21st Century. Before going any further, check the box and make sure that all the correct parts came with your iPod.

Things you have and things you need

The fifth-generation iPod box includes earphones, a CD-ROM with the iTunes software for the Mac and Windows PC, and the USB cable you can use to connect your iPod to a computer. You can get accessories, including an AC power adapter, separately — for example, the iPod AV Connection Kit offers the adapter, AV cables, Apple Remote, and the iPod Universal Dock with adapters for all models.

The accessories don't stop there — you might also have a carrying case and some other goodies, many of which we describe in this book. They are available at the online Apple Store (www.apple.com/store).

You also need a few things that don't come with the iPod:

- ✔ **A PC or Mac to run iTunes:** On a PC, iTunes requires Windows 2000 or XP, a 500 MHz Pentium-class processor or faster, and a minimum of 128MB (256MB or more recommended). With a Mac, iTunes requires Mac OS X 10.2.8 or newer for connecting with FireWire (OS X 10.3.4 or newer for connecting via USB or for using AirPort Express); a 500 MHz G3 processor or better; and at least 256MB of RAM. The iTunes installer for the PC also installs the newest version of QuickTime, replacing any older version you might have. Macs have QuickTime preinstalled; however, you might need to upgrade your version of QuickTime to the newest version to use purchased music from the iTunes Music Store in other iLife applications on a Mac.

- ✔ **A PC to run Musicmatch Jukebox** *(alternative to iTunes):* You can alternatively use the iPod with Musicmatch Jukebox and a 300 MHz or faster PC with at least 96MB of RAM running Windows 98, Windows Me, 2000, or XP (with at least 128MB of RAM).

  If you're using Musicmatch, visit the companion Web site at www.dummies.com/go/ipod4e to discover the requirements to run it.

- ✔ **USB connection:** PCs must have USB 2.0 (also called a *high-powered USB*) for fifth-generation iPods and iPod nano; you can use FireWire (also called IEEE 1394) with older models. All current-model Macs provide USB 2.0, and all Macs provide FireWire. See the sidebar, "USB or FireWire: That is the question," in this chapter for more information about FireWire and USB 2.0.

- ✔ **FireWire (also called IEEE 1394) cable** *(alternative to USB):* Although older iPod models came with a FireWire cable, fourth- and fifth-generation iPods are supplied with just a USB cable for connecting to either a Mac or a PC. However, you can use a FireWire cable, available from the Apple Store, to connect any iPod with a dock connector to the AC power supply to provide power. You can also use FireWire with first-, second-, and third-generation iPods to connect to your computer. Fourth- and fifth-generation iPods and iPod nano use USB to connect to your computer. If you have an older computer that offers the slower USB 1.0 or 1.1 standard and a newer iPod that updates only via USB, consider upgrading your computer to get faster throughput with USB 2.0 when updating your iPod.

- ✔ **iTunes 6.0.5 or newer:** You can download Mac or Windows versions for free from the Apple Web site (www.apple.com/itunes). The CD-ROM supplied with current-model iPods should have both versions of iTunes as well. Older models, still available in stores and online, might include versions of iTunes as old as version 4.5 — which is fine because version 4.5 works. (It just doesn't have all the features of 6.4.) You can download a newer version at any time to replace it.

✔ **Musicmatch Jukebox for PCs** *(alternative to iTunes):* CD-ROMs supplied with some older iPod models provided Musicmatch Jukebox instead on iTunes. You can use Musicmatch Jukebox if you don't meet the requirements to run iTunes.

✔ **Applications for managing contacts and calendars** *(optional):* Mac users can install Address Book (for managing contacts) and iCal (for managing calendars), both of which can synchronize your iPod with contacts and calendars. Both are available for free from www.apple.com. Windows users can use Outlook or Outlook Express for creating a contacts list and calendars for an iPod.

Using USB or FireWire cables

Current iPod models — the fifth generation and iPod nano — are supplied with a cable that has a USB connector on one end and a flat dock connector on the other end to connect to a dock or to the iPod itself. You can connect the USB end to either the AC adaptor or the computer's USB 2.0 port.

FireWire (called IEEE 1394 in PC circles) is another high-speed connection and power cable, supported by all generations except the current fifth-generation iPod. Fifth-generation iPods and iPod nano use USB to connect to the computer, not FireWire, so if you have the latest video iPod or iPod nano, you can skip all discussions about FireWire — unless you want to use a FireWire cable just to provide power to your iPod.

An older USB port works for synchronizing your iPod, but it doesn't provide power to the iPod. If all you have is an older USB port, you can use it to synchronize your fifth-generation iPod or iPod nano, and then use a FireWire cable (available from the Apple Store) to provide power by connecting it to a FireWire-compatible AC power adapter.

The connection on the bottom of the iPod is the same as the connection on the back of the dock. Plug the flat connector of the cable into the iPod or dock, and then plug the USB connector on the other end into the USB port on your computer.

iPod shuffle offers only a USB connector: Remove the cap from one end and connect it directly to the USB or USB 2.0 connection on your Mac. You can also use an iPod shuffle Dock or a USB extension cable (available from Apple at www.ipod.com/store).

USB or FireWire: That is the question

Current fifth-generation iPods and iPod nano models use USB to connect to computers, so USB is the answer. You can use either a FireWire or USB cable to connect the iPod to the AC power supply, but you must use USB to synchronize your iPod with your computer. That's all you need to know. With iPods older than the fifth-generation, you can use FireWire or, in some cases, USB. If you use a Mac, FireWire is the choice to make unless your Mac offers USB 2.0 and you're using an iPod mini, iPod nano, fifth-generation iPod, or iPod shuffle — all of which support USB 2.0. The iPod shuffle supports only USB and USB 2.0, so you have no choice but to use the USB or USB 2.0 connection.

Why so complicated? Technology marches on, leaving older iPod models and computers to talk in an ancient tongue (in this case, FireWire). At one time, it was a question of speed and convenience. FireWire hustled data at rates up to 400 Mbps over its cable. That was typically fast enough — with FireWire, you could transfer an entire CD's worth of music in less than ten seconds.

But engineers are never happy; they keep making things better. USB (Universal Serial Bus) has been around for a while, connecting hundreds of nifty devices to PCs. Such nifty devices include keyboards, pointing devices, external hard drives, keychain-sized flash drives, printers, scanners, and much more. USB proponents envied FireWire, which is more than 30 times faster than USB version 1.1, which offers a speed of only 12 Mbps. So they developed a more advanced generation of USB. Version 2.0 has a transfer rate of 480 Mbps — that's 40 times faster than the first version and comparable with FireWire.

Both FireWire and USB 2.0 connections are plug-and-play: You can plug them in at any time whether your computer is on or off. Depending on the device that you use with these connections, FireWire or USB 2.0 can provide power to the device. For example, fourth- and fifth-generation iPods, iPod nano, and iPod shuffle can draw power from a USB 2.0 connection, and all can draw power from a FireWire connection.

Have we made your choice easier yet for older iPod models? If you have a PC with USB 2.0 (which is more common than one with FireWire), go with it. The only drawback is that with an iPod older than the fourth generation, you might not be able to get power from the connection (depending on the PC), so you can't recharge its battery from your PC. You then need to get a FireWire cable and a FireWire AC adapter to recharge its battery. To connect older-model iPods, you can add FireWire to your PC with an expansion card such as the FireCard 400 CardBus card from Unibrain (www.unibrain.com), which plugs into a PC desktop or laptop CardBus slot. Laptop PCs made as far back as 1999 offer CardBus slots. Desktop PCs typically let you add expansion cards inside the PC, and there are many IEEE 1394 expansion cards available on the market. Before you buy a FireWire/IEEE 1394 card, make sure that it's compatible with your hardware and operating system. Apple offers approved FireWire expansion cards at the online Apple Store (http://store.apple.com/1-800-MYAPPLE/WebObjects/AppleStore). And, of course, Apple Macs offer built-in FireWire support.

If you have trouble installing your FireWire or USB 2.0 card into a PC or using your iPod with it, see Chapter 26 for troubleshooting tips.

First- and second-generation models offer only a standard FireWire connection, so you can use a standard Mac-style FireWire cable to connect the iPod to the Mac's FireWire connection. Plug the six-pin connector of a standard FireWire cable into the iPod, and plug the six-pin connector on the other end to the FireWire port on your Mac. (The six-pin connector is marked by the Y symbol that resembles a radiation symbol.)

USB and FireWire have been a part of every Mac since at least 2000. (To find out more about USB and FireWire, see the sidebar, "USB or FireWire: That is the question," in this chapter.)

Third-generation full-size iPod models don't support USB 2.0 on the Mac; you must use FireWire.

If you have a Windows PC, you can add FireWire support for older-model iPods. Most PCs already have USB 2.0, which is all you need to provide power to your fifth-generation iPod or iPod nano and to synchronize it with your PC. Although you can use a low-powered USB 1.0 or 1.1 connection, it doesn't supply power to most iPod models.

However, FireWire can provide power to fifth-generation iPod models and iPod nano models.

FireWire/IEEE 1394 expansion cards are available for PCs in various formats: Some offer the standard six-pin port found on Macs, and some offer a four-pin port that is also used in camcorders. If your card has a six-pin port, you can plug your iPod FireWire cable directly into it.

For cards with four-pin ports, Apple provides the FireWire cable adapter, as shown in Figure 1-6, and you can hook it up to the standard six-pin connector at the end of your FireWire cable. The small four-pin connector on the adapter plugs into the four-pin port on the FireWire card. Then plug the other end of your cable to your iPod or your dock. You can purchase a special FireWire/ IEEE 1394 cable that has a six-pin plug on one end and a four-pin plug on the other — look for it in well-stocked electronics stores that sell digital camcorders, because many camcorders use such a cable.

The FireWire cable adapter used to be supplied with full-size fourth-generation iPods but is not supplied with iPod mini, iPod nano, or fifth-generation iPods, which use USB 2.0 to connect to your computer. You can purchase a FireWire cable adapter from the Apple Store.

Don't use another USB device in a chain, or a USB 2.0 hub, to connect your iPod — unless the hub is a powered hub. Note that a USB keyboard typically acts like a USB 1.1 hub, but is not powered. Therefore it can't provide power to the iPod and might slow down performance.

Figure 1-6: The FireWire cable adapter for connecting to a FireWire card that has a four-pin port.

Powering Up Your iPod

All iPods come with essentially the same requirement: power. Fortunately, each iPod also comes with a battery and a way of charging it — either directly from your computer or by using a cable and an AC power adapter that works with voltages in North America and many parts of Europe and Asia. (See Chapter 21 for information about plugging into power in other countries.)

First- and second-generation iPod models offer a Mac-style FireWire connection on the top of the iPod. The power adapter also sports a FireWire connection, so all you need is a standard six-pin FireWire cable to plug in.

Third-, fourth-, and fifth-generation models — as well as iPod nano and iPod mini — use a dock that offers FireWire and USB connections. The dock can also connect to your home stereo through a line-out connection.

A FireWire or USB connection to a Mac provides power to the iPod and recharges the battery as long as the Mac isn't in sleep mode. A FireWire connection to a FireWire/IEEE 1394 card in a PC might not be able to provide power — check with the card manufacturer. The smaller four-pin connections for FireWire/IEEE 1394 cards typically don't supply power to the iPod.

If your iPod shows a display but doesn't respond to your touch, don't panic — check the Hold switch on top of the unit and make sure that it's set to one side so that the orange bar disappears (the normal position). You use the Hold switch for locking the buttons, which prevents accidental activation.

You might notice that the iPod's display turns iridescent when it gets too hot or too cold, but this effect disappears when its temperature returns to normal. iPods can function in temperatures as cold as 50 degrees and as warm as 95 degrees (Fahrenheit) but work best at room temperature (closer to 68 degrees).

If you leave your iPod out in the cold all night, it might have trouble waking from sleep mode, and it might even display a low-battery message. Plug the iPod into a power source, wait until it warms up, and try it again. If it still doesn't wake up or respond properly, try resetting the iPod as we describe in "Resetting Your iPod," later in this chapter.

Facing Charges of Battery

You can take a six-hour flight from New York City to California and listen to your iPod the entire time — and with some models, listen all the way back on the return flight — without recharging. All iPod models use the same type of built-in, rechargeable lithium-ion battery with the following power specs:

- ✔ The first-, second-, and third-generation iPod models offer up to 8 hours of battery power.
- ✔ The fourth-generation models and the iPod shuffle offer up to 12 hours.
- ✔ iPod mini offers up to 18 hours.
- ✔ The color-display fourth-generation models offer 15 hours of music playing time or 5 hours of photo display with music.
- ✔ iPod nano offers 24 hours of music playing time or 5 hours of photo display with music.
- ✔ The fifth-generation iPod models offer between 14 and 20 hours of music playing time, between 3.5 and 6.5 hours of video playing time, or between 4 and 6 hours of photo display with music.

However, keep in mind that playback battery time varies with the type of encoder that you use for the music files in iTunes. (Chapter 18 has more information about encoders.) It also varies depending on how you use your iPod controls and settings.

The iPod battery recharges automatically when you connect the iPod to a power source — for example, it starts charging immediately when you insert it into a dock that's connected to a power source (or to a computer with a powered FireWire or USB connection). It takes only four hours to recharge the battery fully for all models, and only three hours for an iPod nano.

Need power when you're on the run? Look for a power outlet in the airport terminal or hotel lobby — the battery fast-charges to 80 percent capacity in two hours. After the first two hours, the battery receives a trickle charge for the next two hours until fully charged.

Don't fry your iPod with some generic power adapter — use *only* the power adapter supplied with the iPod from Apple or a certified iPod adapter such as the power accessories from Belkin and other vendors.

A battery icon with a progress bar in the top-right corner of the iPod display indicates how much power is left. When you charge the battery, the icon turns into a lightning bolt inside a battery. If the icon doesn't animate, the battery is fully charged. You can also use your iPod while the battery is charging or disconnect it and use it before the battery is fully charged.

To check the battery status of an iPod shuffle, press the battery status button on the back (the long button above the Apple logo and below the position switch for setting the iPod shuffle to shuffle songs or play them in order). If the battery status light is green, the iPod shuffle is fully charged; if yellow, the charge is low; if red, very little charge is left, and you need to recharge it. If no light is visible, the iPod shuffle is completely out of power, and you need to recharge it to use it.

Maintaining battery life

The iPod's built-in, rechargeable lithium-ion battery is, essentially, a life-or-death proposition. After it's dead, it can be replaced, but the replacement might cost more than $50 (some services may charge less for older models). If your warranty is still active, you should have Apple replace it — don't do it yourself because opening the iPod invalidates the warranty.

Fortunately, the battery is easy to maintain. We recommend *calibrating* the battery once soon after you get your iPod — that is, run it all the way down (a full discharge) and then charge it all the way up (which takes four hours). Although this doesn't actually change battery performance, it does improve the battery gauge so that the iPod displays a more accurate indicator.

Unlike nickel-based batteries that require you to fully discharge and then recharge in order to get a fuller capacity, the iPod lithium-ion battery prefers a partial rather than a full discharge, so avoid frequent full discharges after the initial calibration. (Frequent full discharges can lower battery life.)

Lithium-ion batteries typically last three years or more and are vulnerable to high temperatures, which decrease their life spans considerably. Don't leave your iPod in a hot place, such as on a sunny car dashboard, for very long.

For a complete description of how Apple's lithium-ion batteries work, see the Apple Lithium-ion Batteries page at www.apple.com/batteries.

The bottom of the iPod warms up when it's powered on. The bottom functions as a cooling surface that transfers heat from inside the unit to the cooler air outside. The iPod's carrying case acts as an insulator, so be sure to remove the iPod from its carrying case before you recharge it.

Keeping the iPod in its carrying case when charging is tempting but also potentially disastrous. The iPod needs to dissipate its heat, and you could damage the unit by overheating it and frying its circuits, rendering it as useful as a paperweight. To get around this problem, you can purchase one of the heat-dissipating carrying cases available in the Apple Store. Alternatively, Marware (`www.marware.com`) offers a variety of sporty cases for about $30 to $40.

Even when not in use, your iPod drinks the juice. If your iPod is inactive for 14 days, you must recharge its battery — perhaps the iPod gets depressed from being left alone too long.

Saving power

Full-size iPods include a hard drive, and whatever causes the hard drive to spin causes a drain on power. Your iPod also has a *cache* — a memory chip holding the section of music to play next. The iPod uses the cache not only to eliminate skipping when something jostles the hard drive, but also to conserve power because the drive doesn't have to spin as much.

If you use the AIFF or WAV formats for importing music into iTunes (or Musicmatch Jukebox), don't use these formats with your iPod — convert the music first, as we describe in Chapter 19. These formats take up way too much space on the iPod hard drive and fill up the iPod cache too quickly, causing skips when you play them and using too much battery power because the drive spins more often. (See Chapter 5 for bringing content into iTunes. Chapter 18 provides detailed information about these formats.)

The following are tips on saving power while using your iPod:

- **Pause:** Pause playback when you're not listening. Pausing (stopping) playback is the easiest way to conserve power.

- **Back away from the light:** Use the iPod backlight sparingly. Select Backlight from the iPod main menu to turn it on or off, or turn the Backlight Timer setting to a number of seconds, or to Off, in the iPod's Settings menu. (Choose Settings from the main menu.) Don't use the backlight in daylight if you don't need it.

- **Hold it:** Flip the Hold switch to the locked position (with the orange bar showing) to make sure that controls aren't accidentally activated. You don't want your iPod playing music in your pocket and draining the battery when you're not listening.

- **You may continue:** Play songs continuously without using the iPod controls. Selecting songs and using Previous/Rewind and Next/Fast-Forward require precious energy. Not only that, but the hard drive has to spin more often when searching for songs, using more power than during continuous playback.

Always use the latest iPod software and update your software when updates come out. Apple is constantly trying to improve the way your iPod works, and many of these advancements relate to power usage.

Replacing your battery

Apple customers aren't always happy campers. Early iPods came with batteries that couldn't be replaced, but all it took were a few premature battery failures and quite a few customer complaints for Apple to institute a battery-replacement service. Apple also offers a special AppleCare warranty for iPods.

You can't remove or replace the iPod internal battery yourself. You need Apple to replace it if it dies.

If your iPod isn't responding after a reset (see "Resetting Your iPod" in this chapter for how to reset your iPod), follow the troubleshooting steps in Chapter 26. If these steps don't restore your iPod to working condition, you might have a battery problem. Go to the Apple support page for the iPod (www.apple.com/support/ipod) and click the iPod Service FAQ link to read frequently asked questions and answers about iPod support. Then click the iPod Battery Service Request Form link on the support page and follow the instructions to request service and return your iPod for a replacement.

The only time we had to do this (with a 30GB iPod), Apple required us to send just the iPod unit itself, without the power adapter or any other accessories, to Apple's service facility. Within a week, Apple sent back a brand-new iPod (same model).

Thumbing Through the Menus

After you bring content into iTunes and update your iPod, you're ready to play. The design of the iPod lets you hold it in one hand and perform simple operations by thumb. Even if you're all thumbs when pressing small buttons on tiny devices, you can still thumb your way to iPod heaven.

The iPod's unique circular scroll wheel makes scrolling through an entire music collection quick and easy. With your finger or thumb, scroll clockwise on the wheel to scroll down a list, or counter-clockwise to scroll up. As you scroll, options on the menu are highlighted. Use the Select button at the center of the scroll wheel to select whatever is highlighted in the menu display.

In full-size third-generation models, the touch-sensitive buttons above the scroll wheel perform simple functions when you touch them. (First- and second-generation models aren't touch-sensitive, so you need to press them.)

Current fifth-generation iPods, iPod nano, iPod mini, and fourth-generation iPods (including color-display models) provide a click wheel that offers the same functions as the scroll wheel *and* the clickable buttons. It has pressure-sensitive buttons underneath the top, bottom, left, and right areas of the circular pad of the wheel. These areas tilt as you press them, activating the buttons.

The iPod main menu for fifth-generation models, shown in Figure 1-7, offers the following selections:

- ✔ **Music:** Select music by playlist, artist, album, song, genre, or composer, or select an audio book.

- ✔ **Photos:** Select photos by photo album or select individual photos in the photo library. This selection appears only on color-display models.

- ✔ **Videos:** Select videos by playlist or by type (movies, music videos, TV shows, or video podcasts). This selection appears only on fifth-generation models.

- ✔ **Extras:** View and set the clock and alarm clock, view contacts, view your calendar, view notes, and play games.

✔ **Settings:** Adjust display settings, menu settings, the backlight timer, the clicker, and the date and time.

✔ **Shuffle Songs:** Play songs from your music library in random order.

✔ **Now Playing:** This selection appears only when a song is playing — it takes you to the Now Playing display.

iPod	
Music	>
Photos	>
Videos	>
Extras	>
Settings	>
Shuffle Songs	

Figure 1-7: The fifth-generation iPod main menu.

The iPod main menu for fourth-generation models and iPod nano is the same as fifth-generation models, but without the Videos selection.

Third-generation models offer the following menu selections:

✔ **Music:** Select music by playlist, artist, album, song, genre, or composer, or select an audio book.

✔ **Playlists:** Select a playlist to play.

✔ **Extras:** View and set the clock and alarm clock, view contacts, your calendar, or notes, and play games.

✔ **Settings:** Set display settings, menu settings, the backlight timer, the clicker, and the date and time.

✔ **Backlight:** Turn on or off the backlighting for the iPod display.

✔ **Now Playing:** This selection appears only when a song is playing — it takes you to the Now Playing display.

The main menu for first- and second-generation iPods and iPod mini offers the following selections:

- **Playlists:** Select a playlist to play.
- **Browse:** Select music by playlist, artist, album, song, genre, or composer, or select an audio book.
- **Extras:** View and set the clock and alarm clock, view contacts, view your calendar, view notes, and play games.
- **Settings:** Set display settings, menu settings, the backlight timer, the clicker, and the date and time.
- **Backlight:** Turn on or off the backlighting for the iPod display.
- **Now Playing:** This selection appears only when a song is playing — it takes you to the Now Playing display.

Pressing the iPod Buttons

The buttons on full-size iPod models do various tasks for song playback:

- **Previous/Rewind:** Press once to start a song over. Press twice to skip to the previous song. Press and hold to rewind through a song.
- **Menu:** Press once to go back to the previous menu. Each time you press, you go back to a previous menu until you reach the main menu.
- **Play/Pause:** Press to play the selected song, album, or playlist. Press Play/Pause when a song is playing to pause the playback.
- **Next/Fast-Forward:** Press once to skip to the next song. Press and hold Next/Fast-Forward to fast-forward through the song.

The buttons and scroll wheel on full-size iPods can do more complex functions when used in combination:

- **Turn on the iPod.** Press any button.
- **Turn off the iPod.** Press and hold the Play/Pause button.
- **Disable the iPod buttons.** To keep from accidentally pressing the buttons, push the Hold switch to the other side so that an orange bar appears (the locked position). To reactivate the iPod buttons, push the Hold switch back to the other side so that the orange bar disappears (the normal position).

✔ **Reset the iPod.** You can reset the iPod if it gets hung up for some reason. (For example, it might get confused if you press the buttons too quickly.) This operation resets the iPod, essentially restarting the iPod's hard drive. It doesn't change the music or data on the iPod. See "Resetting Your iPod," later in this chapter to find out how to reset your iPod.

✔ **Change the volume.** While playing a song (the display reads Now Playing), adjust the volume with the scroll wheel — clockwise turns the volume up, counterclockwise turns the volume down. A volume slider appears on the iPod display, indicating the volume level as you scroll.

✔ **Skip to any point in a song.** While playing a song (the display says Now Playing), press and hold the Select button until the progress bar appears to indicate where you are in the song, and then use the scroll wheel to scroll to any point in the song. Scroll clockwise to move forward and counterclockwise to move backward.

Setting the Language

Wiedergabelisten? Übersicht? (Playlists? Browse?) If your iPod is speaking in a foreign tongue, don't panic — you're not in the wrong country. You might have purchased an iPod that's set to a foreign language. More likely, someone set it to a different language accidentally or on purpose (as a practical joke). Fortunately, you can change the setting without having to know the language that it's set to.

To set the language, no matter what language the menu is using, follow these steps:

1. **Press the Menu button repeatedly until pressing it doesn't change the words on the display or until you see the word *iPod*.**

   If pressing the Menu button no longer changes the display, you're at the main menu. With fourth- and fifth-generation models and iPod nano, the menu displays the word *iPod* no matter what language is selected — and you know you're at the main menu.

2. **Choose the third option from the top on fourth-generation iPods without color displays. Choose the fourth option from the top on iPod mini, iPod models with color displays, and older models. (In English, this is the Settings option.)**

   Scroll clockwise until the item is highlighted, and then press the Select button. The Settings menu appears.

3. **Choose the third option from the bottom of the Settings menu (which, in English, is the Language option).**

   The Language menu appears.

4. **Choose the language that you want to use. (English is at the top of the list.)**

If these steps don't do the trick, the menu may have been customized (something you can discover how to do in Chapter 22). Someone could have customized it previously, or perhaps you accidentally pressed buttons that customized the menu. To get around this problem, you can reset all the iPod settings back to the defaults. (Unfortunately, resetting your iPod to the default settings wipes out any customizations that you've made. You have to redo any repeat/shuffle settings, alarms, backlight timer settings, and so on.)

Follow these steps to reset all your settings, no matter what language displays:

1. **Press the Menu button repeatedly until pressing it doesn't change the words on the display or until you see the word *iPod*.**

   If pressing the Menu button no longer changes the display, you're at the main menu. With fourth-generation and fifth-generation models and the iPod nano, the menu displays the word *iPod* no matter what language is selected — and you know you're at the main menu.

2. **Choose the third option from the top on fourth-generation iPods without color displays. Choose the fourth option from the top on iPod mini, iPod models with color displays, and older models. (In English, this is the Settings option.)**

   The Settings menu appears.

3. **Choose the option at the bottom of the menu (in English, the Reset All Settings option).**

   The Reset All Settings menu appears.

4. **Choose the second menu option (in English, the Reset option; the first menu option is Cancel).**

   The Language menu appears.

5. **Choose the language you want to use. (English is at the top of the list.)**

The language you choose now applies to all the iPod menus. But don't pull that practical joke on someone else!

Chapter 2

Setting Up iTunes and Your iPod

An iPod without iTunes is like a CD player without CDs. Sure, you can use utility programs from sources other than Apple to put music, podcasts, and videos on an iPod. (See Chapter 25 if you don't believe us.) But iTunes gives you access to the vast online iTunes Music Store, and it's excellent for managing content on your computer and synchronizing your content library with your iPod.

This chapter explains how to set up your iPod with iTunes on the Mac or for Windows. It also explains how to set up the iPod Software, which provides the intelligence inside your iPod. With a history of different models and software configurations, getting the right iPod Software for your iPod would be downright confusing if Apple didn't provide one downloadable installer that takes care of everything. Fortunately, Apple provides exactly that: an updater/installer for Mac and Windows that recognizes the type of iPod you have and installs the correct software.

Setting Up the Software for Windows

Setting up your Windows software is a quick and easy process. As of this writing, the CD-ROMs supplied with iPods offer iTunes for Windows and iPod Software in one installation. If the CD-ROM doesn't contain the newest versions — for example, if the iPod sat on a store shelf for a few months — you might want to install it first and then visit the Apple Web site to download the most up-to-date versions. See the "Downloading and Installing Software Upgrades" section for more information.

Before installing iTunes and iPod Software for Windows, make sure that you're logged on as a Windows administrator user. Quit all other applications before installing and disable any antivirus software.

The iTunes installer also installs the newest version of QuickTime, replacing any older version you might have. QuickTime is Apple's multimedia development, storage, and playback technology. Although Windows users aren't required to use QuickTime beyond its use by iTunes, QuickTime is a bonus for Windows users because it offers digital video playback.

iPods that were sold before iTunes became available for Windows (in the fall of 2003) don't include iTunes on the CD-ROM. The older iPod CD-ROMs install Musicmatch Jukebox. If you plan on using iTunes for Windows, which requires Windows XP or Windows 2000, download the newer iTunes and iPod installers from the Apple Web site.

If you're using Musicmatch, visit the companion Web site at `www.dummies.com/go/ipod4e` to find out how to install it.

Installing the Windows software

To install iPod Software for Windows from the CD-ROM, *do not* connect the iPod to your computer — leave it disconnected. Place the CD in your CD drive and follow these steps:

1. **Double-click the CD-ROM icon in Windows Explorer.**

   The CD-ROM's AutoPlay feature starts the installation process. If the installer doesn't open automatically, right-click the CD-ROM icon in the My Computer window and choose AutoPlay from the shortcut menu that appears.

2. **In the first dialog that appears, choose the language that you want to use and then click OK.**

   The language shortcut menu lets you choose from quite a number of languages. After clicking OK, the InstallShield Wizard, so familiar to Windows users, takes over and launches the installer. The Welcome to the iPod Installer dialog appears with photos of cute people using iPods.

3. **Click Next in the Welcome dialog.**

   A dialog appears, asking for your iPod's serial number, as shown in Figure 2-1.

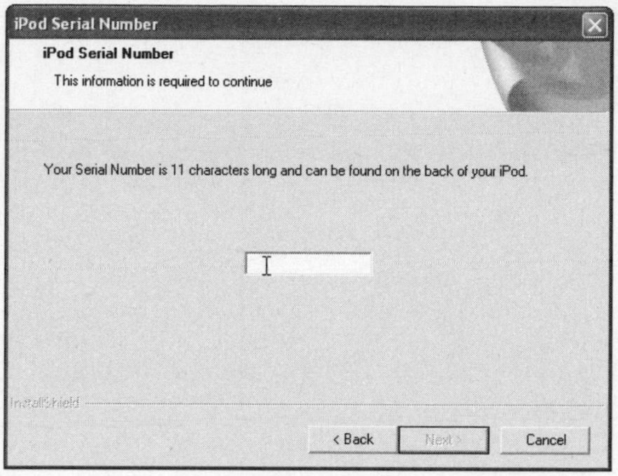

iPod Serial Number

This information is required to continue

Your Serial Number is 11 characters long and can be found on the back of your iPod.

InstallShield   < Back   Next >   Cancel

Figure 2-1:
You need
your iPod
serial
number
during the
installation
process.

4. **Type your iPod serial number and then click Next.**

   You can find the serial number of the back of your iPod (use a magnifying glass) or on the side of its packaging.

   After you click Next, the installer displays the country/region dialog.

5. **Select your country or region and then click Next.**

   Click the Show All button to display all countries rather than just the countries that use the language you selected in Step 2.

   After you click Next, the installer displays the registration dialog.

6. **Fill out the registration information and then click Next.**

   Register your copy of the software with Apple to take advantage of Apple support. Fields marked with an asterisk (*) are required — your name and e-mail address.

   After you click Next, the installer displays the Choose Destination Location dialog, as shown in Figure 2-2.

7. **Select a destination folder for the iPod for Windows software and then click Next.**

   The iPod folder contains the iPod software. By default, the installer assumes that you want to store the iPod folder in the Program Files folder of your C: drive (which is just peachy, unless you like to defy the system designers at Microsoft by putting programs in other places). Click Browse to use Windows Explorer if you dare locate a different folder.

   After selecting a folder (or keeping the default), click Next. The installer takes care of installing the iPod software. When finished, the iTunes installer dialog appears.

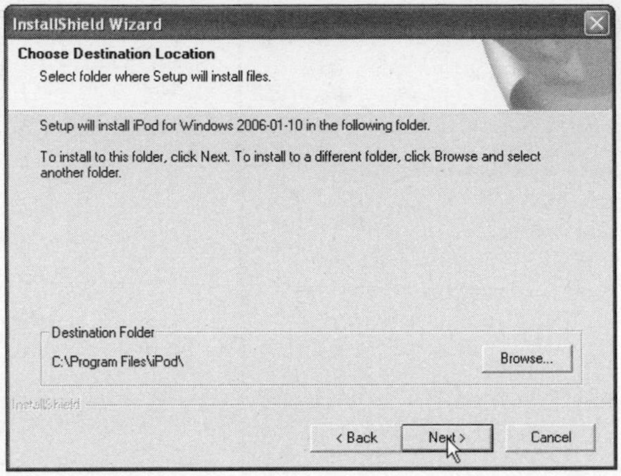

InstallShield Wizard

Choose Destination Location
Select folder where Setup will install files.

Setup will install iPod for Windows 2006-01-10 in the following folder.

To install to this folder, click Next. To install to a different folder, click Browse and select another folder.

Destination Folder
C:\Program Files\iPod\   Browse...

< Back   Next >   Cancel

Figure 2-2:
Choose a destination folder for the iPod software.

8. **Click Next to start the iTunes installer.**

   After clicking Next, the installer displays the License Agreement dialog.

9. **Click the I Accept the Terms of the License Agreement option and then click Next.**

   Apple's License Agreement appears in the installer window, and you can scroll down to read the agreement. You must choose to accept the agreement, or the installer goes no further.

   After clicking Next (which is active only if you accept), the installer displays the About iTunes information.

10. **Read the About iTunes information and click Next.**

    The installer displays important "read me" information about the latest iTunes features, and you can scroll down to read the entire information.

    After clicking Next, the installer displays the Setup Type dialog, as shown in Figure 2-3.

11. **Select the appropriate options for your iTunes setup and then click Next.**

    Here are your options:

    - **Install desktop shortcuts:** You can install shortcuts for your Windows desktop for iTunes.

    - **Use iTunes as the default player for audio files:** We suggest turning this option on, allowing iTunes to be the default audio content player for all audio files it recognizes. If you're happy with your audio player, you can deselect this option, leaving your default player setting unaffected.

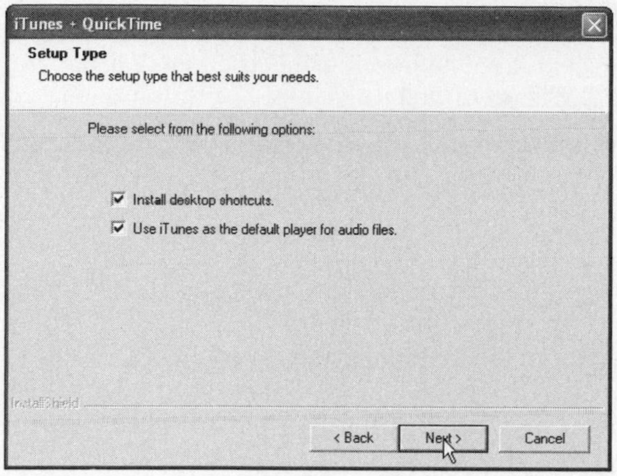

Figure 2-3:
Setup
options for
the iTunes
installation
in Windows.

After clicking Next, the installer displays the Choose Destination Location page, as shown in Figure 2-4.

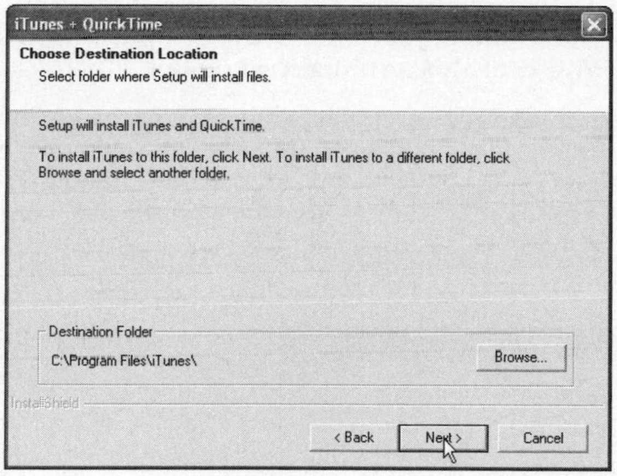

Figure 2-4:
Choose a
Windows
destination
folder for
the iTunes
application.

12. Select a destination folder for iTunes and then click Next.

By default, the installer assumes that you want to store the program in the Program Files folder of your C: drive (which is an excellent place to store it, unless you have other ideas). If you want to use a different folder, click Browse to use Windows Explorer to locate the desired folder.

After you click Next, the installer displays the iTunes + QuickTime dialog, showing a nice, cute couple playing iPods.

13. **Click Next.**

    After you click Next, the installer finishes the installation and displays the InstallShield Wizard Complete dialog.

14. **Choose the option to restart your computer and then click Finish.**

    Restarting your Windows PC after installing software is always a good idea.

iTunes for Windows, iPod Software for Windows, and QuickTime are now installed on your PC. To start using iTunes, double-click the iTunes program or use your Start menu to locate iTunes and launch it.

Using the iPod Setup Assistant for Windows

When you connect a new iPod for the first time, iTunes displays the Setup Assistant. Follow these steps to set up your iPod:

1. **With iTunes open, connect your iPod to the computer with a USB cable (or FireWire cable for an older iPod model).**

   iTunes recognizes your iPod and opens the iPod Setup Assistant to get you started. If for some reason your iPod is not recognized in a few minutes, see "Using the iPod Updater" later in this chapter. The Setup Assistant displays a dialog that lets you give your iPod a name, as shown in Figure 2-5.

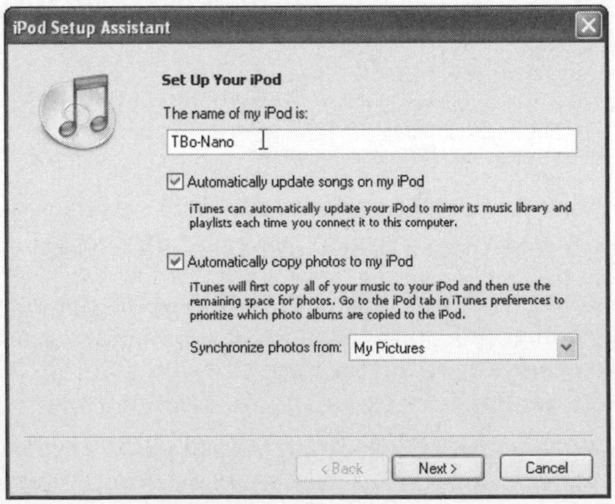

Figure 2-5:
Set up your iPod's name and automatic options by using the iPod Setup Assistant for an iPod nano.

2. Give your iPod a name, set automatic options, and then click Next.

If you plan on sharing several iPods among several computers, it's a good idea to give your iPod a name.

If you want to copy your entire iTunes music library, leave the Automatically Update Songs on My iPod option selected. This option creates a mirror image of your music library on the iPod, including all playlists and audio files, every time you connect your iPod. (Don't worry. You can always change this setting later; see Chapter 12.) If you want to copy only a portion of your library to the iPod, deselect this option.

For an iPod shuffle, the Setup Assistant displays an option to copy songs randomly. If you leave the Automatically Choose Songs for My iPod option selected, iTunes copies a random selection of songs to your iPod shuffle. You can always choose to fill your iPod shuffle with a different selection by clicking the Autofill button, as we describe in Chapter 12.

If you have a color-display iPod model, including iPod nano (used in Figure 2-5), select the Automatically Copy Photos to My iPod option if you want to copy all the photos in your Pictures folder to your iPod. Leave it deselected if you want to transfer photos later.

If you turn on both the option to copy photos automatically and the option to copy songs automatically, iTunes copies the songs first and then copies photos up to the limit of the iPod's capacity. (See Chapter 11 to find out about transferring photos to your color-display iPod.)

After you click Next, the Setup Assistant moves on to the dialog for registering your iPod.

3. Click the Register button to register your iPod, and then click Finish.

The Setup Assistant allows you to register your iPod with Apple to take advantage of Apple support.

Your iPod's name now appears in the iTunes Source pane under the Music Store selection.

If you selected the automatic update feature in the Setup Assistant, the iPod name appears grayed out in the Source pane, and you can't open it. However, your iPod quickly fills up with the music from your iTunes music library. Of course, if you're just starting out, you probably have no tunes in your library. Your next step is to import music from CDs, buy music online, or import music from other sources (see Chapter 4).

If you deselect the automatic update feature, the iPod name appears just like any other source in the Source pane. You can then add songs manually, as we describe in Chapter 12.

If iTunes displays a dialog with the message that a new version of iTunes is available and asks whether you would like to download it now, click Yes to download the new version. iTunes launches your Web browser and takes you right to the iTunes download page — see "Downloading and Installing Software Upgrades," later in this chapter.

Using the iPod Updater

If your iPod isn't recognized by iTunes, try the following steps:

1. **Launch the iPod Updater program by double-clicking the program icon or choosing Start➪iPod➪iPod Updater.**

   The iPod Updater displays `Plug in an iPod to update it` in the iPod Updater window. You can now plug your iPod into the computer.

2. **Connect your iPod and wait for iPod Updater to recognize it.**

   Connect your iPod as we describe in Chapter 1. iPod Updater recognizes it and displays its name. If iPod Updater doesn't recognize your iPod, skip to Step 4.

   If your iPod needs to be updated with new software, the Update button is active.

3. **If you need new software, click the Update button to update the iPod's internal software.**

   We describe this in more detail in Chapter 26. iTunes now recognizes your iPod.

   If the updater doesn't recognize the iPod by name, it checks to see whether the iPod needs to be reformatted. If the iPod needs reformatting, the Updater tells you to reformat the iPod and deactivates the Update button, as shown in Figure 2-6. This situation leaves you no other option except to use the Restore button to restore the iPod to its factory condition, which includes reformatting the iPod for Windows. If your iPod is formatted for Mac use, it displays N/A for Name and Capacity.

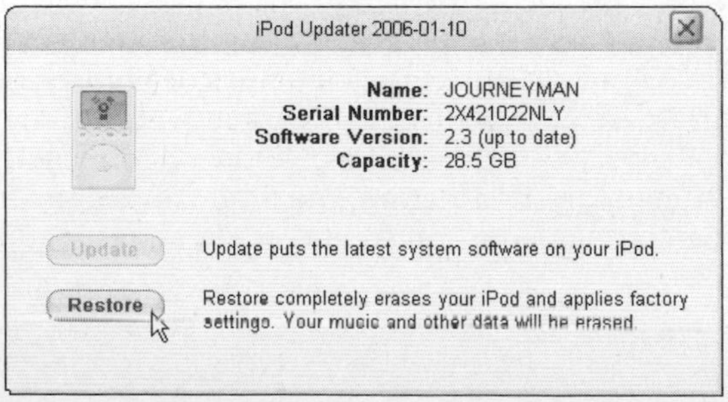

Figure 2-6:
Use the iPod Updater to restore an iPod and reformat it for Windows use.

iPod Updater 2006-01-10

Name: JOURNEYMAN
Serial Number: 2X421022NLY
Software Version: 2.3 (up to date)
Capacity: 28.5 GB

Update Update puts the latest system software on your iPod.

Restore Restore completely erases your iPod and applies factory settings. Your music and other data will be erased.

4. **If necessary, click the Restore button to restore the iPod, and click Restore again to continue.**

After you click Restore, the iPod Updater displays a warning dialog. Click Restore to continue with the restoration. The iPod Updater erases and reformats the hard drive and restores the iPod to its factory settings. When it finishes restoring, it displays `Restore is complete.` `Please disconnect iPod from PC and connect it to the` `external power supply to allow firmware reflash.`

5. **Disconnect the iPod from the computer and connect it to AC power.**

The iPod needs AC power to do a firmware refresh. (*Firmware* is software encoded in hardware.) Disconnect your iPod carefully and then connect it to your power adapter. The iPod performs a firmware refresh operation that takes a few minutes. After you've disconnected the iPod, the iPod Updater displays its opening dialog.

6. **Connect the iPod to the computer again.**

iPod Updater now recognizes your iPod.

7. **Close the iPod Updater but leave your iPod connected.**

Close the iPod Updater by clicking the Close box in the upper-right corner. Because your iPod is still connected, iTunes starts automatically and displays the iPod Setup Assistant dialog inside the iTunes window. If iTunes doesn't start automatically, start iTunes and wait for it to recognize your iPod.

If your computer or iTunes still has trouble recognizing your iPod, see Chapter 26 where we cover more troubleshooting tips.

Setting Up the Software for a Mac

As a Mac user, you probably already have iTunes installed because all Macs sold since 2003 (and many before that time) are preinstalled with iTunes and Mac OS X, and you also get iTunes if you install Mac OS X on an older machine. The most up-to-date version of iTunes as of this writing is version 6.0.5.

The version of iTunes that's provided with the Mac might be the newest version; then again, it might not be. Software updates occur very rapidly. If you really want the latest version, go directly to the Apple Web site to get it. You can download iTunes for free, as we describe in "Downloading and Installing Software Upgrades," later in this chapter.

You can set your Mac to automatically download the latest version of iTunes when it becomes available. Simply use Software Update from the Mac OS X System Preferences window. Click the Check Now button to check for a new version. If one exists, it appears in a window for you to select. Click the check mark to select it and then click Install to download and install it.

Installing the Mac software

To install the iPod software from the CD-ROM, open the CD-ROM and then double-click the Install iPod Software package file to unpack and install it. Then follow these steps:

1. **Click Continue after the installer's Welcome page appears.**

   The installer needs to run a program to check your computer and make sure it's capable of running iTunes. After it runs the program, the installer displays the Important Information page.

2. **Read the Important Information page and click Continue.**

   The installer displays important "read me" information about the latest iTunes features. If you like, click Save to save the Important Information page as a document or click Print to print it.

3. **Read the License Agreement and click Continue to go to the second page. Click the Agree button and then click Continue again.**

   You can scroll down to read the agreement. You must choose to accept the agreement by clicking the Agree button, or the installer goes no further. After clicking Agree, the installer displays the Select a Destination page.

   Optional: Before you click the Agree button, you can click Save to save the license agreement as a document or click Print to print it. No lawyers are present when you do this; it's all up to you.

4. **Select the destination volume and then click Continue.**

   The installer asks for the destination volume (hard drive), as shown in Figure 2-7, which must be a Mac OS X startup drive — any other drive is marked by a red exclamation point, indicating that you can't install the software there. iTunes is installed in the Applications folder on the Mac OS X startup drive, and the iPod Software Updater is installed in the Utilities folder inside the Applications folder. After you click Continue, the installer asks if you want to customize the installation.

5. **Click Install (or Upgrade) to proceed with the installation.**

As an alternative, you can customize your installation by clicking Customize, selecting each package you want to install, and then clicking Install. The CD-ROM installer skips installing iTunes if you already have a version as current as (or newer than) the one on the CD-ROM.

6. Click Close when the installer finishes.

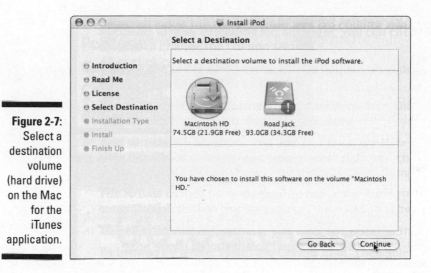

Figure 2-7: Select a destination volume (hard drive) on the Mac for the iTunes application.

You can now launch iTunes by double-clicking the iTunes application or clicking the iTunes icon in the Dock.

Using the iPod Setup Assistant for the Mac

To set up your iPod with a Mac, connect it to the Mac as we describe in Chapter 1. When you first connect your iPod to a Mac, iTunes automatically starts, and the iPod Setup Assistant appears like a butler, ready to help you set it up. Follow these steps with the iPod Setup Assistant:

1. Open iTunes and connect your iPod to the Mac with a USB cable (or FireWire cable for an older iPod model).

iTunes recognizes your iPod and opens the iPod Setup Assistant to get you started. The Setup Assistant displays a dialog that lets you give your iPod a name, as shown in Figure 2-8.

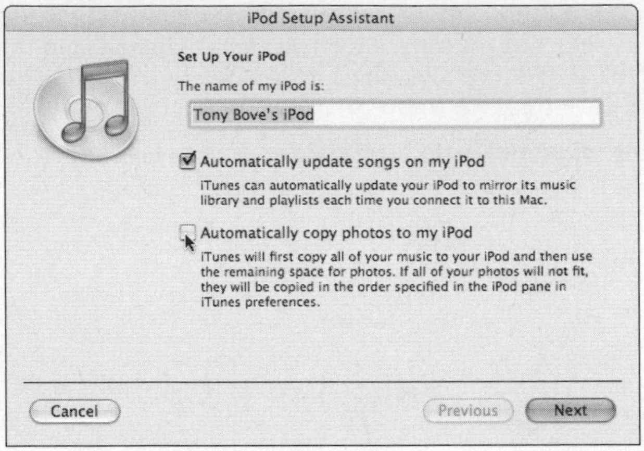

Figure 2-8:
Set up your
iPod with
the iPod
Setup
Assistant.

2. **Give your iPod a name, set automatic options, and then click Next.**

Giving your iPod a name is a good idea if you plan on sharing several iPods among several computers.

If you want to copy your entire iTunes music library, leave the Automatically Update Songs on My iPod option selected. This option creates a mirror image of your music library on the iPod, including all playlists and audio files, every time you connect your iPod. (Don't worry. You can always change this setting later; Chapter 12 tells you how.) If you want to copy only a portion of your library to the iPod, deselect this option.

If you have a color-display iPod model, select the Automatically Copy Photos to My iPod option if you want to copy all the photos in your iPhoto library to your iPod. Leave it deselected if you want to transfer photos later. This option copies (or updates) your entire iPhoto library to the iPod every time you connect your iPod.

If you turn on both the option to copy photos automatically and the option to copy songs automatically, iTunes copies the songs first and then copies photos from the iPhoto library up to the limit of the iPod's capacity. (See Chapter 11 to find out about transferring photos to your color-display iPod.)

If you have an iPod shuffle, the iTunes Setup Assistant displays an option to copy songs randomly, as shown in Figure 2-9. If you leave the Automatically Choose Songs for My iPod option selected, iTunes copies a random selection of songs to your iPod shuffle. You can always choose to fill your iPod shuffle with a different selection (see Chapter 12).

After you click Next, the Setup Assistant moves on to the dialog for registering your iPod.

3. Click the Register button to register your iPod, and then click Done.

The Setup Assistant allows you to register your iPod with Apple to take advantage of Apple support.

Your iPod's name now appears in the iTunes Source pane under the Music Store selection.

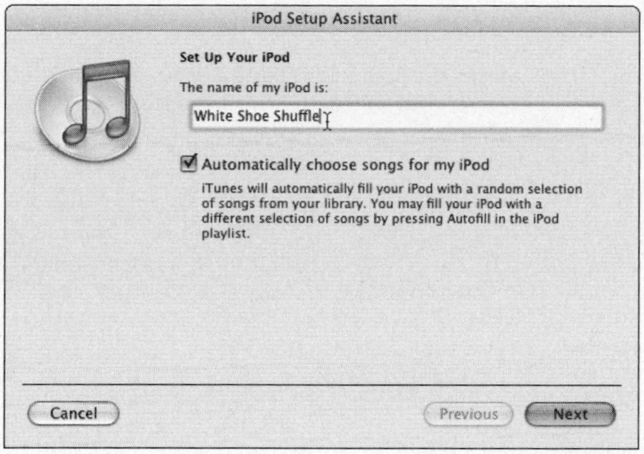

Figure 2-9:
Set up your
iPod shuffle
with the
iPod Setup
Assistant.

> iPod Setup Assistant
>
> **Set Up Your iPod**
>
> The name of my iPod is:
>
> White Shoe Shuffle
>
> ☑ **Automatically choose songs for my iPod**
> iTunes will automatically fill your iPod with a random selection
> of songs from your library. You may fill your iPod with a
> different selection of songs by pressing Autofill in the iPod
> playlist.
>
> Cancel   Previous   Next

If you selected the automatic update feature in the iPod Setup Assistant, the iPod name appears grayed out in the Source pane, and you can't open it. However, your iPod quickly fills up with the music from your iTunes music library — that is, if you *have* music in your library.

If you deselected the automatic update feature, the iPod name appears just like any other source in the Source pane, and you can copy songs to it manually, as we describe in Chapter 12. Of course, if you're just starting out, you probably have no tunes in your library. Your next step is to import music (see Chapter 4).

After finishing setup, the iPod icon appears on the Finder Desktop. If you leave your iPod connected to the Mac, the iPod appears on the Desktop and in iTunes whenever you start iTunes.

To see how much free space is left on the iPod, click the iPod icon on the desktop and choose File⇨Get Info. The Finder displays the Get Info window with information about capacity, amount used, and available space. You can also use the About command on the iPod, which is available on the Settings menu: Choose Settings⇨About. The iPod information screen appears with capacity and available space.

Downloading and Installing Software Upgrades

If iTunes displays a dialog with the message that a new version of iTunes is available and asks whether you would like to download it now, click Yes to download the new version. iTunes launches your Web browser and takes you right to the iTunes download page.

Apple upgrades iTunes and iPod Software regularly to add new features and fix bugs. The best way to stay updated with the latest version is to get in the habit of downloading upgrades over the Internet.

To download iTunes for Mac or Windows, go to the Apple iTunes page on the Web (www.apple.com/itunes), select the appropriate version (Mac or Windows), and then click the Download iTunes button, as shown in Figure 2-10. Follow the instructions to download the installer to your hard drive.

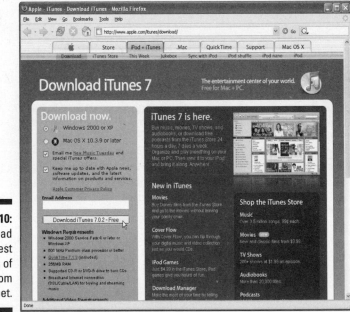

Figure 2-10:
Download the newest version of iTunes from the Internet.

You can set your Mac to automatically download the latest version of iTunes and iPod Software when they become available — just use Software Update from the Mac OS X System Preferences window. Click the Check Now button to check for a new version. If one exists, it appears in a window for you to select. Select it and click Install to download and install it.

If you use a Mac, launch the downloaded installer to unpack and install iTunes, and follow the instructions in "Setting Up the Software for a Mac," which appears earlier in this chapter.

If you use Windows, double-click the iTunesSetup.exe file to install iTunes, and follow the instructions in "Setting Up the Software for Windows," earlier in this chapter.

As with the iTunes software, the version of the iPod software that's provided with your iPod on CD-ROM might not be the newest version — especially if the iPod sat on a store shelf for a few months.

To download the newest version of the iPod software for Mac or Windows, go to Apple's iPod download page on the Web (www.apple.com/ipod/download) and select the appropriate version (Mac or Windows). Follow the instructions to download the installer to your hard drive. Pick a location on your hard drive to save the installer. Then launch the installer to unpack and install the iPod software.

Chapter 3

Getting Started with iTunes

More than half a century ago, jukeboxes were the primary and most convenient way for people to select the music they wanted to hear and share with others, especially newly released music. Juke joints were hopping with the newest hits every night. You could pick any song to play at any time, but you had to insert a coin and pay for each play. Radio eventually supplanted the jukebox as the primary means of releasing new music to the public, and the music was free to hear — but you couldn't choose to play any song you wanted at any time.

Today, using iTunes, you can have a digital jukebox *and* a radio in your computer. Click a button to play any song anytime you want, or click a radio station and play a broadcast. Connect your computer to a stereo amplifier in your home or connect speakers to your computer, and suddenly your computer is the best jukebox in the neighborhood.

This chapter gives you an overview of what you can do with iTunes, and you get started in the simplest way possible: using iTunes to play music tracks on a CD. You can use iTunes just like a jukebox, only better — you don't have to pay for each song you play, and you can play some or all of the songs on an album in any order.

What You Can Do with iTunes

You can download songs, audio books, and videos from the Internet and copy them to iTunes, or you can copy songs and audio books from CDs directly into your iTunes library. You can also buy music and videos online at the iTunes Music Store or subscribe to *podcasts* (feeds that transfer new audio files, such as weekly radio broadcasts, automatically). iTunes downloads content from the store and puts it in your library, making it immediately available for playing. You can then burn the audio content onto a CD or transfer the content to an iPod. You can even use iTunes to listen to Web radio stations and add your favorite stations to your music library.

Transferring songs from a CD to your computer is called *ripping* a CD (to the chagrin of the music industry old-timers who think that users intend to destroy the discs or steal the songs). Ripping an entire CD's worth of songs is quick and easy, and track information, such as artist name and title, arrives automatically over the Internet for most commercial CDs. (You can add the information for rare CDs, custom-mix CDs, live CDs, and others that are unknown to the database.)

You can also add digital video files to your iTunes library — either by choosing videos from the iTunes Music Store (such as TV shows, music videos, and even free movie trailers) or by downloading standard video files in the MPEG-4 format from other sources on the Internet. You can also create your own videos with a digital camcorder or with the iSight camera built into every MacBook and copy them to iTunes to view on your iPod. You can also convert a television signal (or any analog video signal) by using products such as EyeTV 250 from Elgato Systems (www.elgato.com) Although you can't use iTunes to transfer video content from a DVD, you can use other software to convert DVDs to digital video files, and you can transfer video content from older VHS players by using a digital video camcorder — see Chapter 20 for more details.

iTunes gives you the power to organize content into playlists and burn any set of songs, audio books, and podcasts in your library to CD, in any order. You can even set up dynamic smart playlists that reflect your preferences and listening habits. iTunes offers an equalizer with preset settings for all kinds of music and listening environments, and it gives you the ability to customize and save your own personalized settings with each song, audio book, or podcast.

The Mac and Windows versions of iTunes are virtually identical, with the exception that dialogs look a bit different between the two operating systems. There are also a few other differences, mostly related to the different operating environments — the Windows version lets you import Windows Media (WMA) songs, and the Mac version, like most Mac applications, can be controlled by AppleScript programs. Nevertheless, as Apple continues to improve iTunes, the company releases upgrades to both versions at the same time, and the versions are free to download.

Opening the iTunes Window

You can run iTunes anytime to add music, audio books, podcasts, Web radio stations, TV shows, and other videos, and to manage your iTunes library. You don't have to connect your iPod until you're ready to transfer content to it (as we describe in Chapter 12).

When you launch iTunes, your library and other sources of content appear. Figure 3-1 shows the iTunes window on the Mac, and Figure 3-2 shows the Windows version.

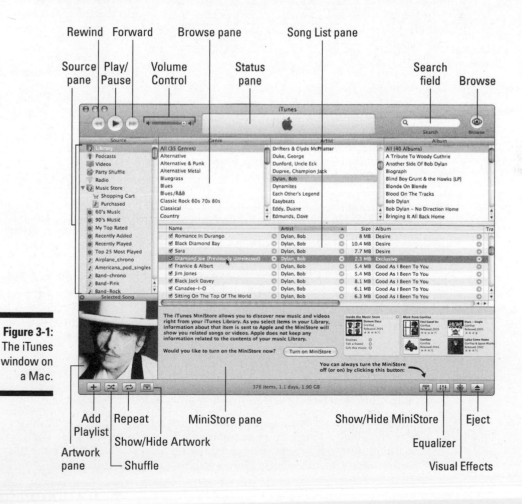

Figure 3-1:
The iTunes window on a Mac.

Rewind Forward Browse pane Song List pane

Source Play/ Volume Status Search
pane Pause Control pane field Browse

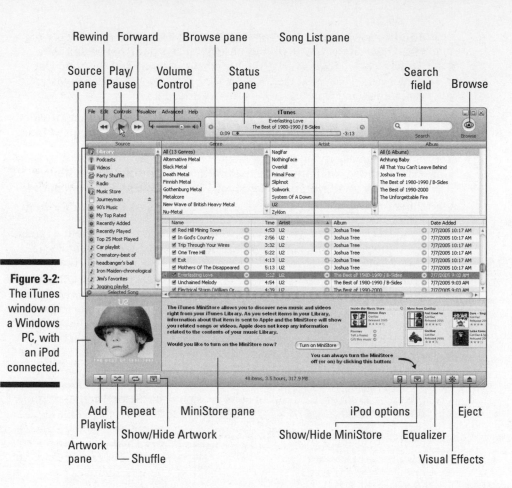

Figure 3-2:
The iTunes
window on
a Windows
PC, with
an iPod
connected.

Add
Playlist Repeat MiniStore pane iPod options Eject

Artwork
pane Show/Hide Artwork Show/Hide MiniStore Equalizer

Shuffle Visual Effects

The iTunes window offers a view of your library and your sources for content,
as well as controls for organizing, importing, and playing content, as follows:

✔ **Source pane:** Displays the source of content, which can be Library (your
iTunes library), Podcasts (the podcasts you've subscribed to), Videos
(the videos you've added), Party Shuffle (a dynamic playlist), Radio
(access to Web radio), Music Store (the iTunes Music Store), your iPod
(if it's connected), and your playlists.

✔ **Song List pane and Browse pane:** Depending on the source that's
selected in the Source pane, these panes display a list of the content in
your library, your podcasts, your videos, the Party Shuffle list, Web
radio stations, the iTunes Music Store, your iPod, or your playlist.

✔ **MiniStore pane:** The MiniStore pane makes suggestions for what to get
from the iTunes Music Store based on what you're listening to. There's
no obligation to buy anything, and you can dispense with this pane if it
bothers you (see "Using the iTunes MiniStore" in this chapter).

✔ **The Browse button:** The Browse button in the upper-right corner toggles between Browse view (with the Song List pane below and the Browse pane above with genre, artist, and album) and the Song List pane by itself. Browse view isn't available when viewing a playlist, podcasts, the Party Shuffle, or the Radio selection.

✔ **Status pane:** When a song, audio book, radio station, podcast, or video is playing, the artist name, piece title (if known), and the elapsed time display in this pane.

✔ **Search field:** Type in this field to search your library. You can also use the search field to peruse a playlist or to look within the iTunes Music Store.

✔ **Player buttons — Forward/Next, Play/Pause, and Previous/Rewind:** Control the playback of content in iTunes.

✔ **Playlist buttons — Add, Shuffle, Repeat:** Add playlists and shuffle or repeat playback of playlists.

✔ **Volume control:** You can change the volume level in iTunes by dragging the volume control slider in the upper-left section of the iTunes window to the right to increase the volume, or to the left to decrease it. The maximum volume of the iTunes volume slider is the maximum set for the computer's sound.

✔ **iPod Options button:** If your iPod is connected (refer to Figure 3-2), the iPod Options button is also available to set iPod preferences.

✔ **Miscellaneous buttons — Show/Hide Artwork, Show/Hide MiniStore, Equalizer, Visual Effects, Eject:** Display or hide artwork (either your own or the artwork supplied with purchased songs and videos), the MiniStore pane, the equalizer, and visual effects. The Eject button ejects a CD or iPod. However, whereas a CD actually pops out of some computers, iPods are hard drives, and ejecting them simply removes *(unmounts)* the drives from the system.

If you don't like the width of the Source pane, you can adjust it by dragging the shallow dot on the vertical bar between the Source pane and the Song List pane and Browse pane. You can also adjust the height of the Song List and Browse panes by dragging the shallow dot on the horizontal bar between them. To resize the iTunes window on a Mac, drag diagonally from the bottom-right corner. In Windows, drag the edges of the window horizontally or vertically.

Playing CD Tracks in iTunes

iTunes needs content. You can get started right away by ripping music from CDs into your library, but for more instant gratification, you can *play* music right off the CD without importing it. Maybe you don't want to put the music into your library yet. Maybe you just want to hear it first, as part of your Play First, Rip Later plan.

Insert any music CD or even a CD-R that someone burned for you. The song tracks appear in the iTunes song list as generic, unnamed tracks with numbers rather than actual song titles. The Browse button changes to an Import button when a CD is inserted, in anticipation of ripping the CD.

After you insert the CD, iTunes displays a message about accessing the Gracenote CDDB on the Internet, and then iTunes presents the track information for each song automatically, as shown in Figure 3-3. (Gracenote CDDB is a song database on the Internet that knows the track names of most commercial CDs but not homemade mix CDs. You can read about it and editing song information in Chapter 9.)

Figure 3-3:
CD track
info appears
after iTunes
consults the
Internet.

When you play a CD in iTunes, it's just like using a CD player. To play a CD from the first track, click the Play button. (If you clicked somewhere else after inserting the disc, you might have to click the first track to select it before clicking the Play button.) The Play button then turns into a Pause button, and the song plays.

When the song finishes, iTunes continues playing the songs in the list in sequence until you click the Pause button (which then toggles back into the Play button) or until the song list ends. You can skip to the next or previous song by using the arrow keys on your keyboard or by clicking the Forward button or the Back button (next to the Play button). You can also double-click another song in the list to start playing it.

You can press the spacebar to perform the same function as clicking the Play button; pressing it again is just like clicking the Pause button.

The Status pane above the list of songs tells you the name of the artist or the song title (if known), as well as the elapsed time of the track. When you click the artist name, the artist name disappears, and the song title appears. If you click the song title, the artist name comes back up. If you click the Elapsed Time status, the status changes to the remaining time and then, with another click, to the total time. (One more click brings you back to the elapsed time.)

Eject a CD by clicking the Eject button or by choosing Controls⇨Eject Disc. Another way to eject the CD is to click the Eject icon next to the CD's name in the Source pane. You can also right-click the CD's name and choose Eject from the contextual menu.

Rearranging and repeating tracks

You can rearrange the order of the tracks to automatically play them in any sequence you want — similar to programming a CD player. Click the up arrow at the top of the first column in the song list (refer to Figure 3-3), and it changes to a down arrow, and the tracks appear in reverse order.

To change the order of tracks that you're playing in sequence, just click and hold the track number in the leftmost column for the song, and then drag it up or down in the list. You can set up the tracks to play in a completely different sequence.

Skipping tracks

To skip tracks so that they don't play in sequence, deselect the check box next to the song names. iTunes skips deselected songs when you play the entire sequence.

To remove all check marks from a list, press ⌘ on a Mac or Ctrl in Windows while clicking a check mark. Select an empty check box while pressing ⌘ or Ctrl to add check marks to the entire list.

Repeating a song list

You can repeat an entire song list by clicking the Repeat button, which you find below the Source pane on the left side of the iTunes window (or by choosing Controls⇨Repeat All). When it's selected, the Repeat button shows blue highlighting. Click the Repeat button again to repeat the current song (or choose Controls⇨Repeat One). The button changes to include a blue-highlighted numeral 1. Click it once more to return to normal playback (or choose Controls⇨Repeat Off).

TIP The Shuffle button, located to the left of the Repeat button, plays the songs in the list in random order, which can be fun. You can then press the arrow keys on your keyboard or click the Back and Forward buttons to jump around in random order.

Displaying visuals

The visual effects in iTunes can turn your display into a light show that's synchronized to the music in your library. You can watch a cool visual display of eye candy while the music plays — or leave it on like a lava lamp.

 Click the Visual Effects button in the bottom-right corner of the iTunes window to display visual effects. An animation appears in the iTunes window and synchronizes with the music.

In addition to the animation replacing the iTunes song list, an Options button replaces the Import button in the upper-right corner of the iTunes window. You can click the Options button to open the Visualizer Options dialog, as shown in Figure 3-4.

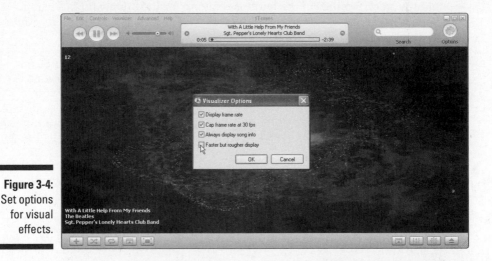

Figure 3-4:
Set options
for visual
effects.

The Visualizer Options dialog offers the following options that affect the animation (but not the performance of iTunes when it's playing music):

 ✔ **Display Frame Rate:** Displays the frame rate of the animation along with the animation.

 ✔ **Cap Frame Rate at 30 fps:** Keeps the frame rate at 30 fps (frames per second) or lower, which is roughly the speed of video.

- ✔ **Always Display Song Info:** Displays the song name, artist, and album for the song currently playing, along with the animation.

- ✔ **Use OpenGL (Mac only):** You can choose to use OpenGL, the most widely used standard for three-dimensional graphics programming, to display very cool animation with faster performance.

- ✔ **Faster but Rougher Display:** The animation plays faster, with rougher graphics. Select this option if your animation plays too slowly.

The Visualizer menu in iTunes gives you even more control over visual effects. You can choose Visualizer➪Small or Visualizer➪Medium to display the visual effects in a rectangle inside the iTunes window, or choose Visualizer➪Large to fill the iTunes window. Choosing Visualizer➪Full Screen sets the visual effects to fill up the entire screen. When displaying the full-screen visual effects, you can click the mouse button or press Escape (Esc) to stop the display and return to iTunes. Choosing Visualizer➪Turn Visualizer On is the same as clicking the Visual Effects button: It displays the visual effects.

While the animated visual effects play, press Shift-/ (as if you're typing a question mark) to see a list of keyboard functions. Depending on the visual effect, you might see more choices of keyboard functions by pressing Shift-/ again.

To turn off the visual effects display, click the Visual Effects button again. You can leave the effects on (except when in full-screen mode) even while opening the equalizer because you still have access to the playback controls.

You can enhance iTunes with plug-ins that provide even better visuals. For example, SpectroGraph from Dr. Lex displays a spectrogram of the music, and Cover Version from imagomat displays the album cover artwork. You can find these and many others at PluginsWorld.com (`http://itunes.pluginsworld.com`).

Using the iTunes MiniStore

If you turn on the iTunes MiniStore pane, which appears below the Song List and Browse panes, it makes suggestions for what to buy from the iTunes Music Store based on what you're listening to. No, celebrity DJs and music historians aren't choosing what shows up here; your peers are. The MiniStore informs the online store about the songs you select whenever the MiniStore pane is open. The store simply shows you music that other listeners purchased when they purchased the music you're playing. You can click any item in the MiniStore pane to go right to the iTunes Music Store page for that item — see Chapter 4 for details about using the music store.

The MiniStore operates only if you give it permission first. When you first start iTunes, the MiniStore is not yet turned on (refer to Figures 3-1 and 3-2); it shows only the Turn On MiniStore button until you turn it on. To turn on the MiniStore pane's function, click the Turn On MiniStore button inside the MiniStore pane. After turning it on, the MiniStore pane appears at the bottom of the window, as shown in Figure 3-5, offering suggestions as you play the content in your library.

Figure 3-5:
Turn on the
MiniStore to
see choices
from the
online store
based on
your
selections.

If you turn on the MiniStore, iTunes transmits information back to the store about the songs you select whenever the MiniStore pane is *open*. The iTunes MiniStore does *not* transmit the current song data if the MiniStore pane is hidden. Click the Show/Hide MiniStore button to show or hide the MiniStore pane (or choose Edit➪Show MiniStore or Edit➪Hide MiniStore).

If the MiniStore can't find the artist for the song you're playing, it displays No Match and offers choices that are simply in the same genre, along with New Releases, Today's Top songs and Top Albums. If you select an audio book or TV show in your library, you'll see the top-selling audio books or TV shows in the MiniStore. If you don't have an iTunes Music Store available for your country, you see the U.S. store, just as Chuck Berry once sang, "Anything you want, we got right here in the U.S.A."

Chapter 4

Shopping at the iTunes Music Store

*W*hen Apple announced its online music service, Apple chairman Steve Jobs remarked that other services put forward by the music industry tend to treat consumers like criminals. Steve had a point. Many of these services cost more and add a level of copy protection that prevents consumers from burning more than one CD or using the music they bought on other computers or portable MP3 players.

Record labels had been dragging their feet for years, experimenting with online sales and taking legal action against online sites that allowed free downloads and music copying. Although the free music attracted millions of listeners, the free services were under legal attack in several countries, and the digital music that was distributed wasn't of the highest quality (not to mention the widespread and sometimes intentional misspellings in the song information and artist names). Consumers grew even warier when the Record Industry Association of America (RIAA), a lobbying organization looking out for the interests of record companies, began legal proceedings against people for illegal copyright infringement — people who possibly thought they were downloading free music.

No one should go to jail for being a music junkie. Consumers and the industry both needed a solution, so Apple did the research on how to make a service that worked better and was easier to use, and the company forged ahead with the iTunes Music Store. By all accounts, Apple has succeeded in offering the easiest, fastest, and most cost-effective service for buying music online for your computer and iPod. The iTunes Music Store even offers gift certificates that you can e-mail to others and allows accounts that you can set up for others (such as children) with credit limits but without the need to use a credit card. Apple adds new features to the store almost every week.

In this chapter, we show you how to sign in and take advantage of what the iTunes Music Store has to offer.

Visiting the iTunes Music Store

You can visit the iTunes Music Store by connecting to the Internet and using iTunes or America Online (AOL). You can even click a Launch Music Store link on Apple's Web site, or a similar link on Web sites that are iTunes affiliates with songs for sale (such as www.rockument.com). The link automatically launches your installed copy of iTunes and opens the Music Store.

As of this writing, the iTunes Music Store offers millions of songs, with most songs available for download at the price of 99 cents each and entire albums available for download at less than the CD price. You can play the songs on up to five different computers, burn CDs, and use the songs on the iPod. The store also offers audio books from Audible.com, free movie trailers, and free *podcasts*. (Podcasts are similar to syndicated radio shows, but you can download them into iTunes and listen to them at your convenience on your computer and iPod.) You can even find music videos and TV shows that you can purchase, download into iTunes, and use with your fifth-generation iPod.

As with most online music services, the music you buy online is not as high in audio quality as music on a commercial CD, although most people can't tell the difference when playing the music on car stereos or at low volume. In Chapter 18, we explain why there is a quality tradeoff to reduce the space the music occupies on the hard drive or flash memory of your iPod. The quality of the music sold in the iTunes Music Store is comparable to the quality you get when *ripping* (copying) your CDs into iTunes by using the MP3 or AAC formats, which we explain in Chapter 18. And although you do get a bit of song information such as artist, song titles, the album title, and cover artwork, the iTunes Music Store currently doesn't provide extensive liner notes that you might find on a commercial CD. We hope that soon the store will offer the equivalent of a complete jewel-case booklet when purchasing entire albums.

The iTunes Music Store is part of iTunes version 4 and newer. If you're running an older version of iTunes, download the newest version, as we describe in Chapter 2.

You can preview any song or video for up to 30 seconds (and audio books and podcasts up to about 90 seconds), and if you have an account set up, you can buy and download songs, audio books, podcasts, and videos immediately. We don't know of a faster way to purchase content.

To open the iTunes Music Store, you have at least four choices:

- ✔ **Click the Music Store option in the Source pane.** The Music Store's home page opens, as shown in Figure 4-1.

- ✔ **Click any link in the MiniStore pane.** The Music Store's home page opens and automatically switches your Source pane selection to Music Store. The MiniStore pane offers suggestions based on the music you select in your library — you can turn this feature on or off by clicking the Show/Hide MiniStore button (see Chapter 3 for details).

- ✔ **Follow a music link in iTunes.** Click the *content link* (the gray-circled arrow next to a song or video title, artist name, or album title) to go to a Music Store page related to the song or video, artist, or album. iTunes performs a search in the Music Store by using the content information. If nothing closely related turns up, at least you end up in the Music Store, and you might even find music you like that you didn't know about.

- ✔ **Go to iTunes on AOL and click the iTunes link.** If you use AOL, you can browse or search the AOL music area for songs and click the iTunes link to automatically launch iTunes and go to the Music Store.

If you need to fire up your modem and log on to your Internet service to go online, do so before clicking the Music Store option or following a music link.

The Music Store uses the iTunes Song List and Browse panes to display its wares. You can check out content to your heart's content although you can't buy songs and videos unless you have a Music Store account set up. You can use the Choose Genre pop-up menu to specify music genres, or you can click links for new releases, exclusive tracks, and so on.

We use the term *pop-up menu* for menus on the Mac that literally pop up from dialogs and windows; the same type of menu in Windows actually drops down and is called a *drop-down menu*. We use pop-up menu for both.

The iTunes Music Store also provides buttons on a gray bar just above the advertised albums and videos in the Song List pane. The left and right triangle buttons work just like the Back and Forward buttons of a Web browser, moving back a page or forward a page. The button with the Home icon takes you to the iTunes Music Store home page. The Browse button in the upper-right corner switches the view between Browse view (with the Song List and Browse panes both open) and Song List view (with only the Song List pane open).

iTunes Music Store home page   Switch between Browse and Song List views.

Back   Forward   Sign In button

Figure 4-1:
The iTunes
Music Store
home page.

Setting Up an Account

You need an account to buy music. To create an iTunes Music Store account, follow these steps:

1. **In iTunes, click the Music Store option in the Source pane or click a music link or MiniStore pane link.**

   The Music Store's home page appears (refer to Figure 4-1), replacing the iTunes Song List pane and Browse pane.

2. **Click the Sign In button in the upper-right area of the window to create an account (or sign in to an existing account).**

   If you already have an account that you've logged on to before using iTunes, the account name appears in place of the Sign In button.

   After clicking the Sign In button, iTunes displays the account sign-in dialog, as shown in Figure 4-2.

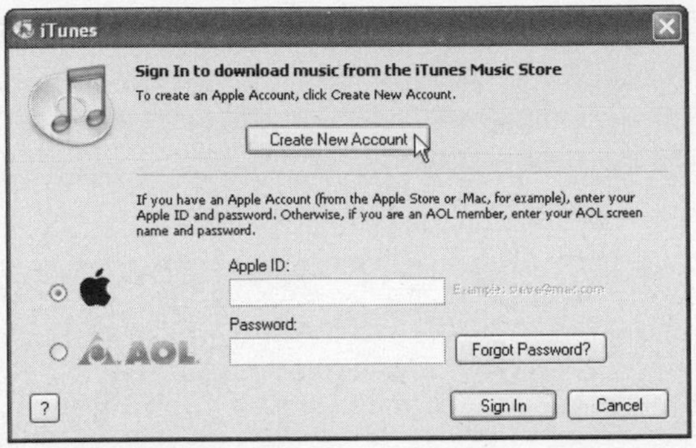

Figure 4-2:
The sign-in
dialog for
the iTunes
Music
Store.

If you already set up an account with the iTunes Music Store, with the .Mac service, with other Apple services (such as the Apple Developer Connection), or with AOL, you're halfway there. Type your ID and password and then click the Sign In button. Apple remembers the personal information that you put in previously, so you don't have to re-enter it every time you visit the Music Store. If you forgot your password, click the Forgot Password? button, and iTunes provides a dialog to answer your test question. If you answer correctly, iTunes then e-mails your password to you.

3. Click the Create New Account button.

iTunes displays a new page, replacing the iTunes Music Store home page with the terms of use and an explanation of steps to create a new account.

4. Click the Agree button and then fill in your personal account information.

iTunes displays the next page of the setup procedure, shown in Figure 4-3, which requires you to type your e-mail address, password, test question and answer (in case you forget your password), birth date, and privacy options.

5. Click the Continue button to go to the next page of the account setup procedure, and then enter your credit card information.

The entire procedure is secure, so you don't have to worry. The Music Store keeps your personal information (including your credit card information) on file, and you don't have to type it again.

6. Click Done to finish the procedure.

You can now use the iTunes Music Store to purchase and download music to play in iTunes and use on an iPod.

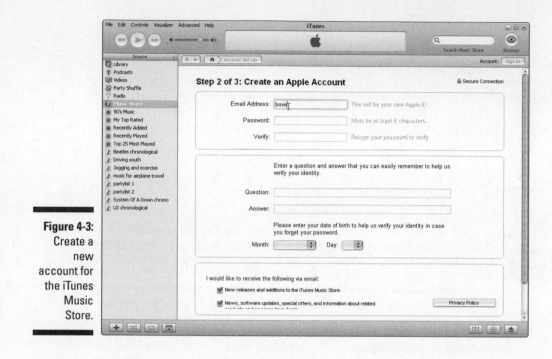

Figure 4-3:
Create a
new
account for
the iTunes
Music
Store.

If you use AOL and the AOL Wallet feature, you can assign payment for your Music Store account to your AOL Wallet. AOL Wallet contains your billing and credit card information for purchases. AOL Wallet automatically fills information into the text boxes of the account setup pages so that you don't have to.

Click the Choose Store button in the top-left corner of the iTunes Music Store page to choose online music stores in other countries. iTunes displays a page of buttons with flags of other countries — click one to go to the home page for the iTunes Music Store for that country. For example, the music store in France displays menus in French and features hit songs and TV shows for the French market.

Browsing and Previewing Songs

The iTunes Music Store home page is loaded with specials and advertisements to peruse. You can also use the Genre pop-up menu to see only those specials and ads for a particular genre. You can click just about anything on the home page to get more information: today's top-ten songs and top-ten videos, exclusive offerings, albums, artists' names, and more.

What if you're looking for music in a particular genre? You can browse the store by genre and artist name in a method similar to browsing your iTunes library. To browse the store, click the Browse button in the top-right corner of the iTunes window. iTunes displays the store's offerings categorized by genre, and within each genre, by artist and album. Select a genre in the Genre column, then a subgenre in the Subgenre column, then an artist in the Artist column, and finally an album in the Album column, which takes you to the list of songs from that album that are available to preview or purchase, as shown in Figure 4-4.

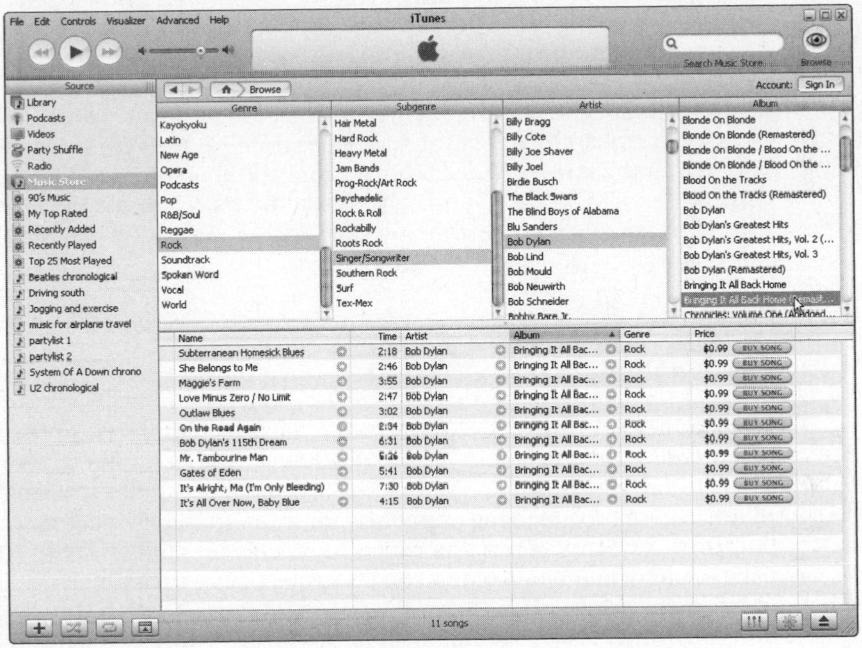

Figure 4-4:
Browsing
the Music
Store for
artists and
albums.

To see more information about a song or the album that it came from, click the *music link* (one of the gray-circled arrow buttons in the Song List pane):

- ✔ Clicking the arrow in the Artist column takes you to the artist's page of albums.

- ✔ Clicking the arrow in the Album column takes you to the album page.

- ✔ Clicking the arrow in the Genre column takes you back to the genre's specials page (or the home page).

Our only complaint about browsing by artist is that artists are listed alphabetically by first name — you have to look up Bob Dylan under *Bob*.

To preview a song, click the song title in the song list, and then click the Play button or press the spacebar.

By default, the previews play on your computer off the Internet in a stream, so you might hear a few hiccups in the playback. Each preview lasts about 30 seconds. Just when you start really getting into the song, it ends — but if the song is irresistible, you can buy it on the spot.

If you have a slow Internet connection — especially if it's slower than 128 Kbps — the preview might stutter. Choose iTunes⇨Preferences on a Mac or Edit⇨Preferences on a Windows PC and click the Store tab to see the Store preferences. In the Store preferences, click the Load Complete Preview before Playing option to turn it on.

If you know specifically what you're looking for, you can search rather than browse. The Search field in the top-right corner of the iTunes window lets you search the iTunes Music Store for just about anything. Type part of a song title or artist name to quickly search the store, or use the Power Search feature to narrow your search. (See the "Power searching" section later in this chapter.)

Browsing the charts

What do Louis Armstrong, Roy Orbison, the Beach Boys, Dean Martin, and Mary Wells have in common? Each one had a top-ten hit in the charts for 1964. So says *Billboard,* the weekly magazine for the entertainment industry that has kept tabs on song popularity for more than half a century. The iTunes Music Store offers pop charts for each year going back to 1946, so you can probably find some of the songs that you grew up with.

You can't find *every* song that made the charts — only the songs that the iTunes Music Store offers.

To find the charts, click the Billboard Charts link on the home page, or select Charts at the very top of the Genre column. From the Charts column, you can select Billboard Hot 100, Billboard Top Country, or Billboard Top R&B (rhythm & blues).

Don't like the songs that *Billboard* chose? Try selecting Radio Charts from the Genre column and then pick a city in the United States in the middle column. Now you can find out what songs were hits in your hometown, no matter where you are at the moment.

Power searching

You're serious about music, and you desire the power to search for exactly what you want. Click the Power Search link on the iTunes Music Store home page to go to the Power Search page, as shown in Figure 4-5. (At the time of this writing, power searching didn't work for TV shows.)

Figure 4-5: Use Power Search to find a song in the Music Store.

You can fill in the song title, the artist name, and the album title, or just fill in one of those text boxes (for example, if all you know is the song title). You can narrow your search by picking a genre from the Genre pop-up menu and by adding a composer name. After you fill in as much as you know, click the Search button.

Browsing celebrity and published playlists

Do you want to be influenced? Do you want to know what influenced some of today's music celebrities and buy what they have in their record collections? Scroll down the iTunes Music Store home page and click a celebrity name in the Celebrity Playlists pane, or click the Celebrity Playlists link to go to the page of celebrity playlists.

A typical celebrity playlist offers about an album's worth of songs from different artists. You can preview or buy any song in the list or follow the music links to the artist or album page.

The Music Store home page lists some of the celebrity playlists, but a lot more aren't listed there (over 250 the last time we checked). To see all the celebrity playlists, click the See All button at the bottom of the Celebrity Playlist links on the home page.

You can also be influenced by other Music Store buyers and do a little influencing yourself. Click the iMix link on the Music Store home page to check out playlists that have been contributed by other consumers and published in the Music Store. iMixes offer 30-second previews of any songs in the playlist. To find out how to publish your own iMix playlist, see Chapter 10.

You can also include a Web link (URL) to an iTunes Music Store page in an e-mail message or other document so the reader can click the link to go directly to the store page. Drag any link, track, or graphic from a Music Store page to an e-mail message or document you are composing, and iTunes copies the link. You can also Ctrl-click (Mac) or right-click (Windows) the item and choose Copy iTunes Music Store URL.

Browsing and Previewing TV Shows and Videos

The uncool thing about video stores — besides the weird people who hang out in them — is the lack of any ability to preview videos before you buy them. And the only way to preview TV shows is to watch TV. However, you can use the online iTunes Music Store to preview short films, music videos, and TV shows before you buy them. Most shows offer 30 seconds of previewing time.

To find TV shows, do one of the following:

✔ Click the TV Shows link in the list of Music Store links on the home page. The store displays advertisements for the most popular TV shows, and a list of Today's Top Ten TV Shows.

✔ Select TV Shows from the Genre column, then a TV show in the Shows column, and a season of episodes in the Seasons column.

To find short films, click the Short Films link in the list of Music Store links on the home page. The Music Videos link on the iTunes Music Store home page takes you to the Music Videos page.

To preview a TV show, short film, or music video, click the title in the list and then click the Play button or press the spacebar. (Short films are actually videos on the computer, so we use "videos" from now on.) The video plays in the Artwork pane in the lower-left corner of the iTunes window, as shown in Figure 4-6. If the Artwork pane isn't visible, click the Show/Hide Artwork button to display it. Click the iTunes Play/Pause, Forward/Next, and Previous/Rewind buttons to control playback, and use the iTunes volume slider to control the volume, just like with songs. For more details about playing videos in iTunes, see Chapter 6.

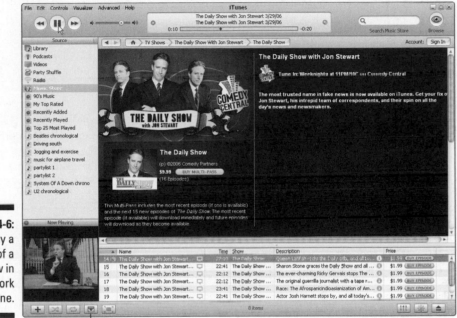

Figure 4-6:
Play a preview of a TV show in the Artwork pane.

Show/Hide Artwork

You can play the video in a larger, separate window, as shown in Figure 4-7, by clicking inside the Artwork pane while the video is playing. You can then control video playback by using the separate window's controls: Click the right-facing triangle on the bottom-left side of the window to play the video and click it again to pause the video. Drag the slider to move forward or backward through the video. You can click the Rewind or Fast-Forward buttons in the bottom-right corner of the window to move backward or forward through a video.

The iTunes Music Store also offers music videos for sale. You can select and buy a music video, either as part of an album package or separately, and download the video into iTunes just like a song. The video file appears in your Purchased list just like any other song. See the "Buying and Downloading Content" section for more info.

Figure 4-7:
Play a
preview of a
TV show in
a small
window.

Playing Free Movie Trailers

Free movie trailers are just a click away. The Movie Trailers link on the iTunes Music Store home page takes you to a Movie Trailers page. Click an advertisement, thumbnail, or title to go to the movie trailer's page, and click the link for the trailer (usually called "Trailer" or "Teaser"). Then click the Small button to select a small video window size for quicker downloading, the Medium button for a medium-sized window, or the Large button for a larger video window size for better viewing, as shown in Figure 4-8.

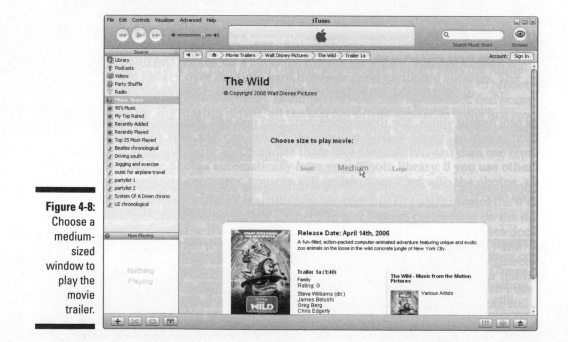

Figure 4-8:
Choose a
medium-
sized
window to
play the
movie
trailer.

It might take some time to download the video before it starts to play. After the QuickTime player controls appear in the iTunes window, as shown in Figure 4-9, you can click the movie's Play button (the right triangle next to the Sound button) to play the video.

Figure 4-9:
Play the movie trailer in a medium-sized window.

You can play music in your iTunes library while waiting for a Music Store page or video to download over the Internet. Double-click the Music Store option in the Source pane to open the Music Store in a separate window. With two windows, you can use the first window to play music in your library while using the second to browse the Music Store and download a video. The first window stops playing music when you use the second window to play a video or select a song to preview or buy.

Browsing and Subscribing to Podcasts

Podcasting is a popular method of publishing audio files to the Internet, enabling people to subscribe to a feed and receive new audio files automatically. Similar to a tape of a radio broadcast, you can save a podcast and play it back at your convenience, both in iTunes on your computer and on your iPod. A podcast can be anything from a single song to a commentary-hosted radio show.

The iTunes Podcast page on the iTunes Music Store lets you browse, find, preview, and subscribe to thousands of podcasts, all of which are free of charge. You don't need an account to browse the store and subscribe to podcasts.

To find podcasts in the iTunes Music Store, do one of the following:

✔ Click the Podcasts link located among the Music Store links on the home page. The store displays the Podcast page, with advertisements for popular podcasts and a list of Today's Top Podcasts. You can click the pop-up menu under Today's Top Podcasts, as shown in Figure 4-10, to see the most popular podcasts in specific categories.

You can also get to the Podcast page by clicking Podcasts in the iTunes Source pane and then clicking Podcast Directory at the bottom of the Song List view.

✔ Search from the Podcast page of the iTunes Music Store (refer to Figure 4-10). Scroll down just a bit, and in the left column, enter your search terms in the search field just above the Search All Podcasts pop-up menu. Use the Search All Podcasts pop-up menu to narrow your search by podcast title or author.

Figure 4-10: Select a category to see the popular podcasts in that category.

✔ Browse all podcasts in a particular category by clicking the Browse button in the top-right corner and then selecting Podcasts (alphabetized under P) in the Genre column, as shown in Figure 4-11. Select a category from the Category column and a subcategory from the Subcategory column.

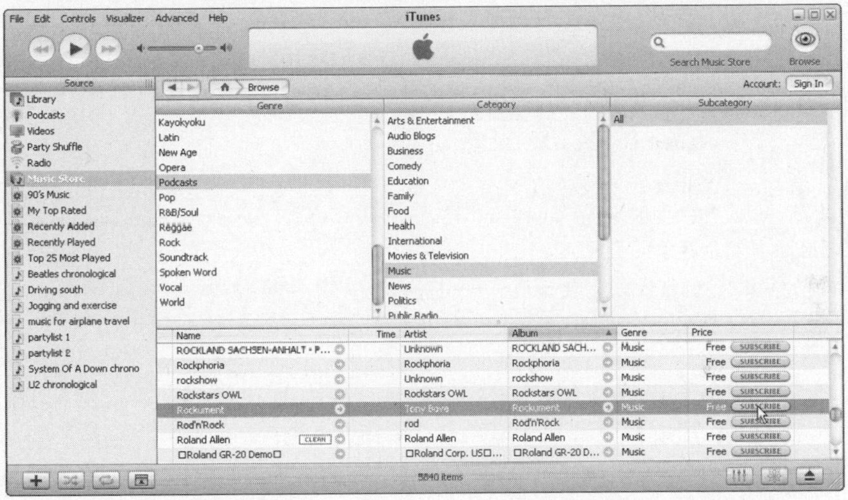

Figure 4-11: Browse all podcasts in a particular category.

After you select a podcast, the store displays the podcast's specific page in the iTunes Music Store, as shown in Figure 4-12, with all available podcast episodes in the song list. (There are two episodes in Figure 4-12 for the Rockument podcast.)

To select, play, and subscribe to a podcast, follow these steps:

1. **Choose a podcast in the Music Store.**

   The Music Store offers a description, a Subscribe button to receive new podcasts, and a link to the podcast's Web site for more information. The page also lists the most recent podcast. Some podcasters offer several podcasts in one feed. You can click the lowercase *i* icon on the far-right podcast listing margin to display separate information about the podcast.

2. **To preview the podcast, click the Play button or press the spacebar.**

   You can play a preview of any podcast in the list. iTunes plays the podcast for about 90 seconds just like a Web radio station, streaming to your computer. To jump ahead in a podcast or play the entire podcast episode, you must first subscribe to the podcast. By subscribing, you download a set of podcast episodes to your computer.

3. **Click the Subscribe button to subscribe to the podcast.**

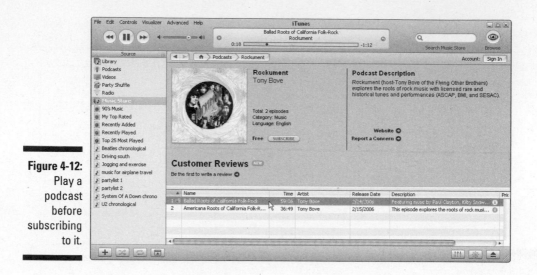

Figure 4-12:
Play a
podcast
before
subscribing
to it.

In typical Apple fashion, iTunes first displays an alert to confirm that you want to subscribe to the podcast.

4. Click OK to confirm.

iTunes downloads the podcast to your computer and switches to the Podcasts selection in the Source pane. iTunes displays your newly sub-scribed podcast in the song list, as shown in Figure 4-13.

5. (Optional) Get more episodes of the podcast.

When you subscribe to a podcast, you get the current episode. However, each podcast can contain multiple episodes. To download previously available episodes, click the triangle next to the podcast name in the song list (refer to Figure 4-13) to see the individual episodes, and then click the Get button next to an episode to download it.

6. To play the podcast in full, select it and click the Play button.

You can now play the podcast just like any other song in your iTunes library. The blue dot next to a podcast means you haven't yet played it. As soon as you start listening to a podcast, the dot disappears. For more information about playing podcasts, see Chapter 6.

Anyone can create a podcast and then submit it to the store by following Apple's published guidelines. (Click the Submit a Podcast link on the Podcast page in the store.) In fact, the Rockument and the Flying Other Brothers music podcasts, available in the iTunes Music Store (and from www.rockument. com), are produced by one of this book's authors. You can find out more about creating podcasts in *Podcasting For Dummies,* by Tee Morris and Evo Terra (Wiley).

Figure 4-13:
The
subscribed
podcasts
appear in
the Podcast
song list.

You can play the podcast, incorporate it into playlists, and make copies and burn CDs as much as you like. If you don't like the podcast, simply delete it from your iTunes library and update your iPod.

Buying and Downloading Content

As you select songs, audio books, and videos, you can purchase them and download each of them to your computer immediately. Alternatively, you can gather your selections in a virtual shopping cart first to see your choices and decide whether to purchase them before downloading them all at once.

Depending on how you set up your account, you can buy and download the content immediately with the 1-Click option or place the items in your Music Store Shopping Cart temporarily, to purchase and download later. You can change your Music Store shopping method at any time.

Each time you buy music, you get an e-mail from the iTunes Music Store with the purchase information. It's nice to know right away what you bought.

Your decision to download each item immediately or add to a shopping cart and download later is likely based on how your computer connects to the Internet. If you have a slow connection such as a phone line, you probably want to use the shopping cart to avoid tying up the phone with each download.

Using 1-Click

Apple offers 1-Click technology in the iTunes Music Store so that with one click, your digital content immediately starts downloading to your computer — and the purchase is done.

With 1-Click, you click the Buy button — whether the item is a song, an album, a TV show episode, or an audio book. For example, if you select a song in the song list, click the Buy Song button in the far-right column for the song. (You might have to scroll your iTunes Music Store window to see the far-right column.) When you select a TV show episode, click the Buy Episode button in the far-right column. You can click the Buy Album button in an album advertisement. With 1-Click, iTunes complies immediately.

The store displays a warning dialog to make sure that you want to buy the item, and you can then go through with it or cancel. If you click the Buy button to purchase it, the song, album, audio book, or video downloads automatically shows up in your iTunes library. The Music Store keeps track of your purchases over a 24-hour period and charges a total sum rather than for each single purchase.

1-Click seems more like two clicks. If you really want to use only one click to buy a song, select the Don't Warn Me About Buying Songs option in the warning dialog so that you never see it again.

Using the shopping cart

You don't have to use the 1-Click technology. Instead, you can add items to the shopping cart to delay purchasing and downloading until you're ready. With the shopping cart, the store remembers your selections, allowing you to browse the store at different times and add to your total without making any purchases final. You can also remove items from the cart at any time. When you're ready to buy, you can purchase and download the items in your cart in one fell swoop.

If you switch to the shopping cart method (see the following section, "Changing your Store preferences"), the Buy button changes to an Add button — as in Add Song, Add Album, Add Episode, and so on. After adding items, you can view your shopping cart by clicking the triangle next to the Music Store option in the Source pane to show the Music Store selections (see Figure 4-14) and selecting the Shopping Cart option.

The shopping cart appears with your selections listed in the Song List pane, and recommendations from the store appear along the top of the window. Albums appear with a triangle next to their name, which you can click to open and see the album's songs. As you can see in Figure 4-14, albums, individual songs, music videos, TV episodes, and audio books are listed in alphabetical order by artist name (or TV show name, as in *Alfred Hitchcock Presents* and *Monk*).

Figure 4-14: View your shopping cart before purchasing the items from the Music Store.

When you're ready to purchase everything in your shopping cart, click the BUY NOW button in the lower-right corner of the Shopping Cart pane to close the sale and download all the items at once. Alternatively, you can click the Buy (for an album) or Buy Song buttons for each item that you want to purchase.

To delete items from your shopping cart, select them and press Delete/Backspace. A warning appears asking whether you're sure that you want to remove the selected items. Click Yes to go ahead and remove the selections from your shopping cart.

Purchased songs also appear in a special Purchased playlist under the Music Store option in the Source pane. You can see the list of all the songs that you purchased by clicking the triangle to expand the Music Store option in the

Source pane and then clicking the Purchased option. The Song List pane and Browse pane change to show the list of songs that you purchased (which includes audio books). To see videos you purchased, select the Videos option in the Source pane.

Changing your Store preferences

You can change your shopping method by choosing iTunes⇨Preferences on the Mac or by choosing Edit⇨Preferences in Windows. In the Preferences window, click the Store button. The Store Preferences window appears.

You can set the following features:

- ✔ Change from 1-Click to Shopping Cart or vice versa. 1-Click is the default.

- ✔ When you purchase a collection of songs, such as an iMix prepared by other music store visitors or a list of iTunes Essentials chosen by the store staff, you set iTunes to automatically assign the collection to a new playlist by selecting the Automatically Create Playlists When Buying Song Collections option. For details about using playlists, see Chapter 10.

- ✔ If you select the Play Songs After Downloading option, the songs that you buy start playing as soon as they completely download to your iTunes library.

- ✔ For better playing performance (fewer hiccups) with previews over slow Internet connections, select the Load Complete Preview before Playing option. (It's deselected by default.)

If you use more than one computer with your Music Store account, you can set the preferences for each computer differently and still use the same account. For example, your home computer might have a faster connection than your laptop on the road, and you can set your iTunes preferences accordingly — the home computer could be set to 1-Click, and the laptop could be set to shopping cart.

Resuming interrupted downloads

All sales are final — you can't return the digital merchandise. However, the download must be successful — you have to receive all of it — before the Music Store charges you for the purchase. If for any reason the download is interrupted or fails to complete, your order remains active until you connect to the store again.

iTunes remembers to continue the download when you return to iTunes and connect to the Internet. If for some reason the download doesn't continue, choose Advanced➪Check for Purchases to continue the interrupted download. You can also use this command to check for any purchased music that hasn't downloaded yet.

If your computer's hard drive crashes and you lose your information, you also lose all your digital content — you have to purchase and download them again. However, you can mitigate this kind of disaster by backing up your content library, which we describe in detail in Chapter 13 — including backing up video files. You can also burn your purchases to an audio CD, as we describe in Chapter 14.

Redeeming gift certificates and prepaid cards

If you're the fortunate recipient of an iTunes Music Store gift certificate, all you need to do is go to the Music Store in iTunes and set up a new account if you don't already have one. Recipients of gift certificates can set up new accounts without having to provide a credit card number. As a recipient of a gift, you can simply click None for the credit card option and use the gift certificate as the sole payment method.

You can receive gift certificates on paper, delivered by the postal service, or by e-mail. You can also receive a prepaid card with a fixed balance. To redeem a certificate, click the Gift Certificate link on the iTunes Music Store home page and then click the Redeem Now button. Then type the number printed on the lower-right edge of the certificate or supplied in the e-mail, click the Redeem button to credit your account, and then sign in to your account or set up an account. To redeem the amount of a prepaid card, click the iTunes Music Cards link on the iTunes Music Store home page, enter the 16-digit code exactly as it appears on the prepaid card, click the Redeem Now button, and then sign in or set up your account.

If you use Apple's Mail program or access your .Mac e-mail through the Safari Web browser, you can redeem a gift certificate that was sent by e-mail by clicking the Redeem Now button at the bottom of the e-mail message. This button launches iTunes with the Music Store option selected in the Source pane, and the certificate's number shows up automatically. Click the Redeem button to credit your account, and then sign in to your account (if you already have an account) or set up an account (see "Setting Up an Account," earlier in this chapter).

The balance of your gift certificate (how much you have left to spend) appears right next to your account name in the iTunes Music Store window and is updated as you make purchases.

Managing Your Account

Online stores record necessary information about you, such as your credit card number, your billing address, and so forth. You can change this information at any time, and you can also take advantage of Music Store account features, such as sending gift certificates and setting up allowance accounts.

Viewing and changing account information

Life is unpredictable. As John Lennon sang in "Beautiful Boy (Darling Boy)," "Life is what happens to you while you're busy making other plans." So if your billing address changes, or you need to switch to another credit card, or you need to change your password for any reason, you can edit your account information at any time.

To see your account information in the Music Store, click the Account button that shows your account name. iTunes displays a dialog for you to enter your account password. Then click the View Account button to see your account in the store.

Your account page displays your Apple ID, the last four digits of the credit card that you use for the account, your billing address, your most recent purchase, and your computer authorizations. (See "Authorizing computers to play purchased music," later in this chapter.) You can click buttons to edit your account information and credit card and to buy or redeem gift certificates and set up allowances.

Viewing your purchase history

In the rock 'n' roll lifestyle, you might recall songs from the '60s but not remember what you bought last week. To view your purchase history, go to your account page by clicking the Account button (top-right corner) and typing your password in the dialog that appears. Click the View Account button and, on your account page, click the Purchase History button.

The Music Store displays the items that you purchased, starting with the most recent. If you bought a lot of songs, not all of them appear on the first page. To see the details of previous purchases, click the arrow to the left of the order date. After viewing your history, click Done at the bottom of the history page to return to your account page.

Setting up allowances

Do you trust your kids with your credit card? You don't have to answer that — you can sidestep the entire issue by providing an *allowance account* for that special someone who wants to buy music on your credit card. With an allowance account, you can set the amount of credit to allow for the account each month — from $10–$200 in increments of $10. You can change the amount of an allowance or stop it at any time.

To use an allowance account, the recipient must be using iTunes version 4 or newer and live in a country where the iTunes Music Store is available on the Internet (such as the United States).

You can set up the allowance account yourself or define an allowance on an existing account. The recipient signs in to the account and types his or her password — no credit card required. When the recipient reaches the limit of the allowance, that account can't buy anything else until the following month. iTunes Music Store saves any unused balance until the next Music Store purchase.

To set up an allowance account, click the Allowance link on the Music Store home page. iTunes takes you to the Allowance page in the Music Store, where you can enter your name, your recipient's name, the monthly allowance amount (using the Monthly Allowance pop-up menu), and your recipient's Apple ID and password.

Click Continue to proceed with the account setup process, and then follow the instructions to finish setting up the account.

To stop an allowance or change the amount of an allowance account, go to your account page by clicking the Account button that shows your account name (in the top-right corner) and then type your password in the dialog that appears. Click the View Account button and scroll the account page until you see the Setup Allowance button; click this button to go to the Allowance page.

Sending gift certificates

A song is a gift that keeps on giving every time the recipient plays the song. A gift of a music video or TV show might commemorate a special occasion. Besides, you can't go wrong giving a Music Store gift certificate to that special person who has everything.

Before sending a gift certificate, first make sure that the recipient can run iTunes 4 or newer versions. Also, he or she must be able to run iTunes 6 for video. (You might want to subtly suggest to the future recipient in an e-mail that it's time to download the newest version of iTunes, just to find out whether he or she has the requisite system configuration — see Chapter 1.)

To buy a gift certificate to send to someone, click the Gift Certificates link on the Music Store home page. iTunes takes you to the Gift Certificates page in the Music Store.

Click the Buy Now button to purchase a gift certificate. You then have three options:

- **Send a printed certificate by snail mail by clicking U.S. Mail.** iTunes launches your browser to connect to the online Apple Store, which lets you enter your name, the recipient's name and address, the amount of the certificate, and a personal message. Click Continue and follow the instructions to finish the process.

- **Send a certificate as an e-mail message by clicking Email.** iTunes displays a page that lets you enter your name, the recipient's name and address, the amount of the certificate, and a personal message. Click Continue and follow the instructions to finish the process.

- **Print a certificate yourself, on your own printer, to give to someone.** Click Print, and iTunes displays a page that lets you enter your name, the recipient's name and address, the amount of the certificate, and a personal message. Click Continue and follow the instructions to finish the process.

To set up or change the amount of a gift certificate, go to your account page by clicking the Account button that shows your account name and typing your password in the dialog that appears. Click the View Account button and scroll the account page until you see the Gift Certificate button; click it to go to the Gift Certificates page.

Authorizing computers to play purchased music

The computer that you use to set up your account is automatically authorized by Apple to play the songs, audio books, and videos that you buy. Fortunately, the content isn't locked to that computer — you can copy your purchased songs, audio books, and videos to other computers and play them with iTunes. When you first play them on the other computers, iTunes asks for your Music Store account ID and password to authorize that computer. You can have up to five computers authorized at any one time.

Purchased songs, audio books, and videos need to be downloaded or copied to one of your authorized computers before you can copy them from the added computer to an iPod.

If you want to delete one computer and add another computer, you can remove the authorization from a computer by choosing Advanced⇨Deauthorize Computer on that computer. If you need to deauthorize a computer that no longer works, you can contact Apple through its Music Store support page (www.apple.com/support/itunes/authorization.html).

Remember to deauthorize your computer before you upgrade it, sell it, or give it away. Also, we recommend that you deauthorize your computer before upgrading your RAM, hard drive, or other system components. Otherwise, the upgraded system might count as another authorized computer. If you've reached five authorizations due to system upgrades or failed computers, you can reset your authorization count by clicking Deauthorize All on the Account Information screen. You can do this only once a year. The Deauthorize All button appears only if you have at least five authorized computers and you haven't used the option in the last 12 months.

Chapter 5

Bringing Content into iTunes

*T*hree excellent reasons to bring your music CDs into iTunes, or to download media files from the iTunes Music Store into iTunes, are

✔ To preserve the content forever

✔ To play the content easily from your computer (without having to fumble with discs)

✔ To take the content in your iPod with you

In this chapter, we show you how to store content in your iTunes library. A song or video in digital format can be kept in that format in a file on any number of digital media storage devices — so even if your CDs, DVDs, and hard drive fail, your backup copy (assuming that you made a backup copy on a safety CD or disk) is still as perfect as the original digital file. You may make any number of digital copies with no technical limitations on playing the copies except those imposed by the iTunes Music Store for content that you purchase.

As you add more content, your iTunes library becomes your entertainment center, and you can find any item you want to play faster than opening a CD jewel case, as we show in Chapter 8. Your iTunes library also manages your content and makes it easy to transfer some, or all of it, to your iPod (see Chapter 12).

Adding Music

Bringing music tracks from a CD into iTunes is called *ripping* a CD. We're not sure why it's called that, but Apple certainly took the term to a new level with an ad campaign for Macs that featured the slogan *Rip, Mix, Burn.* Burning a mix CD was the hip thing to do a few years ago. With iTunes, you can still rip and mix, but if you have an iPod, you no longer need to burn CDs to play your music wherever you go.

Ripping, in technical terms, is the process of extracting the song's digital information from an audio CD, but in common terms it also includes the process of compressing the song's digital information and encoding it in a particular sound file format. The ripping process is straightforward, but the import settings that you choose affect sound quality, hard drive space (and iPod space), and compatibility with other types of players and computers.

Setting the importing preferences

Although importing music from an audio CD takes a lot less time than playing the CD, it still takes time, so you want your import settings to be correct before starting. To do this

1. **Choose iTunes⇨Preferences⇨Advanced on a Mac or Edit⇨ Preferences⇨Advanced in Windows.**

   The iTunes Preferences dialog, with the Advanced tab showing, opens.

2. **Click the Importing tab.**

   The importing preferences appear, as shown in Figure 5-1.

The Importing preferences tab offers the following options, which you set before ripping a CD:

- **Import Using:** Set this pop-up menu to the encoder. For more information about encoders, see Chapter 18.

- **Setting:** Set this pop-up menu to High Quality or better for most music. You can change this setting to get better quality or use hard drive space more efficiently, as we describe in Chapter 19.

- **Play Songs While Importing:** Select this check box to play the songs at the same time that you start ripping them. This option slows down the speed of importing, but hey — you get to listen to the music right away.

- **Create Filenames with Track Number:** Select this check box to include the track number in the filenames created by iTunes for the songs that you rip. Including the track number makes it easier to find tracks on an iPod when using a car's audio controls — if you've connected your iPod to a car stereo system, which Chapter 21 covers.

- **Use Error Correction When Reading Audio CDs:** Although it reduces the speed of importing, select this check box to use error correction if you have problems with audio quality or if the CD skips. (Not every skipping CD can be imported even with error correction, but it might help.)

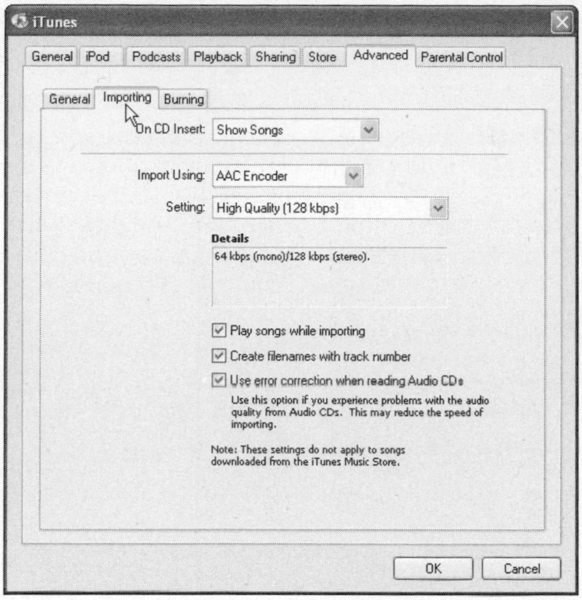

Figure 5-1:
Set your
importing
preferences
for ripping
CDs.

The Import Using pop-up menu gives you the opportunity to set the type of encoding — this choice is perhaps the most important — and the Setting pop-up menu offers different settings depending on your choice of encoder. For example, in Figure 5-1, we chose the AAC Encoder with a high-quality setting; in Figure 5-2, we switch to the MP3 Encoder in the Import Using pop-up menu, and we're in the process of choosing Higher Quality from the Setting pop-up menu.

Encoding is a complicated subject that requires a whole chapter to explain. (In fact, Chapter 18 provides an in-depth look if you want to know more.) For a quick and pain-free ripping session, select from among the following encoders in the Import Using pop-up menu based on how you plan to use your iTunes library:

✔ **AAC Encoder:** We recommend AAC for all uses. (However, AIFF or WAV is better if you plan to burn another CD with the songs you ripped and not use them in your iPod.) Select the High Quality option from the Setting pop-up menu.

You can convert a song that's been ripped in AIFF, Apple Lossless, or WAV to AAC or MP3. However, ripping a CD with one encoder might be more convenient. After that, you can rip it again with a different encoder. For example, you might import *Sgt. Pepper's Lonely Hearts Club Band* with the AAC encoder for use in your Mac and iPod and then import it again with the AIFF encoder. You might call the album Sgt. Pepper-2, for example, in order to burn songs onto a CD. After burning the CD, you can delete Sgt. Pepper-2 to re-claim the hard drive space.

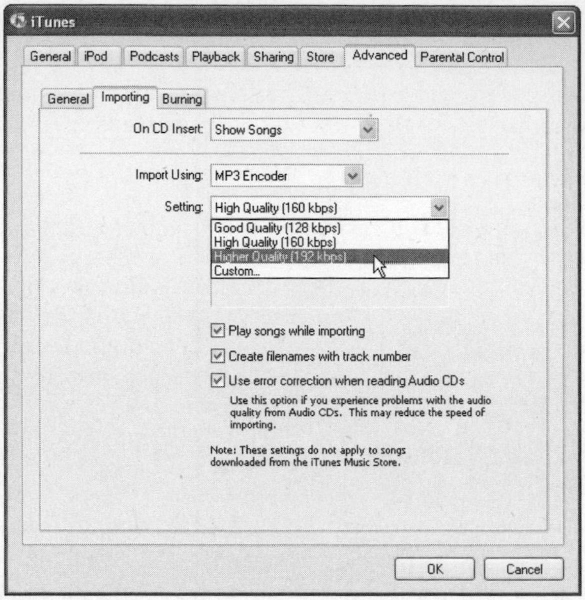

Figure 5-2:
Set the
quality
setting for
the encoder
you've
chosen for
importing.

✔ **AIFF Encoder:** Use AIFF if you plan to burn the song to an audio CD using a Mac (use WAV for Windows). AIFF offers the highest possible quality, but it takes up a lot of space (about 10MB per minute). If you use AIFF, select the Automatic option from the Setting pop-up menu. Don't use AIFF format for songs that you intend to transfer to your iPod; convert them first to AAC or MP3.

✔ **Apple Lossless Encoder:** Use the Apple Lossless encoder for songs that you intend to burn onto audio CDs as well as for playing on iPods. The files are just small enough (about 60–70 percent of the size of the AIFF versions) that they don't hiccup on playback.

✔ **MP3 Encoder:** Use the MP3 format for songs that you intend to burn on MP3 CDs or that you intend to use with MP3 players or your iPod — it's universally supported. If you use MP3, we recommend selecting the Higher Quality option from the Setting pop-up menu.

✔ **WAV Encoder:** WAV is the high-quality sound format that's used on PCs (like AIFF), but it also takes up a lot of space (about 10MB per minute). Use WAV if you plan on burning the song to an audio CD or using WAV with PCs. If you use WAV, select the Automatic option from the Setting pop-up menu. Don't use WAV for songs that you intend to transfer to your iPod. Convert them first to AAC or MP3, as we describe in Chapter 19.

Ripping music from CDs

After checking your importing preferences to be sure that your settings are correct, you're ready to rip. To rip a CD, follow these steps:

1. **Insert an audio CD.**

   The songs appear in your song list as generic, unnamed tracks at first. If your computer is connected to the Internet and the CD is in the Gracenote database, iTunes automatically retrieves the track information. If necessary, establish your connection to the Internet and then choose Advanced⇨Get CD Track Names to get the track information. If you don't want to connect to the Internet or if your CD isn't recognized by the Gracenote database, you can type the track information (see Chapter 9).

2. **(Optional) Deselect the check boxes next to any songs on the CD that you don't want to import.**

   iTunes imports the songs that have check marks next to them; when you remove the check mark next to a song, iTunes skips that song.

3. **(Optional) To remove the gap of silence between songs that segue together, select those songs and choose Advanced⇨Join CD Tracks.**

   This gap happens often with music CDs. The tracks are separate, but the end of one song merges into the beginning of the next song. You don't want an annoying half-second gap between the songs. For example, in Figure 5-3, we already joined the first two songs of the *Sgt. Pepper's Lonely Hearts Club Band* album because they run together, and we're in the process of using Join CD Tracks to join the last three songs.

Import

Figure 5-3: Join songs to avoid the audible gap between them.

To select multiple songs, click the first one, press ⌘ on a Mac or Ctrl in Windows, and click each subsequent song. To select several consecutive songs in a row, click the first one, hold down Shift, and then click the last one.

Be sure to check the importing preferences before actually ripping the CD.

4. **Click the Import button.**

   The Import button is at the top-right corner of the iTunes window. The status display shows the progress of the operation. To cancel, click the small *x* next to the progress bar in the status display.

   iTunes plays the songs while it imports them. You can click the Pause button to stop playback, but the importing continues. If you don't want to listen to the songs as they import, you can deselect the Play Songs While Importing check box in the iTunes Preferences dialog. (See the earlier section, "Setting the importing preferences.")

   iTunes displays an orange, animated waveform icon next to the song that it's importing. When iTunes finishes importing each song, it displays a check mark next to the song, as shown in Figure 5-4. (On a color monitor, the check mark is green.) iTunes chimes when it finishes the import list.

5. **When all the songs are imported, eject the CD by clicking the Eject button at the lower-right corner of the iTunes window.**

   You can also choose Controls⇨Eject Disc to eject the disc, or click the Eject icon next to the disc name in the Source pane.

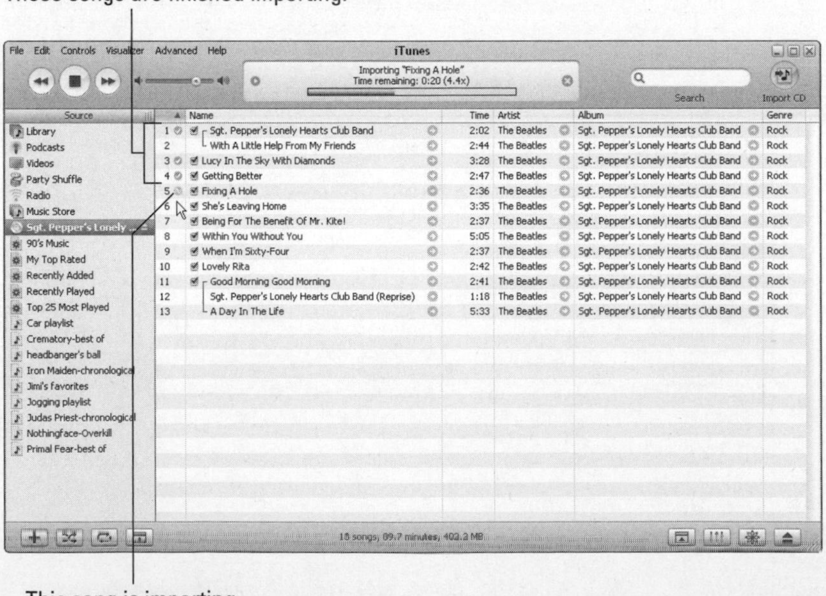

These songs are finished importing.

Figure 5-4:
iTunes
shows a
check mark
to indicate
it's done
ripping the
song.

This song is importing.

Adding music files

The quality of the music that you hear depends initially on the quality of the source. Web sites and services offering music files vary widely. Some sites provide high-quality, legally derived songs that you can download, and some sites provide only streaming audio that you can play, but not save, on your hard drive or on a CD (such as a Web radio station).

The allegedly illegal file-sharing services offering MP3 files might vary in quality. Unauthorized copies of songs might be saved in a lower-quality format to save space and download time, so beware of less-than-high-quality knockoffs.

You can download the music file or copy it from another computer to your hard drive. After you save or copy an MP3 file — or for that matter an AIFF or WAV file — on your hard drive, you can simply drag it into the iTunes window to bring it into your library. If you drag a folder or disk icon, all the audio files that it contains are added to your iTunes library. You can also choose File⇨ Add to Library as an alternative to dragging.

When you add a song to your iTunes library, a copy of the song file is placed inside the iTunes Music folder — as long as you have your preferences set for iTunes to "Copy files to iTunes music folder when adding to library" (the default setting) in the General pane of the Advanced tab of iTunes Preferences dialog. See Chapter 13 for details on storing music in your iTunes Music folder.

If you want iTunes to store only links to song files on the hard drive and not copy the files when you add songs, you can turn off the default copy files option by doing the following:

1. **Choose iTunes⇨Preferences (Mac) or Edit ⇨Preferences (Windows).**

2. **Click the Advanced tab in the iTunes Preferences dialog.**

3. **Click the General tab under the Advanced tab.**

4. **Turn off the "Copy files to iTunes music folder when adding to library" setting.**

You can check out the contents of your music folder using the Finder on a Mac or Windows Explorer on a Windows PC. On the Mac, the iTunes Music folder lives in the iTunes folder inside the Music folder in your Home folder. The path to this folder is *your home folder*/Music/iTunes/iTunes Music. In Windows, the iTunes Music folder resides in the iTunes folder inside the My Music folder of the My Documents folder in your user folder. The path to this folder is *Your User folder*\My Documents\My Music\ iTunes\iTunes Music. These are the default locations; you can change the default folder:

1. **Choose iTunes⇨Preferences on a Mac or Edit⇨Preferences in Windows.**

2. **Click the Advanced tab in the iTunes Preferences dialog.**

3. **Click the General tab under the Advanced tab.**

4. **Choose a new location for the music folder.**

When you bring a song file into iTunes, the song is copied into a new file in the iTunes library without changing or deleting the original file. You can then convert the song to another format. For example, you can convert an AIFF file to an MP3 file while leaving the original intact. Find out about converting your songs to a different format in Chapter 19.

MP3 CDs are easy to add because they are essentially data CDs. Simply insert them into your CD-ROM drive, open the CD in the Finder, and drag and drop the MP3 song files into the iTunes window. Downloaded song files are even easier — just drag and drop the files into iTunes. If you drag a folder or CD icon, all the audio files it contains are added to your iTunes library.

You can bring any sound into iTunes, even music from scratchy old vinyl records or sound effects recorded through a microphone, as we describe in Chapter 20. You might want to import unusual sounds or digitize and preserve rare music that can't be found anywhere else.

How do you get stuff like that into iTunes? On a Mac, you can use GarageBand, which is part of the iLife suite (available from the Apple Store and pre-installed on all new Macs), or use a sound-editing program such as CD Spin Doctor (part of the Toast package) or Sound Studio. These programs typically record from any analog source device such as a tape player or even a turntable. Sound Studio lets you record and digitize directly to your hard drive on a Mac running OS X. Some Mac models include a free copy of Sound Studio. (You can find it in the Applications folder.) You may also download a copy from Felt Tip Software (www.felttip.com/products/soundstudio) and use it for two weeks before having to pay $49.99 for it. CD Spin Doctor from Roxio (www.roxio.com) for Mac OS X provides special features for recording music from old vinyl records.

Many commercial applications are available to choose from that work with Windows, including Roxio's Easy CD Creator 8. You may also use Musicmatch Jukebox to record sound through a PC's line-in connection. If you're using Musicmatch, visit the companion Web site at www.dummies.com/go/ipod4e.

AIFF- or WAV-encoded sound files occupy too much space in your music library and iPod. Voice recordings and sound effects tend to be low-fidelity and typically don't sound any better in AIFF or WAV format than they do in formats that save hard drive space. Also, sound effects and voice recordings are typically mono rather than stereo. You can save hard drive and iPod space and still have quality recordings by converting these files to MP3 or AAC formats, changing them from stereo to mono in the process, and leaving the original versions intact. We describe converting songs in Chapter 19.

Adding Audio Books

Do you like to listen to audio books and spoken magazine and newspaper articles? Not only can you bring these files into iTunes, but you can also transfer them to an iPod and take them on the road, which is much more convenient than taking cassettes or CDs.

Audible is a leading provider of downloadable, spoken audio files. Audible lets you authorize computers to play the audio files — just like the iTunes Music Store; see Chapter 4. Audible does require that you purchase the files, and Audible's content is also licensed by Apple to be included in the iTunes Music Store in the Audio Books category. Audible content includes magazines and radio programs as well as books.

To import Audible files, follow these steps:

1. **Go to www.audible.com and set up an account if you don't already have one.**

2. **Select and download an Audible audio file.**

   Files that end with .aa are Audible files.

3. **Drag the Audible file to the iTunes window.**

   If this is the first time that you've added an Audible file, iTunes asks for your account information. You enter this information once for each computer that you use with your Audible account.

To disable an Audible account, open iTunes on the computer that you no longer want to use with the account, and choose Advanced⇨Deauthorize Computer. In the Deauthorize Computer dialog that appears, select the Deauthorize Computer for Audible Account option and click OK.

You need to be online to authorize a computer or to remove the authorization from that computer.

Adding Podcasts

You can add podcasts to your iTunes library by subscribing to them in the iTunes Music Store, as we describe in Chapter 4, or by subscribing to them directly from Web sites that host them. Similar to a tape of a radio broadcast, you can save and play a podcast at your convenience — both in iTunes on your computer and on your iPod.

A podcast can be anything from a single song to a commentary-hosted radio show. Podcasts are saved in the MP3 format and may be used with any media player, device, or application that supports MP3, including your iPod. The podcast producer uses Real Simple Syndication (RSS) technology to publish the podcast. RSS feeds are typically linked to an RSS or eXtensible Markup Language (XML; the language of RSS) button. With a feed reader, aggregator application, or browser plug-in, you can automatically check RSS-enabled Web pages and display updated stories and podcasts. RSS is supported directly by some Web browsers, including Apple's Safari for Mac OS X.

With iTunes, you can play a podcast, incorporate it into playlists, make copies, and burn CDs with it as much as you like. If you don't like the podcast, simply delete it from your iTunes library and update your iPod to delete it from your iPod. You can listen to most common podcast file formats in iTunes, including MP3, AAC, WAV, and M4B.

Subscribing to podcasts

The Podcasts section of the iTunes Music Store offers access to thousands of podcasts, but over a million podcasts are out there, many of which are available only by visiting their Web sites. You can subscribe to podcasts directly from iTunes without ever visiting the online store. However, the store makes it easy to subscribe to the podcasts so check there first. Turn to Chapter 4 to subscribe to podcasts in the store.

By *subscribing,* we mean simply listing the podcast in your iTunes Podcasts pane so that new episodes are downloaded automatically. It's like a magazine subscription that's updated with a new issue every month or so. You don't have to register or fill out any form. You don't have to provide an e-mail address or any other information. Your copy of iTunes automatically finds new podcast episodes and downloads them to your computer.

The best way to subscribe to a podcast is through the iTunes Music Store. If you can't find a podcast in the store and you know how to find its Web site, use your browser and then go to that Web site. To subscribe to a podcast on a Web page, follow these steps:

1. **In your browser, Control-click (Mac) or right-click (Windows) the podcast's RSS2 link on the Web page.**

   Look for the RSS2 link on the Web page — many sites use an icon, as shown in Figure 5-5.

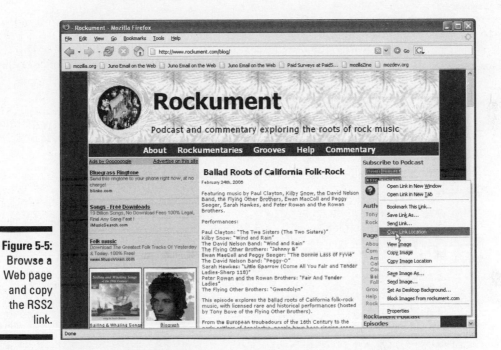

Figure 5-5:
Browse a
Web page
and copy
the RSS2
link.

2. **Copy the podcast's RSS2 link.**

   Copy the link — choose Copy Link in Safari, or Copy Link Location in Firefox. The link should look something like `http://www.rockument.com/blog/?feed=RSS2` when you paste it.

3. **In iTunes, choose Advanced⇨Subscribe to Podcast.**

   The Subscribe to Podcast dialog opens, as shown in Figure 5-6.

4. **Paste the RSS link by choosing Edit⇨Paste and then click OK.**

   As an alternative, you can also press ⌘-V on a Mac or Ctrl-V in Windows.

Figure 5-6:
Paste the
RSS2 link
into the
Subscribe to
Podcast
dialog.

iTunes downloads the podcast to your computer and switches to the Podcasts selection in the Source pane. It displays your newly subscribed podcast in the song list.

5. Click the *i* icon to see information about the podcast.

You can click the lowercase *i* icon on the far-right podcast listing margin, as shown in Figure 5-7, to display separate information about the podcast's newest episode.

6. Select the podcast and then click the Play button.

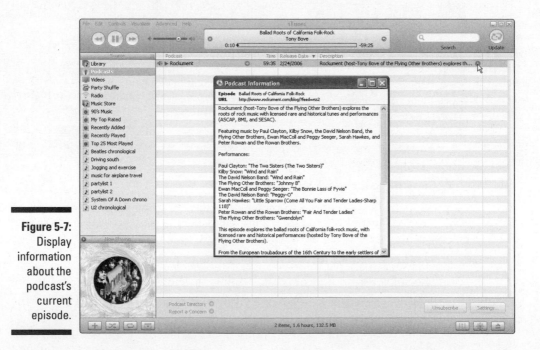

Figure 5-7:
Display
information
about the
podcast's
current
episode.

You can now play the podcast just like a song in your iTunes library. The podcast might be long, but it's still just a song. You can use the iTunes playback controls to fast-forward, rewind, or play the podcast from any point. The blue dot next to a podcast means you haven't played it yet. As soon as you start listening to a podcast, the dot disappears.

Podcasts don't show up in Party Shuffle unless you drag them into the Party Shuffle playlist (see Chapter 6). Podcasts can't be shared over a network, and you can't include podcasts with Autofill when updating an iPod shuffle.

If the podcaster embedded a photo in an audio podcast file or included a link to a video from the file, the photo or video content appears in the Artwork pane.

Updating podcasts

Many podcast feeds provide new material on a regular schedule. iTunes can check these feeds automatically and update your library with new podcast episodes. You can, for example, schedule iTunes to check for new podcast episodes — such as news, weather, traffic reports, and morning talk shows — before you wake up and automatically update your iPod. When you get up, you have new podcast episodes to listen to in your iPod.

To check for updates manually, select Podcasts in the Source pane and click the Update button (which replaces the usual Browse button). All subscribed podcast feeds are updated immediately when you click Update, and iTunes downloads the most recent (or all) episodes, depending on how you set your podcasts preferences to schedule podcast updates.

Scheduling podcast updates

To set your podcast preferences so iTunes can check for new podcasts automatically, choose iTunes➪Preferences on a Mac or Edit➪Preferences in Windows. In the iTunes Preferences dialog, click the Podcasts tab to display the podcast preferences, as shown in Figure 5-8.

You can schedule your podcasts with these settings:

- **Check for New Episodes:** Choose to check for podcasts every hour, day, week, or manually — meaning whenever you want.

- **When New Episodes Are Available:** You can download the most recent one (useful for news podcasts), download all episodes (useful for music podcasts you might want to keep), or nothing so that you can use the Update button to update manually as you need.

✔ **Keep:** Choose to keep all episodes, all unplayed episodes, the most recent episodes, or previous episodes.

Keeping unplayed episodes is useful for news podcasts — if you've already played an episode, or a portion of it, you don't need it anymore, but you probably want to keep the ones you haven't played yet. iTunes automatically deletes podcast episodes that you don't want to keep.

✔ **Set Which Podcasts Are Copied to Your iPod:** Click the iPod Preferences button next to this option to change the updating preferences for your iPod. See Chapter 12 for details on setting up your iPod for automatic updating, including choosing podcasts for the update.

If you copy podcasts automatically during an update of your iPod, as we describe in Chapter 12, don't set iTunes to keep only your unplayed episodes. If you listen to part of a podcast episode on your iPod and then update your iPod, the podcast episode disappears from iTunes. You can always recover a lost episode by choosing to download all episodes on the Podcasts tab of the iTunes Preferences dialog.

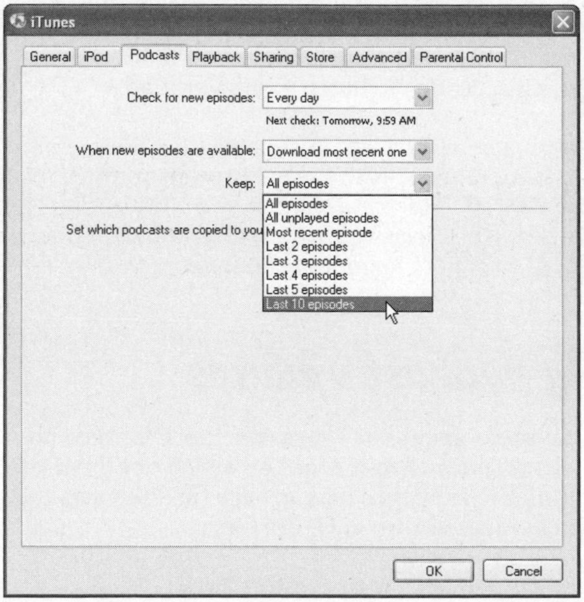

Figure 5-8:
Set your
podcast
preferences
to auto-
matically
check for
new
updates.

Adding Videos

Besides purchasing and downloading videos from the iTunes Music Store, as we describe in Chapter 4, you can also download videos from the Internet or copy them from other computers and bring them into iTunes to use with your video-enabled iPod.

You can watch QuickTime and MPEG-4 movies (files that end in .mov, .mpg, or .mp4) in iTunes and use them in a video-enabled iPod. *QuickTime,* Apple's digital video file format, is installed on every Mac. It's also installed on PCs along with the Windows version of iTunes. QuickTime is used extensively in the digital video production world for making DVDs and movies for the Web. Music videos, movie trailers, and other videos you can buy on the iTunes Music Store are in the QuickTime format. MPEG-4 (Motion Picture Expert Group Version 4) is a standard format for digital video that works on just about any computer that plays video.

You can drag the video into iTunes just like a song file. Drag each video file from the Mac Finder or Windows desktop to the Library, directly to a playlist in the iTunes Source pane, or to the Videos view on the right side of the iTunes window, as shown in Figure 5-9.

Figure 5-9:
Bring a
video file
into iTunes.

The video files you drag into iTunes, along with the ones you purchased from the iTunes Music Store, are all on display in the Videos section of your iTunes library — click Videos in the Source pane (refer to Figure 5-9).

Video files are organized in folders and stored in the music library on your hard drive just like song files. You can find the video file's location on your hard drive and its type by choosing File➪Get Info.

You can create your own QuickTime or MPEG-4 video files with a suitable video-editing application such as iMovie for the Mac (part of the iLife software suite that includes iTunes), or Apple's QuickTime Pro for Windows, available from the Apple Store.

Chapter 6

Playing Content in iTunes

In This Chapter

▶ Adjusting your computer volume

▶ Playing songs on your stereo through a wireless AirTunes connection

▶ Playing songs, podcasts, audio books in iTunes

▶ Playing videos in iTunes

*I*f you like to entertain folks by spinning tunes and playing videos at home or at parties, iTunes could easily become your media jockey console. Imagine how much music you could choose from with an iTunes library that can grow as large as your hard drive — and you can fit more than 20,000 songs, or 64 days of nonstop music, in about 100GB of hard drive space. When we last checked the Apple store, you could buy a 2-terabyte external drive for either Mac or PC that would probably hold enough music to run a radio station. But that's not all — you can manage your videos and favorite TV shows and play them in full-screen mode on your computer running iTunes.

Your computer is already a mean multimedia machine with the ability to mix sounds, photos, and videos. You can play music through your computer's built-in speakers or through headphones, but you'll get better results with high-quality external speakers. You can even connect your home computer to an excellent stereo for high-quality sound. The same is true for video: You can use iTunes to play video on your computer's display, or you can pipe it out to a larger television or display monitor — even a video projector — to get a bigger picture.

Changing the Computer's Output Volume

You can control the volume and other characteristics of the sound coming out of your computer's speakers, headphones, or external speakers. Even if you connect your computer to a stereo amplifier with its own volume and equalizer controls, it's best to get the volume right at the source — your computer and iTunes — and then adjust the output volume as you please on your stereo or external speaker unit.

You control the volume by using your computer system's audio controls. iTunes also controls the volume, but that control is within the range of the computer's volume setting. For example, if you set your computer's volume to half and set iTunes volume to full, you get half volume because the computer is limiting the volume to half. If you set your computer volume at half and also reduce the iTunes volume to half, you actually get *one-quarter* volume — half the computer's setting. You can further adjust the sound after it leaves your computer with your stereo system or external speakers with controls.

The appropriate volume depends entirely on your preferences for hearing music, audio books, or video soundtracks, but in general, the maximum level of output from your computer is preferable when connecting to a stereo system or speakers with volume controls. After setting your computer to the maximum volume, adjust the iTunes volume or your stereo or speaker volume (or both) to get the best sound. When using the computer's speakers or headphones, the computer's volume and the iTunes volume are the only volume controls that you have, so after adjusting the volume on your computer to the maximum level (or lower if you prefer), adjust the iTunes volume.

Adjusting the sound on a Mac

The Mac was built for sound from the very start. Making and playing music has been part of the Mac culture since day one, when Steve Jobs introduced the original Mac to an audience with sound coming from its small speaker. (It played synthesized speech and simple tones, but it was the first personal computer with built-in sound.)

Today's Mac comes with built-in or external speakers and at least one headphone/line-out connection that you can use to connect external speakers or a stereo system. Mac OS X lets you configure output speakers and control levels for stereo speakers and multichannel audio devices.

If you use external speakers, headphones, or a stereo system, make sure that you connect these devices properly before adjusting the volume.

To adjust the volume on your Mac, follow these steps:

1. **Choose System Preferences from the Apple menu or the Dock and then click the Sound icon.**

Otherwise, press Option and a volume control key simultaneously as a shortcut. You can have iTunes open and playing music while you do this.

2. **In the Sound preferences window, click Output and select the sound output device.**

   If you have headphones or external speakers attached to the headphones connection on your Mac, a Headphones option appears in the list of sound output devices, as shown in Figure 6-1; if not, an External Speakers or Internal Speakers option appears. If you have external speakers *and* a pair of headphones attached to your Mac, you should see both and be able to set their volumes separately.

3. **Adjust the volume.**

   You can do any of the following:

   - Drag the slider to adjust the volume as you listen to music.
   - Select the Mute check box to silence your Mac.
   - Drag the Balance slider to put more music in the left or right channels.

4. **Close the Preferences window by choosing System Preferences⇨Quit System Preferences, by clicking the red button in the upper-left corner of the window, or pressing ⌘-Q.**

   The Sound preferences window isn't like a dialog — when you change settings, you can hear the effect immediately without having to click an OK button. (There isn't an OK button, anyway.)

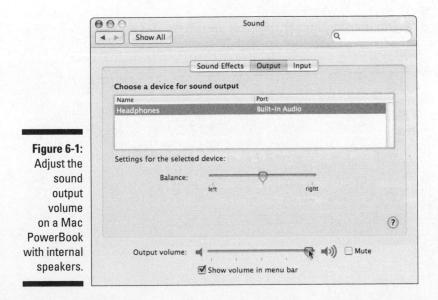

Figure 6-1:
Adjust the sound output volume on a Mac PowerBook with internal speakers.

Adjusting the sound in Windows

Windows XP and Windows 2000 let you configure output speakers and control levels for stereo speakers and multichannel audio devices.

Use the Sounds and Audio Devices Properties dialog to change the volume. To open this window, choose Start➪Control Panel, and click the Sounds and Audio Devices icon. Then click the Volume tab.

As shown in Figure 6-2, the Sounds and Audio Devices Properties dialog offers the Device Volume slider — drag this slider to set the volume. You can also silence your PC by selecting the Mute check box.

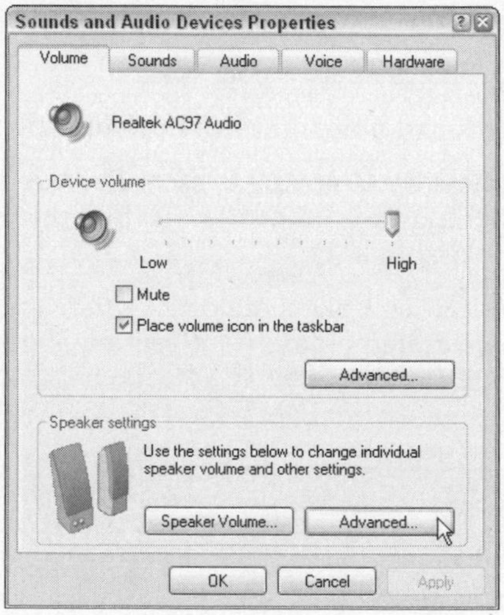

Figure 6-2:
Adjust the sound output volume on a PC.

If you select the Place Volume Icon in the Taskbar option and your sound card supports changing the volume with software, a sound icon appears in the notification area of Windows. You can then change the volume quickly without having to open the Sounds and Audio Devices Properties dialog — simply click the speaker icon and drag the slider that pops up. For more information about adjusting sound on a PC, see *PCs For Dummies,* 10th Edition, by Dan Gookin (Wiley).

Using AirTunes for Wireless Stereo Playback

You want to play the music in your iTunes library, but your stereo system is in another room, and you don't want wires going from one room to the other. What you need is an AirPort in your home — specifically, AirPort Express with AirTunes, which lets you play your iTunes music through your stereo or powered speakers in virtually any room of your house, without wires. The only catch is that your computer must be within range of the AirPort Express.

Apple's AirPort technology provides Wi-Fi wireless networking for any AirPort-equipped Mac or PC that uses a Wi-Fi–certified IEEE 802.11b or 802.11g wireless card or offers built-in Wi-Fi. For more about AirPort, see *Mac OS X Tiger All-in-One Desk Reference For Dummies,* by Mark L. Chambers (Wiley).

To use a stereo system or powered speakers with AirTunes, connect the system or speakers to the audio port on the AirPort Express. iTunes automatically detects the connection.

If you already have a wireless network in place, you can add AirPort Express and AirTunes without changing anything. Connect the AirPort Express Base Station to the stereo system or powered speakers, and plug the Base Station into an electrical outlet. The AirPort Express Base Station wirelessly links to your existing wireless network without requiring any change to the network.

You can use several AirPort Express Base Stations — one for each stereo system or set of powered speakers, in different rooms — and then choose which stereo/speaker system to use in the pop-up menu.

To use AirTunes and the AirPort Express, follow these steps:

1. **Install the software supplied with the AirPort Express on CD-ROM, which includes support for AirTunes.**

2. **Connect your stereo or a set of powered speakers to the audio port of the AirPort Express.**

   You can use an optical digital or analog audio cable. (Both are included in the AirPort Express Stereo Connection Kit available from the Apple Store.) Which cable you use depends on whether your stereo or set of powered speakers has an optical digital or analog connection.

3. **Plug the AirPort Express into an electrical outlet.**

   Use the AC plug that came with the AirPort Express or the power extension cord included in the AirPort Express Stereo Connection Kit. The AirPort Express turns on automatically when connected to an electrical outlet. The status light glows yellow while AirPort Express is starting up. When it starts up completely, the light turns green.

4. **On your computer, set your preferences in iTunes to look for speakers connected to your computer wirelessly by using AirTunes.**

Set your iTunes preferences to look for AirTunes speakers by choosing iTunes➪Preferences on a Mac or Edit➪Preferences in Windows, and click the Advanced button and then the General tab. Select the Look for Remote Speakers Connected with AirTunes option in the Advanced General pane, as shown in Figure 6-3.

In the Advanced General pane, you can also deselect the Disable iTunes Volume Control for Remote Speakers option so that you can control those speakers separately (a setting you should use if connecting to a stereo with a volume control). Leaving this option deselected enables you to control the volume from iTunes.

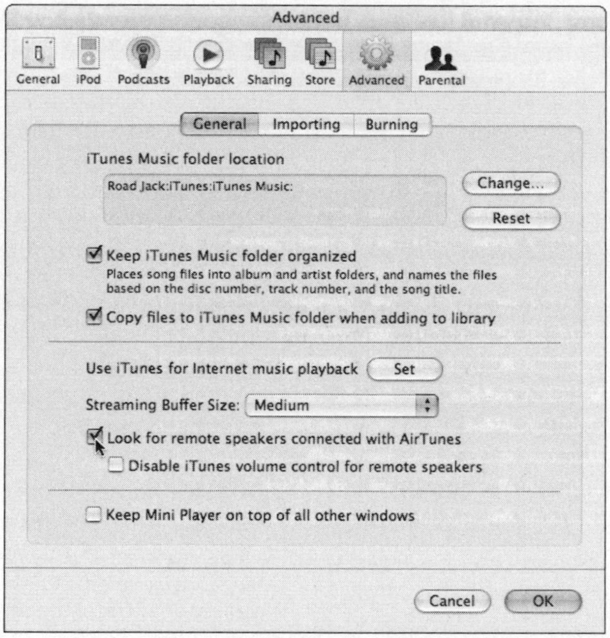

Figure 6-3:
Select the option to look for speakers connected wirelessly to your computer using AirTunes.

After turning on the option to look for AirTunes-connected speakers, a Computer button appears in the lower-right corner of the iTunes window.

5. **Click the Computer button and then select the AirTunes-equipped network.**

Clicking the Computer button displays a pop-up menu with any available wireless AirTunes networks, as shown in Figure 6-4. You can select the AirTunes network to play music ("Little Net Buddy" in Figure 6-4). From that point on, iTunes plays music through the AirTunes network rather than the computer. To play music through speakers connected to the computer (or through the computer's built-in speakers), choose Computer from the pop-up menu.

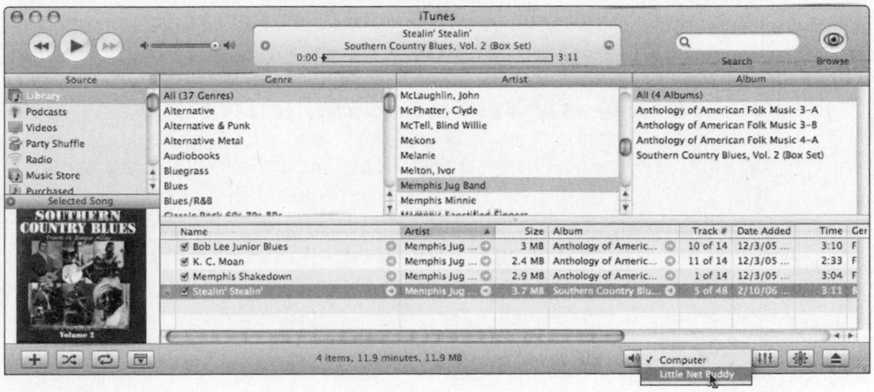

Figure 6-4:
Choosing
the AirTunes
network
"Little Net
Buddy" to
play music.

The AirPort Express is small enough to fit in the palm of your hand — and it travels well because all it needs is a power outlet. You can take your laptop and AirPort Express to a friend's house or party, connect the AirPort Express to the stereo system and a power outlet, and then use your laptop anywhere in its vicinity to play DJ. You can even use portable powered speakers in a hotel room without wires and use a hotel room's LAN-to-Internet access with an AirPort Express to connect your wireless computer and other wireless computers in the room to the Internet.

Playing Songs

When you've found a song you want to play (see Chapter 8 for searching details), simply select it in the Song List pane and click the Play button. The Play button turns into a Pause button while the song plays. When the song finishes, iTunes continues playing the songs in the list in sequence until you click the Pause button (which then toggles back into the Play button) or until the song list ends. This setup is useful if you selected an album; not so great if you selected a song at random and don't want to hear the next one. (Fortunately, you can arrange songs in playlists so that they play back in exactly the sequence you want; see Chapter 10 for details.)

You can skip to the next or previous song by pressing the right- or left-arrow keys on your keyboard, respectively, or by clicking the Forward or Back buttons next to the Play button. You can also double-click another song in the list to start playing it.

TIP

Press the spacebar to perform the same function as the Play button; press the spacebar again to pause.

You can choose songs to play manually, but iTunes also provides several automated features so that you can spend less time prepping your music selection and more time enjoying it.

Queuing up tunes with Party Shuffle

Playlists, described in Chapter 10, are great for organizing music in the order that you want to play it, but you can have iTunes serve up songs at random by using Party Shuffle. It's not a dance step or pub game — *Party Shuffle* is a dynamic playlist that automatically generates a semi-random selection in a list that you can modify on the fly. With Party Shuffle at work, you might even find songs in your library you forgot about or rarely play — Party Shuffle always throws a few rarely played songs into the mix.

To use Party Shuffle, follow these steps:

1. **Click Party Shuffle in the Source pane.**

   The Song List pane and Browse pane are replaced with the Party Shuffle track list and settings at the bottom, as shown in Figure 6-5.

Figure 6-5:
Adjust the settings for Party Shuffle.

2. **Select a source from the Source pop-up menu below the Party Shuffle track list.**

   You can select Library (for the entire library) or any playlist (including a smart playlist; see Chapter 10 for details) as the source for music in Party Shuffle. If you select a playlist, Party Shuffle limits its choices to songs from that playlist.

3. **Set the following options:**

   - **Recently Played Songs:** Choose how many songs should remain in the Party Shuffle list after they are played. You can drag already-played songs (even though they are grayed out after playing) to a spot later in the list to play them again.

   - **Upcoming Songs:** Choose how many songs should be listed as upcoming (not yet played). By displaying upcoming songs first, you can decide whether to rearrange the list or delete songs from the Party Shuffle playlist before they are played.

   - **Play Higher Rated Songs More Often:** Check this option to have iTunes add more high-rated songs to the random list. Using this option, you weight the randomness in favor of higher-rated songs. See Chapter 9 to find out how to add ratings to songs.

4. **(Optional) If you don't like the order of songs, you can rearrange them. If you dislike any songs, you can eliminate them.**

   You can rearrange the order of songs in Party Shuffle by dragging songs to different positions in the Party Shuffle list. Eliminate songs by selecting them in the Party Shuffle list and pressing Delete/Backspace (or choosing Edit⇨Clear). Don't worry — the songs are not deleted from your library, just from the Party Shuffle playlist.

5. **Play Party Shuffle by selecting the first song and clicking the Play button or pressing the spacebar.**

   You can start playing the first song or any song on the list. (When you pick a song in the middle to start playing, the songs before it are grayed out to show that they won't play.)

6. **Add, delete, or rearrange songs even while Party Shuffle plays.**

   While the Party Shuffle list plays, you can add songs in one of two ways:

   - Open Party Shuffle in a separate window by double-clicking the Party Shuffle item in the Source pane. You can then drag songs from the main iTunes window — either from the Library or from a playlist — directly into position in the Party Shuffle track list.

   - Without opening Party Shuffle in a separate window, you can switch to the library or a playlist and drag the song to the Party Shuffle item in the Source pane. When you add a song to Party Shuffle, it shows up at the end of the track list. You can then drag it to a new position.

You can add one or more albums to the Party Shuffle track list by dragging the albums; the songs play in album order. You can also add all the songs by an artist by dragging the artist's name. Party Shuffle acts like a dynamic playlist — you add, delete, and change the order of songs on the fly.

Cool DJs mix the Party Shuffle window with other open playlist windows — just double-click the playlist item in the Source pane to open it in a separate window, as shown in Chapter 10. You can then drag songs from different playlist windows to the Party Shuffle window while Party Shuffle plays, adding songs in whatever order you want in real time.

Cross-fading song playback

You can often hear a song on the radio fade out as another song immediately fades in right over the first song's ending. This is a *cross-fade,* and with iTunes, you can smoothly transition from the ending of one song to the beginning of the next one. Ordinarily, iTunes is set to have a short cross-fade of one second — the amount of time between the end of the fade in the first song and the start of the fade in the second song.

What's totally cool is that you can cross-fade between two songs in iTunes even if they're from different sources — the songs could be in your library, in a shared library, on CD, or even on one (or more!) iPods connected to your computer and playing through iTunes (as we describe in Chapter 16). You could play DJ at a party with a massive music library on a laptop and still augment that library with one or more iPods and any number of CDs, and the songs cross-fade to the next just like on the radio or at a dance party with a professional DJ.

You can change the amount of the cross-fade by choosing iTunes⇨Preferences on a Mac or Edit⇨Preferences in Windows, and then clicking the Playback button. The Playback preferences dialog appears, as shown in Figure 6-6.

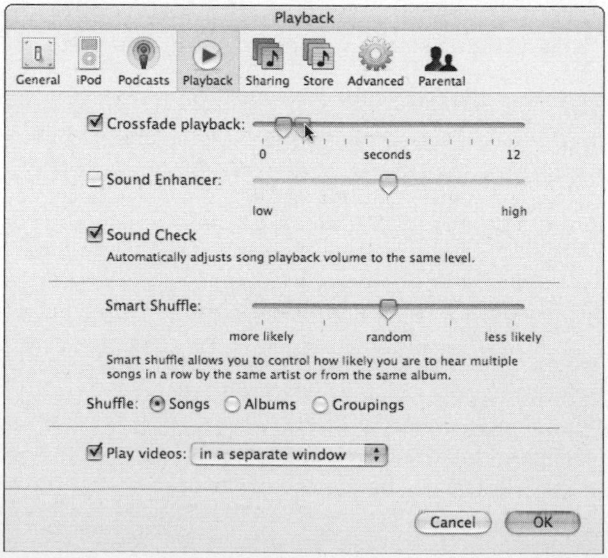

Figure 6-6:
Set the cross-fade between songs.

In the Playback preferences dialog, select the Crossfade Playback option and then increase or decrease the amount of the cross-fade by dragging the slider. Each notch in the slider is one second. The maximum amount of cross-fade is 12 seconds. With a longer cross-fade, you get a longer overlap from one song to the next — the second song starts before the first one ends. To turn off the cross-fade, deselect the check box.

Playing Streaming Radio

Radio stations from nearly every part of the world are broadcasting on the Internet. You can tune in to Japan-A-Radio for the top 40 hits in Japan, or Cable Radio UK for tunes from the south coast of England, or Radio Darvish for traditional Persian music. You can also check out the local news and sports from your hometown, no matter where you are. You can listen to talk radio and music shows from all over the country and the world.

By *radio,* we really mean a *streaming broadcast.* A streaming broadcast sends audio to your computer in a protected stream of bits over the Internet. Your computer starts playing the stream as soon as the first set of bits arrives, and more sections are transferred while you listen, so that you hear it as a continual stream. Broadcasters can use this technology to continually transmit new content, just like a radio station. Of course, real radio stations also make use of this technology to broadcast their programs over the Internet.

In addition, thousands of Web sites offer temporary streaming audio broadcasts all the time. A rock group on tour can offer a broadcast of a special concert, available for only one day. You might want to tune in weekly or monthly broadcasts, such as high-tech talk shows, news programs, documentaries, sporting events . . . the list is endless. You can even have access to private broadcasts, such as corporate board meetings.

You can't record or save a song from a streamed broadcast without special software. Nor can you play a streaming broadcast on your iPod, except as a podcast. (See Chapter 5 about adding podcasts.)

Listening to a radio station

iTunes offers a set of links to radio stations on the Internet, so you might want to try these first. Follow these steps:

1. **Select the Radio option in the Source pane.**

   The iTunes window displays a list of categories of radio stations.

2. **Click the Refresh button to retrieve the latest radio stations.**

   More Web radio stations are added all the time. The Refresh button in the top-right corner of the iTunes window (taking the place of the Browse button) connects iTunes to the Internet to retrieve the latest list of radio stations for each category.

3. **Open a category to see a list of stations in that category.**

   Click the triangle next to a category name to open the list of radio streams in that category, as shown in Figure 6-7. Some large radio stations offer more than one stream.

4. **Select a stream and click the Play button.**

   To select a stream, click its name in the iTunes Song List pane. (Actually, it's the Radio Station List pane now because you selected Radio in the Source pane.) Within seconds, you hear live radio off the Web.

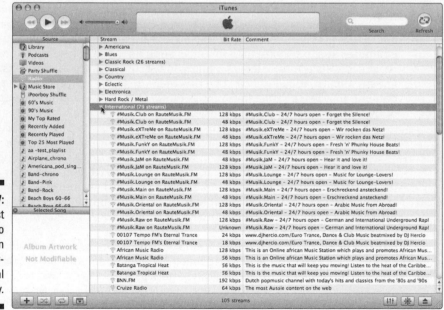

Figure 6-7:
Open a list of radio streams in the International category.

If you use a dialup modem connection to the Internet, you might want to choose a stream with a bit rate of less than 56 Kbps for best results. The Bit Rate column (refer to Figure 6-7) shows the bit rate for each stream.

TIP

iTunes creates a buffer for the audio stream so that you hear continuous playback with fewer Internet-related hiccups than most Web radio software. The buffer temporarily stores as much of the stream as possible, adding more of the stream to the end of the buffer as you play the audio in the buffer. If you hear stutters, gaps, or hiccups when playing a stream, set your buffer to a larger size by choosing iTunes⇨Preferences (Mac) or Edit⇨Preferences (Windows). In the Preferences dialog, click the Advanced button and then the General tab, and then choose a size from the Streaming Buffer Size pop-up menu.

Creating a playlist of your radio stations

Car radios offer preset stations activated by you pressing a button. Of course, you first need to tune in to the station of your choice to set that button. You can save your radio station choices in an iTunes playlist, and the process is easy:

1. **Select a radio station stream.**

2. **Drag the stream name to the bottom of the list of playlists in the Source pane.**

    iTunes creates a playlist using the stream name. You can add more radio streams to the same playlist by dragging their names over the new playlist name in the Source pane.

Drag as many streams as you like to as many playlists as you like. You can click any playlist name and rearrange that playlist as you want, dragging stream names as you would drag song names. See Chapter 10 to discover how to create and use playlists.

Radio streams in your playlists play only if you are connected to the Internet.

To quickly create a playlist from selected radio streams, first select the streams just as you would select multiple songs and then choose File⇨New Playlist from Selection.

Adding a radio station to iTunes

You can tune in to any broadcast on the Internet. All you need to know is the Web address, also known as the *URL* (Uniform Resource Locator), which is the global address of documents and other resources on the Web. You can find most URLs from a Web site or e-mail about a broadcast.

Follow these steps to add a Web broadcast to your iTunes library:

1. **Choose Advanced⇨Open Stream.**

    The Open Stream dialog appears, with a URL text field for typing a Web address.

2. **Type the exact, full URL of the stream.**

   Include the `http://` prefix, as in `http://64.236.34.141:80/stream/1014`.

   If you're connected to the Internet, iTunes automatically retrieves the broadcast and places it at the end of your song list.

3. **Click OK.**

As of this writing, iTunes supports only MP3 broadcasts. You can find lots of MP3 broadcasts from SHOUTcast (`www.shoutcast.com`) and Live365.com (`http://live365.com`).

Playing Podcasts

Podcasts you subscribe to show up in the Song List pane that appears when you select the Podcasts option in the Source pane. You can add podcast episodes to your library by subscribing to them in the iTunes Music Store (see Chapter 4) or on a Web site (see Chapter 5). To play a podcast episode, follow these steps:

1. **Select the Podcasts option in the Source pane.**

   The podcasts appear in the Song List pane.

2. **Select the podcast in the Podcasts list and click the triangle to see its episodes.**

   The triangle rotates, and a list of episodes appears beneath the podcast, as shown in Figure 6-8.

3. **Select the podcast and click the Play button.**

   You can use the iTunes playback controls to fast-forward or rewind the podcast or play it from any point. The blue dot next to a podcast means you haven't yet played it. As soon as you start listening to a podcast, the dot disappears.

When you play a podcast, iTunes remembers your place when you stop listening to it, just like a bookmark in an audio book. iTunes resumes playing from the bookmark when you return to the podcast to play it.

Some podcasts are enhanced to include chapter marks and photos. When you play an enhanced podcast in iTunes, a bookmark menu icon appears to the right of the status display at the top of the iTunes window, as shown in Figure 6-9. Click this icon to display a pop-up menu offering the podcast's chapter marks, artwork, and chapter start times, as shown in Figure 6-10.

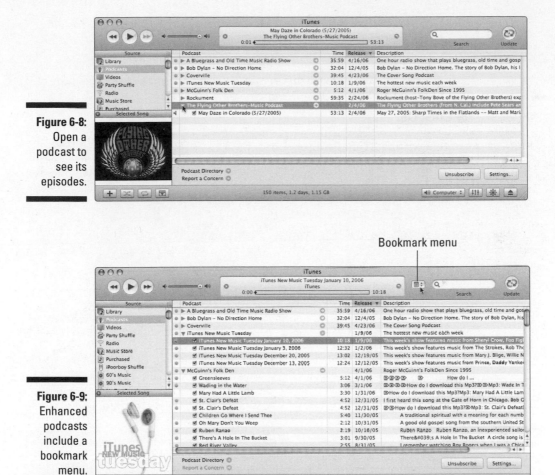

Figure 6-8:
Open a
podcast to
see its
episodes.

Bookmark menu

Figure 6-9:
Enhanced
podcasts
include a
bookmark
menu.

If the podcaster embedded a photo in an audio podcast file or included a link to a video from the file, the photo or video content appears in the Artwork pane.

You can drag a podcast to the Source pane to create a new playlist, as shown in Figure 6-11, which takes on the name of the podcast. (For example, dragging The Flying Other Brothers–Music Podcast to the Source pane in Figure 6-11 creates The Flying Other Brothers–Music Podcast playlist.) For more information about playlists, see Chapter 10.

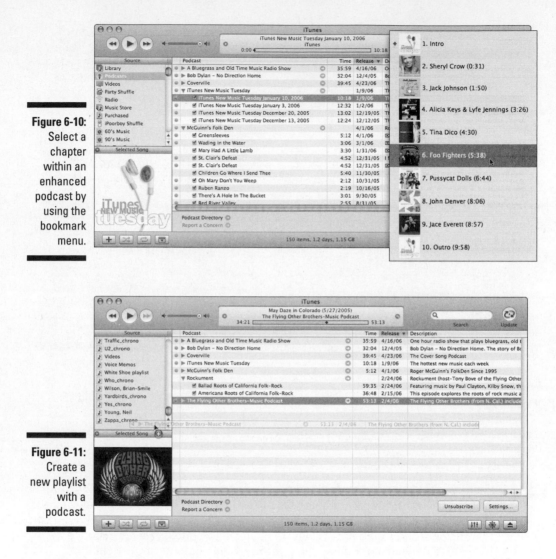

Figure 6-10: Select a chapter within an enhanced podcast by using the bookmark menu.

Figure 6-11: Create a new playlist with a podcast.

Playing Audio Books

You can store and play audio books, articles, and spoken-word titles just like songs in iTunes — you can find them under the Artist name in your library, as we describe in Chapter 8. (You can download titles from www.audible.com; see Chapter 5.)

To play an audio book, select it just like you would a song and click the Play/Pause button. You can use the iTunes playback controls to fast-forward or rewind the audio book or play it from any point.

Audio books from Audible and the iTunes Music Store are enhanced to include chapter marks. When you play any of these audio books in iTunes, a bookmark menu icon appears to the top right of the iTunes window display (refer to Figure 6-9). Click this icon to display a pop-up menu offering the audio book's chapter marks, as shown in Figure 6-12.

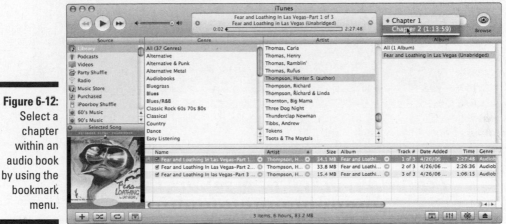

Figure 6-12: Select a chapter within an audio book by using the bookmark menu.

Playing Videos

Your iTunes library is ready to play your video collection — the videos you bought and downloaded from the iTunes Music Store (see Chapter 4) and the ones you dragged into iTunes from other sources (see Chapter 5).

To watch a video in iTunes, select it in your library or playlist and click the Play/Pause button. Use the iTunes Play/Pause, Forward/Next, and Previous/ Rewind buttons to control playback and the iTunes volume slider to control the volume, just like with songs.

The video appears in the Artwork pane in the lower-left corner of the iTunes window, as shown in Figure 6-13. If the Artwork pane isn't visible, click the Show/Hide Artwork button.

You can view your video two ways: by opening it in a separate window or by filling the entire display with the video.

Figure 6-13:
A video
appears in
the Artwork
pane.

Show/Hide Artwork   Full-Screen Video

Playing a video in a separate window

To watch a video in a separate window, click the video as it plays in the Artwork pane. To make this setting permanent, set your iTunes preferences to play video in a separate window. Open iTunes Preferences by choosing iTunes⇨Preferences (Mac) or Edit⇨Preferences (Windows), and click the Playback button. Choose the In a Separate Window option from the Play Videos pop-up menu, as shown in Figure 6-14. From that point on, videos in your library play in a separate window that offers QuickTime playback controls, as shown in Figure 6-15.

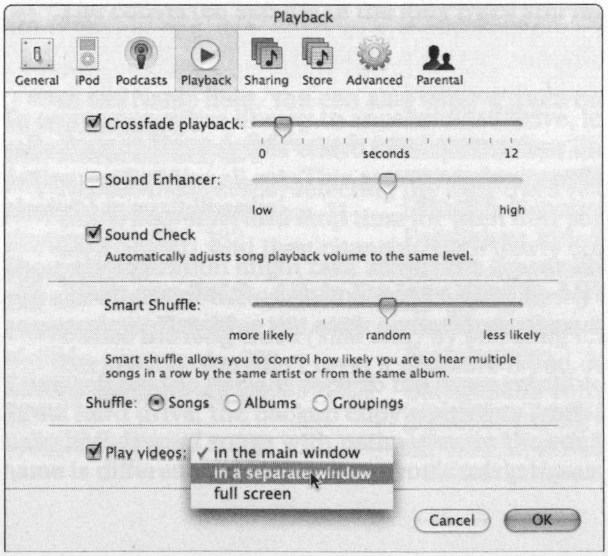

Figure 6-14:
Change
video
playback to
a separate
window.

The QuickTime video buttons offer more control over playback in the separate window: Click the right-facing triangle on the bottom-left side of the
window to play or pause, and drag the slider to move forward or backward
through the video (refer to Figure 6-15). Click the rewind or fast-forward buttons on the bottom-right side of the window to move backward or forward
through a video.

Playing a video full-screen

 To watch the video on the full screen, click the Full-Screen Video button
(refer to Figure 6-13). This button doesn't appear unless you're playing a
video.

After clicking the Full-Screen Video button, video fills your screen and plays.
Pressing any key during playback stops full-screen video and returns you to
the iTunes window.

For many, the computer display is just fine for viewing videos full-screen; the
picture clarity on a Mac, for example, is better than any comparably sized
television (even Mac PowerBooks and iBooks). However, if you want to connect your PC to a television, follow the instructions that came with your PC.
(Most likely you'll use the same cables that you would use to connect an iPod
to a television; see Chapter 16.)

You can connect a Mac to a television that offers an S-video connection or standard RCA video and audio connections. After connecting to the television, follow these steps:

1. **Choose System Preferences from the Apple menu.**

   The System Preferences window appears with icons for each set of preferences.

2. **Click the Displays icon in the System Preferences window.**

   The Display preferences window appears. Depending on the type of display, you might see tabs for different panes.

3. **Click the Display tab for the Display preferences pane if it isn't already selected.**

   The preferences appear with settings for your display.

4. **Click the Detect Displays button.**

   The Mac detects the television and sets it to the appropriate resolution. For more about setting display resolutions on the Mac, see *Mac OS X Tiger All-in-One Desk Reference For Dummies,* by Mark L. Chambers (Wiley).

If you don't see a picture on your television, check to be sure your television is set to the correct input source — video in (RCA) or S-video in (if you use an S-video cable). You can also use other types of video equipment. For example, a video recorder that accepts RCA or S-video input can record the video, and a video projector can display it on a large screen.

Chapter 7

Sharing Content Legally

· ·

In This Chapter

▶ Sharing content purchased from the iTunes Music Store

▶ Using a local area network to share an iTunes library

▶ Copying media files to other drives and computers

▶ Copying from Macs to PCs and vice versa

· ·

Hey, it's your content after you buy it — that is, to the extent that you can make copies for yourself. You want to play your music and videos anywhere and even share them with your friends. It's only natural.

iTunes lets you share a library over a local area network (LAN) with other computers running iTunes. You can also copy the content files to other computers without any restrictions on copying, although protected content has playback restrictions. You can easily share the music that you rip from your CDs: After the music becomes digital, you can copy it endlessly with no subsequent loss in quality. You can also share the songs, audio books, podcasts, and videos that you download. Of course, if the songs, audio books, and videos are in a protected format (such as content bought from the iTunes Music Store), the computers that access the shared library must be authorized to *play* the content. Whether the computers are connected to the LAN by cable (such as Ethernet) or by wireless technology (such as Apple's AirPort), you can share your library with other computers — up to *five* other computers in a single 24-hour period.

In this chapter, we show you how to bend the rules and share your iTunes library with others. (After all, your parents taught you to share, didn't they?)

Sharing Content from the iTunes Music Store

To a limited extent, you can share the content that you buy online from the iTunes Music Store. Apple uses a protected form of the AAC encoder for the songs — the music filenames use the extension .m4p for protected music rather than .m4a for music in the regular AAC format. (Read all about audio format encoders in Chapters 18 and 19.) Therefore, more than with most other services, the rights of artists are protected while also giving you leeway in using the music. Apple uses a protected video format for TV shows, music videos, and short films that you can buy in the online store — the filenames use the extension .m4v or .mp4 for protected video rather than .mpg for video in the standard MPEG-4 format.

The protection used with iTunes Music Store content lets you do the following:

- **Create backups.** You can download the content files and make as many copies as you want (even burn them onto data CDs and DVDs).

- **Copy content to iTunes libraries on other computers.** Play songs and videos on up to five separate computers. See Chapter 4 to find out how to authorize your computers.

- **Copy content to iPods.** Copy the music and videos to as many iPods as you want. See Chapter 12 for automatic and manual iPod updating.

- **Burn up to seven CDs.** Burn seven copies of the same playlist containing protected songs to an audio CD — but no more. You can also burn data CDs and DVDs with content files for backup purposes. See Chapter 14 for tips on CD and DVD burning.

- **Share content over a network.** Up to five computers running iTunes on a LAN can play the content in your shared library in a 24-hour period.

You can also play music in your library over a wireless connection to a stereo amplifier or receiver by using AirTunes and AirPort Express, which we cover in Chapter 6.

You might also want to know where the songs, audio books, and videos are stored on your hard drive so that you can copy the content to other computers and hard drives and create a backup of your entire library. You might want to move the library to another computer because computers just keep getting better year after year. To find the location of your content files, see Chapter 13.

Sharing Content on a Network

If you live like the Jetsons — with a computer in every room that's connected by a wireless or wired network — iTunes is made for you. You can share your iTunes library with other computers in the same network. These computers can be either PCs that run Windows or Macs — as long as they run iTunes. If they can communicate with each other over the network, iTunes can share a content library with up to five PCs in a single 24-hour period. The restriction

I fought the law, and the law won: Sharing and piracy

Apple CEO Steve Jobs gave personal demonstrations of the iTunes Music Store and the iPod to Paul McCartney and Mick Jagger before introducing the online music store. According to Steven Levy at *Newsweek* (May 12, 2003), Jobs said, "They both totally get it." The former Beatle and the Stones' frontman are no slouches — both conduct music-business affairs personally and have extensive back catalogs of music. They know all about the free music-swapping services on the Internet, but they agree with Jobs that most people are willing to pay for high-quality music rather than download free copies of questionable quality.

We think the solution to piracy is not technology because determined pirates always circumvent it with newer technology and because only consumers are inconvenienced.

Giving music away is, of course, the subject of much controversy. For example, some services (such as the original Napster) were closed by court order whereas others flourish in countries that don't have copyright laws as strict as the United States' laws. (Napster is back, but it no longer provides the same type of music sharing.)

The songs available from some free sharing services are mostly low-quality MP3 audio files, which sound about as good as an FM radio broadcast, although some sources of free music offer higher-quality MP3 audio files. The iTunes Music Store offers licensed music in a high-quality format comparable to MP3, and we prefer the original authorized version of the song — not some knock-off that might have been copied from a radio broadcast.

As for making copies for personal use, the law is murky at best. It depends on what you mean by *personal use*. For example, Apple's iLife software suite for the Mac allows you to use these music files in creative projects. You can, for example, put together a music video to show your friends by using iMovie to combine some video footage that you shot with your camcorder along with the latest hit by Eminem. However, don't expect to see it on MTV or VH1. Your local public access cable TV station can't even play it unless you first obtain the broadcast rights (which typically include contacting the music publisher, the record label, and the artist — good luck).

Can you legally use a pop song as a soundtrack for a high school yearbook slideshow? Given the ability to use music for educational purposes, it sounds legal to us. Still, you should ask a lawyer. If you're interested in obtaining the rights to music to use in semipublic or public presentations or even movies and documentaries for public distribution, you can contact the music publisher or a licensing agent. Music-publishing organizations, such as the Music Publishers' Association (www.mpa.org), offer information and lists of music publishers as well as explanations of various rights and licenses.

to five in a 24-hour period is yet another one of the imposed rules of record labels and video producers.

When you share content on a network, the content is *streamed* over the network from the computer that contains the library (the *library computer*) to the computer that plays it. A stream arrives in the receiving computer bit by bit; the computer starts playing the stream as soon as the first set of bits arrive, and more sections are transferred while you listen. The result is that the recipient hears music and sees video as a continual stream. Broadcasters use this technology to continually transmit new content (just like a radio station). The content isn't copied to the receiving computer's library, and you can't burn the shared library songs onto a CD or copy the songs to an iPod.

Sharing an iTunes library can be incredibly useful for playing content on laptops, such as PowerBook, that support the wireless AirPort network. You can manage a very large content library on a desktop computer with a large hard drive, and then play content on the laptop or notebook computer with a smaller hard drive without having to copy files to the smaller hard drive.

Sharing your library with other computers

To share your iTunes library — turning your computer into the library computer — follow these steps:

1. **Choose iTunes⇨Preferences (Mac) or Edit⇨Preferences (Windows) and then click the Sharing tab.**

   The Sharing dialog appears, as shown in Figure 7-1, offering options for sharing music.

2. **Select the Share My Music option.**

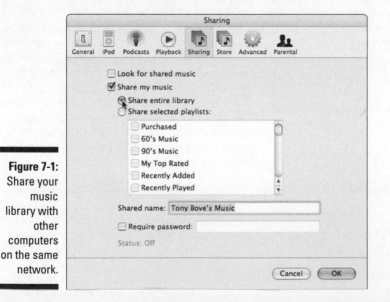

Figure 7-1: Share your music library with other computers on the same network.

3. **Select either the Share Entire Library option or the Share Selected Playlists option and then choose the playlists to share.**

4. **Type a name for the shared library. Also, add a password if you want.**

   The name that you choose appears in the Source list for other computers that share your library. The password restricts access to only those who know it.

   Pick a password that you don't mind sharing with others; for example, your name is a good password, but your ATM PIN isn't.

   iTunes displays a `Reminder: Sharing music is for personal use only` message.

5. **Click OK.**

Before turning off sharing for your library, you must first notify anyone sharing the library to eject the shared library. Otherwise, iTunes displays a warning dialog allowing you to continue (and break off the connection to the shared library) or to leave sharing turned on for the moment.

Accessing a shared library

You can access the content from the other computers on the network by following these steps:

1. **Choose iTunes⇨Preferences on a Mac or Edit⇨Preferences in Windows and click the Sharing tab.**

   The Sharing dialog appears and offers options for sharing content. Refer to Figure 7-1.

2. **Select the Look for Shared Music option.**

   The shared libraries or playlists appear in the Source pane. Figure 7-2 shows a shared library in the Source pane.

3. **Click the triangle next to a shared library entry in the Source pane, as shown in Figure 7-3, to see the shared playlists. Play them as you normally would.**

   iTunes fills the view on the right with the artists and content from the shared library.

4. **When you're finished listening, click the tiny Eject button that appears to the right of the shared library name in the Source pane.**

A shared library

Figure 7-2:
Select the music library that's shared by iTunes running on another network computer.

Eject button

Figure 7-3:
Open the list of playlists in the shared music library.

Copying Media Files

You can copy content freely from your iTunes window to other hard drives and computers or copy the content folders from the iTunes Music folder to other hard drives and computers. On a Mac, you can use the Finder to copy content files as well as dragging stuff out of the iTunes window into folders or hard drives. Windows PCs offer several methods, including using Windows Explorer to copy files.

By default, the files are organized in folders by artist name and by album title (or book, video, or TV show title) within the iTunes Music folder — unless you change options in the Advanced section of iTunes Preferences (see Chapter 13). For example, copying an entire album, or every song by a specific artist, is easy — just drag the folder to a folder on another hard drive.

You can find out the location of any content item by selecting the item in iTunes and choosing File➪Get Info. Click the Summary tab in the Get Info dialog to see the Summary options. Although you can change the location of your iTunes library, most people leave the library in its default location — inside the iTunes Music folder in the iTunes folder on the startup hard drive.

On the Mac, the iTunes Music folder can be found by default at *your home folder*/Music/iTunes/iTunes Music. On a Windows PC, the iTunes Music folder can be found at *your user folder*/My Documents/My Music/iTunes/iTunes Music.

Your playlists, including the library itself (which is in some ways a giant playlist), are stored as eXtensible Markup Language (XML) files in the iTunes folder along with your iTunes Music folder.

The easiest way to copy an album from a folder on a hard drive into your iTunes library is to drag the album's folder over the iTunes window and drop the folder there. If you drop it into the Source pane, iTunes creates a playlist of the album's songs using the album name. To copy individual songs, you can drag the song files over the iTunes window and drop them in the Song List pane. When you add a piece of content (song, video, podcast, or audio book) to your iTunes library, a copy is placed inside the iTunes Music folder.

Copying Files between Macs and PCs

Song files are not small, album folders filled with songs are quite large, and video files are far larger than song files. Copying a library from a Mac to a PC — or vice versa — is not a simple task because of the enormity of these file sizes.

Attaching a file to an e-mail message is the most popular method of transferring a file to someone. However, when you attach a file to an e-mail message, the attached file is encoded in a format that increases the size of the attachment by up to 40 percent. Many e-mail servers in the world won't accept an attachment larger than 5MB; some won't accept attachments larger than 4MB. Don't even think about e-mail: *If the file is over four, it won't go through the door.* (Four megabytes, that is, and the door is the limitation of your Internet service provider's e-mail server.) If you use a .Mac e-mail account, the limitation is 10MB.

Well, heck, just about every jazz tune and Grateful Dead jam we listen to in iTunes is larger than 3MB. A song compressed in the AAC or MP3 format is typically between 2MB and 10MB, so you might get by with one pop song attached to an e-mail, but that's it.

How do you transfer larger amounts of content? One way is with an external FireWire or a USB hard drive formatted for a PC — an iPod installed for Windows would do nicely. You can find out about using an iPod as a hard drive in Chapter 23. A Mac recognizes the iPod when you plug it in even though the drive is formatted for Windows; you can copy files directly to the hard drive and then take the hard drive over to your PC. You need FireWire or USB to connect an external drive.

On a LAN, you can share forever. If your computers communicate over a LAN, they can share files . . . even large ones. To copy large files or entire folders between two Macs in a LAN, all you do is allow personal file sharing on your Mac.

Allowing personal file sharing sounds like a liberal thing to do — inviting all sorts of mischief and voyeurism — but you control what others can do. (The converse is true: If someone wants to make a file or folder available to *you* over a LAN, all he or she has to do is enable personal file sharing.)

Mac OS X makes it very easy to share files and folders with Windows computers. You can enable Windows file sharing on the Mac, or you can access the Windows computer from a Mac. To access a Windows PC from a Mac, you need a valid user ID and password for an account on the Windows computer. You can go right to that account's Home directory on the Windows computer and use your Mac to copy folders and files to and from the Windows computer. For more information about file sharing on a Mac (specifically between Mac and Windows computers on a network), see *Mac OS X Tiger All-in-One Desk Reference For Dummies,* by Mark L. Chambers (Wiley).

Copying very large song files over the Internet is a bit more complex, involving the use of a communication application such as iChat AV or one that offers the File Transfer Protocol (FTP). Although you can easily download an

MP3 song file from a Web page or an FTP site with any browser (all you need is the Web or FTP address — and a user ID and password if the site is protected), you can't *send* the file to a protected site with most browsers unless the site is set up for this function. One easy way to share your files from a Mac is to use the .Mac service to create a Web page that accommodates anyone with the right password, even Windows-using folks, to visit and download files you put there. For information about setting up a .Mac account, see *iLife '04 All-in-One Desk Reference For Dummies,* by the very authors who wrote the book in your hands (Wiley).

To make it easy for others to copy files to and from a Mac at their convenience, enable FTP access for the Mac. To do this

1. **Open System Preferences.**

2. **Click the Sharing icon.**

3. **Click the Services button.**

4. **Select the FTP Access option.**

   A message at the bottom of the Sharing pane provides the address of your FTP server on your Mac — something like `ftp://192.168.1.246`.

5. **Give the address to those with an account on your computer so that they can access files and folders by using a Web browser, an FTP client such as Fetch, or Mac OS X.**

   If you've turned on the firewall in Mac OS X, click the Firewall button in the Sharing preferences and select the FTP Access option; this allows FTP access through the firewall.

How about transferring files to other FTP sites such as a password-protected site that requires the use of an FTP client? You have several options:

✔ **Use an FTP client,** such as Fetch or RBrowser 4 for Mac OS X or FTP Explorer for Windows. You can find Fetch at `http://fetchsoftworks.com` for $25 as of this writing. You can use it for several weeks before paying for it. RBrowser 4 (`www.rbrowser.com`) is free to download and use and looks a bit like the Mac Finder. FTP Explorer (`www.ftpx.com`) is shareware you can use for a month before paying $35. (Students and faculty members can use it for free.)

✔ **Use the FTP function inside another application,** such as Macromedia Dreamweaver.

✔ **Use a free Terminal application,** such as the one supplied with Mac OS X, found in the Utilities folder inside your Applications folder, which offers FTP. For instructions, see *Mac OS X Tiger All-in-One Desk Reference For Dummies,* by Mark L. Chambers (Wiley).

Most FTP utilities and functions within applications provide an easy way to copy files. For example, Fetch provides a drag-and-drop interface for transferring any type of file with FTP servers. After you establish a connection with the FTP server by typing the appropriate information (the FTP server name, your ID, your password, and the directory that you have access to), you can drag files to and from the FTP server window via the Finder, or you can browse folders to select files and then use the Get and Put Files buttons.

You can send an entire folder of files, such as an album of songs or an artist folder with multiple albums, by stuffing the folder (or even a set of folders) into a compressed *Zip file*. (Zip is a standard compression format.) Select the files or folders and Control-click (Mac) or right-click (Windows) the selection. In Mac OS X, choose Create Archive; in Windows, choose WinZip (or similar Zip utility that installs itself into Windows menus).

You can then transfer the Zip file to the FTP server in one step. Although the Zip file formats compress other types of files, the files won't get any smaller if your music files are already compressed as MP3 or AAC. However, the format offers a compact way of sending an entire folder of files.

Part II
Managing Your Media Content

The 5th Wave   By Rich Tennant

"I could tell you more about myself, but I think the playlist on my iPod says more about me than mere words can."

In this part . . .

Visit this part to find out how to organize the content in your iTunes library.

- Chapter 8 describes how to browse your iTunes library, change viewing options, and search for songs, artists, albums, videos, and TV shows.

- Chapter 9 describes how to add information, artwork, and ratings for each content item and then edit the info in iTunes.

- Chapter 10 shows you how to build playlists of songs and entire albums in iTunes, including smart playlists.

- Chapter 11 explains how to import photos from digital cameras and videos from digital camcorders into your computer to use with your iPod.

- Chapter 12 describes updating your iPod or iPod shuffle with content automatically or manually by using iTunes. It also covers how to edit playlists and content information directly on your iPod.

- Chapter 13 shows you how to make backup copies of your iTunes library and move your library to another hard drive.

- Chapter 14 is a guide to burning audio and MP3 CDs and data DVDs, as well as printing CD jewel-case inserts and song listings.

Chapter 8

Searching, Browsing, and Sorting in iTunes

*Y*ou rip a few CDs, buy some songs and videos from the iTunes Music Store, and then watch your iTunes library fill up with content. That list keeps getting longer and longer; as a result, your library is harder to navigate.

The iTunes library is awesome, even by everyday jukebox standards. Though previous versions were limited to a paltry (!) 32,000 files per library and you had to create multiple libraries to get around that limit, the current version (actually all versions newer than version 4) can hold virtually an unlimited number of files. The limit depends entirely on how much space you have on your hard drive.

Consider that a 60GB iPod can hold about 15,000 audio files in the AAC format — enough music to last at least a month even if played 24 hours each day! Even if you keep your iTunes library down to the size of what fits on your iPod, you still have a formidable collection at your fingertips. If your music collection is getting large, organize it to make finding songs easier. After all, finding U2's "I Still Haven't Found What I'm Looking For" is a challenge even in a library of only 32,000 songs.

This chapter shows you how to search, browse, and sort your iTunes library. You can find any song, video, audio book, or podcast in seconds. You can change the viewing options to make your library's display more useful. Display songs sorted by artist, album, genre, or other attributes or sort TV shows by season or episode.

Browsing and Listing Your Library Content

Overwhelmed by the long list of content in your iTunes library? Try browsing: Switch from Song List view to Browse view to find songs more easily.

The iTunes window includes the Browse/Song List pane that offers a view of your library and your sources for content depending on which choice you select in the Source pane, as follows:

- **Library:** Lists the entire library of songs, videos, TV shows, podcasts, and audio books in the Song List pane (someday Apple will change the name of this pane to "List" because it includes more than songs). Click the Browse button in the upper-right corner to toggle between Browse view (with the Song List pane below and the Browse pane above with genre, artist, and album) and the Song List pane by itself.

- **Podcasts:** Lists only the podcasts you've subscribed to. (The Browse button changes to Update — see Chapter 5 for podcast updating information.)

- **Videos:** Lists only the videos you've added to your library. You can click Browse to navigate your video selections by Genre (type of video), Artist, and Album (title of TV season or video).

- **Party Shuffle:** Lists the Party Shuffle playlist (see Chapter 6 for tips on using the Party Shuffle feature).

- **Radio:** Lists the Web radio stations you can play. Radio station content is streamed to your computer but not stored in your library.

- **Music Store:** The iTunes Music Store, which has its own browser. You've been there before — see Chapter 4.

- **Playlist entries:** Smart playlists and regular playlists appear below the Music Store choice. See Chapter 10 for information about playlists.

Browsing Videos and TV Shows

As the newest member of the iTunes content family, video has a method of browsing that we expect to evolve and thus gain more features. It's amazing that iTunes is still called *iTunes* given the capacity for managing video content, but that might change someday soon. (Unless Apple can persuade the rest of the world to start calling videos *tunes;* we prefer *toons.*)

To browse videos — and only videos — select Videos in the Source pane. The Song List pane changes to show thumbnail images of the videos, as shown in Figure 8-1.

Click the Browse button in the upper-right corner to switch to Browse view. iTunes organizes your video content by Genre, Artist, and Album, as shown in Figure 8-1. For TV shows, the Artist is the title of the show, and the Album is the show season title.

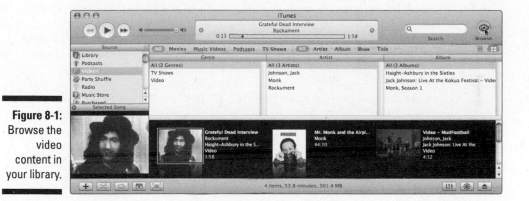

Figure 8-1: Browse the video content in your library.

To see the videos in a list (see Figure 8-2), rather than as thumbnail images, click the List button in the upper-right corner of the Video Browse pane. Next to the List button is the Thumbnails button with four tiny rectangles (in an oval when selected). Click the Thumbnails button to change the Song List view back to the Thumbnails view.

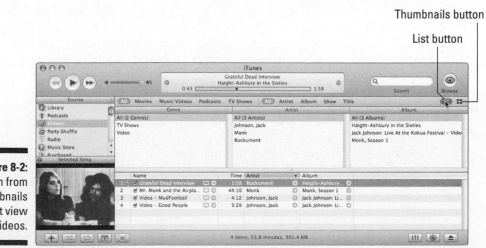

Figure 8-2: Switch from thumbnails to a list view of videos.

The Video Browse pane also has buttons along the top for displaying different genres of video — All, Movies, Music Videos, Podcasts (video podcasts only), and TV Shows. Click the All, Artist, Album, Show, or Title button to sort the list.

Browsing by Artist and Album

To view all the albums in your library in Browse view, select the Library option in the Source pane and then click the Browse button in the upper-right corner. iTunes organizes your library by genre, artist, and album, which makes finding the right tunes easier, as shown in Figure 8-3. When you select an album in Browse view, iTunes displays only the songs for that album.

Click the Browse button again to return to the Song List view. The Browse button toggles between Browse and Song List views.

Figure 8-3: Click the Browse button to browse the iTunes library.

The Browse view sorts the songs by genre, artist, and album. (The Genre column appears only if you leave the Show Genre When Browsing option turned on in the General dialog of iTunes Preferences.) Click a genre in the Genre column to see artists in that genre or click All at the top of the Genre column to see all artists for all genres. When you click an artist in the Artist column (the middle column; see Figure 8-4), the album titles appear in the Album column (on the right).

If you don't get track information from the Internet for each song (as we show in Chapter 5) or if you add the track information yourself by using the Song Information pane (as we describe in Chapter 9), iTunes displays a blank space for the Artist and Album name along with Track 01 and so on for each track. However, that makes browsing for a song or artist by name difficult.

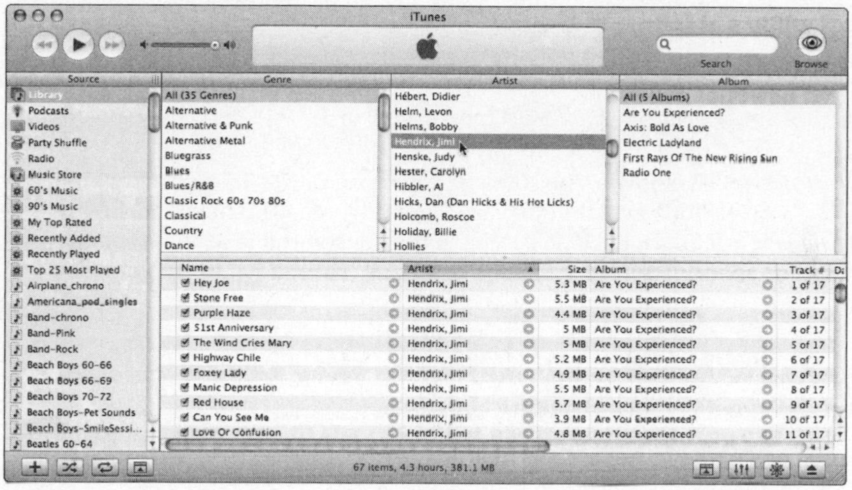

Figure 8-4:
Select an
artist to see
the list of
albums for
that artist.

To see more than one album from an artist at a time, press ⌘ (Mac) or Ctrl (Windows) and then click each album name.

When you click different albums in the Album column, the Song List pane displays the songs from that album. The songs are listed in proper track order, just as the artist, producer, or record label intended, assuming that the correct track information has been downloaded from the Internet or entered into the Song Information pane, as we describe in Chapter 9.

To see all the songs in the library in Browse view, select All at the top of each of the columns — Genre, Artist, and Album.

Note: iTunes considers Clash and The Clash to be different music groups, although it sorts them properly under C. We show you how to edit the artist name and other information in Chapter 9.

Understanding the Column Headings

iTunes can combine all your content in the Song List pane when you click the Library option in the Source pane. The column headings don't change, but they have different meanings for the following types of content:

- **Songs and music videos:** The Name is the title of the song or music video; the Artist is the band, artist, or performer. The Album is the title of the CD or LP on which the song appeared. For music videos, the Name is typically the title of an album associated with the song in the music video.

- **Podcasts:** The Name is the title of the podcast episode (as in "Ballad Roots of California Folk-Rock"), the Artist is the name of the podcast author (as in Tony Bove), and the Album is the name of the podcast (as in *Rockument*).

- **Audio books:** The Album is typically the book's title (as in *Fear and Loathing in Las Vegas*), and the Name is typically the title of a set of chapters (as in *Fear and Loathing in Las Vegas*-Part 1 of 3).

- **TV shows:** The Name is the name of the TV show episode (as in "Mr. Monk and the Airplane"), the Artist is the name of the show (as in *Monk*), and the Album is the season (as in *Monk,* Season 1).

Understanding the content indicators

When you make choices in iTunes, it displays an action indicator next to each content item to show you what it's doing. Here's a list of the indicators and their meanings:

- **Orange waveform:** iTunes is importing the song.

- **Green check mark:** iTunes finished importing the song.

- **Exclamation point:** iTunes can't find the song, video, TV show episode, audio book, or podcast episode.

  If you move or delete the item accidentally, you can move the item back into iTunes by dragging its file from your hard drive into the iTunes window. (To find content files on your hard drive, see Chapter 13.)

- **Broadcast icon:** The item is on the Internet and plays as a stream.

- **Black check mark:** The item is marked for the next operation such as importing from an audio CD or playing in sequence.

  Click to remove the check mark.

- **Speaker:** The song, video, audio book, or podcast is playing.

- **Chasing arrows:** iTunes is copying the content item from another location or downloading it from the Internet.

Altering the headings

iTunes lets you customize the Song List view. The list starts out with the Name, Time, Artist, Album, Genre, My Rating, Play Count, and Last Played categories. You might have to drag the horizontal scroll bar along the bottom of the song list to see all these columns. You can display more, less, or different information in your song list.

Customize your Song List view in the following ways:

- **Make a column wider or narrower.** As you move your cursor over the divider between two columns, the cursor changes to a vertical bar with opposing arrows extending left and right; you can click and drag the divider to change the column's width.

- **Change the order of columns.** Click a column heading and drag the entire column to the left or right.

  You can't change the position of the Name column and the narrow column to its left, which displays indicators.

- **Add or remove columns.** The Size (for file size), Date and Year (for the date the album was released or any other date you choose for each song), Bit Rate, Sample Rate, Track Number, and Comment are all editable:

  a. Choose Edit➪View Options.

  b. Select the columns that you want to appear in the song list from the View Options dialog (see Figure 8-5).

  You can also change the view options by ⌘-clicking (Mac) or Ctrl-clicking (Windows) any of the column headings in the song list in either Browse or Song List view.

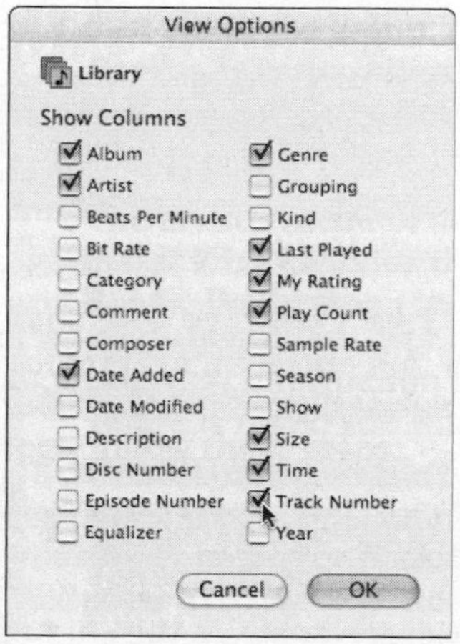

Figure 8-5:
The viewing options for the song list.

View Options

Library

Show Columns

☑ Album   ☑ Genre
☑ Artist   ☐ Grouping
☐ Beats Per Minute ☐ Kind
☐ Bit Rate   ☑ Last Played
☐ Category   ☑ My Rating
☐ Comment   ☑ Play Count
☐ Composer   ☐ Sample Rate
☑ Date Added   ☐ Season
☐ Date Modified ☐ Show
☐ Description ☑ Size
☐ Disc Number ☑ Time
☐ Episode Number ☑ Track Number
☐ Equalizer   ☐ Year

Cancel   OK

Browse view includes a Genre column on the left side. If you don't need a Genre column, you can remove it from the Browse view (or add it back):

1. **Choose Preferences. (Choose iTunes⇨Preferences on a Mac or Edit⇨ Preferences in Windows.)**

2. **Click the General button at the top of the Preferences window.**

3. **In the General dialog, disable the Show Genre When Browsing option, which is on by default.**

Sorting content by the headings

With just a little know how, you can use the viewing options to sort the listing of items. Whether you're using Browse view or viewing the entire content list, the column headings double as sorting options.

For example, clicking the Time heading reorders the items by their duration in ascending order from shortest to longest. If you click the Time header again, the sort is reversed, starting with the longest item. You can sort by any column heading such as Artist, Album, Track, Date Added, and Ratings.

You can tell whether the sort is in ascending or descending order by the little arrow indicator in the heading. When the arrow points up, the sort is in *ascending order;* when pointing down, it's in *descending order.*

Alternatively, you can sort the list in alphabetical order. Click the Artist heading to sort all the items in the list by the artist name in alphabetical order (arrow pointing up). Click it again to sort the list in reverse alphabetical order (arrow pointing down).

Searching for Content

As your iTunes library grows, you might find the usual browsing and scrolling methods that we describe earlier in this chapter too time-consuming. Let iTunes find your content for you!

If you want to search the entire library in Browse view, first click the All selection at the top of the Genre and Artist columns to browse the entire library before typing a term in the Search field. Or, if you prefer, click the Browse button again to return to the Song List view, which lists the entire library.

Locate the Search field — the oval field in the top-right corner to the left of the Browse button — and follow these steps:

1. **Click in the Search field and type several characters of your search term.**

   Use these tips for successful searching:

   • *Specify your search* with a song title, an artist, or an album title.

   • *Narrow your search* by typing more characters. Using fewer characters results in a long list of possible songs.

   • *Case doesn't matter.* The Search feature ignores case. For example, when we search for *miles,* iTunes finds "Eight Miles High," "Forty Miles of Bad Road," "She Smiles like a River," and everything by Miles Davis.

2. **Look through the results, which display while you type.**

   The search operation works immediately, as shown in Figure 8-6, displaying, in the song list, any matches in the Name, Artist, and Album columns.

Figure 8-6: Search for anything by typing any part of the name, artist, album, or title.

If you're in Browse view with an artist and a particular album selected, you can't search for another artist or song. Use browsing with searching to further narrow your search.

3. Scroll through the search results and then click an item to select it.

To back out of a search so that the full list appears again, you can either click the circled X in the Search field (which appears only after you start typing characters) or delete the characters in the Search field. You see the entire list in the library's song list, just like before you began your search. All the Items are still there and remain there unless you explicitly remove them. Searching manipulates only your view of the items.

Finding the Content's Media File

Getting lost in a large library is easy. While you browse your library, you might want to return quickly to view the current item playing. While your file plays, choose File⇨Show Current Song (or press ⌘-L on a Mac or Ctrl-L in Windows as a shortcut). iTunes shows you the currently playing item.

You can also show the location of the media file for any content item. This trick comes in handy when you want to copy a song or video file to another hard drive or over a network, or when you want to open it in another application. Choose File⇨Show Song File (or press ⌘-R on a Mac or Ctrl-R in Windows as a shortcut), and iTunes gives control to the operating system (Mac or Windows), which displays the folder containing the media file. Choosing File⇨Show Song File also works with audio books, videos, podcasts, and even TV shows.

You can show the file if it's on your hard drive but not if it's in a shared library on another computer. See Chapter 13 for more details on looking for media files.

Showing Duplicate Items

As your library grows larger, you might want to check for duplications. Some songs that appear on artist CDs also appear on compilation or soundtrack CDs. If you rip them all, you could have duplicate songs that take up space on your hard drive. You might even have duplicate videos, audio books, or podcast episodes.

On the other hand, maybe you want to find different versions of the same song by the same artist. iTunes can find all the songs with the same title by the same artist quickly even when the songs appear on different albums.

To show duplicate items in the song list, choose Edit⇨Show Duplicate Songs. iTunes displays all the duplicate items in alphabetical order in the song list. If iTunes is in Browse view, you see all the duplicate items in artist order. Click the artist to see the duplicate items for that artist, as shown in Figure 8-7.

To stop showing duplicate items and return to your previous view (either Song List or Browse view), click the Show All Songs button below the list of duplicates.

Figure 8-7: Show duplicate items for each artist.

Deleting Content

Deleting stuff might seem counterproductive when you're trying to build up your iTunes library, but sometimes you just have to do it. You might have to delete

✔ **Versions of songs:** You might have ripped a CD twice — once in AIFF format to burn the songs onto another CD and once in AAC format for your library and iPod. You can delete the AIFF versions in your library after burning your CD (as we describe in Chapter 14).

✔ **Songs from playlists:** You can delete songs from playlists while still keeping the songs in your library. When you delete a song from a playlist, the song is simply deleted from the list — not from the library. You can delete playlists as well without harming the songs in the library. You have to switch to the Library option in the Source pane to delete songs from the library. (See Chapter 10 for more information about playlists.)

✔ **Any song, audio book, podcast, video, album, or artist from the library:**

   • **Podcasts:** Select the Podcasts option in the Source pane and then select any podcast or podcast episodes. Press Delete/Backspace (or choose Edit⇨Clear) to delete them.

   • **Videos or TV shows:** Select the Videos option in the Source pane and then select any video or TV show episodes or seasons. Press Delete/Backspace (or choose Edit⇨Clear).

   • **Any item from the library:** Select the Library option in the Source pane and then select the item. Press Delete/Backspace (or choose Edit⇨Clear). In the first warning dialog that appears, click Yes to remove the selected item from the library.

Deleting a content item from the iTunes library removes the item from your library, but it doesn't remove it from your hard drive until you agree. iTunes displays a second warning — Some of the selected files are located in your iTunes Music folder. Would you like to move these files to the Trash? — and then you can click Yes to trash them, No to keep them in your music folder, or Cancel to cancel the operation.

✔ **An entire album or everything by a certain artist:** Select the album (or artist) in Browse view and then press Delete/Backspace (or choose Edit⇨ Clear). If you choose to move the album or artist folder to the Trash, the album or artist folder is deleted from your hard drive; otherwise, it remains in your iTunes Music folder.

If you leave music files and folders in your iTunes Music folder, you can add them back to your iTunes library by dragging and dropping them into the iTunes window.

You can delete multiple items in one clean sweep. Press Shift while you click to select a range of items. Alternatively, press ⌘ (Mac) or Ctrl (Windows) when you click each item to add it to the selection. Then press Delete/ Backspace (or choose Edit⇨Clear).

Chapter 9

Adding and Editing Information in iTunes

In This Chapter

▶ Retrieving information online

▶ Editing information for each content item

▶ Adding information, album artwork, comments, and ratings

*O*rganization depends on information. You expect your computer to do a lot more than just store a song with Track 01 as the only identifier.

Adding all the information for your iTunes content seems like a lot of trouble, but you can get most of the information automatically from the Internet — without all that pesky typing. Adding song information is important because you certainly don't want to mistakenly play "My Guitar Wants to Kill Your Mama" by Frank Zappa when trying to impress your classical music teacher with the third movement of Tchaikovsky's *Pathétique Symphony,* do you? And because videos you make yourself or convert from other sources don't have this information, you have to enter some information to tell them apart.

This chapter shows you how to add information to your content library in iTunes and edit it for better viewing so that you can organize your content by artist, album name, genre, composer, and ratings. You can then sort the Song List or Browse view using this information by clicking the column headings.

Retrieving Song Information

Why bother entering information if someone else has already done it for you? You can easily get information about most music CDs from the Internet — assuming that you can connect to the Internet. The online database available for iTunes users holds information for millions of songs on commercial CDs and even some bootleg CDs.

Retrieving information automatically

When you pop a commercial music CD into your computer running iTunes, iTunes automatically looks up the information for that CD on the Internet and fills in the information fields (name, artist, album, and so on). You don't need to do anything to make this happen. You can also edit the information after iTunes fills in the fields. This feature is available only for music CDs as of this writing.

If iTunes isn't doing this automatically, you might need to set iTunes to use the Internet. During the iTunes setup process, iTunes is set up automatically to connect to the Internet and play music from the Internet. However, if you install other software that plays Internet content, you might want to set up iTunes as your default Internet music player. Just follow these steps:

1. **Choose iTunes⇨Preferences (Mac) or Edit⇨Preferences (Windows).**

   The iTunes Preferences dialog appears with buttons along the top.

2. **Click the Advanced tab.**

   The preferences on the Advanced tab appear.

3. **Click the General tab.**

   The General Advanced preferences appear.

4. **Click the Set button next to Use iTunes for Internet Music Playback.**

   With this option enabled for a modem connection, iTunes triggers your modem automatically (like a Web browser), calls your Internet service provider (ISP), and completes the connection process before retrieving the track information.

You can always stop an automatic modem connection at any time. This is a good idea if your ISP or phone service charges extra fees based on time usage. When iTunes finishes grabbing the song information from the Internet, switch to your remote connection program without quitting iTunes, terminate the Internet connection, and then switch back to iTunes.

Retrieving information manually

You can connect manually to the Internet at any time (for example, by using a modem connection) and retrieve the song information when you're ready to use it. After you connect to the Internet, choose Advanced⇨Get CD Track Names.

Even if you automatically connect to the Internet, the song information database on the Internet (Gracenote CDDB) might be momentarily unavailable, or you might have a delayed response. If at first you don't succeed, choose Advanced⇨Get CD Track Names again.

Using the Gracenote database

The first time we popped a commercial music CD into our computer, song information appeared like magic. iTunes automatically displayed the song names, album title, and artist names. How did it know? This information isn't stored on a standard music CD in digital form, but iTunes has to recognize the disc somehow.

The magic is that the software knows how to reach out and find the information on the Internet — in the Gracenote CDDB service. CDDB stands for (you guessed it) *CD Database.* The site (www.gracenote.com) hosts CDDB on the Web and searches for music CDs by artist, song title, and other methods. The iTunes software already knows how to use this database so you don't have to!

Gracenote recognizes an audio CD by taking into account the number, sequence, and duration of tracks. (This is how the database recognizes CD-Rs that are burned with the identical songs in the same order.) The database keeps track of information for most of the music CDs that you find on the market.

Although the database doesn't contain any information about personal or custom CDs, people can submit information to the database about such CDs. You can even do this from within iTunes: Type the information for each track while the audio CD is in your computer and then choose Advanced⇨Submit CD Track Names. The information that you enter is sent to the Gracenote CDDB site, where the good people who work tirelessly on the database check out your information before including it. In fact, if you spot a typo or something erroneous in the information that you receive from the Gracenote CDDB, you can easily correct it. Just use the Submit CD Track Names command to send the corrected version back to the Gracenote site. The good folks at Gracenote appreciate the effort.

Entering Content Information

You have to enter the information for certain media, including CDs that aren't known by the Gracenote CDDB, custom CD-Rs, and videos and audio books that you bring into iTunes from sources other than the iTunes Music Store. No big deal, though; just follow these steps:

1. **Click directly in the information field, such as Artist, in either Browse or Song List view.**

2. **Click again so that the mouse pointer turns into an editing cursor.**

3. **Type text directly into the information field.**

After grabbing the song information from the Internet or typing it, iTunes keeps track of the information for the CD even if you just play the CD without importing it. The next time you insert the CD, the song information is automatically filled in.

Editing the Information

Retrieving ready-made song information from the Internet is a great help, but you might not always like the format it comes in. You might want to edit artist and band names or other information. For example, we like to list solo artists by last name rather than by first name. (Gracenote CDDC lists artists by first name.) For example, we routinely change *Miles Davis* to *Davis, Miles*.

Other annoyances sometimes occur in the CDDB such as bands with *The* at the beginning of their names, such as The Who, The Band, The Beatles, and The Beach Boys. Even though these names sort correctly (in alphabetical order under their proper names), we dislike having *The* before the band name, so we routinely remove it.

In either Browse or Song List view, you can edit the content information by clicking directly in the specific track's field (such as the Artist field) and then clicking again so that the mouse pointer turns into an editing cursor. You can then select the text and type over it — or use the Copy, Cut, and Paste commands on the Edit menu — to move tiny bits of text around within the field. As you can see in Figure 9-1, we changed the Artist field to *Beck, Jeff.*

Figure 9-1:
Click inside a field to edit the information.

You can edit the Song Name, Artist, Album, Genre, and My Ratings fields in the song list. However, editing this information by choosing File⇨Get Info is easier. Keep reading to find out why.

Editing multiple items at once

Editing in the content list is fine if you're editing the information for one item, but typically you need to change all the tracks of an audio CD. For example, if a CD of songs by Bob Dylan is listed with the artist as *Bob Dylan,* you might want to change all the songs at once to *Dylan, Bob.* Changing all the information in one fell swoop is fast and clean, but like most powerful shortcuts, you need to be careful because it can be dangerous.

You can change a group of items in either Browse or Song List view. Follow these steps to change a group of items at once:

1. **Select a group of content items by clicking the first song and then pressing Shift while you click the last song.**

   All the items between the first and last are highlighted. You can extend a selection by Shift-clicking other items or add to a selection by ⌘-clicking (Mac) or Ctrl-clicking (Windows). You can also remove items already selected by ⌘-clicking (Mac) or Ctrl-clicking (Windows).

2. **Choose File⇨Get Info or press ⌘-I (Mac) or Ctrl-I (Windows).**

   A warning message displays: `Are you sure you want to edit information for multiple items?`

   Speed-editing the information in multiple items at once can be dangerous for your library organization. If, for example, you change the song title, the entire selection has that song title. Be careful about what you edit when using this method. We recommend leaving the Do Not Ask Me Again check box cleared so that the warning appears whenever you try this.

3. **Click Yes to edit information for multiple items.**

   The Multiple Song Information dialog appears, as shown in Figure 9-2.

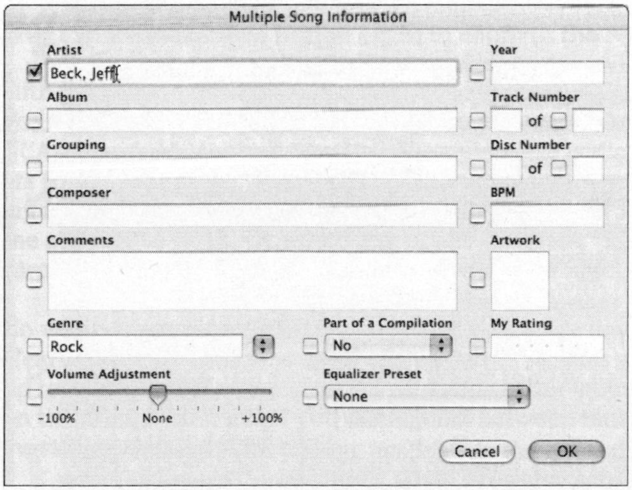

Figure 9-2:
Change the field info for multiple songs at once.

4. **Edit the field you want to change for the multiple songs.**

   When you edit a field, a check mark appears automatically in the check box next to the field. iTunes assumes that you want that field changed in all the selected items. Make sure that no other check box is selected except the field that you want, which is typically the Artist field and per-haps the Genre field and Artwork field if you're adding cover art for an entire album.

5. **Click OK to make the change.**

   iTunes changes the field for the entire selection of songs.

You can edit the song information immediately after inserting the CD, before importing the audio tracks from the CD. The changes you make to the track information for the CD are imported along with the music. What's interesting is that when you access the library without the audio CD, the edited version of the track information is still there, in iTunes. iTunes remembers the edited song information until the next time you insert that audio CD.

Editing fields for a song

Although the track information grabbed from the Internet is enough for identi-fying songs in your iTunes library, some facts — such as composer credits — aren't included. Adding composer credits is usually worth your while because you can then search and sort by composer and create playlists. Videos and audio books might also have information in their fields that you want to change or have blank fields that could use some helpful information. Locate a single item — song, video, or audio book — and choose File⇨Get Info (or press ⌘-I on a Mac or Ctrl-I in Windows). You see the song's information dialog, as shown in Figure 9-3.

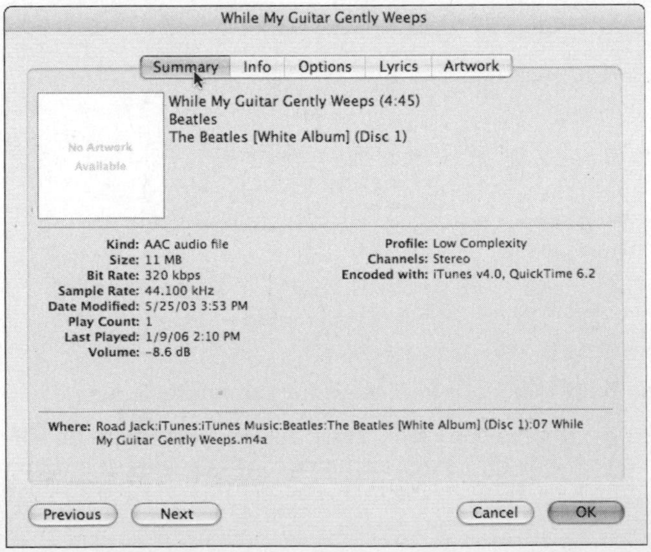

While My Guitar Gently Weeps

| Summary | Info | Options | Lyrics | Artwork |

No Artwork Available

While My Guitar Gently Weeps (4:45)
Beatles
The Beatles [White Album] (Disc 1)

Kind: AAC audio file
Size: 11 MB
Bit Rate: 320 kbps
Sample Rate: 44.100 kHz
Date Modified: 5/25/03 3:53 PM
Play Count: 1
Last Played: 1/9/06 2:10 PM
Volume: –8.6 dB

Profile: Low Complexity
Channels: Stereo
Encoded with: iTunes v4.0, QuickTime 6.2

Where: Road Jack:iTunes:iTunes Music:Beatles:The Beatles [White Album] (Disc 1):07 While My Guitar Gently Weeps.m4a

Previous   Next   Cancel   OK

Figure 9-3:
The information dialog.

When you select one item, the information dialog appears; when you select multiple songs, the Multiple Song Information dialog appears. Be careful when selecting multiple songs and using the Get Info command.

The information dialog offers the following tabs:

- ✔ **Summary:** The Summary tab (as shown in Figure 9-3) offers useful information about the media file format and location on your hard drive, the file size, and the information about the digital compression method (bit rate, sample rate, and so on).

- ✔ **Info:** The Info tab allows you to change the name, artist, composer, album, genre, year, and other information. You can also add comments, as shown in Figure 9-4.

- ✔ **Options:** The Options tab offers volume adjustment, choice of equalizer preset, ratings, and the start and stop times for each item. You can assign up to five stars to an item.

- ✔ **Lyrics:** The Lyrics tab offers a text field for typing or pasting lyrics (or any text).

- ✔ **Artwork:** The Artwork tab allows you to add or delete artwork for the item. Read how to add artwork in the upcoming section, "Adding Album Cover Art or Images."

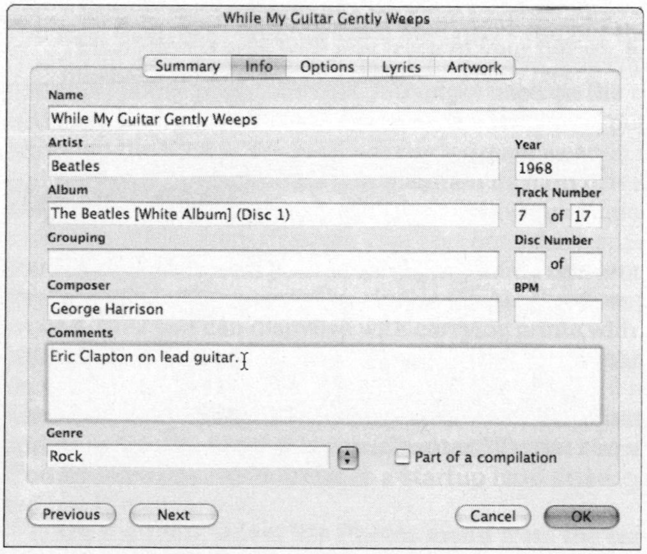

Figure 9-4:
View and edit information from the Info tab.

While My Guitar Gently Weeps

| Summary | Info | Options | Lyrics | Artwork |

Name
While My Guitar Gently Weeps

Artist / **Year**
Beatles / 1968

Album / **Track Number**
The Beatles [White Album] (Disc 1) / 7 of 17

Grouping / **Disc Number**
/ of

Composer / **BPM**
George Harrison /

Comments
Eric Clapton on lead guitar.

Genre
Rock ▢ Part of a compilation

Previous Next Cancel OK

To move through an album one item at a time (without closing and reopening the information dialog), click the Previous or Next buttons in the bottom-left corner of the dialog.

Adding a rating

iTunes also allows you to rate your content. The cool thing about ratings is that they're *yours*. You can use ratings to mean anything you want. For example, you can rate songs based on how much you like them, whether your mother would listen to them, or how they blend into a work environment. Then you can use the My Top Rated playlist to automatically play the top-rated songs in the library. You find out more about playlists in Chapter 10. You can also rate videos based on your watching habits as well as audio books and podcasts.

To add a rating to a content item, click the Options tab, as shown in Figure 9-5. Drag inside the My Rating field to add stars — the upper limit is five stars (for the best).

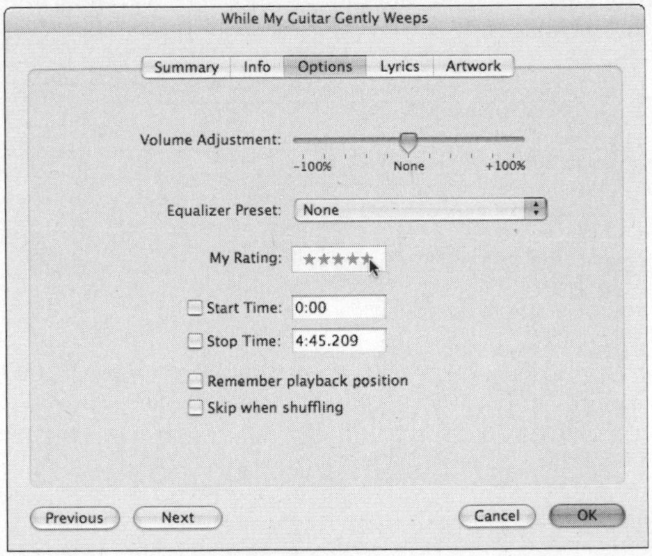

Figure 9-5:
Add a rating
to a song
from the
Options tab.

While My Guitar Gently Weeps

Summary | Info | Options | Lyrics | Artwork

Volume Adjustment: |————————▽————————|
-100%   None   +100%

Equalizer Preset: None

My Rating: ★★★★★

☐ Start Time: 0:00

☐ Stop Time: 4:45.209

☐ Remember playback position
☐ Skip when shuffling

Previous   Next   Cancel   OK

You might have noticed the My Top Rated playlist in the Source pane. This playlist is an example of a *smart playlist* — a playlist that updates when ratings are changed. The My Top Rated playlist plays all the top-rated songs in your library.

Adding Album Cover Art or Images

Songs that you buy from the iTunes Music Store typically include an image of the album cover art or a photo of the artist. Audio books, podcasts, videos, and TV shows also have thumbnail images that serve as cover art. You can see the artwork in the lower-left corner of the iTunes window by clicking the Show/Hide Artwork button, as shown in Figure 9-6. The artwork changes for each item or album that you select.

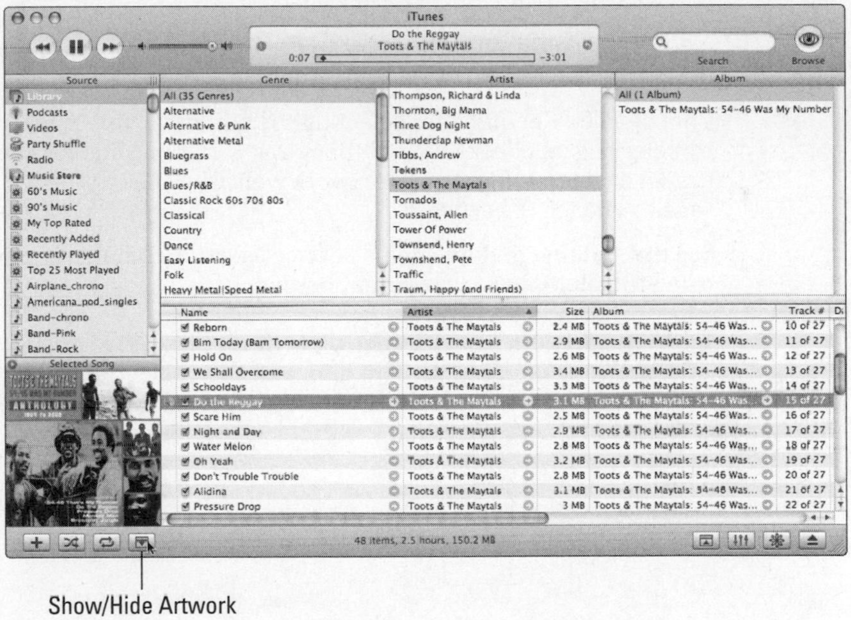

Figure 9-6: Show the artwork for a song.

Show/Hide Artwork

Unfortunately, you don't get free artwork when you rip an audio CD. With a scanner, however, you can scan the cover art and save it in a graphics format that iTunes (and its underlying graphics technology, *QuickTime*) understands — JPEG, GIF, PNG, TIFF, or Photoshop. With a Web browser, you can visit Web pages to scout for suitable art; just Control-click (Mac) or right-click an image (Windows) to download and save the image on your hard drive.

To add artwork to one or more items, select it (or them) in your iTunes library and do one of the following:

✔ **Drag the artwork's image file from a desktop folder into the artwork viewing area (the bottom-left corner of the iTunes window).**

To add artwork for an entire album of songs (rather than just individual songs), select the album in Browse view first or select all the songs in the album in Song List view. Then drag the image file into the artwork viewing area.

✔ **Add artwork to a single song through the information window.**

Choose File➪Get Info and click the Artwork tab in the Get Info dialog. Click the Add button, browse your hard drive or network for the image file, and then select the file. Click OK.

✔ **Add artwork for multiple songs in the Multiple Song Information dialog.**

Choose File➪Get Info after selecting the album, enable the Artwork field by selecting its check box and then drag a graphics file for the cover art from a desktop folder to the Artwork well. Click Yes to the warning message to change the artwork.

See the "Editing multiple items at once" section to find out more about using the Multiple Song Information dialog.

To remove the artwork from an item, view the artwork in a larger window or resize the artwork, choose File➪Get Info, and then click the Artwork tab. You can add a different image, add several images, delete the images with the Add or Delete buttons, or resize images with the size slider.

Chapter 10

Organizing iTunes Content with Playlists

*T*o organize your content for different operations, such as copying to your iPod or burning a CD, you make a *playlist* — a list of the items that you want in the sequence that you want to play them.

You can use playlists to organize your music playback experience. For example, you can make a playlist of love songs from different albums to play the next time you need a romantic mood or compile a playlist of surf songs for a trip to the beach. We create playlists specifically for use with an iPod on road trips and generate other playlists that combine songs from different albums based on themes or similarities. For example, we have a jazz playlist for cruising around the city at night, a classic rock playlist for jogging in the morning, a playlist of short films mixed with TV shows for a long airplane ride, and a playlist of rain songs to celebrate rainy days.

You can create as many playlists of songs, audio books, podcast episodes, and videos in any order that you like. The items and their files don't change, nor are they copied — iTunes simply creates a list of the item names with links to the actual items and their files.

You can even create a *smart playlist* that automatically includes items in the playlist based on the criteria you set up, and the smart playlist removes items that don't match the criteria. The information included in iTunes (see Chapter 9) is very useful for setting up the criteria. For example, you can define the criteria for a smart playlist to automatically include songs from a particular artist or songs that have the highest rating or fit within a particular musical genre.

Creating Playlists

You need to create a playlist to burn a CD, but playlists can also make it easier to play items you like without browsing the entire library looking for them. You can create playlists of individual songs or entire albums. You can also include audio books, TV shows, videos, podcast episodes, and Web radio stations in playlists.

Song playlists

You can drag individual songs into a playlist and rearrange the songs to play in any sequence you want.

To create a playlist, follow these steps:

1. **Click the Add Playlist button or choose File⇨New Playlist.**

   The Add Playlist button, in the bottom-left corner of the iTunes window under the Source pane, creates a new playlist in the Source pane named *untitled playlist*.

2. **In the Source pane, click the *untitled playlist* and type a new descriptive name for the playlist.**

   After you type a new name, iTunes automatically sorts it into alphabetical order in the Source pane, underneath the preset smart playlists and other sources.

3. **Select the library in the Source pane and then drag songs from the library to the playlist.**

   Drag one song at a time (as shown in Figure 10-1) or drag a group of songs, dropping them onto the playlist name in the Source pane. The initial order of songs in the playlist is based on the order in which you drag them to the list. Of course, you can rearrange the songs in any order after dragging them, as we show in the next step.

4. **Select the playlist in the Source pane and then drag songs to rearrange the list.**

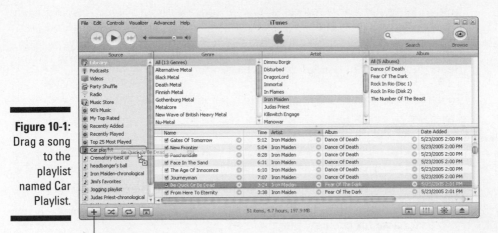

Figure 10-1:
Drag a song
to the
playlist
named Car
Playlist.

Add Playlist

To move a song up the list and scroll at the same time, drag it over the up arrow in the first column (the song number); to move a song down the list and scroll, drag it to the bottom of the list. To move a group of songs at once, select them (press Shift to select a range of songs or press ⌘ on a Mac or Ctrl in Windows to select specific songs) and then drag them into a new position.

You can drag songs from one playlist to another. Only links are copied, not the actual files. Besides dragging songs, you can also rearrange a playlist by sorting the list: Click the Name, Time, Artist column headings, and so on. When you double-click a playlist, it opens in a new window that displays the song list.

To open a playlist in a new window, double-click the playlist icon next to the playlist name in the Source pane. You can then select the Library option to browse your entire library and drag items to the separate playlist window.

To create a playlist quickly, select the group of songs that you want to make into a playlist. Choose File⇨New Playlist from Selection — or drag the selection to the white area underneath items in the Source pane. A new playlist appears in the Source pane, and you can then type a name for the playlist.

Album playlists

Making a playlist of an album is simple. Select the Library option in the Source pane and drag an album from the Album list in the Browse view to the white area below the items in your Source pane. iTunes automatically creates a new playlist named after the album.

You might want to play several albums of songs without having to select each album when you play them. For example, you might want to use an iPod on that long drive from London to Liverpool to play The Beatles' albums in the order they were released (or perhaps the reverse order, reversing The Beatles' career from London back to Liverpool).

To create a playlist of entire albums in a particular order, follow these steps:

1. **Create a new playlist.**

   Create a playlist by clicking the Add Playlist button under the Source pane or by choosing File➪New Playlist.

   A new playlist named untitled playlist appears in the Source pane.

2. **In the Source pane, click the *untitled playlist* and type a new descriptive name for the new playlist.**

3. **Select the Library option in the Source pane and then click the Browse button to find the artist.**

   The Album list appears in the right panel.

4. **Drag the album name over the playlist name.**

5. **Select and drag each subsequent album over the playlist name.**

   Each time you drag an album, iTunes automatically lists the songs in the proper track sequence.

You can rename a playlist at any time by clicking inside its name and typing a new one. Also, in case you forget which songs are in which playlists, you can see all the playlists that include a particular song. In Browse or Song List view, press Control on a Mac and click the song; in Windows, right-click the song and choose Playlists from the pop-up menu. The playlists that include the song are listed in the submenu.

Podcast playlists

You can add podcast episodes to your playlists or you can even create a playlist consisting entirely of podcast episodes. However, podcasts are a slightly different animal than albums or songs. You can drag individual podcast episodes to a playlist; however, if you drag a podcast by its name, iTunes adds to the playlist only the episodes you've listened to (even if only for a second). To add episodes that you haven't heard, you have to select the episodes and then drag them to the playlist.

To add a single podcast episode to a playlist, follow these steps:

1. **Click the Add Playlist button or choose File⇨New Playlist.**

   The Add Playlist button is in the bottom-left corner of the iTunes window under the Source pane.

   A new playlist named *untitled playlist* appears in the Source pane.

2. **In the Source pane, click the *untitled playlist* and type a new descriptive name for the playlist.**

   After you type a new name, iTunes automatically sorts it into alphabetical order in the Source pane, underneath the preset smart playlists and other sources.

3. **Select the Podcasts option in the Source pane, and then open a podcast by clicking the triangle next to its name.**

   The podcast opens to reveal its episodes. (See Chapter 6 for details on opening podcasts and playing podcast episodes.)

4. **Drag episodes from the Podcasts list to the playlist.**

   Drag one episode at a time or drag a selection of episodes and then drop them onto the playlist name in the Source pane. The initial order of episodes in the playlist is based on the order in which you drag them to the list. Of course, you can rearrange the episodes in any order after dragging them, as we show you in the next step.

5. **Select the playlist in the Source pane and then drag episodes to rearrange the list.**

   To move an episode up the list and scroll at the same time, drag it over the up arrow in the first column (the item number); to move an episode down the list and scroll, drag it to the bottom of the list. To move multiple episodes at once, select them (press Shift to select a range of episodes, ⌘ on a Mac, or Ctrl in Windows to select specific episodes) and then drag them into a new position.

You can also create a playlist consisting only of podcast episodes, just like creating a playlist from an album. Follow these steps:

1. **Create a new playlist.**

   Create a playlist by clicking the Add Playlist button under the Source pane or by choosing File⇨New Playlist.

   A new playlist named *untitled playlist* appears in the Source pane.

2. **In the Source pane, click the *untitled playlist* and type a new descriptive name for the new playlist.**

3. **Select the Podcasts option in the Source pane and then select a podcast by name.**

4. **Drag the podcast name over the playlist name.**

   iTunes adds the current podcast episode and any other episodes you've already heard to the playlist. Note, however, that episodes you haven't listened to aren't included. You have to drag unheard episodes directly.

Video playlists

You can drag individual videos and TV shows into a playlist and rearrange them to play in any sequence you want.

To create a video playlist, follow these steps:

1. **Click the Add Playlist button or choose File⇨New Playlist.**

   The Add Playlist button, in the bottom-left corner of the iTunes window under the Source pane, creates a new playlist in the Source pane named *untitled playlist*.

2. **In the Source pane, click the *untitled playlist* and type a new descriptive name for the playlist.**

   After you type a new name, iTunes automatically sorts it into alphabetical order in the Source pane, underneath the preset smart playlists and other sources.

3. **Select the Videos option in the Source pane and then drag videos from the library to the playlist.**

   Drag one video at a time or drag a selection of songs, dropping them onto the playlist name in the Source pane. The initial order of videos in the playlist is based on the order in which you drag them to the list.

4. **Select the playlist in the Source pane and then drag videos to rearrange the list.**

   To move a video up the list and scroll at the same time, drag it over the up arrow in the first column (the item number); to move a video down the list and scroll, drag it to the bottom of the list. To move a group of videos at once, select them (press Shift to select a range of items, or ⌘ on a Mac or Ctrl in Windows to select specific songs) and then drag them into a new position.

You can mix videos with songs and other items in a playlist — for example, mixing songs and music videos, songs and a video documentary, or just a selection of TV shows, music, podcasts, and audio books. However, if you transfer the playlist to an iPod that doesn't play video, the iPod skips the videos.

Deleting items from a playlist

You can delete items from playlists while keeping the items in your library. When you delete an item from a playlist, the item is simply deleted from the list — not from the library. You can also delete playlists without harming the content in the library. Switch to the Library option in the Source pane to delete items from the library.

To delete an item from a playlist, select the playlist in the Source pane and then select the item. Press Delete/Backspace or choose Edit⇨Clear. In the warning dialog that appears, click Yes to remove the selected item from the list.

You can also completely delete an item from your library from within a playlist by selecting the item and pressing ⌘-Option-Delete (Mac) or Ctrl-Alt-Backspace (Windows).

To delete a playlist, select the playlist in the Source pane and then press Delete/Backspace or choose Edit⇨Clear.

Using Smart Playlists

Near the top of the Source pane under the Music Store option, indicated by a gear icon, you can find the *smart playlists*. iTunes comes with a few sample smart playlists, such as the My Top Rated and Recently Added playlists, and you can create your own. Smart playlists add items to themselves based on prearranged criteria, or *rules*. For example, when you rate your content items, My Top Rated changes to reflect your new ratings. You don't have to set anything up — My Top Rated and Recently Added are already defined for you.

Of course, smart playlists are ignorant of your taste in music or video — you have to program them with rules by using the information in iTunes (see Chapter 9). For example, you can create a smart playlist that uses the Year field to grab all the songs from 1966. This list might include The Beatles ("Eleanor Rigby"), Frank Sinatra ("Strangers in the Night"), The Yardbirds ("Over Under Sideways Down"), and Ike and Tina Turner ("River Deep, Mountain High") in no particular order — a far-out playlist, no doubt, but not necessarily what you want. Use other fields of the information you entered such as ratings, artist name, or composer to fine-tune your criteria. You can also use built-in functions such as *Play Count* (the number of times the item was played) or *Date Added* (the date the item was added to the library).

Creating a smart playlist

To create a new smart playlist, choose File⇨New Smart Playlist. The Smart Playlist dialog appears (as shown in Figure 10-2), offering the following choices for setting criteria:

✔ **Match the Following Rule:** From the first pop-up menu (see Figure 10-2), you can select any of the categories used for information, such as Composer or Last Played. From the second pop-up menu, you can choose an operator, such as the greater-than or less-than operators. The selections that you make in these two pop-up menus combine to express a rule such as `Year is greater than 1966`. You can also add multiple conditions by clicking the + button (on the right) and then decide whether to match all or any of these conditions. The check mark next to this option, which is automatically turned on when you set rules, tells iTunes to use the rules.

✔ **Limit To:** You can limit the smart playlist to a specific *duration,* measured by the number of songs (items), time, or size in megabytes or gigabytes, as shown in Figure 10-3. You can have items selected by various methods, such as random, most recently played, and so on.

✔ **Match Only Checked Songs:** This option selects only those songs or other items that have a check mark beside them, along with the rest of the criteria. Selecting and deselecting items is an easy way to fine-tune your selection for a smart playlist.

✔ **Live Updating:** This allows iTunes to continually update the playlist while you play items, add or remove items from the library, change their ratings, and so on.

A smart playlist for recent additions

Setting up rules gives you the opportunity to create playlists that are smarter than the ones supplied with iTunes. For example, we created a smart playlist with criteria (as shown in Figure 10-3) that does the following:

✔ Includes any item added to the library in the past week that also has a rating greater than three stars.

✔ Limits the playlist to 72 minutes of music to be sure it fits on a 74-minute CD even with gaps between the songs. It also refines the selection to the most recently added if the entire selection becomes greater than 72 minutes.

✔ Matches only selected items.

✔ Performs live updating.

Figure 10-3:
Use multiple conditions and a time limit for a smart playlist.

After setting up the rules, click OK. iTunes creates the playlist with a gear icon and the name *untitled playlist* or whatever phrase you used for the first condition (such as the album or artist name). You can click in the playlist field and then type a new name for it.

Editing a smart playlist

To edit a smart playlist, select the playlist and choose File⇨Edit Smart Playlist (or press Control on a Mac or right-click in Windows the playlist and then choose Edit Smart Playlist from the pop-up menu). The Smart Playlist window appears with the criteria for the smart playlist.

For example, to modify the smart playlist so that items with a higher rating are picked, simply add another star or two to the My Rating criteria.

You can also choose to limit the playlist to a certain number of items, selected by various methods such as random, most recently played, and so on.

Creating an iMix

Amateur disk jockeys, rejoice! The iTunes Music Store offers the iMix section for sharing your iTunes playlists with other iTunes users. Although you can submit a playlist of any items to be published in the iMix section of the store, only items available from the store are actually published — unavailable items are skipped.

Browsers in the iTunes Music Store can view the playlist by entering the iMix section and clicking any playlist. See Chapter 4 for information about navigating the iTunes Music Store, playing short preview clips, and buying content.

To create an iMix, follow these steps:

1. **Select the playlist in your iTunes library and choose File➪Create an iMix.**

   iTunes displays a warning dialog before accessing the iTunes Music Store to publish your playlist.

2. **Click the Create button in the warning dialog.**

   iTunes displays the music store sign-in dialog.

3. **Enter your ID and password and then click Publish.**

   iTunes selects the Music Store option in the Source pane and displays the iMix Music Store page. You see the iMix playlist that will be published, which includes only available items from the store.

4. **Edit the title and description for the iMix playlist and then click the Publish button.**

iTunes publishes the playlist in the iMix section of the store. Others can browse the playlist and buy any songs.

Chapter 11

Managing Photos and Videos

*T*aking photos has never been easier. Digital cameras and photo-editing software combine to turn computers into digital darkrooms — no need for a real darkroom with smelly chemicals and film-processing equipment. In fact, you no longer need film. Making videos is also easier than ever before. People use camcorders to record everything from violent weather and police chases to home bloopers, weddings, and school plays. Digital technology makes video editing easy, cheaper, and more fun to make, opening up entirely new possibilities.

Your vacation photos and videos are priceless to you, preserving special memories. Family gatherings, vacations, and weddings don't happen every day. You want to take these pictures and videos with you when you visit friends and relatives. However, you don't want to lug a slideshow projector and a carousel loaded with expensive slides, or wait for a video service to transfer your videos from camcorder media to VHS cassettes that you can play in your neighbor's VCR. Why not use your iPod instead?

All color-display iPod models can play photos and slideshows, and the fifth-generation video iPod can play videos. The full-size iPod models that display color also connect easily with televisions and video equipment, so that you can show slideshows or videos to a larger audience. You can organize your digital photo library on your computer and then transfer the photos directly to a color-display iPod in one easy step — and still keep your color-display iPod synchronized when you add more photos to your library.

This chapter tells you all you need to know about digital cameras and camcorders to get your photos and videos into your computer to organize them.

Getting Your Photos into Your Computer

Digital photography is truly instant gratification. You see the results immediately and can then take more pictures based on what happened an instant before. When you run out of room on your memory card, connect your digital camera or card reader to your computer, download the photos to a computerized photo library, and delete them from the memory card. Then go back and take more pictures!

Don't have a digital camera? You still like to use that old film camera your grandmother gave you? Don't worry. You can use a scanner to scan photographic prints, or you can send your film rolls to a photo service that converts the film to digital images and places the images on a CD or the Web.

Using a computer to organize and archive all your digital photos makes sense. You can organize massive quantities of photos in the photo library in your computer. You can also add keywords, titles, and film roll information to each photo automatically, which helps make locating a particular photo very easy. Keep the photos you like and delete the ones you don't like. If you have a color printer, obtaining extra prints is as easy as using the Print command. You can even e-mail the photos to a service for high-quality prints.

Photo library software, such as iPhoto on the Mac, or Adobe Photoshop Elements or Photoshop Album on a Windows PC, can organize any number of photos; the number is limited only by available hard drive space. At an average size of 2MB per photo (many photos occupy less space), you can store 10,000 photos on a 20GB hard drive. Of course, you can expand a photo library over multiple hard drives or create multiple libraries. The number of digital photos you can manage has no practical limit.

Most importantly, you can take your photos with you, safely tucked into your iPod. On a Mac, you can use iPhoto (version 4.0.3 or newer) to import photos into your computer and organize them into albums. You can then use iTunes to transfer photos automatically from your iPhoto library. If you use other photo-editing programs, you can still update your iPod with the photos, as we describe in Chapter 12. However, the album organization in iPhoto synchronizes automatically with your iPod.

On Windows, you can use Adobe Photoshop Album (version 1.0 or newer) or Photoshop Elements (version 3.0 or newer) to import photos into your computer and organize your photos into collections. You can then use iTunes to transfer photos automatically from your Photoshop Album or Photoshop Elements library. If you use other photo-editing programs, you can still update your iPod with the photos, as we describe in Chapter 12. However, the collections in Photoshop Album and Photoshop Elements synchronize automatically with your iPod.

Connecting a digital camera or memory card reader

To import photos to your computer, connect your digital camera to your computer.

Digital cameras typically come with a special USB or FireWire cable that has a very small connector on one end for the camera and a larger connector on the other end for the computer's USB or FireWire port. However, if both ends are the same on the cable you're using, it doesn't matter which end is plugged into the camera or the computer.

Be sure to power up your camera — most digital cameras have a power-on switch to save battery life. Connect your camera before you turn it on because the computer might not recognize some camera models unless they're turned on while connected. If the computer doesn't recognize your camera, try turning off the camera and then turning it on again.

If your camera has an AC adapter, run the camera off the adapter when importing photos to save the camera's battery time. If your camera has a sleep mode, make sure that you disable or set it to a time increment long enough for your images to import. Importing 50 photos generally takes about 1 minute with most digital cameras using a USB 2.0 connection; it may take up to half an hour with a USB 1.1 connection.

A digital camera memory card is like an extra roll of film. A memory card reader is useful if you take lots of pictures and use additional cards. Rather than connecting your camera to your computer every time you want to transfer pictures, leave the card reader connected to the USB connection on your computer and then put the camera's memory card in the card reader. If you use multiple memory cards, this method is especially convenient. Some Media Center PCs running Windows include built-in card readers.

iPhoto can import photos from a card reader, just as it does with a camera, using the same steps. Many Windows applications supplied with digital cameras can also import photos from memory card readers. For example, Preclick Silver Photo Organizer (www.preclick.com) can import photos from CDs, memory card readers, and digital cameras that can connect by USB or FireWire.

Importing your photos

To import pictures from a digital camera, connect the camera to your computer and then launch a photo application such as iPhoto on a Mac, or the photo application supplied with your camera. Although different cameras have different applications, they generally provide instructions for these four steps:

1. **Connect your camera and then set your application to import mode.**

   After connecting your digital camera, your application offers a simple method of importing photos from the camera into your computer. Set up the application so that it's ready to import. For example, in Adobe Photoshop Album, click the Get Photos button and then choose Digital Camera or Scanner.

   iPhoto automatically changes to indicate that it recognizes your camera, as shown in Figure 11-1. Depending on the type of camera or memory card reader you're using, iPhoto displays a camera icon, a disk icon, or a memory card reader icon. Our Canon PowerShot SD550 displays a camera icon.

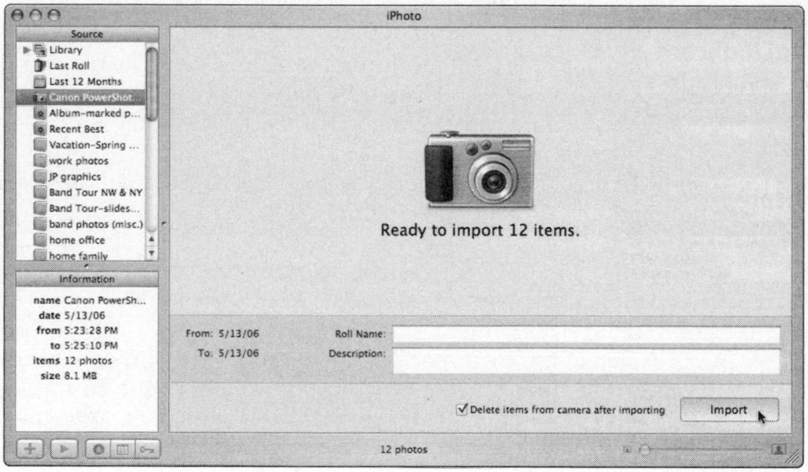

Figure 11-1: iPhoto is in import mode, ready to import photos from a digital camera.

2. **Choose whether to delete the photos in your camera after importing.**

   Most camera applications offer an option to delete photos from your camera as soon as they're imported. Many cameras have a delete function, so you don't need to use this option. However, using this option enables you to import and delete photos in the camera in one step. With the photos in the photo library, you no longer need to keep copies in your camera or on a memory card, and you can make room for new photos. In iPhoto, you can import photos and delete them from your camera in one step by selecting the Delete Items from Camera After Importing option at the bottom of the iPhoto window.

3. Start the importing process by choosing an import command or clicking an import button.

As you import the photos, your photo application stores them in its photo library and displays them. For example, when iPhoto finishes importing, it displays a small image for each photo in the photo library, as shown in Figure 11-2. The size of the images in the viewing area is controlled by the zoom slider in the lower-right corner of the iPhoto window, just underneath the viewing area. These small versions of your images, which can be reduced to very small, are *thumbnails*.

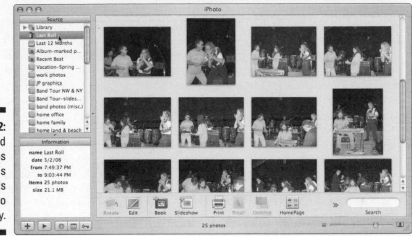

Figure 11-2: Imported photos appear as thumbnails in the photo library.

4. Eject, power down, and disconnect the camera.

To eject the camera on a Windows PC, right-click the camera icon, choose Eject from the pop-up menu, and then disconnect the camera. Another method is to click the Safely Remove Hardware icon in the bottom-right corner of the screen. When the Safely Remove Hardware shortcut menu appears, either select the IEEE 1394 device (if you use FireWire) or the USB Mass Storage device (if you use USB). When the alert dialog appears, click OK and then disconnect the camera.

To eject the camera on a Mac, drag the camera icon over the Eject icon to properly eject the camera.

Although nothing really happens when you eject the camera (nothing actually ejects from the machine, nor do any doors open), you might find that if you don't eject, as required with some cameras, your images might not delete from the camera even if you have the delete option enabled.

Organizing photos into albums or collections

You've probably seen photo albums with plastic sleeves for holding photographic prints. A digital photo album is similar in concept but holds digital photo files instead of prints. In both cases, an album is simply a way of organizing photos and placing them in a proper sequence. You select the photos from your photo library and arrange them in the order you want. iPhoto uses *album* as its term; Adobe Photoshop Elements and Photoshop Album call the album a *collection*. We use the term *album* for both.

You can use photo albums to assemble photos from special events (such as a vacation) or to display a particular subject (such as your favorite nature photos). If you have more photos in your library than what you want to put on your iPod, consider organizing albums specifically for transfer to the iPod and for automatic updating. The order that your photos appear in the album is important because it defines the order of photos in a slideshow on your iPod. You can also use albums to organize photos for a slideshow, QuickTime movie, or Web page.

You can make as many albums as you like using any images from your photo library. Because the albums are lists of images, they don't use disk space by copying the images. Instead, the actual image files remain in the photo library. Like an iTunes playlist, a photo album is a reference list of photos in your library. You can include the same photo in several albums without making multiple copies of the photo and wasting disk space.

Organizing photos with iPhoto

To assign photos to an album in iPhoto, follow these steps:

1. **Select Library in the iPhoto Source pane.**

   The photos in your library appear as thumbnails in the viewer tab.

2. **Click the Add Photo Album button.**

   The + button is underneath the Source pane; refer to Figure 11-2. Alternatively, choose File⇨New Album or press ⌘-N.

   The New Album dialog appears.

3. **Type the album name and then click OK.**

4. **Select photos in your library and then drag them into the album.**

   When you click a photo, you know the photo is selected when an outline appears around it. You can select a block of multiple photos by clicking the first photo and pressing Shift while clicking the last one. The first and last photo — and all the photos in between — are selected automatically. You can also add individual photos to a selection by ⌘-clicking each photo.

A number appears (see Figure 11-3), showing the number of selected photos in the range.

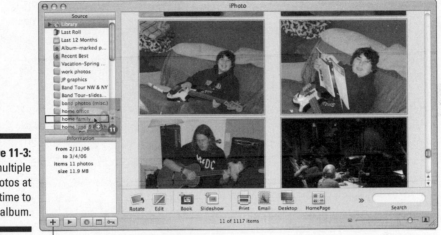

Figure 11-3: Add multiple photos at one time to an album.

Click this button to add an album.

5. **Click the photo album name in the Source pane to rearrange the photos in the album.**

When you click an album name in the Source pane, only the photos you dragged to the album appear in the viewer tab, not the entire library. You can reorder pictures within the album by simply dragging them to a different position.

iPhoto also lets you create *smart albums*. Smart albums add photos to themselves based on prearranged criteria. For example, you can set up a smart album that decides which photos to include based on the ratings you assign to them, such as only the highest-rated photos taken during the last six months.

To create a smart album in iPhoto, follow these steps:

1. **Choose File⇨New Smart Album and then type a name for the album in the Name field.**

2. **Set the conditions for including photos in the smart album.**

   Make your selections from the pop-up menus. Select a condition from the first pop-up menu and then choose a comparison, such as a greater-than or less-than sign, from the second pop-up menu.

3. **Combine conditions for better results.**

   To add additional matching conditions, click the + button. Then decide whether to match any of these conditions by choosing the option you want from the pop-up menu next to Match.

4. **When you finish, click OK to save your smart album.**

iPhoto automatically updates your smart album when any photo that matches the criteria is added to or removed from the library.

Organizing photos in Photoshop Album

Windows users can assign photos to a collection by using Adobe Photoshop Album. Follow these steps:

1. **Click the Collections tab.**

2. **Click the Create New Collection button.**

   The Create Collection dialog appears.

3. **Type the collection name and then click OK.**

4. **Select photos and then drag them into the collection.**

   You can select multiple photos by clicking the first one and pressing Ctrl while clicking more photos.

5. **Select the check box next to the collection name to view the collection and rearrange the photos in the collection.**

   You can reorder pictures within the album by simply dragging them to a different position.

Importing Videos into Your Computer

Making home movies is nothing new. If you have a camcorder, you know that you can create a video — you simply point and shoot. But even if you're extremely careful when shooting, you usually end up with a lot of video that you don't want. When you play it back, it looks like a typical home movie — amateurish, disjointed, and confusing. Even with the best camcorders that let you edit scenes on the fly, you can't edit an entire video easily.

Before digital video software such as iMovie (Mac) or Adobe Premiere (Windows), you had to rent or buy thousands of dollars worth of video-editing gear and use complicated software to edit videos. Most home users couldn't afford that equipment so they had no easy way to edit their videos. With video-editing software, though, you can navigate freely from scene to scene in any manner and then save your edits and changes in digital format on a hard drive without the use of videotape. Digital copies are exact duplicates with no quality loss in the copies. Therefore, you can edit to your heart's content without ever sacrificing the original quality of the video.

The essential piece of movie-making equipment you need, besides the video-editing software, is a digital video (DV) camcorder. You can use this camcorder not only to record your own videos but also to convert older video source material (such as a VHS tape) to a digital format that you can use with iTunes. Software such as iMovie can control the digital camcorder for both recording directly to the hard drive and transferring digital video from the camcorder's cassette. You can connect an older camcorder, VCR, or even a DVD player to just about any digital camcorder and then transfer the content to your computer hard drive. (To read about transferring video from DVDs, see Chapter 20.)

Transferring video from a digital video camcorder

Camcorders not only record video onto digital media such as DV tape, but they also can play back the video you record. Recording and playing video are accomplished in two separate modes:

- **Camera mode** records the video. When your camcorder is in camera mode, its microphone and lens are ready to record when you press the Record button.

- **VTR (video tape recorder)** or **VCR mode** plays back the video you record. When the camera is in VTR/VCR mode, the camcorder plays what was recorded after you press the Play button. (You can also rewind and fast forward.) Some camcorders call this feature *edit mode*.

To use your camcorder with video-editing software, such as iMovie (Mac) or Adobe Premiere (Windows), connect the camcorder and let the software do the rest.

To import your video to your computer, follow these steps:

1. **Connect the camcorder to the computer with a FireWire or USB cable. (Your digital camcorder likely came with one.)**

   These cables are also available commercially. (FireWire is also known as *IEEE 1394 DV terminal* or *i.Link.*) These cables have a camcorder-style (very small), square connector on one end and a standard FireWire connector for the computer on the other end. PCs generally have USB connections if your camcorder supports USB.

2. **Turn your camcorder to camera mode or VTR/VCR mode.**

   If you're recording video directly to a hard drive without using DV tape, choose camera mode. If you're importing prerecorded video from DV tape cassette, choose VTR/VCR mode.

3. **Use the video-editing software to import video from the camcorder.**

   For example, iMovie automatically detects the camcorder and switches to camera mode. Click Import to start importing the video. In Adobe Premiere, choose File⇨Capture and then click the Record button to start capturing the footage onto your hard drive.

Before you start transferring video from your camcorder to your computer, make sure to disable the camcorder's sleep mode or set it to a time increment long enough for your video to play in full at normal speed. If possible, connect AC power to the camcorder during this process to save battery life. Having the camera go into sleep mode or having the batteries die while you're transferring video to your computer could cost you time; you might need to start transferring video again from the beginning of the cartridge.

Video on VHS tape or other types of videotape or cassette can be brought into a program, such as iMovie or Adobe Premiere, through your DV camcorder. DV camcorders typically have a video-in connection for S-video or RCA-type cables. Connect your older camcorder or VCR (or even a DVD player, cable or satellite receiver, or any device that outputs video with RCA or S-video connectors) to your DV camcorder. Then follow the instructions that came with your DV camcorder to record from the video-in connection. Some camcorders have a special Record button for recording from analog sources in VTR/VCR mode (separate from the button for recording video in camera mode). After you start the recording process, the video played on the analog device records in digital format on the DV camcorder's tape. This process preserves the video in digital format before bringing it into your computer. You can then follow the preceding steps to import the video from the DV camcorder tape to your computer.

Some DV camcorders allow you to pass the analog video straight through the camcorder to the computer without prerecording it to DV tape or digital media in the camcorder, saving the extra step and expense of prerecording before importing. For example, the Canon ZR60 offers an analog-digital converter mode that doesn't require prerecording the material first.

Creating video files for iTunes and iPod

Video-editing software lets you edit and improve your imported video clips, add transitions and special effects, and even edit the soundtrack. The final result is a digital video file on your computer's hard drive, which you can save in a format acceptable to iTunes and your iPod.

To bring a video file into iTunes, simply drag it into the iTunes window or over the iTunes icon, or choose File➪Add File to Library. After the video is in your iTunes library, you can play it just like the videos you can buy from the iTunes Music Store.

iTunes accepts a number of different video file formats, including QuickTime `.mov` and `.mpg` files as well as files in the MPEG-4 format and encoded with the H.264 standard, which are typical export options in a number of video-editing programs. The *QuickTime* video technology comprises a collection of digital video file formats that offer many choices for quality, compression, picture size, and playback format.

Use your video-editing program to save or export a video project as a video file and then bring your video file into iTunes to play or copy it to your iPod (see Chapter 12). For example, in iMovie on a Mac

1. **Choose File➪Share and then click the QuickTime button to export a digital video file.**

2. **Choose Expert Settings from the Compress Movie For pop-up menu (see Figure 11-4).**

3. **Click the Share button to display the Save Exported File As dialog.**

4. **Click the Options button to define your digital video settings.**

   You can set the file format, data rate, image size, and frame rate, which control the picture and audio quality.

Although explaining all these digital video settings and formats is beyond the scope of this chapter, you need to know which format to use for which purpose. Although just about all digital video formats play well on computers, some show better picture quality on a television or video monitor than others. Only two formats — standard MPEG-4 and H.264-encoded MPEG — play on iPods. Here's the difference between the two:

Figure 11-4:
Choose
expert
settings to
export an
iMovie
project as a
video file.

✔ **Displaying on an iPod:** H.264 encoding is better. You can set your video image size to 320 x 240 pixels with a data rate up to 768 Kbps and a frame rate up to 30 frames per second (fps). Although it might not look as good as standard MPEG-4 encoding on a television, most people don't know the difference, and the file size is usually smaller.

✔ **Displaying on a television connected to your iPod:** MPEG-4 is better. You can set your image size to 480 x 480 pixels with a data rate up to 2.5 Mbps and a frame rate up to 30 fps. Although it might not look as good as H.264 on the iPod display, it looks better on a television.

Although you can easily convert files to an iPod-ready format, it's also time-consuming. With some settings, computers can take half a day or more to convert a two-hour video file into a format useful for your iPod. Picking the right format and the proper settings in advance in your video-editing software is a good idea; otherwise, you might have to redo your conversions. We describe software for converting video files in Chapter 20.

iTunes provides an option for converting videos in the iTunes library into a format that looks better when you play them on an iPod display. To convert a video to H.264 for use in your iPod

1. **Select the video in your iTunes library, Control-click (Mac) or right-click (Windows) the selected video.**

2. **Choose Convert Selection for iPod (or choose Advanced⇨Convert Selection for iPod).**

   The selected videos are automatically copied, and the copies are converted to H.264 at a width of 320 pixels. The original versions remain unchanged.

You can also use software utilities to convert video from a variety of sources, including DVDs, into iPod-compatible video formats you can import into iTunes. See Chapter 20 for more information.

Chapter 12

Updating Your iPod with iTunes

*i*Tunes puts content on your iPod. iTunes can fill your iPod very quickly and keep it updated every time you connect it. (iTunes can also keep your iPod synchronized with contacts and calendars; see Chapter 25.)

iTunes lets you decide whether to copy some or all of your songs, audio books (which are considered songs), photos, videos, and podcasts. The choice is easy if your iTunes library is small enough to fit in its entirety on your iPod — and you can see the size of your library in GB (gigabytes) at the bottom of the iTunes window in the center. If your library is less than 55GB and you have a 60GB iPod, simply copy everything. Copying your entire library is just as fast as copying individual items, if not faster, and you don't have to do anything except connect the iPod to your computer.

This chapter shows you how to set up iTunes to automatically update your iPod with everything. Of course, this chapter also shows how to update your iPod selectively, choosing which items to automatically copy. You can also update your iPod manually, copying items directly. iTunes is flexible in that you can use either or *both* options to update your iPod. For example, you can update your iPod with all your songs but only some of your videos and podcasts, or all songs and videos but very few photos. You can even update your iPod automatically with the songs in playlists, copy other music not in playlists directly to your iPod, and delete songs from your iPod if you need to make more room.

This chapter explains how to set your preferences for updating and change them when you need to. It also explains how to fill an iPod shuffle automatically or manually and how to manage space on an iPod shuffle.

Updating Your iPod Automatically

The default setting for a new iPod is to update itself automatically, *synchronizing* to your iTunes library: The iPod matches your library exactly, item for item, playlist for playlist. If you made changes in iTunes after the last time you synchronized, those changes are automatically made in the iPod when you synchronize again. If you added or deleted content in your iTunes library, that content is added or deleted in the iPod library.

The same is true of photos — the default setting is to copy them all. The catch is that photos are in a different library. If you store photos in an iPhoto library on a Mac or in a program such as Adobe Photoshop Album in Windows, you can transfer photos to your iPod automatically and synchronize your iPod to your library so that any changes you make to the photo library are copied to your iPod.

If your iTunes library is too large to fit on your iPod, you can still update automatically and keep your iPod synchronized to a subset of your library, adding new material under your control, in the following ways:

✔ Have iTunes select content automatically according to your ratings, as described in the upcoming section, "Updating your iPod from a larger iTunes library."

✔ Create a *smart playlist* that selects content for you, as described in the later section, "Updating by playlist."

✔ Limit the transfer and synchronization of photos to albums or collections rather than the entire photo library, as we describe later in the section, "Choosing photos and photo albums to transfer."

✔ Select which videos to transfer, as we describe later in "Choosing videos to transfer."

Before you actually connect your iPod to a computer to automatically update, keep these things in mind:

✔ **iTunes remembers your updating preferences** for each iPod you connect from the last time you updated the iPod. If you already set your preferences to update automatically, iTunes starts to automatically update the iPod. If you already set your preferences to update manually, iTunes makes the iPod active in the iTunes Source pane.

✔ **To prevent an iPod from automatically updating,** press ⌘-Option (Mac) or Ctrl-Alt (Windows) as you connect the iPod, and keep pressing until the iPod name appears in the iTunes Source pane.

✔ **If you connect your iPod to another computer running iTunes,** you might be in for a surprise. When you connect an iPod previously linked to another computer, ITunes displays the message: `This iPod is linked to another iTunes music library. Do you want to change the link to this iTunes music library and replace all existing songs and playlists on this iPod with those from this library?` If you don't want to change your iPod to have this other music library, click No. Otherwise, iTunes erases your iPod and updates your iPod with the other computer's iTunes library. By clicking No, you change that computer's iTunes preferences to manually update, thereby avoiding automatic updating.

✔ **Content stored remotely** (such as songs shared from other iTunes libraries on a network) is not synchronized because it isn't physically on your computer. See Chapter 7 for more info on how to share iTunes files over a network with iTunes.

When your iPod is set to update automatically (the entire library, or by either playlist or selected song), the iPod song list and the iPod entry in the Source pane are grayed out in the iTunes window. Because you manage the contents automatically, you don't have direct access to the songs in the iPod using iTunes. For direct access, see "Updating Your iPod Manually," later in this chapter.

Synchronizing your iPod with your library

Your iPod is set up by default to automatically synchronize with your iTunes library. Just follow these simple steps:

1. **Connect the iPod to your computer.**

2. **Wait for the updating to finish and then click Eject to eject the iPod.**

   Wait until the iTunes Status pane (at the top) reads `iPod update is complete`. You can then click the iPod Eject button, which appears in the bottom-right corner of the iTunes window.

   You can also eject the iPod by dragging the iPod icon on the Desktop to the Trash on the Mac; in OS X 10.3, you can click the Eject icon next to the iPod icon in the Finder Sidebar. In Windows, you can use various methods, such as right-clicking the iPod icon and choosing Eject.

3. **Disconnect your iPod from your computer.**

   Don't disconnect your iPod until it tells you that it's safe to do so with the `OK to disconnect` message.

Updating your iPod from a larger iTunes library

If your iTunes library is too large to fit on your iPod, you can still update automatically and keep your iPod synchronized to a subset of your library. When you first use your iPod, iTunes displays a message if your library is too large to fit, saying it will copy as many files as possible. You can click OK for iTunes to do this or Cancel to stop the updating process.

After clicking OK, iTunes tries its best to fit everything, but because it has to cut something, it skips the photos and displays a `Some photos were not copied to the iPod . . .` message. Click OK because you have no choice, and iTunes continues updating with everything else. If you already have photos on your iPod, iTunes asks whether you want to delete them to gain more iPod space. You can click Yes or No to this question, and iTunes keeps on updating until it finishes.

If, however, you're still short of space even after skipping photos, iTunes displays a message that it can create a special selection — actually a playlist — specifically for updating your iPod, along with Yes and No buttons:

✔ **If you click Yes,** iTunes creates a new playlist (titled *Your iPod name* Selection) and displays a message telling you so. Click OK, and iTunes updates your iPod by using the new playlist. iTunes also sets your iPod to update automatically by playlist, as we describe later, in the section "Updating by playlist."

✔ **If you click No,** iTunes updates automatically until it fills your iPod without creating the playlist.

Either way, iTunes decides which songs and albums to include by using the ratings that you set for each song. iTunes groups album tracks together and computes an average rating and play count for the album. It then fills the iPod, giving higher priority to albums with play counts and ratings greater than zero. You can therefore influence the decisions that iTunes makes by adding ratings to songs or entire albums (see Chapter 9 to do so).

Changing Your Update Preferences

Change your iPod preferences by following these steps:

1. **Connect the iPod to your computer.**

Your iPod must be connected for you to change the update preferences.

iTunes starts automatically if it isn't already running. If you're connecting your iPod for the first time, it synchronizes automatically with the iTunes library. If you want to prevent this from happening, press ⌘-Option (Mac) or Ctrl-Alt (Windows) as you connect the iPod, keeping them pressed until the iPod name appears in the iTunes Source pane.

2. **Select the iPod in the iTunes Source pane.**

   Your iPod appears in the Source pane with the name you gave it when you installed the iPod software (see Chapter 2).

3. **Click the iPod Options button in the bottom-right corner of the iTunes window.**

   The iPod Options button appears only when an iPod is connected and selected in the Source pane. You can also choose iTunes➪Preferences (Mac) or Edit➪Preferences (Windows) and click the iPod tab — whether or not the iPod is selected in the Source pane (although it has to be connected).

   The iPod preferences appear, as shown in Figure 12-1.

4. **Click the Music tab.**

   The Music tab might already be selected; if not, click it to show the Music preferences.

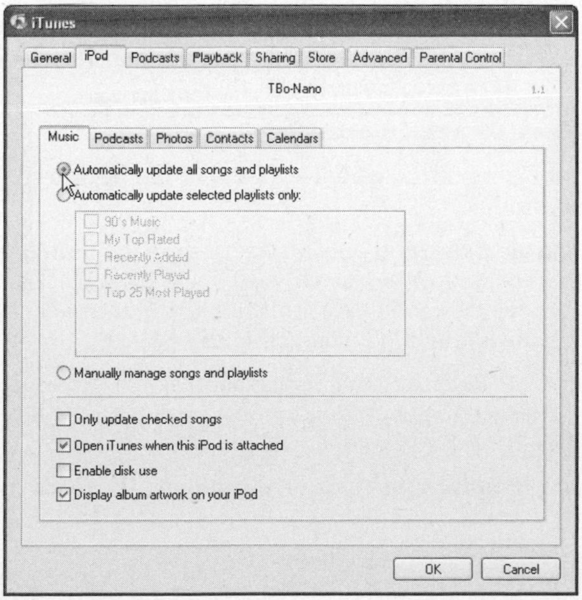

Figure 12-1:
Switch iPod Music updating methods in the iPod preferences dialog.

5. Select the music update preferences you want.

If you select the Automatically Update All Songs and Playlists option, iTunes displays a warning message asking you to confirm the update preference you chose (see Figure 12-2). Be sure that you want to use this option before selecting it; see "Updating Your iPod Automatically," earlier in this chapter. Click OK to go ahead (confirming that you want to change to automatic update).

Figure 12-2:
Confirm that you want to update your iPod automatically with all the music in your library.

6. Change other iPod music preferences as you want.

Other preferences that you might want to change include the Open iTunes when This iPod Is Attached option, which launches iTunes automatically when turned on. If this option is off, you have to start iTunes by launching it yourself. Other options appear, depending on the iPod model — for example, the Display Album Artwork on Your iPod option appears only for iPod models with color displays.

7. Click OK to close the Preferences dialog.

8. Click the iPod Eject button, which appears in the bottom-right corner of the iTunes window.

Another way to eject the iPod on a Mac is to drag the iPod icon on the Desktop to the Trash — or in Mac OS X 10.3, click the Eject icon next to the iPod icon in the Finder Sidebar. You can also Control-click (Mac) or right-click (Windows) the iPod icon and choose Eject.

After you eject the iPod, the iPod displays an `OK to disconnect` message in first- and second-generation models, or the iPod main menu in third-generation models.

9. Disconnect the iPod from its dock or disconnect the dock from the computer.

While the updating is in progress, don't disconnect your iPod from the computer until it tells you it's safe to do so. The iPod is a hard drive, after all, and hard drives need to be closed down properly in order for you not to lose any critical data. When it's safe, the iPod displays an `OK to disconnect` message in first- and second-generation models, or the iPod main menu in third-generation, fourth-generation, and fifth-generation models.

Updating Your iPod Selectively

Even if your iTunes library is too large to fit on your iPod, you can still use automatic methods to update your iPod — just be *selective,* choosing which playlists, photo albums, podcasts, and videos to automatically copy.

By updating selectively, you can still make your iPod match at least a subset of your iTunes library. If you make changes to that subset in iTunes, those changes are automatically made in the iPod when you synchronize again. For example, if you change your settings to update by certain playlists, any changes you make to those playlists — adding or deleting songs, for example — are reflected in your iPod the next time you synchronize it to your computer.

Updating by playlist

Updating by playlist is useful when you want to copy selected sets of songs to your iPod every time you connect it to your computer. For example, you can define a set of playlists in your iTunes library to use just for updating an iPod.

Updating automatically by playlist is also an easy way to automatically update an iPod from an iTunes library that is larger than the iPod's capacity.

Before using this update option, create the playlists in iTunes (see Chapter 10) that you want to copy to the iPod. Then follow these steps:

1. **Connect the iPod to your computer.**

   If your iPod is set to automatically update, press ⌘-Option (Mac) or Ctrl-Alt keys (Windows) while connecting the iPod.

2. **Select the iPod name in the iTunes Source pane.**

3. **Click the iPod Options button.**

   The iPod Options button appears only when an iPod is connected and selected in the Source pane. You can also choose iTunes➪Preferences (Mac) or Edit➪Preferences (Windows) and click the iPod tab.

   The iPod preferences appear (see Figure 12-3).

4. **Click the Music tab.**

5. **Select the Automatically Update Selected Playlists Only option.**

6. **In the list box, select each playlist that you want to copy in the update.**

7. **Click OK to close Preferences.**

   iTunes automatically updates the iPod by erasing its contents and copying only the playlists that you selected in Step 6.

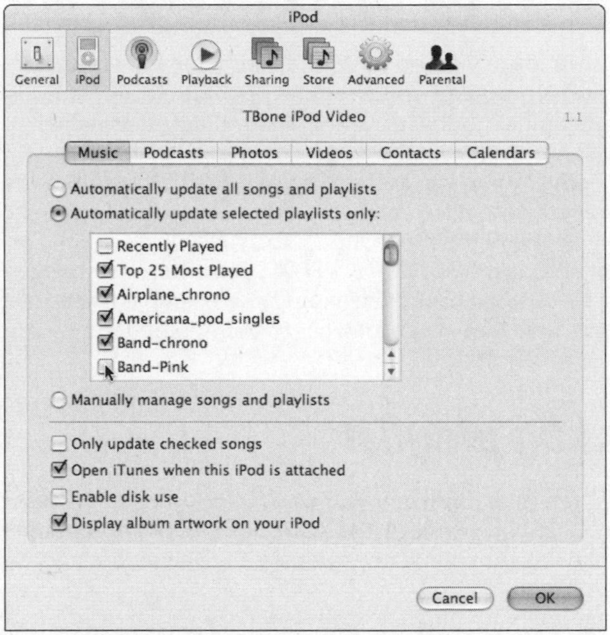

Figure 12-3:
Set the iPod
to auto-
matically
update with
only
selected
playlists.

8. **Wait for the updating to finish and then click the iPod Eject button.**

   Wait until the iTunes Status pane reads `iPod update is complete` before ejecting your iPod.

Updating selected items

You might want to update the iPod automatically but only with selected songs, videos, audio books, or podcast episodes. To use this method, you must first deselect the items you don't want to transfer, because all the items in your iTunes library are selected by default.

To deselect an item, click the check box next to the item so that the check mark disappears. To select an item, click the check box so that the check mark appears. To select or deselect a podcast episode, open the podcast first (see Chapter 6 for information about opening and playing podcasts).

You can quickly select or deselect an entire album by selecting an album in Browse view and pressing ⌘ key (Mac) or the Ctrl key (Windows) while making your selections.

After you deselect the items that you don't want to transfer and select the items you *do* want to transfer, follow these steps:

1. **Connect the iPod to your computer.**

   If your iPod is set to automatically update, press ⌘-Option (Mac) or Ctrl-Alt keys (Windows) while connecting the iPod.

2. **Select the iPod name in the iTunes Source pane.**

   You can select the iPod name even when it's grayed out; as long as you have your iPod connected, you can choose it in the Source pane.

3. **Click the iPod Options button.**

   The iPod Options button appears only when an iPod is connected and selected in the Source pane. You can also choose iTunes⇨Preferences (Mac) or Edit⇨Preferences (Windows) and then click the iPod tab.

   The iPod preferences appear; refer to Figure 12-3.

4. **Click the Music tab.**

5. **Select the Automatically Update All Songs and Playlists option and click OK for the `Are you sure you want to enable automatic updating` message that appears.**

6. **Select the Only Update Checked Songs check box and then click OK to close the dialog.**

   iTunes automatically updates the iPod by copying only the items in the iTunes library that are selected.

7. **Wait for the updating to finish and then click the iPod Eject button.**

   Wait until the iTunes Status pane reads `iPod update is complete` before you eject your iPod.

Choosing podcasts to transfer

Although you can listen to a podcast at any time on your computer, a podcast's real value is that you can take it with you in your iPod. You can keep your iPod synchronized with the most recent podcast episodes automatically. (You can also drag podcast episodes directly to your iPod just like any other item, as we describe in "Updating Your iPod Manually," later in this chapter.)

At first, your iPod is set to update all podcasts automatically. To update your iPod with podcasts you select, follow these steps:

1. **Connect your iPod to your computer. Wait for iTunes to start and for your iPod to be ready in the Source pane.**

   If the iPod is set for automatic updating, wait for the iPod to finish its usual updating or press ⌘-Option keys (Mac) or Ctrl-Alt (Windows) while connecting the iPod to prevent automatic updating.

2. **Choose iTunes⇨Preferences (Mac) or Edit⇨Preferences (Windows).**

3. **Click the iPod tab.**

   iTunes displays the iPod preferences.

4. **Click the Podcasts tab in the iPod preferences.**

   iTunes displays the iPod Podcasts preferences, as shown in Figure 12-4.

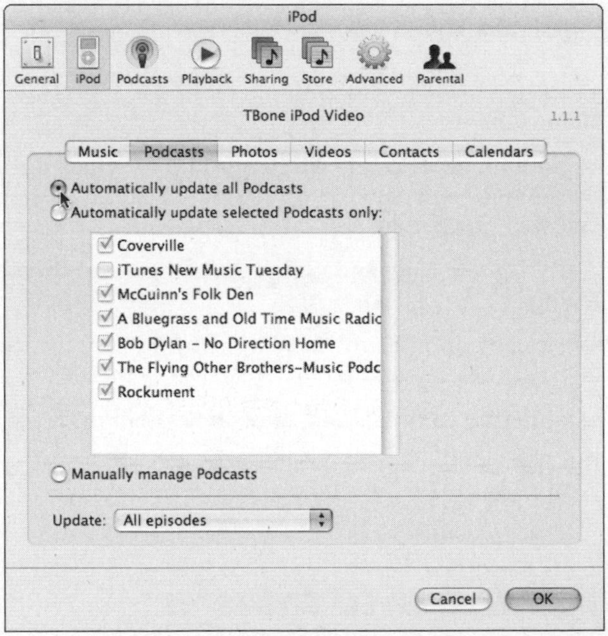

Figure 12-4:
Set your iPod to update automatically with new podcasts.

5. **Select the Automatically Update Selected Podcasts Only option and then select which podcasts you want to update.**

   You can also set the Update pop-up menu to update all episodes, only the most recent episode, or only unplayed episodes, as shown in Figure 12-5.

If you set iTunes to keep only your unplayed episodes, then listen to part of a podcast episode on your iPod, and then update your iPod, the podcast episode disappears from iTunes.

6. **Click OK.**

7. **Wait for the updating to finish and then click the iPod Eject button.**

   Wait until the iTunes Status pane reads `iPod update is complete` before you eject your iPod.

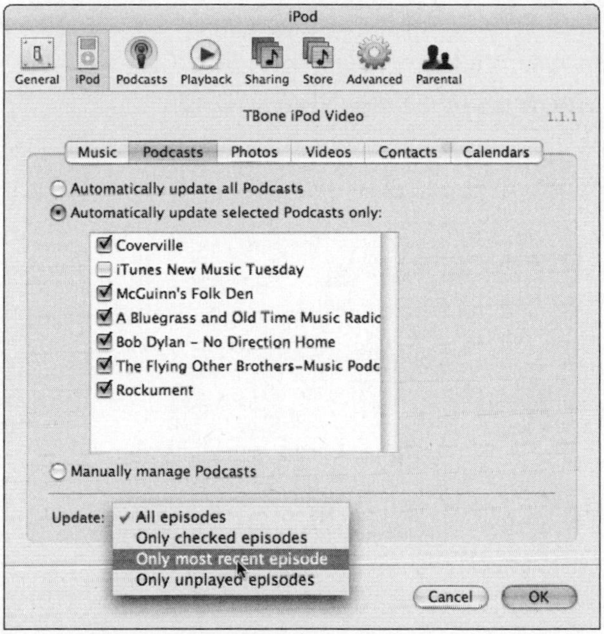

Figure 12-5:
Set your
iPod to be
updated
with only
the recent
episodes of
selected
podcasts.

You can synchronize podcasts with filenames ending with `.m4b` to any iPod and never lose your bookmarked place, whether you listen on your iPod or on your computer.

Choosing videos to transfer

Video takes up a lot of iPod space on a per-minute basis, so if you limit the videos you transfer to your video iPod during an iPod update, you gain extra space for more music, audio books, and podcasts.

At first, your video iPod's update preference is to transfer all videos automatically. To update your iPod with videos selectively, follow these steps:

1. **Connect your iPod to your computer. Wait for iTunes to start and for your iPod to be ready in the Source pane.**

   If the iPod is set for automatic updating, wait for the iPod to finish its usual updating or press ⌘-Option (Mac) or Ctrl-Alt (Windows) while connecting the iPod to prevent automatic updating.

2. **Choose iTunes⇨Preferences (Mac) or Edit⇨Preferences (Windows).**

3. **Click the iPod tab.**

   iTunes displays the iPod preferences.

4. **Click the Videos tab in the iPod preferences.**

   iTunes displays the iPod Videos preferences, as shown in Figure 12-6.

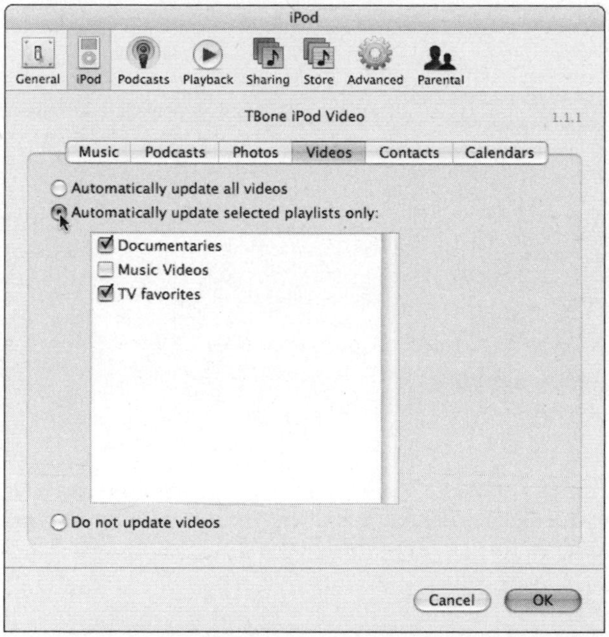

Figure 12-6:
Set your iPod to update automatically with video playlists.

5. **Select the Automatically Update Selected Playlists Only option and then your desired video playlists in the list box.**

   iTunes automatically displays only the playlists that include videos — see Chapter 10 for details about creating playlists.

6. **Wait for the updating to finish and then click the iPod Eject button.**

    Wait until the iTunes Status pane reads `iPod update is complete` before you eject your iPod.

Updating Your iPod with Photos

You can take your pictures with you, safely tucked into your color-display iPod. On a Mac, you can use iPhoto (version 4.0.3 or newer) to import photos into your computer and organize them into albums, as we describe in Chapter 11. You can then use iTunes to transfer photos from your iPhoto library automatically.

With Windows, you can use Adobe Photoshop Album (version 1.0 or newer) or Photoshop Elements (version 3.0 or newer) to import photos into your computer and organize your photos into collections, as we describe in Chapter 11. You can then use iTunes to transfer photos from your photo library automatically.

If you don't have any of these programs, you can use any other photo-editing or -organizing software and store your photos in a folder on your hard drive, or on a CD or server volume. You can then use iTunes to transfer photos from the folder.

Whether you transfer photos from a library or from a folder on your hard drive, you can keep your color-display iPod synchronized with the photo library and its albums or with the subfolders and image files in the folder.

If you connect your color-display iPod to another computer running iTunes, you might be in for a surprise. When you connect an iPod previously linked to another computer, iTunes displays the message: `This iPod is linked to another photo library. Do you want to change the link to this photo library and replace all existing photos on this iPod with those from this library?` If you don't want to change your iPod to have this other photo library, click No. Otherwise, iTunes erases the photos on your iPod and updates your iPod with the other computer's photo library.

Updating the entire photo library

If you store photos in a photo library (for example, in iPhoto on a Mac or Photoshop Elements in Windows), you can transfer photos to your color-display iPod automatically. You can synchronize your iPod to your library so that any changes you make to the library are copied to your iPod. You can also limit the transfer and synchronization to albums or collections rather than the entire library.

To transfer all photos in a library to an iPod and keep your iPod synchronized with your photo library, follow these steps:

1. **Connect the iPod to your computer.**

   Your iPod must be connected for you to change the update preferences. iTunes starts automatically when you connect the iPod to your computer.

2. **Select the iPod in the iTunes Source pane.**

   Your iPod appears in the Source pane with the name you gave it when you installed the iPod software; see Chapter 2.

3. **Click the iPod Options button in the bottom-right corner of the iTunes window.**

   The iPod Options button appears only when an iPod is connected and selected in the Source pane. You can also choose iTunes⇨Preferences (Mac) or Edit⇨Preferences (Windows) and click the iPod tab — whether or not the iPod is selected in the Source pane (although it has to be connected).

   The iPod preferences appear.

4. **Click the Photos tab to view the iPod Photos preferences.**

   The iPod Photo preferences appear, as shown in Figure 12-7.

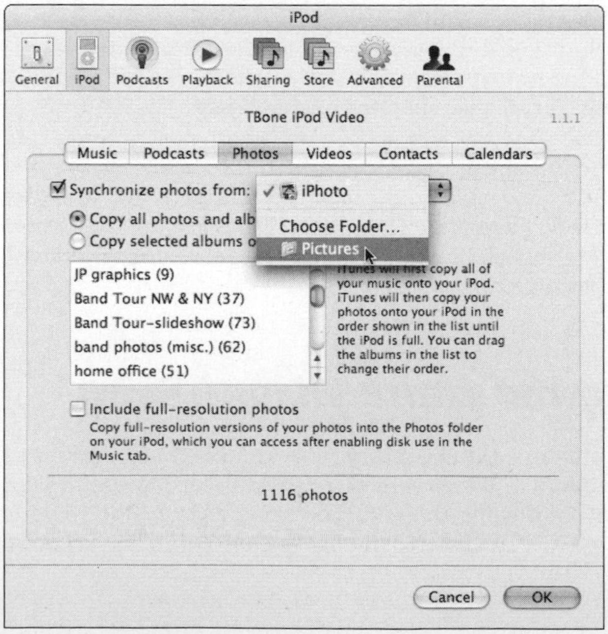

Figure 12-7:
Set your color-display iPod to synchronize with your photo library.

5. **Click the Synchronize Photos From option and select the library from the pop-up menu.**

   The pop-up menu in the figure lists iPhoto; with Windows, your choices are Photoshop Album or Photoshop Elements. You can also choose a folder, such as Pictures on a Mac or My Pictures in Windows. If you're going this way, see the "Transferring image files from a hard drive folder" section, later in this chapter.

6. **Click the Copy All Photos and Albums option.**

7. **Click OK.**

Until you change these preferences, every time you connect your iPod to this computer, iTunes automatically synchronizes the iPod with your entire photo library, keeping the iPod up-to-date with any new photos, improvements to photos, or deletions in your library. Your iPod also copies your photo album assignments so that your photos are organized by album.

Choosing photos and photo albums to transfer

To transfer only photos in specific albums in a library to your iPod and keep your iPod synchronized with these albums (not the entire library), follow these steps:

1. **Connect the color-display iPod to your computer.**

   Your iPod must be connected for you to change the update preferences. iTunes starts automatically when you connect the iPod to your computer.

2. **Select the iPod in the iTunes Source pane.**

3. **Click the iPod Options button in the bottom-right corner of the iTunes window.**

4. **Click the Photos tab to view the iPod Photos preferences.**

   The iPod Photos preferences open, as shown in Figure 12-8.

5. **Click the Synchronize Photos From option and select the library from the pop-up menu.**

6. **Click the Copy Selected Albums Only option.**

7. **In the list box, select each album that you want to copy.**

8. **Click OK.**

Until you change these preferences, every time you connect your iPod to this computer, iTunes automatically synchronizes it with the selected albums in the photo library, keeping your iPod up-to-date with any new photos, improvements to photos, or deletions that occur in those albums.

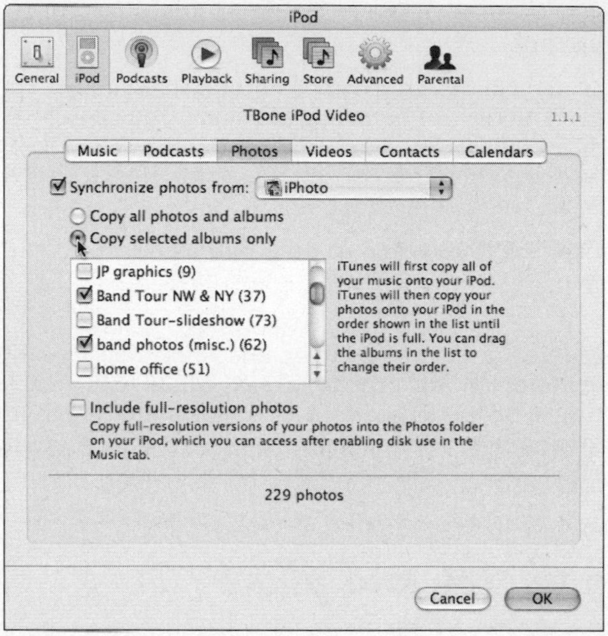

iPod

General iPod Podcasts Playback Sharing Store Advanced Parental

TBone iPod Video   1.1.1

| Music | Podcasts | Photos | Videos | Contacts | Calendars |

☑ Synchronize photos from: 📷 iPhoto ⬍

○ Copy all photos and albums
◉ Copy selected albums only

☐ JP graphics (9)
☑ Band Tour NW & NY (37)
☐ Band Tour–slideshow (73)
☑ band photos (misc.) (62)
☐ home office (51)

iTunes will first copy all of your music onto your iPod. iTunes will then copy your photos onto your iPod in the order shown in the list until the iPod is full. You can drag the albums in the list to change their order.

☐ Include full-resolution photos
Copy full-resolution versions of your photos into the Photos folder on your iPod, which you can access after enabling disk use in the Music tab.

229 photos

(Cancel)   (OK)

Figure 12-8: Set your color-display iPod to synchronize only with selected albums in your photo library.

Transferring image files from a hard drive folder

No matter what photo application you use, you can save photos as image files in a folder on your hard drive and then bring them into your iPod whenever you want. It's rare for an iPod to meet an image file format it doesn't like. Use JPEG (JPG), GIF, TIFF (TIF), Pict, PNG, PSD (Photoshop), PDF, jpg 2000, SGI, and BMP on a Mac. In Windows, use JPEG (JPG), GIF, TIFF (TIF), PNG, and BMP.

To transfer all photos in a folder on your hard drive to an iPod, follow these steps:

1. **Connect the iPod to your computer.**

   Your iPod must be connected for you to change the update preferences. iTunes starts automatically when you connect the iPod to your computer.

2. **Select the iPod in the iTunes Source pane.**

   Your iPod appears in the Source pane with the name you gave it when you installed the iPod software; see Chapter 2.

3. **Click the iPod Options button in the bottom-right corner of the iTunes window.**

   The iPod Options button appears only when an iPod is connected and selected in the Source pane. You can also choose iTunes➪Preferences (Mac) or Edit➪Preferences (Windows), and click the iPod tab — whether or not the iPod is selected in the Source pane (although it has to be connected).

   The iPod preferences appear.

4. **Click the Photos tab to view the iPod Photos preferences.**

   The iPod Photo preferences appear; refer to Figure 12-8.

5. **Click the Synchronize Photos From option and select Choose Folder from the pop-up menu.**

   The Browse dialog opens, showing the files and folders on your hard drive or other storage media (such as a CD-ROM or a server volume).

6. **Browse your hard drive (or other storage media) for the folder containing images and then click Choose (Mac) or OK (Windows).**

   If you want your photos to appear in separate albums on your iPod, create subfolders inside the folder and organize your image files inside these subfolders. iTunes copies the subfolder assignments as if they were album assignments.

7. **Click OK.**

Until you change these preferences, every time you connect your iPod to this computer, iTunes automatically synchronizes your iPod with the folder on your hard drive, keeping your iPod up-to-date with any new photos, changed photos, or deletions.

Transferring full-resolution photos and images

Picture quality with a digital camera is measured by the number of pixels — specific points of information in a picture, also known as the image *resolution*. Digital cameras are often described by the image resolution in millions of pixels, or *megapixels*. Higher megapixel counts usually result in better images. A 2-megapixel camera produces good 4 x 6-inch prints and acceptable 8 x 10-inch prints. A 3-megapixel camera produces very good 4 x 6-inch prints and magazine-quality 8 x 10-inch prints. A 5-megapixel camera produces good quality 10 x 14-inch prints. And so on.

A color-display iPod, by default, doesn't need the full resolution of photos to display them well on televisions and use them with video projectors, which are far lower in resolution than prints; certainly the tiny iPod display doesn't need high resolution in the photos it displays. The more resolution you have, the more space the photo takes up, so during the transfer, the iPod software optimizes photos for video display to save space.

If you intend to use your iPod to transfer images to another computer or to make a backup of your photos in their original resolution, you can set an option to include full-resolution versions of the photos when transferring photos.

To include full-resolution images, follow the steps in the "Choosing photos and photo albums to transfer" section. Before clicking OK, select the Include Full-Resolution Photos option. This option copies the full-resolution photos into the Photos folder of your iPod, which you can access on your computer by enabling your iPod for hard drive use (see Chapter 23).

Updating Your iPod Manually

With manual updating, you can add content to your iPod directly via iTunes, and you can delete content from your iPod, as well. The iPod name appears in the iTunes Source pane, and when selected, its contents appear in the iTunes song list, replacing the library contents.

You might have one or more reasons for updating manually, but here are some obvious ones:

- ✔ Your entire library is too big for your iPod, and you want to copy individual files to the iPod directly.

- ✔ You want to share a single library with several iPods, and you have different playlists that you want to copy to each iPod directly.

- ✔ You share an iPod with others, and you want to copy your content to the iPod without wiping out their contents.

- ✔ You want to copy some songs or videos from another computer's iTunes library without deleting any content from your iPod.

- ✔ You want to edit the playlists and content information directly on your iPod without changing anything in your computer's library.

- ✔ You want to play your iPod through the computer's speakers and take advantage of iTunes playback features (such as cross-fading between two tracks; see Chapter 6).

When you set your iPod to update manually, all contents on the iPod are active and available in iTunes. You can copy items directly to your iPod, delete items on the iPod, and edit the iPod playlists directly.

To set your iPod to update manually, follow these steps:

1. **Connect the iPod to your computer, press ⌘-Option (Mac) or Ctrl-Alt (Windows) to prevent automatic updating.**

   Continue pressing the keys until the iPod name appears in the iTunes Source pane.

2. **Select the iPod name in the iTunes Source pane.**

3. **Click the iPod Options button.**

   The iPod Options button appears only when an iPod is connected and selected in the Source pane. You can also choose iTunes⇨Preferences (Mac) or Edit⇨Preferences (Windows), and click the iPod tab.

   The iPod preferences appear (refer to Figure 12-1).

4. **Click the Music tab.**

5. **Select the Manually Manage Songs and Playlists option.**

   iTunes displays the `Disabling automatic update requires manually unmounting the iPod before each disconnect` message.

6. **Click OK to accept the new iPod preferences.**

   The iPod contents now appear active in iTunes and not grayed out.

Don't disconnect your iPod while it is active in iTunes with the manual updating method. You have to eject the iPod and wait until the iPod displays the message `OK to disconnect` (in first- and second-generation models) or the iPod main menu. You risk making the iPod's hard drive or flash memory unreadable, forcing you to restore the iPod to its original factory condition (see Chapter 26).

Copying items directly

As soon as you set your iPod to manual updating, you can copy items from your iTunes library directly. Follow these steps (with your iPod connected to your computer):

1. **Select Library in the iTunes Source pane (or a playlist).**

   The library's or playlist's songs appear in List or Browse view.

2. **Drag items directly from your iTunes library or playlist over the iPod name in the Source pane, as shown in Figure 12-9.**

   When you drag a playlist name, all the songs associated with the playlist copy along with the playlist itself. When you drag an album title, all the songs in the album are copied.

Figure 12-9:
Copy an
album of
songs
directly from
the iTunes
library to
the iPod.

3. **Wait for the copy operation to finish and then click the iPod Eject button.**

   Wait until the iTunes Status pane reads `iPod update is complete` before ejecting your iPod.

Deleting items on your iPod

With manual updating, you can delete content from the iPod directly. Manual deletion is a nice feature if you just want to go in and delete a song, video, or album to make room for more.

To delete any item in your iPod, set your iPod to manual updating and then follow these steps:

1. **Select the iPod in the iTunes Source pane.**

   The iPod's content appears in List or Browse view, replacing the view of your library.

2. **Select an item on the iPod and press Delete/Backspace or choose Edit⇨
Clear.**

   iTunes displays a warning to make sure you want to do this; click OK to
   go ahead or Cancel to stop. If you want to delete a playlist, select the
   playlist and press Delete or choose Edit⇨Clear.

Like in the iTunes library, if you delete a playlist, the items listed in the playlist are not deleted — they are still on your iPod unless you delete them from
the iPod song list or update the iPod automatically with other content or
playlists.

Creating playlists directly on the iPod

The content information and playlists for your iPod are automatically copied
to your iPod when you update. However, you might want to edit your iPod's
music library separately, perhaps creating new playlists or changing the song
information manually.

To create a new playlist, follow these steps:

1. **Select the iPod in the iTunes Source pane.**

2. **Open the iPod's playlists.**

   Click the triangle next to the iPod name to open the iPod list of playlists,
   as shown in Figure 12-10.

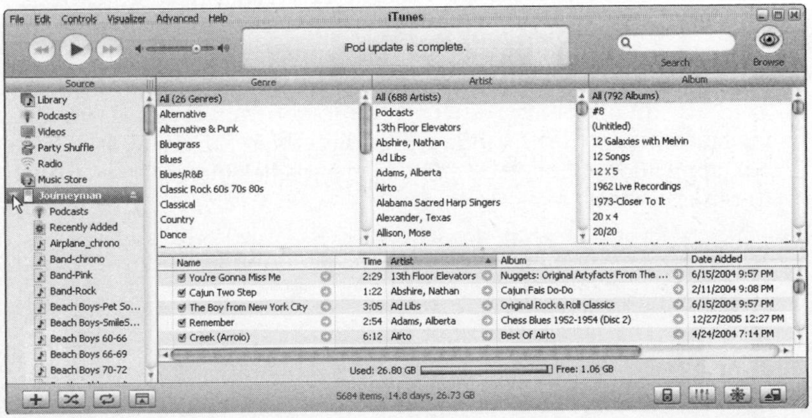

Figure 12-10:
Create a
playlist
here, right
on your
iPod.

3. **Create a new playlist by clicking the Add Playlist button in the bottom-left corner of iTunes under the Source pane or choose File⇨New Playlist.**

   Untitled playlist appears in the Source pane under the iPod entry.

4. **Type a name for the untitled playlist.**

   After you type a new name, iTunes automatically sorts it into alphabetical order in the iPod list.

5. **Drag items from the iPod song list to the playlist.**

   You can also click the Browse button to find items on the iPod more easily.

The order of items in the playlist is based on the order in which you drag them to the list. You can rearrange the list by dragging items within the playlist.

You can create smart playlists on the iPod in exactly the same way as in the iTunes library. A *smart playlist* updates itself when you create it with iTunes and then updates itself every time you connect and select your iPod with iTunes. Read all about smart playlists in Chapter 10.

Editing content information on your iPod

With the iPod selected in iTunes and set for updating manually, you can edit the content information just like you do in the iTunes library by scrolling down the list and selecting items.

After selecting the iPod in the Source pane, click the Browse button. In Browse view, you can browse the iPod library and find songs by artist and album.

You can edit information such as the song name, artist, album, genre, and ratings information for the iPod songs directly in the columns in the song list. To edit song information, locate the song and click inside the text field of a column to type new text.

You might find it easier to edit this information by choosing File⇨Get Info and typing the text into the Information dialog.

iTunes grabs song information from the Internet (as we describe in Chapter 9), but this information typically doesn't include composer credits. If you have the time and inclination to add composer credits, doing so is worth your while because you can then search, sort, and create playlists based on this information. This is particularly important for classical music lovers because iTunes and the iPod make it easy to find songs by the performer/

artist but not by the composer — and sorting by composer is what many classical music fans prefer.

Updating an iPod shuffle

iPod shuffle is designed for quick and convenient music updating — just plug it into your computer and click the Autofill button in iTunes. It also offers automatic compression to fit more songs (or audio books, which are treated as songs) into your iPod shuffle space.

Although Apple proudly advertises its capability to shuffle songs randomly, the key to its success is not that you can shuffle the songs already there, but you can copy random songs to it every time you connect it to your computer. Eventually, you can shuffle through everything in your library if you so wish, by randomly filling your iPod shuffle every time. On the other hand, you can fine-tune your random selection and even reorder the iPod shuffle's playlist to play back in a specific order.

Although you can add songs to your iPod shuffle manually by dragging a play-list or song, you can also automatically fill it without having to set options for automatic updating. Autofill automatically picks songs from your entire iTunes library or from a playlist you select in the Source pane. You can also manage the playlist for your iPod shuffle directly, after using Autofill, to fine-tune your selection.

Using Autofill

To use Autofill to copy songs to your iPod shuffle, follow these steps:

1. **Connect the iPod shuffle to your computer.**

   When you connect an iPod shuffle to your computer, it shows up in the Source pane.

2. **Select the iPod shuffle in the iTunes Source pane.**

   The Autofill pane appears below the Song List pane, as shown in Figure 12-11. The iPod shuffle's songs appear in List or Browse view, replacing the view of your library songs.

3. **Choose your source of music in the Autofill From pop-up menu.**

   Choose either a playlist or Library (for the entire library). If you choose a playlist, Autofill uses only the playlist as the source of music.

4. **(Optional) To pick random songs, select the Choose Songs Randomly option.**

5. **(Optional) To pick only the best songs (if you're choosing them randomly), select the Choose Higher Rated Songs More Often option.**

6. **(Optional) To replace songs already on the iPod shuffle, select the Replace All Songs When Autofilling option.**

   If you don't select this option, iTunes adds the songs without replacing existing songs.

7. **Click the Autofill button to start copying songs.**

   iTunes grabs a subset of your music, creates a playlist, and copies the contents of the playlist to your iPod shuffle.

8. **Wait for the copy operation to finish and then click the iPod Eject button.**

   Wait until the iTunes Status pane reads `iPod update is complete` before ejecting your iPod shuffle.

Figure 12-11:
Autofill your
iPod shuffle
from an
iTunes
playlist.

You can click the Autofill button over and over to create different random playlists. When you get one you like, select all its contents and choose File⇨New Playlist From Selection to create a new playlist that contains the songs generated by Autofill. When you next connect your iPod shuffle, select this new playlist from the Autofill From pop-up menu and click the Autofill button to load the music from the playlist to your shuffle.

TIP

iPod shuffle can play type 2, 3, and 4 Audible.com audio books (including audio books sold by the iTunes Music Store). Unfortunately, iTunes won't automatically add them to the iPod shuffle — you have to add them manually.

Updating manually

iPod shuffle is always set for manual updating. When you connect an iPod shuffle to your computer, you can copy music (or audio books) directly to it, delete items on it, and edit its playlist.

To copy items to your iPod shuffle directly, connect it to your computer and follow these steps:

1. **Select Library in the iTunes Source pane.**

   The library's content appears in a List or Browse view.

2. **Drag items directly from your iTunes library over the iPod shuffle name in the Source pane, as shown in Figure 12-12.**

   When you copy a playlist, all the songs in the playlist are copied. When you copy an album, all the songs in the album are copied.

Figure 12-12: Copy songs directly from the iTunes library to the iPod shuffle.

3. **Wait for the copy operation to finish and then click the iPod Eject button.**

Wait until the iTunes Status pane reads `iPod update is complete` before ejecting your iPod shuffle.

To delete any item in your iPod shuffle, follow these steps:

1. **Select the iPod shuffle in the iTunes Source pane.**

The iPod shuffle songs appear in the List or Browse view, replacing the view of your library songs.

2. **Select one or more songs on the iPod shuffle and press Delete/Backspace or choose Edit⇨Clear.**

iTunes displays a warning to make sure you want to do this; click OK to go ahead or Cancel to stop.

Managing an iPod shuffle playlist

You might not want to make a random choice or even fine-tune a random choice — you might want to take a more deterministic approach to updating the song choices and sequence of your iPod shuffle. You can do this by managing your iPod shuffle playlist manually, and you can manage it without connecting your iPod shuffle.

Connect the iPod shuffle and select it in the iTunes Source pane so you can see its playlist in the Song List view. The song order in the playlist is based either on the order Autofill selected them or the order in which you dragged them. You can rearrange the playing order by dragging songs within the iPod shuffle playlist to new positions in the list. You can also copy songs to the iPod shuffle at any position in the list and delete songs from the iPod shuffle playlist, as described in the previous section, "Updating manually."

The cool thing about an iPod shuffle is that you can also do these things *without* connecting it. Follow these steps:

1. **Connect the iPod shuffle and select it in the Source pane.**

2. **Click the iPod Options button.**

The iPod Options button appears only when an iPod is connected and selected in the Source pane. You can also choose iTunes⇨Preferences (Mac) or Edit⇨Preferences (Windows), and click the iPod tab.

The iPod preferences appear, as shown in Figure 12-13.

3. **Click the Music tab.**

4. **Select the Keep This iPod in the Source List option.**

   Now when you disconnect your iPod shuffle, it remains in the Source pane, and you can continue changing its playlist. Your iPod shuffle is automatically updated the next time you connect it.

5. **(Optional) Select the Only Update Checked Songs option.**

   Select this check box if you want iTunes to copy only songs that are selected in the iTunes library. To use this option effectively, you must first *deselect* songs you don't want to copy. Deselect the check box next to any songs you don't want to copy in the iTunes library. To select a song, click the check box.

6. **Click OK to close the Preferences dialog.**

7. **Click the iPod Eject button or click the Eject icon next to the iPod shuffle name in the Source pane and then disconnect the iPod shuffle.**

   Remember to wait for the `OK to disconnect` message before disconnecting your iPod shuffle.

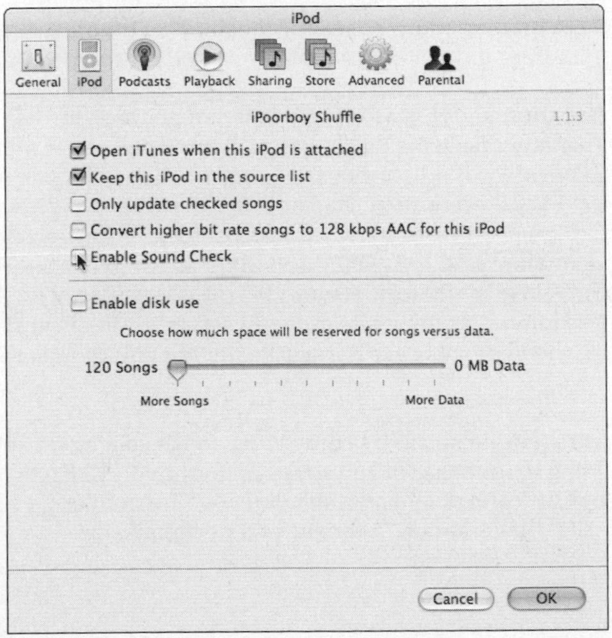

Figure 12-13:
Set iPod shuffle preferences.

iPod

General | iPod | Podcasts | Playback | Sharing | Store | Advanced | Parental

iPoorboy Shuffle   1.1.3

☑ Open iTunes when this iPod is attached
☑ Keep this iPod in the source list
☐ Only update checked songs
☐ Convert higher bit rate songs to 128 kbps AAC for this iPod
☐ Enable Sound Check

☐ Enable disk use

Choose how much space will be reserved for songs versus data.

120 Songs ●————————— 0 MB Data

More Songs   More Data

Cancel | OK

Your iPod shuffle remains in the Source pane even after you disconnect it. Select the iPod shuffle's name in the Source pane and rearrange the playlist as you wish, including copying and deleting songs. When you finish, iTunes saves the iPod shuffle playlist so when you reconnect your iPod shuffle, it is automatically updated to match this playlist.

Managing space on your iPod shuffle

It's a nifty song player! No, it's an external flash drive for data backup! Either way, you can wear the iPod shuffle on your sleeve, which makes it quite convenient for either music or data. To maximize its data potential, see Chapter 23.

To maximize its music potential, connect your iPod shuffle and open iPod preferences — either select the iPod shuffle in the Source pane and click the iPod Options button or choose iTunes⇨Preferences (Mac) or Edit⇨Preferences (Windows) and click the iPod tab.

The iPod preferences (refer to Figure 12-13) include a storage allocation slider with More Songs on the left side and More Data on the right. Drag the slider to the left to open up more space for music. Don't worry — adding more space won't affect any data files already stored on the iPod shuffle.

If the storage allocation slider is as far left as it can go or as far left as you want to take it (leaving space for data), you still have one more method of squeezing music onto the iPod shuffle: the Convert Higher Bitrate Songs to 128 Kbps AAC for This iPod option. This option does just what it says: It converts songs with higher bit rates in either protected or unprotected AAC files or MP3 files into smaller AAC files using 128 Kbps as the bit rate. (For more information about these audio formats and bit rates, see Chapter 18.) It performs this conversion on the fly while copying songs to the iPod shuffle, but it doesn't change the songs in your library. Protected AAC songs retain their protection.

You can save considerable space by converting songs to a lower bit rate. An iPod shuffle holding an average of 180 songs encoded at 192 Kbps in MP3 can hold an average of 260 songs by using this option. The conversion reduces an uncompressed AIFF file to about 7 percent of its original size.

Chapter 13

Gimme Shelter for My Media

You might think that your digital content is safe, stored as-is, on both your iPod and your hard drive. However, demons in the night are working overtime to render your hard drive useless — and at the same time, someone left your iPod out in the rain. (No, not really, but it could happen.)

Copyright law and common sense prohibit you from copying copyrighted content and then selling it to someone else. However, with iTunes you are allowed to make copies of music, videos, audio books, and podcasts you own for your personal use, including copies for your iPod for backup purposes.

In this chapter, you find out how to make a backup of your entire library. This operation is very important, especially if you have songs and videos that don't exist anywhere else in your collection but in your computer. That way, even if your hard drive fails, you still have your iTunes library.

You can't copy content from your iPod to your computer via iTunes. It's a one-way trip from iTunes to your iPod. You can't copy stuff from your iPod with iTunes because record labels and video distributors don't want indiscriminate copying, and Apple complied with their request. You can, however, use *third-party utility programs* (not supported by Apple) to copy content both ways. (More on this topic in Chapter 25.) This chapter describes how to keep a backup of your iTunes library on your computer, another hard drive, or a backup medium so that you don't rely on your iPod as your sole music storage device.

The iTunes Music Store uses the Apple FairPlay technology that protects the rights of copyright holders while also giving you some leeway in how you can use the copyrighted content. You can copy the media files freely so that backup is easy and straightforward on either a PC or a Mac.

Studying Files in the iTunes Library

If you're like that guy in the movie *Diner* who couldn't stand to have his records misfiled, you'll love iTunes and its nice, neat file storage methods. For all content items, iTunes creates a folder named for the artist, and creates folders within the artist folder named for each album. These folders are stored in the iTunes Music folder unless you change your storage preferences.

Finding the iTunes library

The default method of storing content in the iTunes library is to store all media files — including music, videos, podcasts, and audio books — in the iTunes Music folder. With this method, media files that you drag to the iTunes window are copied into the iTunes Music folder without deleting the original files. You need to know where this folder is to copy content folders or back up your library.

iTunes maintains a separate iTunes folder (with a separate iTunes Music folder) in each Home folder (Mac) or user folder (PC). If you share your computer with other users who have Home folders, each user can have a separate iTunes library on the same computer (and, of course, a separate iPod that synchronizes with it). You need only one copy of the iTunes program.

On a Mac, iTunes stores your content library in your Home folder's Music folder. The path to this folder is by default

```
your home folder/Music/iTunes/iTunes Music
```

On a Windows PC, iTunes stores your content library in your user folder. The path to this folder is by default

```
your user folder/My Documents/My Music/iTunes/iTunes Music
```

Changing how files are stored in the library

The default method of organizing files in the iTunes library is to store content files in album and artist folders, naming the files according to the disc number, track number, and title.

For example, the song "Here, There and Everywhere" has the track number and song title in the filename (05 Here, There And Everywhere.mp3). The filename extension even tells you the type of encoding format — in this case, MP3. *Note:* Songs encoded in AAC have the extension .m4a or .m4p (for protected songs purchased from the iTunes Music Store). This song is saved in the Revolver folder (for the album), which is in The Beatles folder (for the artist).

Videos and TV shows follow the same naming conventions (even if they don't make much sense). For example, the TV show *Monk,* episode 13 in season 1, titled "Mr. Monk and the Airplane" (the *song* title), is 13 Mr. Monk and the Airplane.m4v and is stored in the Season 1 folder (the *album*) inside the Monk folder (the *artist*).

What about songs performed by multiple artists, such as duets, or soundtrack albums with multiple artists? Albums and songs designated as part of a compilation are stored in album folders within the Compilations folder rather than within individual artist folders.

To designate a song as part of a compilation, select the song and choose File⇨Get Info, click the Info tab in the information dialog, and then select the Part of a Compilation check box.

To designate an entire album as a compilation album, select the album, choose File⇨Get Info, and then select Yes from the Part of a Compilation pop-up menu. Even if Yes is already selected for the album, choose Yes again to set the check mark for updating.

The filename and location within artist and album folders change when you change the information for a song (or video, audio book, or podcast episode) in the information fields. For example, if you change the song title, the filename also changes. If you change the artist name, the folder name for the artist might change, or the file might move to a new folder by that name. iTunes organizes the files based on the song information.

To make changes to song information without changing the files on your hard drive, choose iTunes⇨Preferences (Mac) or Edit⇨Preferences (Windows) and then click Advanced. On the Advanced tab, click the General tab and then deselect the Keep iTunes Music Folder Organized option.

Keep your iTunes music folder organized — leave the Keep iTunes Music Folder Organized option turned on — if you plan on copying the music files to an iPod that will then be used with a car installation. (We describe car installations in Chapter 21.) Most iPod interfaces for car stereos provide a way to navigate the iPod with the car stereo controls but won't display the proper artist, album, and song titles unless the music folder is organized by the default method.

Maybe you don't want to store copies of your media files in the library — especially if you already have copies stored on your hard drive in another location and need to conserve space. If you want to add content to your iTunes library without copying the files into the iTunes Music folder:

1. **Choose iTunes⇨Preferences (Mac) or Edit⇨Preferences (Windows).**

2. **Click the Advanced tab.**

3. **Click the General subtab in the Advanced pane.**

4. **Deselect the Copy Files to iTunes Music Folder When Adding to Library option.**

The next time you drag a media file into the iTunes window, it stores only a reference in your iTunes library to the file that specifies its actual location. The file isn't copied or moved.

Locating a media file

No matter where you store your iTunes library or your media files, you can find the location of any item by selecting the item, choosing File⇨Get Info, and then clicking the Summary tab of the information dialog. You can see the file type next to the Kind heading of the Summary tab. The Where section tells you where the song is, as shown in Figure 13-1.

If you access shared libraries on a network, you probably have content in your library that isn't actually in your library but is rather part of a shared library or playlist on a network. When you look at the Summary tab of the information dialog for an item in a shared library, the Where section doesn't appear.

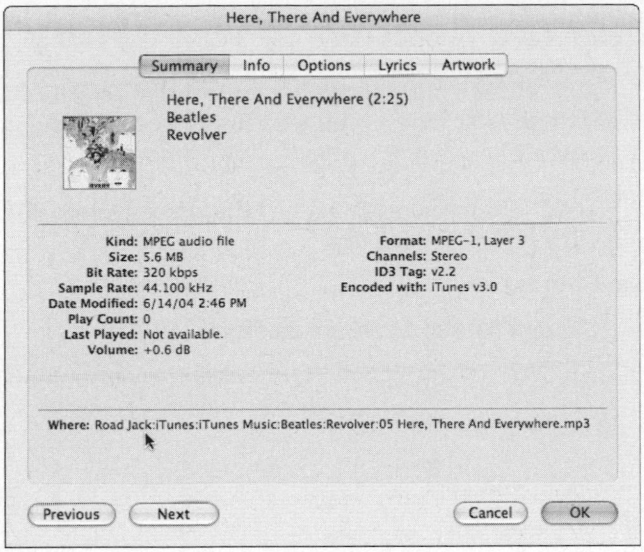

Figure 13-1:
Locate a
media file by
using the
information
dialog.

Manipulating the iTunes Library

If you're like us, your iTunes library is huge. We've nearly filled the internal hard drives of two modern computers, each sporting 80GB of space. (And you thought 80GB would be enough?) What do you do if you want to expand your library, but you run out of space? How do you move your library to a higher-capacity hard drive? What if you have media files all over your hard drive and you need to consolidate them all in once place so you can reclaim drive space? You can do all that and more.

Consolidating the library media files

If you have media files that are stored on different hard drives that are connected to the same computer, you can have iTunes consolidate your library by copying everything into the iTunes Music folder. By first consolidating your library, you make sure that any backup operation you perform is complete.

To consolidate your iTunes library, choose Advanced➪Consolidate Library. The original media files remain where they are, but copies are made in your Music folder.

Changing the location of the library

You can store your iTunes library in a different location on your hard drive or on another hard drive — as long as you tell iTunes where to find it. To change where iTunes stores your content library, follow these steps:

1. **Choose iTunes⇨Preferences (Mac) or Edit⇨Preferences (Windows) and then click the Advanced tab.**

2. **Click the General tab.**

3. **Click the Change button, as shown in Figure 13-2.**

   You can then browse to select another location on any connected hard drive.

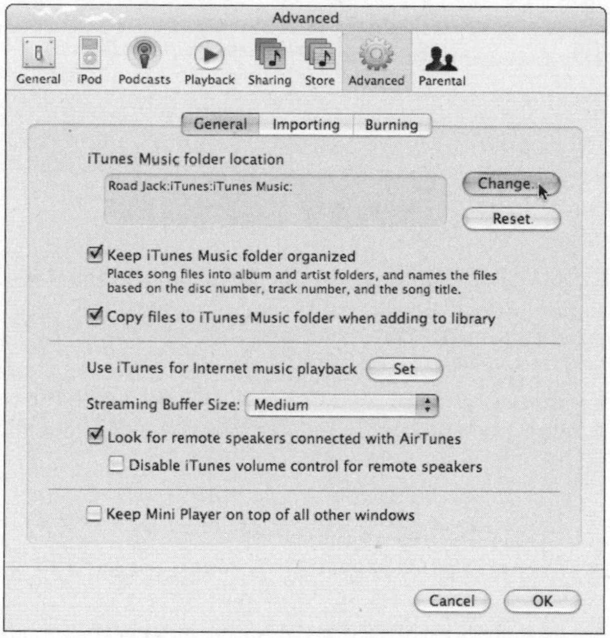

Figure 13-2: Change the location of the iTunes Music folder that contains your entire library.

After selecting a new location, the content you bring into iTunes (by ripping CDs, downloading items from the iTunes store, or dragging media files) is stored in the new location. However, previously imported media files stay where they are. To move the previously imported files to the new library location, drag the media files into the iTunes window so that iTunes stores them automatically in the new location and updates its library file properly. You can then delete the media files you copied from the old library location.

To change the storage location back to the iTunes folder inside the Music folder, click the Reset button in the Preferences window.

Moving your library to another hard drive

To move your entire library to another hard drive (presumably a higher-capacity drive), you can change the location of the library and consolidate the library at the same time. Follow these steps:

1. **Create a folder — name it *iTunes* — on the other hard drive.**

   iTunes is a good name, but you could call it anything, and iTunes can still find it.

2. **Change the location of the iTunes library to the new iTunes folder.**

   To change where iTunes stores the library, see the earlier section, "Changing the location of the library."

   iTunes creates a new iTunes Music folder inside your new iTunes folder.

3. **In the General section of the Advanced pane of the Preferences dialog, select the Copy Files to iTunes Music Folder When Adding to Library and the Keep iTunes Music Folder Organized options and then click OK.**

   These options might already be enabled. Just double-check to make sure that they are selected.

4. **Choose Advanced⇨Consolidate Library.**

   iTunes automatically copies all the media files, along with playlists, into the new iTunes Music folder.

Exporting iTunes playlists

With iTunes, you can export and import a playlist into a different computer to have the same playlist in both places.

You must also copy the songs, videos, podcast episodes, and audio books in the playlist for the playlists on the other computer to work. Better yet, copy the entire artist folders containing the items to keep them organized. Exporting a playlist doesn't copy the items in the playlist. You get a list of items in the XML (eXtensible Markup Language) format but not the content of these items. You still need to copy the actual media files to the other computer.

To export a single playlist, select the playlist and then choose File⇨Export Song List. On a Mac, choose the XML option from the Format pop-up menu in the Save: iTunes dialog and then click the Save button. On a Windows PC, choose the XML option from the Files pull-down menu in the Save dialog.

After exporting a playlist and copying it to another computer, you can import the playlist into iTunes on the other computer by choosing File⇨Import on that computer, selecting the XML file, and then clicking the Choose button. You can also export all the playlists in your library at the same time by choosing File⇨Export Library; then import them into iTunes on the other computer by choosing File⇨Import and selecting the exported XML file.

You can also import playlist files exported from other applications as .m3u files. The .m3u format is supported by applications such as Winamp (www.winamp.com) and VideoLAN Client (www.videolan.org) for managing playlists.

Backing Up the iTunes Library

Backups? You don't need no stinkin' backups?

Yes, don't think twice: Backing up can be inconvenient and can eat up the capacity of all your external hard drives, but it must be done. Fortunately, it's easy to do. With iTunes, you can copy your library to another hard drive on your computer or to another computer. You can burn as many data DVDs as needed to store all the files (see Chapter 14). You can even copy a library from a Mac to a PC and vice versa.

Backing up on the same type of computer

To copy your entire library to another hard drive, locate the iTunes folder on your computer. Drag this entire folder to another hard drive or backup device, and you're all set. This action copies everything, including the playlists in your library.

The copy operation might take some time if your library is huge. Although you can interrupt the operation anytime, the newly copied library might not be complete. Finishing the copy operation is always best.

If you restore the backup copy to the same computer with the same names for its hard drive, the backup copy's playlists work fine. Playlists are essentially XML lists of songs with pathnames to the song files: If the hard drive name is different, the pathnames won't work. However, you can import the playlists into iTunes by choosing File⇨Import, which realigns the playlist pathnames to the new hard drive. Alternatively, you can use the method described in the following section, "Backing up from Mac to PC or PC to Mac."

If you copy just the iTunes Music folder and not the entire iTunes folder, you're copying the files but not your playlists. You still have to export your playlists — see the earlier section, "Exporting iTunes playlists."

If you use a Mac and subscribe to the Apple .Mac service, you can download and use the free Backup software. This software lets you save the latest versions of your files regularly and automatically so that you never have to worry about losing important files. With Backup, you can quickly and easily store files on your *iDisk* (a portion of an Internet hard drive hosted by .Mac) or on CD or DVD as data files — not as CD songs. (See Chapter 14 to read how to burn an audio or MP3 CD.) The iDisk is perhaps the least convenient even though you do get some free space with a .Mac membership. Copying to the iDisk is slow even over a high-speed connection. We use iDisk to transfer individual songs and large files to other people and to back up very important documents. However, you're better off using data DVDs as a backup medium for data and audio CDs for your songs and albums.

Backing up from Mac to PC or PC to Mac

Maybe you use a Mac but you want to transfer your iTunes library to a PC that runs iTunes, or the other way around. Or perhaps you want a foolproof method of copying your entire library to another computer, whether it's a Mac, a PC running Windows, or just a computer that uses a different name for its hard drive (or a different path to the Home folder or user folder).

To back up your iTunes library no matter what the situation is, follow these steps:

1. **Locate your iTunes Music folder on your *old* computer.**

   Locate your iTunes Music folder as described in "Finding the iTunes library," earlier in this chapter. Consider the first computer the *old* computer and the one receiving the copied library the *new* computer.

2. **Download and install iTunes on the new computer.**

   See Chapter 2 for instructions on installing iTunes. If the new computer already has an iTunes Music folder with music that you want to preserve, move that iTunes Music folder to another folder on the hard drive or copy it to another hard drive or storage medium.

3. **Copy the iTunes Music folder from the old computer to the newly installed iTunes folder on the new computer.**

   If you have multiple users on the new computer, make sure that you choose the appropriate Home folder (Mac) or user folder (Windows). The copy operation for a large music library takes a while.

4. **Choose File➪Export Library on the old computer, browse to a location on your hard drive or network, and then click the Save button.**

   When you export your entire library, iTunes creates the XML file `iTunes Music Library.xml` that links to music files and stores all your playlists.

5. **Start iTunes on the new computer.**

6. **Choose File➪Import on the new computer and then import the `iTunes Music Library.xml` file.**

   The music library is now available on the new computer.

The iTunes Music Library file (`iTunes Music Library.xml`) must be located within the iTunes folder where iTunes can find it.

Chapter 14

Baking Your Own Discs with Printed Inserts

. . . .

In This Chapter

▶ Creating a burn playlist

▶ Choosing the right format for burning a disc

▶ Setting the burn preferences

▶ Burning an audio CD, MP3 CD, or data DVD

▶ Printing jewel case inserts and song lists

▶ Troubleshooting tips

. . . .

*O*nce upon a time, when vinyl records were popular, rock radio disk jock-eys who didn't like disco held disco-meltdown parties. People were encouraged to throw their disco records into a pile to be burned or steam-rolled into a vinyl glob. We admit having participated in one such meltdown. However, this chapter isn't about that (nor is it about anything involving fire or heat). Rather, *burning* a disc refers to the process in which the CD drive recorder's laser heats up points on an interior layer of the disc. This simu-lates the pits pressed into commercial CDs that represent digital information.

You burn CDs for a lot of reasons — reason *numero uno* for us is to make safety copies of songs we buy from the iTunes Music Store — in addition to backup copies of the song files on other hard drives. We also like to combine songs from different artists and albums on a single CD (a "custom mix" — not to be confused with *mixing,* which is a production technique for combining tracks into a single song). With iTunes you can even print CD jewel case inserts with the list of songs and liner notes. You can also burn DVD data discs to back up your files.

This chapter burns, er, boils everything down for you by telling you what kind of discs to use, which devices you can use to play the discs, how to get your playlist ready for burning, and what settings to use for burning. You find out what you need to know to make sure that your burns are not meltdowns — the only melting is the music in your ears.

Don't violate copyright law. You can copy content to discs for your own personal use but you are not allowed legally to copy content for any other purpose. Consult a lawyer if you're in doubt.

Selecting Recordable CDs and DVDs

After importing music into your iTunes library, you can arrange any songs in your library into a playlist and then burn a CD using that playlist. (See Chapter 10 for more on creating playlists.) If you have a CD-R, CD-RW, or DVD-R drive (such as the Apple SuperDrive for Macs) and a blank CD-R (*R* stands for recordable), you can create your own music CDs that play in most CD players. You can also include audio books and podcast episodes in a playlist and then burn them onto CDs.

Blank CD-Rs are available in most electronics and computer stores, and even supermarkets. You can also get them online from the Apple Store (not the music store — the store that sells computers and accessories). Choose iTunes⇨Shop for iTunes Products (Mac) or Help⇨Shop for iTunes Products (Windows) to reach the Apple Store online.

The discs are called *CD-R* because they use a recordable format related to commercial audio CDs (which are not recordable, of course). You can also create a disc in the MP3 format (conforming to the ISO 9660 standard) by creating a CD-R with data rather than music, which is useful for backing up a music library or making discs for MP3 CD players.

Many CD burners, such as the Apple SuperDrive, also burn *CD-RWs* (recordable, read-write discs) that you can erase and reuse, but CD players don't always recognize them as music CDs. Some burners can create data DVD-Rs and DVD-RWs also, which are useful for holding data files, but you can use these discs only with computers that have DVD drives. Some commercial DVD players won't recognize a data DVD-R or DVD-RW, but may still recognize an MP3 DVD-R.

You can play MP3 files burned on a CD-R in the MP3 format on any MP3 disc player, on combination CD/MP3 players, on many DVD players, and of course on computers that recognize MP3 CDs (including computers with iTunes).

TECHNICAL STUFF

The little Red Book that launched an industry

The typical audio CD and CD-R uses the CD-DA (Compact Disc-Digital Audio) format, which is known as *Red Book*. This book isn't something from Chairman Mao but is a document (published in 1980) that provides the specifications for the standard CD developed by Sony and Philips. According to legend, this document was in a binder with a red cover.

Also according to legend, in 1979, Norio Ohga, honorary chairman and former CEO of Sony (who's also a maestro conductor), overruled his engineers and insisted that the CD format be able to hold Beethoven's *Ninth Symphony*

(which is 74 minutes and 42 seconds — now the standard length of a Red Book audio CD).

CD-DA defines audio data digitized at 44,100 samples per second (44.1 kHz) and in a range of 65,536 possible values (16 bits). The format for the audio is called PCM (*pulse code modulation*).

To import music into the computer from an audio CD, you have to convert the music to digital sound files by a program, such as iTunes. When you burn an audio CD, iTunes converts the sound files back into the CD-DA format while it burns the disc.

What You Can Fit on a CD-R or DVD

You can fit up to 74 minutes of music on a high-quality CD-R; most can go as high as 80 minutes. The sound files on your hard drive might take up more space than 650MB if they're uncompressed, but you can still fit 74 minutes (or 80 minutes, depending on the disc) because the CD format stores information without error-correction data.

If you burn music to a CD-R in the MP3 format, the disc can hold more than 12 hours worth of music. You read that right — 12 hours on one disc. Now you know why MP3 discs are popular. MP3 discs are essentially CD-Rs with MP3 files stored on them.

If you have a DVD burner, such as the Apple SuperDrive, you can burn data DVD-Rs or DVD-RWs to use with other computers. This approach is suitable for making backup copies of media files (or any data files). A DVD-R can hold about 4,700,000,000 bytes (about 4.38GB).

Creating a Burn Playlist

To burn a CD (actually a CD-R, but most people refer to recordable CD-R discs as *CDs*), you must first define a playlist for the CD. See Chapter 10 to find out how to create a playlist. You can use songs encoded in any format that iTunes supports; however, you get higher-quality music with the uncompressed AIFF and WAV formats or with the Apple Lossless format.

If your playlist includes music purchased from the iTunes Music Store or other online stores in the protected AAC encoding format, some rules might apply. For example, as of this writing, the iTunes Music Store allows you to burn seven copies of the same playlist containing protected songs to an audio CD, but no more.

You can get around this limitation by creating or using a new playlist, copying the protected songs to the new playlist, and then burning more CDs with the new playlist.

Calculating how much music to use

When you create an audio CD playlist, you find out how many songs can fit on the CD by totaling the durations of the songs, using time as your measure. You can see the size of a playlist by selecting it; the bottom of the iTunes window shows the number of songs, the amount in time, and the amount in megabytes for the currently selected playlist, as shown in Figure 14-1.

Figure 14-1:
Check the
duration of
the playlist
below the
song list.

	Name	Time	Artist	Album	Genre	My Rating
1	Diamond Joe (Previously Un...	2:22	Dylan, Bob	Exclusive	Rock	
2	Electrical Storm (William Or...	4:39	U2	The Best of 1990-2000	Rock	
3	Miss Sarajevo (Single Radio ...	4:32	U2	The Best of 1990-2000	Rock	
4	The Hands That Built Ameri...	4:58	U2	The Best of 1990-2000	Rock	
5	Hold Me, Thrill Me, Kiss Me,...	4:45	U2	The Best of 1990-2000	Rock	
6	Hand of Kindness	6:28	Thompson, Richard	Exclusive Songs for iTunes – ...	Rock	
7	Put It There Pal	10:20	Thompson, Richard	Exclusive Songs for iTunes – ...	Rock	
8	Two Left Feet	4:05	Thompson, Richard	Exclusive Songs for iTunes – ...	Rock	
9	Simple Sister	5:52	Procol Harum	Greatest Hits	Rock	
10	Benedictus	4:24	Strawbs	20th Century Masters – The ...	Rock	
11	When You Say	4:32	Fleetwood Mac	Then Play On	Rock	
12	Like Crying Like Dying	2:24	Fleetwood Mac	Then Play On	Rock	
13	Before the Beginning	3:26	Fleetwood Mac	Then Play On	Rock	
14	Sgt. Pepper's Lonely Hearts ...	2:28	McCartney, Paul	Live 8 (Hyde Park, London) – ...	Rock	
15	The Long and Winding Road	3:39	McCartney, Paul	Live 8 (Hyde Park, London) – ...	Rock	

15 songs, 1.1 hours, 65.3 MB

In Figure 14-1, the selected playlist takes 1.1 hours (exactly 1:08:54) to play, so it fits on a standard audio CD. (The 15 songs take up only 65.3MB of hard drive space; they were purchased from the iTunes Music Store and encoded in the compressed and protected AAC format.)

A one-hour playlist of AIFF-encoded music, which might occupy over 600MB of hard drive space, also fits on a standard audio CD. The amount you can fit on a standard audio CD depends on the duration, not the hard drive space occupied by the music files. Although a CD holds between 650MB and 700MB (depending on the disc), the music is stored in a special format known as CD-DA (or Red Book) that fills byte sectors without error-correction and checksum information. Thus, you can fit about 90MB more — 740MB total — of AIFF-encoded music on a 650MB disc. We typically put 1.1 hours (about 66 minutes) of music on a 74-minute or an 80-minute CD-R with many minutes to spare.

Always use the actual duration in hours, minutes, and seconds to calculate how much music you can fit on an audio CD — either 74 or 80 minutes for blank CD-Rs. Leave at least one extra minute to account for the gaps between songs.

You do the *opposite* for an MP3 CD or DVD data disc — you use the actual megabytes to calculate how many song files can fit on a disc — up to 700MB for a blank CD-R. You can fit lots more music on an MP3 CD-R because you use MP3-encoded songs rather than uncompressed AIFF songs.

If you have too many songs in the playlist to fit on a CD, iTunes burns as many songs in the playlist as will fit on the CD (either audio or MP3). Then it asks you to insert another CD to continue burning the remaining songs in the playlist.

If you include in a burn playlist a very long song that you purchased from the iTunes Music Store, you see a dialog telling you to put that long song in its own playlist. Then burn that single-song playlist separately.

Importing music for an audio CD-R

Before you rip an audio CD of songs that you want to burn to an audio CD-R, you might want to change the import settings. Check out Chapter 19 if you need to do this. Use the AIFF, WAV, or Apple Lossless encoders for songs from audio CDs if you want to burn your own audio CDs with music at its highest quality.

AIFF is the standard digital format for uncompressed sound on a Mac, and you can't go wrong with it. WAV is basically the same thing for Windows. The Apple Lossless encoder provides CD-quality sound in a file size that's about 55 to 60 percent of the size of an AIFF- or WAV-encoded file. Both the AIFF encoder and the WAV encoder offer the same custom settings for sample rate, sample size, and channels, which you can set by choosing Custom from the Settings pop-up menu in the Importing section of the Advanced pane of iTunes Preferences. You can choose the automatic settings, and iTunes automatically detects the proper sample rate, size, and channels from the source. Apple Lossless is always set to automatic.

Songs that you purchase from the iTunes Music Store come in a protected format encoded with the AAC encoder. You can't convert this format to anything else, but you can still burn the songs onto CDs and the quality of the result on CD is acceptable. Audio books also come in a protected format that can't be converted, but you can burn them onto CDs with acceptable quality.

The AAC encoder creates an audio file that is similar in audio quality to one created by the MP3 encoder, but takes up less space; both are acceptable to most CD listeners. We think AAC offers a decent trade-off of space and quality and is suitable (although not as good as AIFF or Apple Lossless) for burning to an audio CD. For a complete description of these encoders, see Chapter 18.

Switching import encoders for MP3 CD-R

MP3 discs are essentially CD-Rs with MP3 files stored on them using the ISO 9660 file structure that is standard across computers and players. Consumer MP3 CD players are readily available in consumer electronics stores, including hybrid models that play both audio CDs and MP3 CDs.

You can fit an average of 12 hours of music on a CD using the MP3 format although this amount can vary widely (along with audio quality) depending on the encoding options and settings you choose. For example, you might be able to fit up to 20 hours of mono (monaural) recordings because they use only one channel and carry less information. On the other hand, if you encode stereo recordings at high bit rates (above 192 bits per second), you fit less than 12 hours. If you rip an audio CD, you can set the importing options to precisely the type of MP3 file you want; see Chapter 19.

You can use only MP3-encoded songs to burn an MP3 CD-R. Any songs not encoded in MP3 are skipped and not burned to the CD-R. Audible books and spoken-word titles are provided in an audio format that uses security technologies, including encryption, to protect purchased content. You can't burn an MP3 CD-R with Audible files; any Audible files in a burn playlist are skipped when you burn an MP3 CD-R.

Setting the Burning Preferences

Burning a CD is a simple process, and getting it right the first time is a good idea because when you burn a CD-R, it's done one time — right or wrong. You can't erase content on a CD-R like you can with a CD-RW. Because you can't play a CD-RW in as many CD players, if you want to burn an audio CD, we recommend using a CD-R. Fortunately, CD-Rs are inexpensive, so you won't be out more than a few cents if you burn a bad one. (Besides, they're good as coasters for coffee tables.)

You should set the following options to ensure that you burn your CD right the first time:

- **Sound Check:** Musicians do a sound check before every performance to check the volume of microphones and instruments and their effect on the listening environment. The aptly named Sound Check option in the Burning preferencesdialog (see Figure 14-2) lets you do a sound check on your tunes to bring them in line, volume-wise.

- **A gap between songs:** Another professional touch is to add an appropriate gap between songs, just like commercial CDs.

- **The disc format:** Choosing the appropriate disc format is perhaps the most important choice. Decide whether you're burning an audio CD (CD-R), an MP3 CD (CD-R), or a Data CD (CD-R) or DVD (DVD-R or DVD-RW). Your choice depends on what type of player you are using, or whether you are making a data backup of files rather than a disc that plays in a player.

- **The recording speed:** iTunes typically detects the rating of a blank CD-R and adjusts the recording speed to fit. However, if your blank CD-Rs are rated for a slower speed than your burner or if you have problems creating CD-Rs, you can change the recording speed setting to match the CD's rating.

Follow these steps to set the sound check, the length of the gap between the songs, the disc format, and the recording speed:

1. **Choose iTunes⇨Preferences (Mac) or Edit⇨Preferences (Windows), click the Advanced tab, and then click the Burning tab.**

    The burning preferences appear, as shown in Figure 14-2.

2. **Choose a specific recording speed or the Maximum Possible option from the Preferred Speed pop-up menu.**

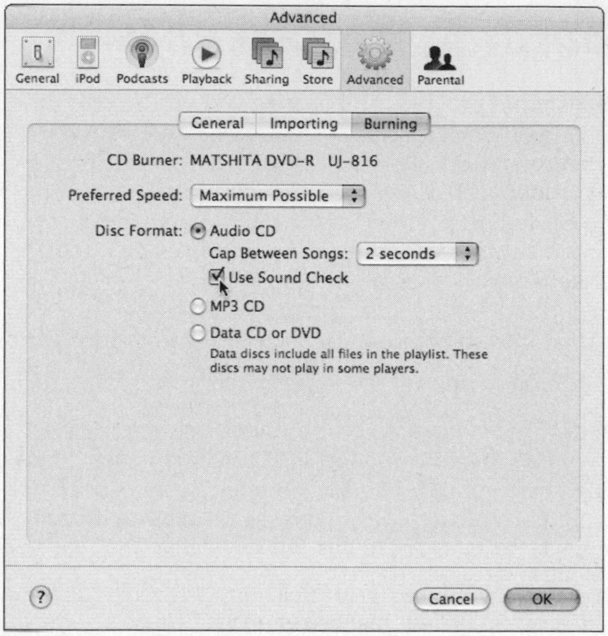

Advanced

General | iPod | Podcasts | Playback | Sharing | Store | Advanced | Parental

General | Importing | **Burning**

CD Burner: MATSHITA DVD–R UJ–816

Preferred Speed: Maximum Possible

Disc Format: ● Audio CD
             Gap Between Songs: 2 seconds
             ☑ Use Sound Check
      ○ MP3 CD
      ○ Data CD or DVD
        Data discs include all files in the playlist. These
        discs may not play in some players.

?   Cancel   OK

Figure 14-2:
The Burning
preferences
dialog.

3. **Choose a disc format:**

- **Audio CD:** Burn a normal audio CD of up to 74 or 80 minutes (depending on the type of blank CD-R) using any iTunes-supported music files, including songs bought from the iTunes Music Store. Although connoisseurs of music might use AIFF- or WAV-encoded music to burn an audio CD, you can also use songs in the AAC and MP3 formats.

- **MP3 CD:** Burn an MP3 CD with songs encoded in the MP3 format. No other formats are supported for MP3 CDs.

- **Data CD or DVD:** Burn a data CD-R, CD-RW, DVD-R, or DVD-RW with the music files. You can use any encoding formats for the songs. *Important:* Data discs won't play on most consumer CD players. They are meant for use with computers. However, data discs are good choices for storing backup copies of music bought from the iTunes Music Store.

4. **(Audio CDs only) Select the Use Sound Check option.**

   Note: This option, for Audio CDs only, works regardless of whether you're already using the Sound Check option in the Playback preferences for iTunes playback. You can select this option for burning without ever changing the preferences for iTunes playback.

5. **(Audio CDs only) Choose an amount from the Gap between Songs pop-up menu.**

You can choose from a gap of 0 to 5 seconds. We recommend leaving the menu set to the default setting of 2 seconds.

6. **Click OK.**

Burning a Disc

After you set the burning preferences, you're ready to start burning. Follow these steps to burn a disc:

1. **Select the playlist and then click the Burn Disc button.**

   The Burn Disc button replaces the Browse button in the upper-right corner of the iTunes window whenever you select a playlist (refer to Figure 14-1).

   A message appears telling you to insert a blank disc.

2. **Insert a blank disc (label side up).**

   iTunes immediately checks the media and displays a message in the status window that the disc is ready to burn.

3. **Click the Burn Disc button again.**

   This time, the button has a radiation symbol. The burn process begins. The "radioactive" button rotates while the burning takes place, and a progress bar appears with the names of the songs displayed while they burn to the disc.

   When iTunes finishes burning the disc, iTunes chimes, and the disc is mounted on the Desktop.

4. **Eject the newly burned disc from your drive and then test it.**

Burning takes several minutes. You can cancel the operation at any time by clicking the X next to the progress bar, but canceling the operation isn't like undoing the burn. If the burn has already started, you can't use that CD-R or DVD-R again.

If the playlist has more music than can fit on the disc using the chosen format, iTunes burns as much as possible from the beginning of the playlist and then asks you to insert another disc to burn the rest. To calculate the amount of music in a playlist, turn to the section, "Calculating how much music to use," earlier in this chapter.

Spoken word fans: Audible audio books with chapter markers are burned onto a CD with each chapter as a separate track.

If you choose the MP3 CD format, iTunes skips over any songs in the playlist that aren't in this format.

Printing Song and Album Information

Putting music on a blank CD-R doesn't change the disc's look in any way, so if you misplace it, how do you know it isn't just another blank? Put it inside a case and include something in print that identifies it.

Don't delete your burn playlist yet, though. You can print the CD jewel case insert, song list, and album notes for the CD you just burned. You can even print the cover art that the iTunes Music Store provides with your purchased songs (even artwork that you add yourself, as described in Chapter 9). If you have a color printer, you can print gorgeous color inserts for your CDs. If you don't have a suitable printer, you can save the printed version as a Portable Document Format (PDF) file that you can print at a Kinko's or similar copy shop.

Select the playlist and choose File⇨Print to see the iTunes Print dialog (as shown in Figure 14-3). You can see all the choices you have for CD jewel case inserts, song listings, and album notes as well as a preview of how they look when printed.

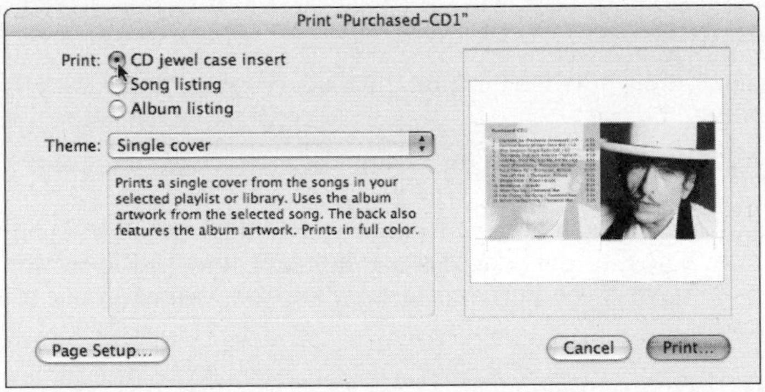

Figure 14-3:
Print a CD
jewel case
insert
directly from
iTunes. It
can include
cover art
provided
with songs.

Print "Purchased-CD1"

Print: ○ CD jewel case insert
○ Song listing
○ Album listing

Theme: Single cover

Prints a single cover from the songs in your selected playlist or library. Uses the album artwork from the selected song. The back also features the album artwork. Prints in full color.

Page Setup...   Cancel   Print...

Printing CD jewel case inserts

Everyone calls the standard CD case a jewel case even though the only precious element in the package is the music. *Jewel cases* have slots for inserting a printed insert or booklet. You can print your own jewel case insert directly from iTunes using the burn playlist.

To print a CD jewel case, select the album you want to print the artwork for, and follow these steps:

1. **Choose File⇨Print.**

2. **In the iTunes Print dialog, select the CD Jewel Case Insert option.**

3. **Choose a theme from the Theme pop-up menu.**

   Choose a theme such as Text Only (without song artwork), Mosaic (with artwork from songs arranged in a mosaic), Single Cover (with one song's artwork), and so on, as shown in Figure 14-4.

Figure 14-4:
Choose a
theme for a
CD jewel
case insert.
Mosaic
(Black &
White) is
shown in
the preview.

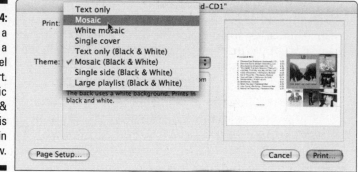

4. **(Optional) Click the Page Setup button to set page layout options, such as landscape or portrait orientation.**

   The CD jewel case themes automatically set the proper orientation, but you can change them in the Page Setup dialog.

5. **Click the Print button and then follow your normal printing procedures.**

Printing song lists and album notes

Cover art for the jewel case is a nice decoration, but if you choose an art-based theme rather than one that lists the songs, you might still want another sheet with a song list to tell which track is which. You might also want a more detailed song list that includes information for each song, such as the composer, the duration, the original album, and perhaps even the rating you assigned in iTunes.

To print a song list, follow these steps:

1. **Choose File⇨Print.**

2. **Select the Song Listing option.**

3. **Choose one of the following themes for the song listing from the Theme pop-up menu:**

   • **Songs:** This theme prints a column for each song name, duration, artist, and album title.

   • **User Ratings:** This theme prints the same columns as the Songs theme and adds a ratings column with the ratings that you assign in iTunes. This theme prints in landscape orientation.

   • **Dates Played:** This theme prints the same columns as the Songs theme and adds columns for the play count and the date last played, set by iTunes when you play songs. This theme prints in landscape orientation.

   • **Custom:** This theme prints the columns as they're set in the iTunes Song List view. You can print any piece of information about the songs that iTunes stores, such as composer, genre, and year. See Chapter 8 to add or change the viewing options for columns in the Song List view.

4. **Click the Print button and then follow your normal printing procedures.**

To print a catalog-style album listing, choose the Album Listing option in the dialog (refer to Figure 14-3). This option prints the album title, artist, song names, and song lengths.

Need a printed list of what's in your library? You can use the Song listing or Album listing options to print a listing of all the content in your iTunes library, rather than just a playlist. Select the Library option in the Source pane. Then choose File⇨Print and choose your printing options. If you want to save paper and create an electronic version, create a PDF file in the Mac or Windows Print dialog.

If you want to print liner notes in a layout that iTunes doesn't offer in its printing themes, you can export the song information to a text file and then edit that information in a word processor or page layout program to make liner notes for the CD. iTunes exports all the song information for a single song, a playlist, an album, songs by an artist, or songs in the library into a text file. Follow these steps:

1. **Select the album, songs, or playlist.**

2. **Choose File⇨Export Song List.**

3. **Browse your hard drive and choose a location to store the song list.**

4. **In the Export Song List dialog, select the Plain Text option from the Format pop-up menu.**

   The Plain Text option is the right choice for you unless you use a double-byte language, such as Japanese or Chinese, for which the Unicode option is the right choice.

5. **Click the Export button.**

To print high-quality labels for CD and DVDs and jewel case covers and inserts using an exported song list, try the Discus Labeling Software (www.magicmouse.com).

Troubleshooting Burns

Murphy's Law applies to everything, even something as simple as burning a CD-R. Don't think for a moment that you're immune to the whims and treacheries of Murphy (no one really knows who Murphy is) who, in all his infinite wisdom, pronounced that anything that *can* go wrong *will* go wrong (and usually at the least convenient time). In this section, we cover some of the most common problems that you might encounter when burning discs.

The best way to test your newly burned disc is to pop it right back into your computer's drive — or, if it's an audio CD, try it on a consumer CD player. On most CD players, an audio CD-R plays just like any commercial audio CD. MP3 CDs play fine on consumer MP3 CD players and also work in computers with CD-ROM and DVD drives.

If the disc works on the computer but not on a commercial CD player, you might have a compatibility problem with the commercial player and CD-R. We have a five-year-old CD player that doesn't play CD-Rs very well, and car players sometimes have trouble with them.

The following list gives some typical problems, along with the solutions, that you might run into when burning a CD:

✔ *Problem:* The disc won't burn.

   Solution: Perhaps you have a bum disc. Hey, it happens. Try using another disc or burning at a slower speed.

✔ *Problem:* In a consumer CD player, the disc doesn't play or stutters while playing.

Solution: This happens often with older consumer players that don't play CD-Rs well, and with some players that are "fussy" about reading less expensive CD-Rs or certain brands. Try the disc in your computer's CD-ROM or DVD drive. If it works there and you set the format to Audio CD, you probably have a compatibility problem with your consumer player.

✔ ***Problem:*** The disc doesn't show tracks on a consumer CD player or ejects immediately.

Solution: Be sure to use the proper disc format. The Audio CD format works in just about all consumer CD players that can play CD-Rs. MP3 CDs work in consumer MP3 CD players and computer CD-ROM and DVD drives. Data CDs or DVDs work only in computer drives.

✔ ***Problem:*** Some songs in your playlist were skipped and not burned onto the disc.

Solution: Audio CD-Rs burn with songs encoded in any format, but you can use only MP3-encoded songs to burn an MP3 CD-R. Any songs not encoded in MP3 — including songs purchased from the iTunes Music Store in protected AAC format — are skipped when burning MP3 CDs. (Any Audible files are also skipped, which can't be put onto an MP3 CD.) If your playlist for an audio CD-R includes music purchased from the iTunes Music Store, some rules might apply — see the section, "Creating a Burn Playlist," earlier in this chapter.

Part III
Playing Your iPod

The 5th Wave   By Rich Tennant

@RICHTENNANT

"I know you can do a lot with an iPod, but dressing one up in G.I. Joe clothes and calling it 'Sarge' is something I never thought of."

In this part . . .

Part III focuses on playing content with your iPod, connecting it to stereos and TVs, and fine-tuning the sound.

✔ Chapter 15 shows you how to locate and play songs, audio books, podcasts, and videos on your iPod; create playlists on the fly; and adjust the iPod's volume.

✔ Chapter 16 is about playing music over home stereos and portable speakers with your iPod, connecting your iPod to a television or video equipment to display video and photos, and using cool accessories for the iPod at home.

✔ Chapter 17 tells you about the iTunes and iPod equalizers and fine-tuning music playback in iTunes and on your iPod.

Chapter 15

Playing iPod Content

For a music lover, nothing compares with the feeling of having so many song choices at your fingertips. Rather than sitting back like a couch potato and soaking up the preprogrammed sounds of radio or CDs, you control the iPod playback and you can pick any song that you want to hear at any time. Shuffle through songs randomly to get an idea of how wide your music choices are or just to surprise yourself or others. Or follow a thread of musical ideas, such as The Kingsmen's version of "Louie Louie" through "All Day and All of the Night" by The Kinks, "Dirty Water" by The Standells, "Little Bit of Soul" by The Music Explosion, The Troggs' "Wild Thing," all the way to the version of "Wild Thing" by Jimi Hendrix.

You might have spent a few minutes creating playlists in iTunes that barely scratch the surface of the huge library that you have in your hands. Now how do you switch songs or playlists while maintaining your jogging pace or avoiding wrecks on the freeway?

With your iPod, you can locate and play music easily, browsing by artist and album, and even by composer — the only exception is iPod shuffle. Selecting a playlist is simple, and if you don't have playlists from iTunes (or you don't want to hear those playlists), you can create a temporary On-The-Go playlist. This chapter shows you how to locate and play content on any iPod. If you have an iPod shuffle, skip to the "Playing an iPod shuffle" section.

Locating Songs on Your iPod

With so many songs on your iPod, finding a particular one can be hard — like finding a needle in a haystack or even trying to find "Needle in a Haystack" by The Velvelettes in a Motown catalog. You can locate songs by searching for artist (or composer), genre, album, playlist.

You can also search for audio books and podcasts by artist (author's name) or album (title).

By artist

Your iPod organizes music by artist, and within each artist by album. Follow these steps to locate a song by artist and then by album:

1. **Select the Music item from the iPod main menu.**

   Scroll the main menu until Music is highlighted, as shown in Figure 15-1, and then press the Select button — the center button in the scroll wheel that selects items in the menu.

   The Music menu appears, as shown in Figure 15-2.

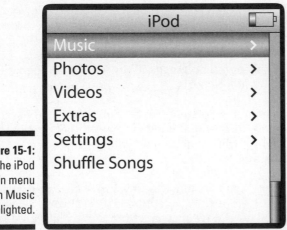

Figure 15-1: The iPod main menu with Music highlighted.

Figure 15-2:
The iPod
Music
menu.

Music menu showing: Playlists, Artists, Albums, Songs, Podcasts, Genres, Composers, Audiobooks

2. **Select the Artists item.**

   The Artists item is second from the top of the Music menu. Scroll the menu until Artists is highlighted and then press the Select button.

   The Artists menu appears.

   To browse by genre, select the Genres item. Then select a genre from the Genres menu to get a list of artists that have songs in that genre (in alphabetical order by artist name).

3. **Select an artist from the Artists menu.**

   The artists' names are listed in alphabetical order by last name or the first word of a group. *Note:* Any leading *The* is ignored, so that *The Beatles* appears where *Beatles* is in the list. Scroll the Artists menu until the artist name (such as *Radiohead* or *Bowie, David*) is highlighted and then press the Select button.

   The artist's menu of albums appears. For example, the Radiohead menu in our iPod includes the selections All, *OK Computer,* and *The Bends;* the Bowie, David menu includes All, *Heroes, Space Oddity, Ziggy Stardust,* and many more.

4. **Select the All item or the name of an album from the artist's menu.**

   The All item is at the top of the artist's menu and should already be highlighted. You can press the Select button to select it or scroll until an album name (or podcast or audio book title) is highlighted and then press the Select button.

Note: Albums are listed in alphabetical order based on the first word. A leading *A* or *The* isn't ignored, so the album *The Basement Tapes* is listed *after* the album *Stage Fright*.

A song list appears after you select either an album choice or All.

5. **Select a song from the list.**

The songs in the album list are in album order (the order that they appear on the album); in the All list, songs are listed in album order for each album.

By album

Follow these steps to directly locate a song by album:

1. **Select the Music item from the iPod main menu.**

Scroll the main menu until Music is highlighted and then press the Select button.

The Music menu appears.

2. **Select the Albums item.**

Scroll the Music menu until Albums is highlighted and then press the Select button.

The Albums menu appears (see Figure 15-3).

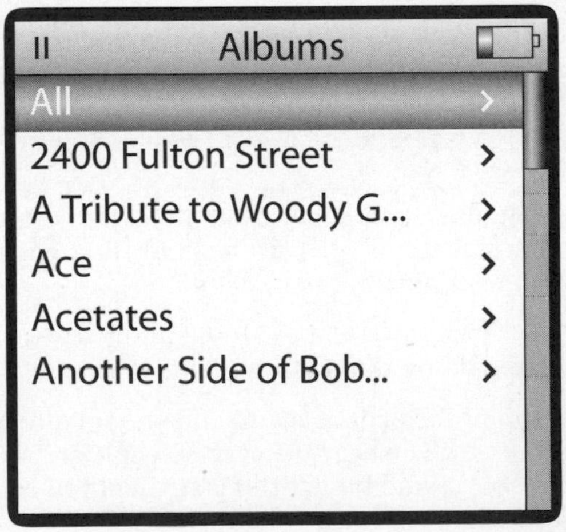

‖	Albums	▭
All		**›**
2400 Fulton Street		›
A Tribute to Woody G...		›
Ace		›
Acetates		›
Another Side of Bob...		›

Figure 15-3:
The Albums
menu.

Select the Composers item to choose a composer and then select a composer from the Composers menu to get a list of songs for that composer.

3. **Select an album from the Albums menu.**

The albums are listed in alphabetical order (without any reference to artist, which might make identification difficult). The order is by first word; a leading *A, An,* or *The* isn't ignored, so the album *The Natch'l Blues* is listed after *Taj's Blues* in the T section rather than the N section. Scroll the Albums menu until the album name is highlighted and then press the Select button.

A song list appears.

You can also find podcasts and audio books in the Albums menu — the album name is the podcast name or audio book title. After selecting a podcast, a list of the podcast's episodes appear by date of release; after selecting an audio book, a list of the audio book episodes (as in Part 1, Part 2, and so on.) are listed in the order that they should be read.

4. Select a song from the list.

The songs in the album list are in the order that they appear on the album. Scroll the list to highlight the song name and then press the Select button.

The artist and song names appear.

By playlist

When you automatically update your iPod from your entire iTunes library, all your playlists in iTunes are copied to the iPod. You can choose to update your iPod with only specified playlists, as we describe in Chapter 12.

Playlists make playing a selection of content in a specific order easy. The playlist plays from the first item selected to the end of the playlist. You can combine songs, podcast episodes, audio books, and videos in a playlist. However, videos are skipped on iPods that can't play video.

Follow these steps to locate a playlist on your iPod:

1. Select the Music item from the iPod main menu.

Scroll the main menu until Music is highlighted and then press the Select button.

The Music menu appears.

2. Select the Playlists item.

The Playlists item is at the top of the Music menu and might already be highlighted. If not, scroll the Music menu until Playlists is highlighted and then press the Select button.

The Playlists menu appears (see Figure 15-4).

Figure 15-4:
The Playlists
menu.

3. **Select a playlist.**

   The playlists are listed in alphabetical order. Scroll the Playlists menu to highlight the playlist name and then press the Select button.

   A list of songs in the playlist appears.

4. **Select a song from the list.**

   The songs in the playlist are in *playlist order* (the order defined for the playlist in iTunes). Scroll up or down the list to highlight the song you want.

Playing a Song

After scrolling the song list until the song name is highlighted, press the Select button to play the selected song or press the Play/Pause button — either button starts playing the song. When the song finishes, the iPod continues playing the next song in the song list.

While a song is playing, the artist name and song name appear along with the album cover (if you have a color-display iPod), and you can use the scroll wheel to adjust the volume. See the section, "Adjusting and Limiting the Volume," later in this chapter.

Press the Play/Pause button while a song is playing to pause the playback.

Repeating songs

If you want to drive yourself crazy repeating the same song over and over, the iPod is happy to oblige. (You might want to try repeating "They're Coming to Take Me Away, Ha-Haaa" by Napoleon XIV, a favorite from the *Dr. Demento* album — and perhaps they will come.) More than likely, you'll want to repeat a sequence of songs, which you can easily do.

You can set the iPod to automatically repeat a single song by following these steps:

1. **Locate and play a song.**

2. **While the song plays, press the Menu button repeatedly to return to the main menu and then select the Settings item.**

   The Settings menu appears.

3. **Scroll the Settings menu until Repeat is highlighted.**

   The Repeat setting displays Off next to it.

4. **Press the Select button once (Off changes to One) to repeat one song.**

   If you press the button more than once, keep pressing until One appears.

You can also press the Previous/Rewind button to repeat a song.

To repeat all the songs in the selected album or playlist, follow these steps:

1. **Locate and play a song in the album or playlist.**

2. **While the song plays, press the Menu button repeatedly to return to the main menu and then select the Settings item.**

   The Settings menu appears.

3. **Scroll the Settings menu until the Repeat item is highlighted.**

   The Repeat setting displays Off next to it.

4. **Press the Select button twice (Off changes to All) to repeat all the songs in the album or playlist.**

Shuffling the song order

Maybe you want your song selections to be surprising and unpredictable, and you want your iPod to read your mind, as the Apple ads suggest. You can *shuffle* the playback of songs so that they play in random order (like an automated radio station without a disk jockey or program guide). With the shuffle feature, you can mix up your song collection and play it back in a jumbled order. See for yourself whether your iPod knows how to pick good tunes without your help.

To turn your iPod into a random song player so that you have no idea what comes next, choose Shuffle Songs from the main menu. Your iPod starts with a random song and continues to select songs randomly — without ever repeating one — until it plays every song in your library.

Although your iPod might seem to play favorites, the shuffle algorithm is truly random, according to Apple. When an iPod does a shuffle, it reorders the songs (like shuffling a deck of cards), and then it plays them back in the new order. If you listen for as long as it takes to complete the list, you hear every song just once.

You can also shuffle songs within an album or playlist, which gives you some control over random playback. For example, you could create a smart playlist for all jazz songs and then shuffle the songs within that jazz playlist.

Follow these steps to shuffle songs in an album or playlist:

1. **Locate and play a song in the album or playlist.**

2. **While the song plays, press the Menu button repeatedly to return to the main menu and then select the Settings item.**

   The Settings menu appears.

3. **Scroll the Settings menu until the Shuffle item is highlighted.**

   The Shuffle setting displays Off next to it.

4. **Press the Select button once (Off changes to Songs) to shuffle the songs in the selected album or playlist.**

You can set your iPod to repeat an entire album or playlist but still shuffle the playing order so that the order is different each time you hear it.

What if you want to play albums randomly, but you don't like when the songs in an album aren't played in proper album order? To shuffle all the albums in your iPod while still playing the songs in normal album order, follow these steps:

1. **Press the Menu button repeatedly to return to the main menu and then select the Settings item.**

   The Settings menu appears.

2. **Scroll the Settings menu until the Shuffle item is highlighted.**

   The Shuffle setting displays Off next to it.

3. **Press the Select button twice (Off changes to Albums) to shuffle the albums without shuffling the songs within each album.**

When the iPod is set to shuffle, it won't repeat a song until it has played through the entire album, playlist, or library.

By default, only songs are included in iPod shuffling. However, you can select podcast episodes, audio books, and videos in iTunes and set an option to include them in shuffles. To do this in iTunes

1. **Select the video, podcast episode, or audio book episode.**

2. **Choose File⇨Get Info.**

3. **Click the Options tab.**

4. **Deselect the Skip When Shuffling option.**

   The next time you update your iPod, any items with this option turned off are included in shuffles.

If you want to exclude a song from shuffles, select the song in iTunes, choose File⇨Get Info, click the Options tab, and then select the Skip When Shuffling option.

Playing Podcasts

Podcasts, naturally, have their own menu on an iPod. Podcasts are organized by podcast name (which is like an album name), and podcast episodes are listed within each podcast in the order that they were released (by date).

To play a podcast episode, follow these steps:

1. **Select the Music item from the iPod main menu.**

   Scroll the main menu until Music is highlighted and then press the Select button.

   The Music menu appears.

2. **Select the Podcasts item.**

The Podcasts item is fifth from the top of the Music menu. Scroll the menu until Podcasts is highlighted and then press the Select button.

The Podcasts menu appears (see Figure 15-5).

Figure 15-5:
The
Podcasts
menu.

3. **Select a podcast from the Podcasts menu.**

The podcast names are listed in alphabetical order by first word. ***Note:*** Any leading *The* isn't ignored, which is why *The Flying Other Brothers-Music Podcast* appears after the *Rockument* podcast. Scroll the Podcasts menu until the podcast name is highlighted and then press the Select button.

The podcast's menu of episodes appears. For example, the *Rockument* podcast menu in our iPod includes the selections "Ballad Roots of California Folk-Rock" and "Americana Roots of California Folk-Rock" listed in order by date from newest to oldest. The *McGuinn's Folk Den* podcast lists the episodes "Molly Malone" first (the newest as of this writing) followed by older episodes going back to the first one we downloaded ("In the Evenin'").

4. **Select and play an episode from the podcast's menu.**

Scroll the episode list until the episode name you want is highlighted and then press the Select button to play the episode.

While a podcast episode is playing, the podcast name and episode title appear, along with the podcast's graphic image (similar to an album cover) if you have a color-display iPod. You can use the scroll wheel to adjust the volume. See the section, "Adjusting and Limiting the Volume," later in this chapter.

Press the Play/Pause button when a podcast episode is playing to pause the playback.

Podcast episodes are automatically set to remember the playback position when you pause an episode. This feature lets you play part of an episode in iTunes and pause, update your iPod, and continue playing the episode on your iPod from where you left off. This feature also works in the opposite way: If you start playing an episode on your iPod and then pause, the podcast episode remembers the playback position so that you can continue playing it in iTunes from where you left off.

To turn off the playback feature

1. **Select a podcast episode in iTunes.**

2. **Choose File⇨Get Info.**

3. **Click the Options tab.**

4. **Deselect the Remember Playback Position option.**

    This option works with any track in your library, letting you resume playback on any song or video as well.

When you update your iPod, any played episodes are deleted if you set iTunes to keep only your unplayed episodes. To make sure that a particular episode stays on your iPod, select it in iTunes, Control-click (Mac) or right-click (Windows) the episode, and choose Mark as Unplayed. You can also change your iPod's preferences for updating with podcasts. See Chapter 12 for details.

Playing Audio Books

Audio books also have their own menu on an iPod. Audio books are organized by title (which also appears in the Albums menu), and episodes of the audio book are listed in the order that they should be read (as in Part 1, Part 2, and so on).

To play an audio book episode, follow these steps:

1. **Select the Music item from the iPod main menu.**

   Scroll the main menu until Music is highlighted and then press the Select button.

   The Music menu appears.

2. **Select the Audiobooks item.**

   The Audiobooks item is at the bottom of the Music menu. Scroll the menu until Audiobooks is highlighted and then press the Select button.

   The Audiobooks menu appears (see Figure 15-6).

Figure 15-6:
The Audiobooks menu.

3. **Select an audio book episode from the Audiobooks menu.**

   The audio book episodes are listed in proper order for each book, with each book title in alphabetical order. *Note:* Like in song titles, any leading *The* isn't ignored, which is why *The Hitchhiker's Guide to the Galaxy: The Tertiary Phase* by Douglas Adams appears below the *Mao II* by Don DeLillo. Scroll the Audiobooks menu until the episode title is highlighted.

4. **Press the Select button to play the highlighted episode.**

While an audio book episode is playing, the book and episode titles appear, along with the book's graphic image (similar to a book cover) on color-display iPods. You can use the scroll wheel to adjust the volume. See the section, "Adjusting and Limiting the Volume," later in this chapter.

Press the Play/Pause button when an audio book episode is playing to pause the playback.

Audio books are automatically set to remember the playback position when you pause an episode. This feature lets you play part of an episode in iTunes and then pause, update your iPod, and continue playing the episode on your iPod from where you left off. This feature also works the opposite way: If you start playing an episode on your iPod and then pause, the audio book episode remembers the playback position so that you can continue playing it in iTunes from where you left off.

To turn off the playback feature

1. **Select the audio book episode in iTunes.**

2. **Choose File⇨Get Info.**

3. **Click the Options tab.**

4. **Deselect the Remember Playback Position option.**

   This option works with any track in your library, letting you resume playback on any song or video as well.

Playing Videos

Fifth-generation iPods can play the videos you store in your iTunes library. You can watch your favorite TV show anytime, anywhere. Check out the NCAA March Madness Basketball Championship while waiting in line for tickets to the next game. Watch Disney animations with your children while waiting for the bus. Get your dose of *The Daily Show with Jon Stewart* while taking the subway to work. Or watch one of our favorites, "Mr. Monk and the Airplane" from the *Monk* TV series, on your next flight.

No video is more portable than iPod video. People are amazed by the crisp, clear picture quality of video iPods, which fit right in your hand and can hold up to 150 hours of video. And it's no wonder that videos have their own menu on the iPod, which helps you distinguish between music videos, TV shows, movies, and video podcasts.

To play a video, follow these steps:

1. **Select the Videos item from the iPod main menu (of course!).**

   Scroll the main menu until Videos is highlighted and then press the Select button.

   The Videos menu appears (shown in Figure 15-7).

Figure 15-7:
The Videos
menu.

2. **Select Video Playlists, Movies, Music Videos, TV Shows, or Video Podcasts.**

   The Videos menu offers these genre choices for types of video. Scroll the menu until the type of video you want is highlighted and then press the Select button. A menu appears for each type of video:

   • **Video Playlists:** The Video Playlists menu lists any video playlists that you created in iTunes and that you enabled for updating to your iPod.

   • **Movies:** The Movies menu lists any videos categorized as Videos by genre.

   • **Music Videos:** The Music Videos menu lists any videos categorized as Music Videos by genre, sorted alphabetically by artist. Scroll to highlight a music video artist and then press the Select button to see a list of music videos by that artist.

   • **TV Shows:** The TV Shows menu lists any videos categorized as TV Shows by genre, sorted alphabetically by show title. Scroll to highlight a show title and then press the Select button to see a list of the TV show episodes.

   • **Video Podcasts:** The Video Podcasts menu lists any videos categorized as Podcast by genre, sorted alphabetically by podcast name. Scroll to highlight a podcast and then press the Select button to see a list of the podcast episodes.

   If you need to change the genre of an item, turn to Chapter 9.

3. **Press the Select button to play the highlighted playlist item, movie, music video, TV episode, or video podcast episode.**

The video fills the screen of your video iPod, and the playback controls work the same way as with songs. You can use the scroll wheel to adjust the volume. See the section, "Adjusting and Limiting the Volume," later in this chapter.

Press the Play/Pause button when a video is playing to pause the playback.

Videos are automatically set to remember the playback position when you pause. This feature lets you play part of a video or TV episode in iTunes and then pause, update your iPod, and continue playing the video or episode on your iPod from where you left off. This feature also works the opposite way: If you start playing a video on your iPod and then pause, the video remembers the playback position so that you can continue playing it in iTunes from where you left off.

To turn off the playback feature

1. **Select the video in iTunes.**
2. **Choose File⇨Get Info.**
3. **Click the Options tab.**
4. **Deselect the Remember Playback Position option.**

   This option works with any track in your library, letting you resume playback on any song as well.

Viewing Photos

You might remember the old days when you carried around fading wallet-sized photo prints that grew creases, rips, and tears the more you showed them around. Now you can dispense with carrying prints with you — all you need is your color-display iPod, which can hold up to 25,000 photos. That's a lot!

Assuming you already organized your photos into albums (Chapter 11) and updated your iPod with photos (Chapter 12), you can see the photos on your iPod by following these steps:

1. **On the iPod, select the Photos menu from the main menu.**

   The Photos menu appears (see Figure 15-8).

Figure 15-8:
The Photos
menu.

2. **Select either Photo Library or the album name in the Photos menu.**

Photo Library displays thumbnail images of all the photos in your iPod. Selecting an album displays thumbnail images of only the photos assigned to that album.

3. **Use the scroll wheel to highlight the photo thumbnail you want and then press the Select button.**

You might have several screens of thumbnails. Use the scroll wheel to scroll through photo thumbnails in a screen and over several screens, or use the Next/Fast-Forward and Previous/Rewind buttons to skip to the next or previous screen. When you select a photo thumbnail, your iPod color display fills up with the photo that you selected.

Setting up a slideshow

Slideshows are a far more entertaining way of showing photos because you can include music and transitions between each pair of photos. You can display your slideshow on the iPod color display or on a television. (See Chapter 16 for details on connecting your iPod to televisions, stereos, video monitors, and video equipment.) Your slideshow settings work with any photo album or with the entire photo library on your iPod.

To set up a slideshow, follow these steps:

1. **On your color-display iPod, select Photos from the main menu and Slideshow Settings from the Photos menu.**

The Slideshow Settings menu appears (see Figure 15-9).

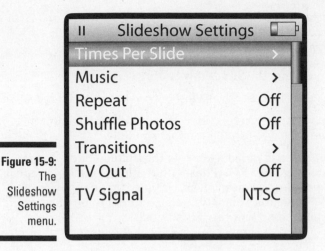

Figure 15-9:
The
Slideshow
Settings
menu.

2. **Select Time Per Slide from the Slideshow Settings menu to set the duration of each slide.**

   You can select choices ranging from 2 to 20 seconds, or Manual to set the slideshow to advance to the next slide only when you click the iPod Next/Fast-Forward button.

3. **Pick music to play by selecting Music from the Slideshow Settings menu and then selecting a playlist.**

   You can choose any playlist in your iPod, including the On-The-Go playlist or the Now Playing choice to play along with your slideshow. You can alternatively choose the From iPhoto option to play the music set in iPhoto (Mac). iPhoto lets you assign an iTunes playlist to an iPhoto album, and that assignment is saved in your iPod. If you copy the playlist to your iPod, it's automatically assigned to the slideshow.

4. **Select a transition to use between photos in the slideshow by choosing Transitions in the Slideshow Settings menu.**

   Wipe Across is our favorite, but you can select versions of the standard Wipe and Push transitions including Push Across, Push Down, Wipe Down, and Wipe Center. Choose Random if you want to use a randomly different transition for each photo change. Choose Off for no transition.

5. **Set the iPod to display the slideshow by choosing TV Out from the Slideshow Settings menu.**

   You have three choices for TV Out:

   • **On** displays the slideshow on a television. (See Chapter 16 for details on the video out connection.) You can also see the slides in large thumbnail form on your iPod, the photo number within the album or library, and the Next and Previous icons.

- **Ask** displays a screen first that asks you to select TV Off or TV On so that you can make the choice each time you play a slideshow.

- **Off** displays the slideshow with full-size images on the iPod.

6. **Select other options from the Slideshow Settings menu:**

- **Repeat:** Select On to repeat the slideshow, or Off to turn off repeating.

- **Shuffle Photos:** Select On to shuffle photos in the slideshow in a random order, or Off to turn off random shuffling.

- **TV Signal:** If traveling or living outside the United States, change your television signal to PAL (Phase Alternating Line) for European and other countries that use PAL as the video standard, or to NTSC (National TV Standards Committee, also referred to humorously as "never the same color") for the U.S. standard.

Playing a slideshow

To play a slideshow, follow these steps:

1. **(Optional) If you want to display the slideshow on a television, connect the color-display iPod to the television first.**

   See Chapter 16 for details on connecting your iPod to a television.

2. **On your iPod, select Photos from the main menu.**

3. **Highlight an album name or Photo Library from the Photos menu and then press the Play/Pause button.**

   Photo Library includes the entire library in the slideshow; highlighting an album includes only the photos in that album.

   You can also start a slideshow by pressing the Select button when you view a photo.

4. **If you previously set the TV Out to Ask, choose TV On or TV Off for your slideshow.**

   TV On displays the slideshow on a television (through the video out connection). You can also see the slides in large thumbnail form on the iPod. TV Off displays the slideshow with full-size images on the iPod.

5. **Use the iPod buttons to navigate your slideshow.**

   If you set Time Per Slide to Manual, press Next/Fast-Forward to move to the next photo and press Previous/Rewind buttons to go back to the previous photo.

If you set Timer Per Slide to a duration, use Play/Pause to pause and play the slideshow.

6. **Press the Menu button to stop the slideshow and return to the Photos menu.**

Creating On-The-Go Playlists

If you don't want to hear the iTunes playlists already in your iPod (or if you haven't created playlists yet), you can create temporary On-The-Go playlists. (*Note:* The On-The-Go playlist feature isn't available in first- and second-generation iPods.) You can create one or more lists of songs, entire albums, podcast episodes, audio books, and videos to play in a certain order, queuing up the items right on the iPod. This option is particularly useful for picking songs to play right before starting to drive a car. (Hel-lo! You shouldn't be messing with your iPod while driving.)

Queued items that you select appear automatically in a playlist called *On-The-Go* on the Playlists menu. (To navigate the Playlists menu, see the "By playlist" section earlier in this chapter.) The On-The-Go playlist remains defined in your iPod until you clear it (delete the songs from the playlist), save it as a new iPod playlist, or update your iPod with new music and playlists — in which case it's copied to your iTunes library and cleared automatically. You can also save any new playlist you create on your iPod in your iTunes library.

Selecting and playing items

To select and then play items on your On-The-Go playlist, follow these steps:

1. **Locate and highlight a song, album title, audio book, podcast episode, or video.**

2. **Press and hold the Select button until the title flashes.**

3. **Repeat Steps 1 and 2 in the order that you want the items played.**

   You can continue to add items to the list of queued items in the On-The-Go playlist at any time. Your iPod keeps track of the On-The-Go playlist until you clear it, save it, or update your iPod automatically.

4. **To play the On-The-Go playlist, scroll the Music menu until Playlists is highlighted and then press the Select button.**

   The Playlists menu appears.

5. **Scroll to the On-The-Go item, which you can always find at the very end of the list in the Playlists menu.**

Deleting items

To delete an item from the On-The-Go playlist in your iPod, follow these steps:

1. **Select the On-The-Go playlist.**

   If you don't see the iPod main menu, repeatedly press the Menu button to return to the main menu. Choose Music from the main menu, scroll the Music menu until Playlists is highlighted, and then press the Select button. The Playlists menu appears. Scroll to the On-The-Go item, which you can always find at the very end of the list in the Playlists menu. Press the Select button, and the list of items in the playlist appears.

2. **Locate and highlight an item to delete it.**

3. **Press and hold the Select button until the title flashes.**

4. **Repeat Steps 2 and 3 for each item you want to delete from the playlist.**

   When you delete items, they disappear from the On-The-Go playlist one by one. The items are still in your iPod — only the playlist is cleared.

Clearing the On-The-Go playlist

To clear the list of queued items in the On-The-Go playlist, follow these steps:

1. **Select the On-The-Go playlist.**

   If you don't see the iPod main menu, repeatedly press the Menu button to return to the main menu. Choose Music from the main menu, scroll the Music menu until Playlists is highlighted, and then press the Select button. The Playlists menu appears. Scroll to the On-The-Go item, which you can always find at the very end of the list in the Playlists menu. Press the Select button, and the list of songs in the playlist appears.

2. **Scroll to the very end of the list and then select the Clear Playlist item.**

   The Clear menu appears, showing the Cancel and Clear Playlist items.

3. **Select the Clear Playlist item.**

   All the items disappear from the On-The-Go playlist. The items are still in your iPod — only the playlist is cleared. If you don't want to clear the playlist, select the Cancel item.

Saving an On-The-Go playlist in your iPod

You might want to create more than one On-The-Go playlist in your iPod, and temporarily save them for transferring to your iTunes library. To temporarily save your On-The-Go playlist in your iPod, follow these steps:

1. **Select the On-The-Go playlist.**

   Choose Music from the main menu and then scroll the Music menu until Playlists is highlighted; then press the Select button. The Playlists menu appears. Scroll to the On-The-Go item. Press the Select button, and the list of items in the playlist appears.

2. **Scroll to the very end of the list and select the Save Playlist item.**

   The Save menu appears, showing the Cancel and Save Playlist items.

3. **Select the Save Playlist item.**

   The On-The-Go playlist is saved with the name *New Playlist 1* (and any subsequent playlists you save are named *New Playlist 2,* and so on). These appear at the very end of the Playlist menu, not in alphabetical order — just above the On-The-Go Playlist item. If you don't want to save the playlist, select the Cancel item.

On-The-Go playlists saved as *New Playlist 1, New Playlist 2,* and so on, are stored temporarily in your iPod until you automatically update the iPod. The On-The-Go playlist is cleared each time you save it as a new playlist, so you can start creating another On-The-Go playlist.

Transferring the playlists to iTunes

While most transfer operations are one way from iTunes to your iPod, you can transfer the On-The-Go playlists back to your iTunes library — but not the content itself (which must already be in the iTunes library). Perhaps the songs you selected (or their order) inspired you somehow, and you want to repeat the experience.

When you automatically update your iPod (as we describe in Chapter 12), the current and other saved On-The-Go playlists (called *New Playlist 1, New Playlist 2,* and so on) are copied to your iTunes library, saved as regular playlists, and cleared from the iPod. The automatic update also places the newly created playlists back in your iPod in proper alphabetical location in the Playlist menu with the names *On-The-Go 1, On-The-Go 2,* and so on.

If you want to change an On-The-Go playlist to a new name, rename it in your iTunes library. The next time you automatically update your iPod, the update changes the playlist names in your iPod to match your iTunes library.

When updating your iPod manually, you can drag the On-The-Go playlist and any saved playlists from your iPod library directly to the iTunes library.

Playing an iPod shuffle

The iPod shuffle is a special model iPod with no display or any controls to select specific songs or albums. The idea behind the iPod shuffle is to load it with songs in the order you want them to play (like a long playlist) and then play the songs in that order or in shuffle (random) order. See Figure 15-10.

To set the iPod shuffle to play songs in the order they were copied, set the position switch to the *play in order* position (the right position marked by the arrows pointing in a circle icon). To set it to play songs in random order, set the position switch to the *shuffle* position (the left position marked by the arrows crossing icon).

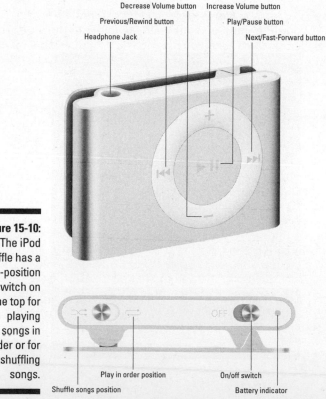

Decrease Volume button   Increase Volume button
Previous/Rewind button   Play/Pause button
Headphone Jack   Next/Fast-Forward button

Figure 15-10:
The iPod shuffle has a two-position switch on the top for playing songs in order or for shuffling songs.

Play in order position   On/off switch
Shuffle songs position   Battery indicator

To play the iPod shuffle songs, press the Play/Pause button. To stop (or pause) playback, press the Play/Pause button again. When you stop playback, the iPod shuffle status light blinks green for a minute.

To navigate songs in the iPod shuffle, press the Previous/Rewind button to skip backward, or the Next/Fast-Forward button to skip forward. Press and hold these buttons to skip more than one song ahead or behind (as if you were fast-forwarding or rewinding a tape). You can start a song over by pressing Previous/Rewind while the song is playing.

If you set the position switch to the *play in order* position, the Previous/ Rewind button skips backward and the Next/Fast-Forward button skips forward in the order the songs were copied to the iPod shuffle. However, if you set the position switch to the *shuffle* position, the playing order is randomized first. Then the Previous/Rewind button skips backward within the same shuffle order, and the Next/Fast-Forward button skips forward within the same shuffle order. For example, suppose your iPod shuffle plays the 14th song, then the 5th song, and then the 20th song. In that case, pressing the Previous/Rewind button during the 20th song takes you back to the 5th song, and pressing it again takes you back to the 14th song. In the same case, pressing the Next/Fast-Forward button skips through the songs in the same shuffle order again: the 14th song, the 5th song, and then the 20th song.

To go immediately to the beginning of an iPod shuffle playlist, press the Play/Pause button three times quickly (within a second).

Adjusting and Limiting the Volume

Because the iPod is quite loud when set to its highest volume, you should turn it down before using headphones.

To adjust the volume on the fly, follow these steps:

1. **Play something on the iPod.**
2. **While the content is playing, change the volume with the scroll wheel.**

   A volume bar appears in the iPod display to guide you. Scroll with your thumb or finger clockwise to increase the volume, and counterclockwise to decrease the volume.

You can also set the maximum volume for your iPod to be lower than the iPod's physical maximum limit so that the volume never reaches the actual maximum no matter what you play. (This protects your ears while listening to content from different sources at different volumes.) To set the new maximum limit, follow these steps:

1. **On your iPod, select Settings from the main menu and Volume Limit from the Settings menu.**

2. **Scroll to set the new maximum volume and then press the Select button.**

   A volume bar appears in the iPod display to guide you. Scroll clockwise to increase the volume or counterclockwise to decrease the volume. While you scroll, a triangle below the volume bar indicates the new limit. Press the Select button to accept the new limit.

   If you set the new limit to a volume less than the actual maximum, the iPod displays a menu that lets you set the combination lock to lock the setting, or you can finish the operation without setting the combination lock.

   If you set the limit to the actual maximum, the iPod resets the limit to the actual maximum and immediately returns you to the Settings menu.

3. **Set the combination lock or choose Done.**

   You can set the combination lock on your iPod to prevent anyone else from changing the settings, including the Volume Limit setting. Choose Set Combination and then press the Select button to set your combination lock. (For more details about setting your iPod combination lock, see Chapter 22.) Choose Done and then press the Select button if you don't need to set the combination lock.

If you have the *Apple iPod Remote* — a handy controller that attaches by cable to the iPod headphone connection — you can use the volume button on the remote to adjust the volume. You can also use the remote controller to play or pause a song, fast-forward or rewind, and skip to the next or previous song. You can disable the buttons on the remote by setting the controller's Hold switch (similar to the iPod Hold switch).

To adjust the volume of an iPod shuffle, press the Volume Up (+) or Volume Down (–) buttons.

Chapter 16

Getting Wired for Playback

The sound quality coming from your iPod is excellent, so why not use it with your home stereo system? Better yet, why not build an excellent home stereo around your iPod — one that truly provides advantages for iPod owners? That's what part of this chapter is all about — connecting your iPod to an audio system for your home, office, patio, den, bathroom, or whatever. The other part of this chapter shows you how to connect a color-display iPod to a television, video monitor, or other video equipment to maximize the quality of the picture. It describes the physical connections that you can make with an iPod to show videos and photo slideshows as if they were playing on DVD players (only they're actually playing from the palm of your hand).

Making Connections

All iPod models enable you to connect your iPod to headphones, to your home stereo with standard audio cables, or to your computer with either FireWire or USB cables.

The connections are as follows for fifth-generation iPods that play video and for iPod nano:

> ✔ **USB/FireWire dock connector:** Fifth-, fourth-, and third-generation models, including iPod mini and iPod nano, have a dock connection. You can use the connection to insert your iPod into a dock, or use the iPod

with a dock connector cable, as shown in Figure 16-1. The dock connector cable has a dock connector on one end (the same type of connection used in docks) and a FireWire or USB connector (or both FireWire and USB connectors with a split cable) on the other.

Figure 16-1:
A fifth-generation video iPod with a dock connector cable attached.

iPod USB/FireWire dock connector cable

✔ **Headphone/line-out:** You can connect headphones or a 3.5 mm stereo mini-plug cable to the headphone/line-out connection (see Figure 16-2). On a color-display iPod, the headphone/line-out connection also serves as an AV (audio-video) connection for displaying slideshows and photos.

✔ **Docks:** Docks come in many sizes and shapes. The iPod Universal Dock available in the optional iPod AV Connection Kit (which you can find in Apple stores and in the online Apple Store) offers three connections:

- A *dock connector* for a FireWire or USB cable connection

- A *headphone/line-out connection* for a stereo mini-plug cable or AV cable (or headphones)

- An *S-video connection* for connecting the dock (and thereby the iPod) to a television monitor to play video output from the iPod

Figure 16-2:
An iPod
nano with a
headphone
cable
attached.

Older iPod models offer the following connections:

- **USB/FireWire dock connector:** Fourth- and third-generation models, including iPod mini, have a dock connection for inserting into a dock. You can also use this connection with a dock connector cable.

- **Headphone/line-out and control socket:** You can connect headphones or a 3.5mm stereo mini-plug cable to the headphone/line-out connection. The combination headphone and control socket connection on top of third- and fourth-generation iPods (see Figure 16-3) lets you plug in accessories, such as remote control devices and voice recorders. The headphone/line-out connection on second-generation models includes an outer ring for connecting the Apple Remote supplied with those models.

- **FireWire (six pin):** First- and second-generation iPods have a six-pin, FireWire-only connection on the top that works with any standard six-pin FireWire cable (see Figure 16-4).

- **Dock:** For fourth- and third-generation iPod models, the dock supplied with the iPod offers two connections — one for the dock connector cable for a FireWire connection, and a headphone/line-out connection for a stereo mini-plug cable (or headphones).

Control socket   Headphone/line out

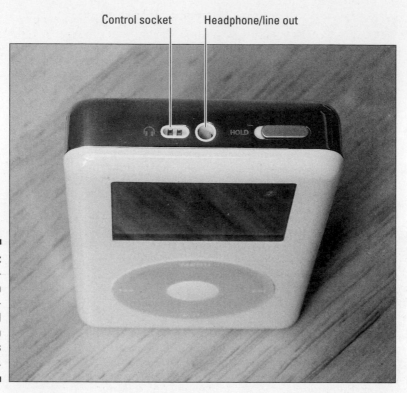

Figure 16-3:
A fourth-
generation
color-
display iPod
with
connections
on top.

Figure 16-4:
A second-
generation
iPod with
connections
on top.

Headphone/line out   FireWire

You can connect the FireWire or USB end of the dock connector cable to the computer (for synchronizing with iTunes and playing the iPod through iTunes, as we describe later in this chapter) or to the power adapter to charge the iPod battery. The FireWire or USB connection to the computer provides power to the iPod as long as the computer's FireWire or USB hardware offers power to the device and the computer isn't in sleep mode. (See Chapter 1 for power information.)

Connecting to a Home Stereo

Home stereo systems come in many shapes and sizes, from an audiophile's monster component racks to a kid's itty-bitty boombox. We're not talking about alarm clock radios but stereos with speakers that allow you to add another input device, such as a portable CD player.

Component-style stereo systems typically include a receiver (which offers a preamp/amplifier with a volume control, and a tuner to receive FM radio). Some separate these functions into separate components such as a preamp, an amplifier, and a tuner. To find a place to connect your iPod or computer to a home stereo, look for RCA-type connections that are marked AUX IN (for auxiliary input), CD IN (for connecting a CD player), or TAPE IN (for tape deck input). All-in-one stereos and boomboxes typically don't have connections for audio input, although you can find exceptions. Look at the back and sides of the unit for any RCA-type connections.

You can connect a CD or tape player to most stereos with RCA-type cables — one (typically red or black) for the right channel, and one (typically white if the other is black, or white or black if the other is red) for the left channel. All you need is a cable with a stereo mini-plug on one end and RCA-type connectors on the other, as shown in Figure 16-5. Stereo mini-plugs have two black bands on the plug, but a mono mini-plug has only one black band.

Figure 16-5: RCA-type connectors (left) and a stereo mini-plug (right).

Follow these steps to connect your iPod to your stereo:

1. **Connect the stereo mini-plug to either the headphone/line-out connection on a dock, or the headphone/line-out connection on the iPod, depending on whether you want to control the volume from your iPod.**

   With the dock connection, you have no control over volume on the iPod. Instead, you use your stereo system or speakers to control the volume.

2. **Connect the left and right connectors to the stereo system's audio input.**

   Use whatever connections are available such as AUX IN, TAPE IN, or CD IN.

   Don't use the PHONO IN connection (for phonograph input) on most stereos. These connections are for phonographs (turntables) and aren't properly matched for other kinds of input devices. If you use the PHONO IN connection, you might get a loud buzzing sound that could damage your speakers.

If you use the iPod's headphone/line-out connection, you can control the volume from the iPod by using the scroll wheel. (See Chapter 15 for volume controls.) This controls the volume of the signal from the iPod. Stereo systems typically have their own volume control to raise or lower the volume of the amplified speakers. For optimal sound quality when using a home stereo, set the iPod volume at less than half the maximum output and adjust your listening volume by using your stereo controls.

Connecting to a TV or Video Input

You can connect your fifth-generation iPod to any television, video projector, or video recorder or player that offers standard RCA video and audio connections, or an S-video connection.

Color-display iPods are supplied with the iPod *AV Cable*, which is a special cable that you can plug in to the headphone/line-out connection of the iPod or to the headphone/line-out connection and S-video connection on the dock supplied with the iPod. (You must use a fourth-generation iPod Photo dock or a fifth-generation iPod dock; other docks do not support video out.) The cable offers RCA video (yellow) and stereo audio (red and white) connectors and an S-video connector, as shown in Figure 16-6, to plug in to your television or video equipment.

You must use the AV Cable supplied with your iPod — Apple warns that others won't work.

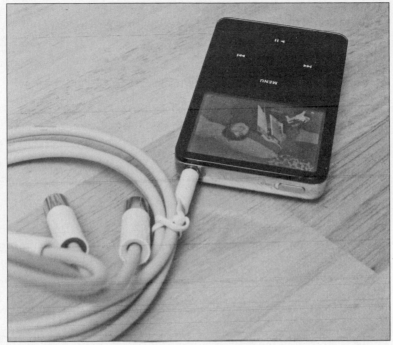

Figure 16-6:
The iPod AV
Cable
provides a
yellow video
RCA-type
connector
as well as
red and
white audio
RCA-type
connectors.

For even better picture quality, use a television or video monitor that supports S-video and your fourth-generation iPod Photo dock or fifth-generation iPod dock. Plug a standard S-video cable into the dock's S-video connection and then plug the other end into your television's S-video connection. Plug the supplied AV Cable into the color-display iPod headphone or dock line-out connection, and the AV Cable stereo audio connectors (but *not* the yellow video connector) into the television. For better sound, plug the AV Cable stereo audio connectors into a stereo system with good speakers.

If you don't see a picture on your television, check that your television is set to the correct input source — video in (RCA) or S-video in (if you use an S-video cable and a fifth-generation iPod dock). You can also use other types of video equipment; for example, a video recorder that accepts RCA or S-video input can record the video, and a video projector can display it on a large screen.

Playing an iPod through iTunes

You can't copy the content from your iPod into your iTunes library using iTunes, but you can use iTunes on your computer to play the content directly from the iPod. You can even connect your friend's iPod to your computer and include your friend's iPod songs in your Party Shuffle. Not only can you do that, but when you play songs from different iPods or from your library, you can cross-fade them (see Chapter 6).

To play the content on your iPod in iTunes, follow these steps:

1. **Connect the iPod to your computer, press ⌘-Option (Mac) or Ctrl-Alt (Windows) to prevent automatic updating.**

2. **Set the iPod to update manually.**

   To set the iPod to update manually, see Chapter 12. (The iPod updates automatically by default, but you can change that.)

3. **Select the iPod name in the iTunes Source pane.**

   After selecting the iPod in the iTunes Source pane, the list of songs on the iPod appears, as shown in Figure 16-7. You can scroll or browse the iPod's library just like the main iTunes library. Click the Browse button to browse the iPod's contents.

Figure 16-7:
Select the iPod in the Source pane and play a song.

4. **(Optional) View the iPod playlists.**

   After selecting the iPod in the iTunes Source pane, you can click the triangle next to its name to view the iPod's playlists.

5. **Click an item in the iPod song list and then click the iTunes Play button.**

What if you want to connect your iPod to a computer other than your own? Or what if a friend arrives with an iPod filled with songs that you'd like to hear, and you want to hear them on your stereo system that's already connected to your computer?

You can either connect your iPod to another computer or connect someone else's iPod to your computer. Either way, iTunes starts and recognizes that the iPod isn't matched to the iTunes library (because it is matched to another computer's iTunes library). iTunes displays a message asking whether you want to change the link to this iTunes music library and replace all existing songs and playlists; it also asks if you want to change the photos. This is important — *click No for each change request.*

Unless you want to change the contents of your iPod to reflect this computer's library, don't click Yes. *If you click the Yes button, iTunes erases the library of your iPod* and then updates your iPod with the library on that computer, including photos and videos. If you're using a public computer with no content in the iTunes library, you end up with an empty iPod. If you're using a friend's computer, your friend's library copies to your iPod, erasing whatever was on your iPod. So don't click Yes unless you really want to completely change the content on your iPod. You've been warned.

With color-display iPods, you also get a similar warning message about changing the link to the photo library and replacing all photos in the iPod. Again, click No to prevent this from happening.

If you connect a Mac-formatted iPod to a Windows computer, you get a warning message about reformatting it. *Don't do it!* Click Cancel. Otherwise, you reformat the iPod and clear all music from it. Then click the Safely Remove Hardware icon and safely eject the iPod from the computer.

Accessories for the iHome

Most of the accessories for the iPod (and hundreds of products are available) are designed for travel, and we describe the best travel accessories in Chapter 21. However, companies also provide docks, speaker systems, and stands for iPods.

For an extremely powerful, single-cabinet, portable speaker system that offers iPod docking and exceptional sound, the stylish, high-quality iPod Hi-Fi from Apple (www.apple.com/ipodhifi) is hard to beat. Housed in a single unit with a dock for the iPod, the Apple iPod Hi-Fi takes up very little space on a table, desk, or bookshelf and also runs on D-cell batteries for taking it outside or on the road as a boom box. You can use the included wireless Apple Remote to control playback from anywhere in the room. When you plug in your fifth-generation iPod or iPod nano, the Hi-Fi adds a Speakers option to the iPod main menu. Select Speakers to see the Speakers menu, which includes a Tone Control option offering Normal, Bass Boost, and Treble Boost settings to tweak the sound coming from the Hi-Fi. The Speakers menu also offers the Backlight option to set your iPod's backlighting while it's connected to the Hi-Fi, and the Large Album Art option to show full-screen art associated with the content.

If you connect a fifth-generation iPod (iPod with video) or fourth-generation iPod Photo running iPod Software 1.0 to an iPod Hi-Fi, the Speakers menu offers a Room Size option instead of Tone Control. You should update your iPod Software, as we describe in Chapter 26.

What if you have multiple iPods from different generations and need to organize your docks and cables? The Belkin Tunesync (www.belkin.com) offers a unique USB cradle that not only offers a place for recharging and syncing your iPods but also adds five additional USB ports.

Need a blast of music for the barbecue out on your patio? The iBoom from Digital Lifestyle Outfitters (www.dlodirect.com) is a 20-watts-per-channel, four-speaker boombox system with a dock for a full-size iPod or iPod mini. iBoom also includes a digital FM radio and an auxiliary input jack for connecting another music source, and it draws power either from an AC adapter or six D-cell batteries (not included). While connected to AC power, the iBoom can recharge your iPod's battery. If you need a more portable solution, check out the battery-powered Portable Folding Speaker System for iPod/ MP3, available from Overstock (www.overstock.com) for about $13. For more solutions that can work in planes, trains, and automobiles — or anywhere for that matter — see Chapter 21.

When your iPod is tethered to a dock and connected to your home stereo, you don't have to be within reach to change the track or the settings. Instead, you can control it remotely. with a wireless remote control. The wireless Apple Remote (see the Apple Web site) provides the usual CD player controls: Play/Pause, Next Track, Previous Track, and volume buttons. It works with Apple's Universal Dock and Hi-Fi.

Ten Technology (www.tentechnology.com) offers the stylish $49.95 naviPod that provides wireless remote control of your iPod with standard Play/Pause, Next Track, Previous Track, and volume controls. The naviPod uses infrared wireless technology with a receiver unit that plugs directly into the control socket on the top of the iPod. The receiver has FireWire and headphone connections on the bottom, which allow you to connect your headphones or hook up your iPod to your computer without removing the naviPod receiver.

Engineered Audio (www.engineeredaudio.com) offers RemoteRemote 2 for about $40. Unlike infrared wireless controls, RemoteRemote 2 is an RF (radio frequency) wireless remote control that works around corners and through walls. With standard Play/Pause, Next Track, Previous Track, and volume controls, RemoteRemote 2 operates in a range up to 100 feet.

Chapter 17

Fine-Tuning the Sound

• •

• •

Sound is difficult to describe. Harder still to describe is how to adjust sound to your liking. Maybe you want more oomph in the lows, or perhaps you prefer highs that are as clear as a bell. Even if you've never mastered a stereo system beyond adjusting the bass and treble controls and the volume control, you can use this limited knowledge of sound to quickly fine-tune the sound in iTunes by using the equalizer settings, as you discover in this chapter.

Sound studio engineers try to make recordings for typical listening environments, so they have to simulate the sound experience in those environments. Studios typically have home stereo speakers as monitors so that the engineers can hear what the music sounds like on a home stereo. In the 1950s and early 1960s, when AM radio was king, engineers working on potential AM radio hits purposely mixed the sound with low-fidelity monaural speakers so that they could hear what the mix would sound like on the radio. (Thank goodness those days are over, and cars offer higher-quality FM radio as well as very high-quality audio systems.)

The reason the engineers did this is because the quality of the sound is no better than the speakers you play them on. As you find out how to adjust and fine-tune the sound coming out of your computer running iTunes and out of your iPod, you also want to use your everyday listening environment as a guide. But if you tweak the sound specifically for your computer speakers or for your home stereo and speakers, remember that with an iPod you have other potential listening environments — different headphones, car stereo systems, portable boomboxes, and so on.

Fortunately iTunes gives you the flexibility of using different equalization set-tings for different songs, audio books, podcasts, and videos. You can also use presets on your iPod. This chapter shows you how to make presets for songs in your library so that iTunes remembers them. What's more, you can use the standard iTunes presets on your iPod or use other iPod settings with the iPod's equalizer. This chapter shows you how.

Adjusting the Sound in iTunes First

Some songs are just too loud. We don't mean too loud stylistically, as in thrash metal with screeching guitars; we mean too loud for your ears when you're wearing headphones or so loud that the music sounds distorted in your speakers. And some songs are just too soft, and you have to turn up the volume to hear them and then turn the volume back down to listen to other songs. You can set the volume in advance in several ways.

Setting the volume in advance

With songs, audio books, podcast episodes, and videos that you already know are too loud (or too soft), consider setting the volume for those items (or even entire albums or podcasts) in advance so that they always play with the desired volume adjustment.

To adjust the overall volume of a particular item in advance so that it always plays at that setting, perform the following steps:

1. **Click an item to select it.**

   To set the volume for multiple songs at once, you can select an entire album in iTunes Browse view or select all the songs. To set the volume for a whole podcast, select it instead of individual episodes.

2. **Choose File⇨Get Info.**

   The information dialog appears.

3. **Click the Options tab.**

   Drag the Volume Adjustment slider left or right to adjust the volume lower or higher, as shown in Figure 17-1. You can do this while playing the file.

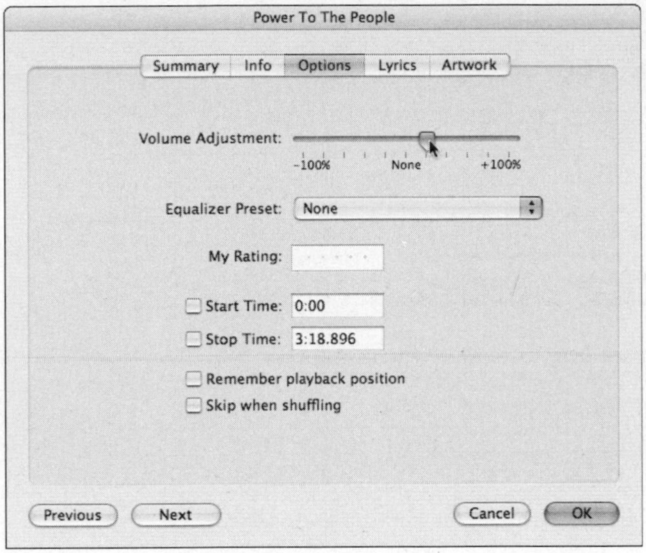

Figure 17-1:
Adjust the
volume
setting for a
song here.

Enhancing the sound

Some home or car stereos offer a sound enhancer button to improve the depth of the sound. iTunes offers a similar option — *Sound Enhancer* — that improves the depth of the sound by enhancing the high and low frequencies. Audiophiles and sound purists would most likely use the equalizer to boost frequencies, but you can use this brute force method to enhance the sound.

To turn on Sound Enhancer, follow these steps:

1. **Choose iTunes⇨Preferences (Mac) or Edit⇨Preferences (Windows).**

   The iTunes Preferences dialog appears.

2. **Click the Playback tab.**

   The Playback preferences appear, as shown in Figure 17-2.

3. **Adjust the Sound Enhancer slider:**

   • *Increase the sound enhancement:* Drag the Sound Enhancer slider to the right toward the High setting. This is similar to pressing the loudness button on a stereo or the equivalent of boosting the treble (high) and bass (low) frequencies in the equalizer (described in "Equalize It in iTunes," later in this chapter).

   • *Decrease the high and low frequencies:* Drag the slider to the left toward the Low setting.

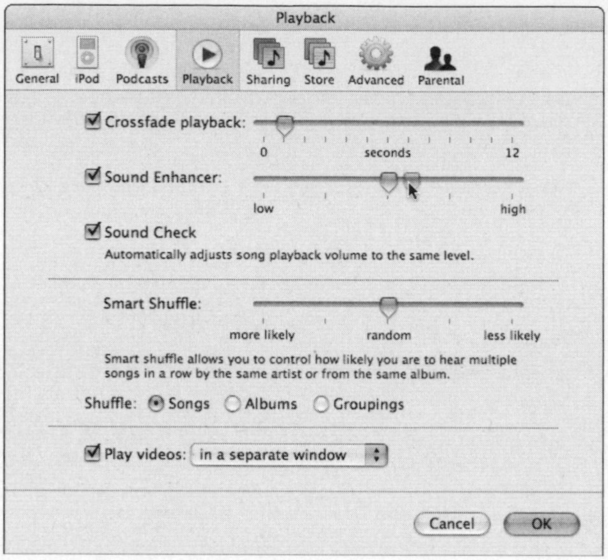

Playback

General iPod Podcasts Playback Sharing Store Advanced Parental

☑ Crossfade playback:
    0   seconds   12

☑ Sound Enhancer:
    low   high

☑ Sound Check
    Automatically adjusts song playback volume to the same level.

    Smart Shuffle:
    more likely   random   less likely

    Smart shuffle allows you to control how likely you are to hear multiple
    songs in a row by the same artist or from the same album.

    Shuffle: ⦿ Songs ◯ Albums ◯ Groupings

☑ Play videos: [in a separate window ⬦]

                    (Cancel) (OK)

Figure 17-2:
Use the
Sound
Enhancer.

The middle setting is neutral, adding no enhancement — the same as turning off the Sound Enhancer by clearing its check box.

Sound-checking the iTunes library

Because music CDs are manufactured inconsistently, discrepancies occur in volume between them. Some CDs play louder than others; occasionally, individual tracks within a CD are louder than others.

You can standardize the volume level of all the songs in your iTunes music library with the Sound Check option. (Musicians do a sound check before every performance to check the volume of microphones and instruments and its effect on the listening environment.) The aptly named Sound Check option in iTunes allows you to do a sound check on your tunes to bring them all into line, volume-wise. This option has the added benefit of applying the same volume adjustment when you play the songs back on your iPod, as described in the upcoming section, "Sound-checking the iPod."

Sound Check scans the audio files, finds each track's peak volume level, and then uses this peak volume information to level the playing volume of tracks so that they have the same peak volume. The sound quality isn't affected, nor is the audio information itself changed — the volume is simply adjusted at the start of the track to be in line with other tracks.

To turn on Sound Check, follow these steps:

1. **Drag the iTunes volume slider to set the overall volume for iTunes.**

   The volume slider is in the top-left corner of the iTunes window, to the right of the Play button.

2. **Choose iTunes⇨Preferences (Mac) or Edit⇨Preferences (Windows).**

   The iTunes Preferences dialog appears.

3. **Click the Playback tab.**

   The Playback preferences appear; refer to Figure 17-2.

4. **Select the Sound Check check box.**

   iTunes sets the volume level for all songs according to the level of the iTunes volume slider.

5. **Click OK.**

   The Sound Check option sets a volume adjustment based on the volume slider on all the songs so that they play at approximately the same volume.

The operation takes a while for a large library but runs in the background while you do other things. If you quit iTunes and then restart it, the operation continues where it left off when you quit. You can turn Sound Check on or off at any time.

Sound-checking the iPod

You can take advantage of volume-leveling in your iTunes library with the Sound Check option and then turn Sound Check on or off on your iPod by choosing Sound Check from the iPod Settings menu.

This feature is useful especially when using your iPod in a car or when jogging while listening to headphones because you don't want to have to reach for the volume on the iPod or on the car stereo every time it starts playing a song that's too loud.

The Sound Check option on your iPod works only if you've also set the Sound Check option in your iTunes library. If you need to enable this setting in iTunes, check out the preceding section. On the iPod, choose Settings⇨ Sound Check⇨On from the main menu to turn on the Sound Check feature. To turn it off, choose Settings⇨Sound Check⇨Off.

What's the frequency, Kenneth? The equalizer opportunity

The Beach Boys were right when they sang "Good Vibrations," because that's what music is — the sensation of hearing audible vibrations conveyed to the ear by a medium such as air. Musicians measure pitch by the *frequency* of vibrations per second. The waves can oscillate slowly and produce low-pitched sounds, or they can oscillate rapidly and produce high-pitched sounds. The *amplitude* is a measurement of the amount of fluctuation in air pressure — therefore, amplitude is perceived as loudness.

When you turn up the bass or treble on a stereo system, you're actually increasing the volume, or intensity, of certain frequencies while the music is playing. The equalizer lets you fine-tune the sound spectrum frequencies in a more

precise way than with bass and treble controls. It increases or decreases specific frequencies of the sound to raise or lower highs, lows, and midrange tones. The equalizer adjusts the volume with several band-pass filters all centered at different frequencies, and each filter offers controllable *gain* (the ability to boost the volume).

On more sophisticated stereo systems, an equalizer with a bar graph display replaces the bass and treble controls. An equalizer (EQ in audio-speak) enables you to fine-tune the specific sound spectrum frequencies, which gives you far greater control than merely adjusting the bass or treble controls.

Equalize It in iTunes

The iTunes equalizer (EQ) allows you to fine-tune the specific sound spectrum frequencies in a more precise way than with the typical bass and treble controls you find on home stereos and powered speakers. (See the sidebar on equalizers, later in this chapter.) You can use the equalizer to improve or enhance the sound coming through a particular stereo system and speakers. With the equalizer settings, you can customize playback for different musical genres, listening environments, or speakers.

You might want to pick entirely different equalizer settings for car speakers, home speakers, and headphones. Fortunately, you can save your settings, as described in the upcoming "Saving your own presets" section.

To see the iTunes equalizer, click the Equalizer button, which is the icon with three mixer faders on the bottom-right side of the iTunes window. (On a Mac, you can also choose Window➪Equalizer.)

Adjusting the preamp volume

The *preamp* in your stereo is the component that offers a volume control that applies to all frequencies equally.

Volume knobs generally go up to 10 — except, of course, for Spinal Tap's Marshall preamps, which go to 11.

The iTunes equalizer, as shown in Figure 17-3, offers a Preamp slider on the far-left side. You can increase or decrease the volume in 3 decibel (dB) increments up to 12 dB. *Decibels* are units that measure the intensity (or volume) of the frequencies. You can adjust the volume while playing the music to hear the result right away.

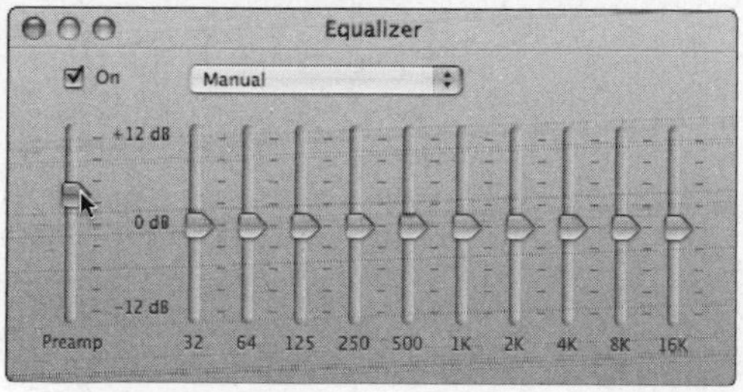

Figure 17-3: Use the Preamp slider to adjust the volume across all frequencies.

If you want to make any adjustments to frequencies, you might need to adjust the preamp volume first if volume adjustment is needed and then move on to the specific frequencies.

Adjusting frequencies

You can adjust frequencies in the iTunes equalizer by clicking and dragging sliders that look like mixing-board faders.

The horizontal values across the equalizer represent the spectrum of human hearing. The deepest frequency ("Daddy sang bass") is 32 hertz (Hz); the midrange frequencies are 250 Hz and 500 Hz; and the higher frequencies go from 1 kilohertz (kHz) to 16 kHz (treble).

The vertical values on each bar represent decibels, which measure the intensity of each frequency. Increase or decrease the frequencies at 3 dB increments by clicking and dragging the sliders up and down. You can drag the sliders to adjust the frequencies while the music is playing so that you can hear the effect immediately.

Using the iTunes presets

iTunes offers *presets,* which are equalizer settings made in advance and saved by name. You can quickly switch settings without having to make changes to each frequency slider. iTunes comes with more than 20 presets of the most commonly used equalizer settings, including ones for musical genres such as classical and rock. You can assign these presets (or your own presets) to a specific item or set of items (songs, audio books, podcast episodes, and videos) in your iTunes library.

These preset settings copy to your iPod along with the content when you update your iPod.

To use an equalizer preset, choose a preset from the pop-up menu in the Equalizer, as shown in Figure 17-4. If something is playing, you hear the effect in the sound immediately after choosing the preset.

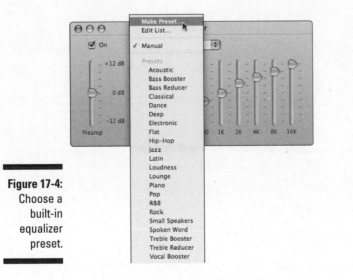

Figure 17-4:
Choose a
built-in
equalizer
preset.

Saving your own presets

Don't settle for the built-in iTunes presets — you can create your own equalizer presets for iTunes. (Unfortunately you can't transfer custom presets to an iPod as of this writing.)

Follow these steps to save your own presets to the iTunes equalizer:

1. **Make the changes that you want to the frequencies by dragging the individual sliders up and down.**

The pop-up menu automatically switches to Manual.

2. **Choose the Make Preset option from the pop-up menu (refer to Figure 17-4) to save your changes.**

   The Make Preset dialog appears, as shown in Figure 17-5.

3. **Enter a descriptive name for your preset in the New Preset Name text box and click OK.**

   The name appears in the pop-up menu from that point on — your very own preset.

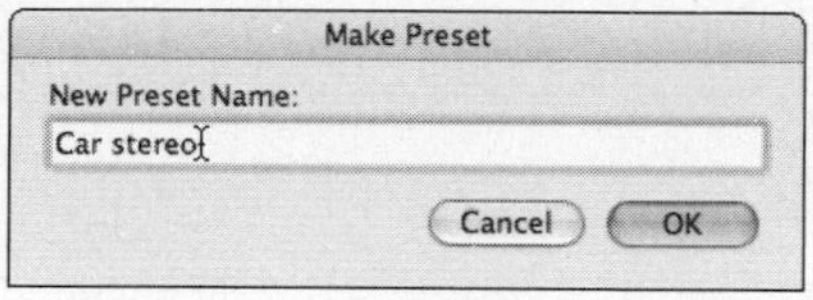

Figure 17-5:
Save your
adjustments
as your own
preset.

Make Preset

New Preset Name:

Car stereo

Cancel   OK

You can rename or delete any preset, including the ones supplied with iTunes (which is useful if you want to recall a preset by another name). Choose the Edit List option from the pop-up menu. The Edit Presets dialog opens, as shown in Figure 17-6. Click Rename to rename a preset, click Delete to delete a preset, and click Done when you finish editing the list.

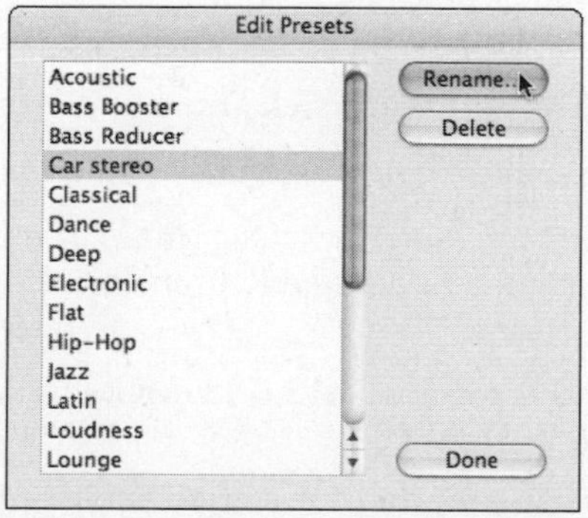

Edit Presets

Acoustic   Rename...
Bass Booster
Bass Reducer   Delete
Car stereo
Classical
Dance
Deep
Electronic
Flat
Hip-Hop
Jazz
Latin
Loudness
Lounge   Done

Figure 17-6:
Rename or
delete
presets.

Assigning equalizer presets

One reason why you go to the trouble of setting equalizer presets is to assign the presets to your iTunes content. The next time you play the item, iTunes uses the equalizer preset that you assigned.

When you transfer the content to your iPod, the standard iTunes preset assignments transfer with the content, and you can choose whether to use the preset assignments when playing the content on your iPod. However, custom presets do not transfer to the iPod.

Assign an equalizer preset to a content item or set of items by following these steps:

1. **Choose Edit⇨View Options.**

   The View Options dialog appears, as shown in Figure 17-7.

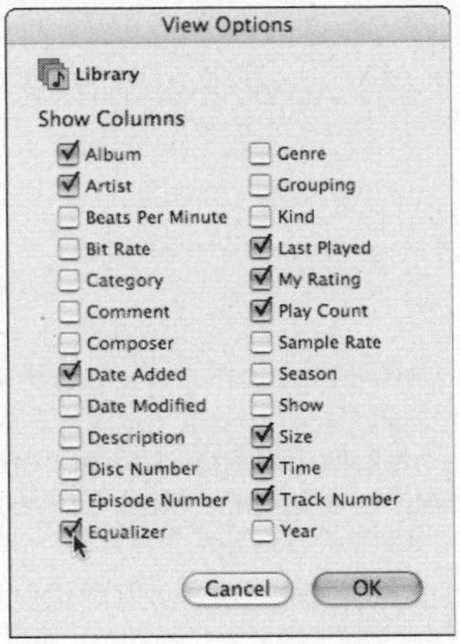

Figure 17-7:
Show the equalizer column to assign presets to songs.

View Options

♫ Library

Show Columns

☑ Album   ☐ Genre
☑ Artist   ☐ Grouping
☐ Beats Per Minute ☐ Kind
☐ Bit Rate   ☑ Last Played
☐ Category   ☑ My Rating
☐ Comment   ☑ Play Count
☐ Composer   ☐ Sample Rate
☑ Date Added   ☐ Season
☐ Date Modified ☐ Show
☐ Description   ☑ Size
☐ Disc Number   ☑ Time
☐ Episode Number ☑ Track Number
☑ Equalizer   ☐ Year

Cancel   OK

2. **Select the Equalizer check box and then click OK.**

   The Equalizer column appears in the song list in the iTunes window.

   You can combine Steps 1 and 2 by Control-clicking (Mac) or right-clicking (Windows) on any song list column heading and then choosing Equalizer.

3. **Locate an item in the list and scroll the list horizontally to see the Equalizer column, as shown in Figure 17-8.**

4. **Choose a preset from the pop-up menu in the Equalizer column.**

   The Equalizer column has a tiny pop-up menu that allows you to assign any preset to a song, audio book, podcast episode, or video.

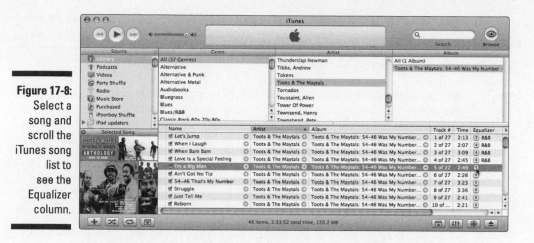

Figure 17-8: Select a song and scroll the iTunes song list to see the Equalizer column.

Equalize It in Your iPod

You leave the back-road bliss of the country to get on the freeway, and now the music in your car doesn't have enough bass to give you that thumping rhythm you need to dodge other cars. What can you do? Without endangering anybody, you can pull over and select one of the iPod equalizer presets, such as Bass Booster.

Yes, your iPod also has a built-in equalizer. Like the iTunes equalizer, the iPod built-in equalizer modifies the volume of the frequencies of the sound. And although you don't have sliders for faders like the iTunes equalizer, you do get the same long list of presets to suit the type of music or the type of environment (everything except Loudness).

The iPod equalizer uses a bit more battery power when it's turned on, so you might have less playing time on your iPod battery.

You can also use the iTunes equalizer to improve or enhance the sound, assigning presets to each song and then updating your iPod.

Choosing an EQ preset on your iPod

To select an iPod equalizer preset, choose Settings➪EQ from the main menu. The EQ is set to Off until you select one of the presets.

Each EQ preset offers a different balance of frequencies designed to enhance the sound in certain ways. For example, Bass Booster increases the volume of the low (bass) frequencies; Treble Booster does the same to the high (treble) frequencies.

To see what a preset actually does to the frequencies, open the iTunes equalizer and select the same preset. The faders in the equalizer show you exactly what the preset does.

The Off setting turns off the iPod equalizer — no presets are used, not even ones you assigned in iTunes. You have to choose an EQ preset to turn on the iPod equalizer.

Applying the iTunes EQ presets

After assigning a standard preset to a content item in iTunes, turn on the iPod equalizer by choosing any EQ setting (other than Off) so that the iPod uses the item's EQ preset for playback. To assign standard presets to items with the iTunes equalizer, see "Assigning equalizer presets," earlier in this chapter.

No matter what EQ preset you choose on your iPod, any item that has an assigned preset uses the assigned preset. That's right — the assigned EQ preset from iTunes takes precedence over the preset in the iPod. Choose the Flat EQ preset in your iPod if you want items that have assigned presets to play with those presets while the rest of the content plays without any EQ adjustment.

If you know in advance that you need to use specific presets for certain songs, assign standard presets to the songs in iTunes *before* copying the songs to the iPod (but not custom presets, which don't transfer to the iPod). If, on the other hand, you don't want the songs fixed to a certain preset, *don't* assign presets to the songs in iTunes. You can then experiment with the presets in the iPod to get better playback in different listening environments.

You can temporarily play an item with an assigned preset by using one of iPod's other EQ settings. Start playing the item on your iPod, and while the item is playing, press the Menu button until you return to the main menu. Choose Settings⇨EQ and select a setting you want to try. The content plays to the end with the new EQ setting. The next time that item is played, it uses the assigned preset as usual.

Part IV
Using Advanced Techniques

The 5th Wave   By Rich Tennant

RICHTENNANT

"After Apple's success with the iPod nano, Microsoft unveils the new 'PC Nano.'"

In this part . . .

This part focuses on what you can do to improve the sound of your music.

- Chapter 18 gives you the info you need to make the right decisions for encoding and compressing sound files and make appropriate tradeoffs of space for quality.

- Chapter 19 describes how to change your encoder and importing preferences and settings for each encoder, to get the best results with digital audio compression.

- Chapter 20 covers other online music sources and explains what you need to do to record sound from various analog sources (including vinyl LPs and tapes) for importing into iTunes.

Chapter 18

Decoding Audio Encoding

As you discover more about digital audio technology, you find that you have more decisions to make about your music than you previously thought, and this chapter helps you make them. For example, you might be tempted to trade quality for space, importing music at average-quality settings that allow you to put more songs on your hard drive and iPod than if you chose higher-quality settings. This method might make you happy today, but what about tomorrow, when iPods and hard drives double or triple in capacity?

On the other hand, you might be very picky about the sound quality, and with an eye toward future generations of iPods and cheap hard drives, you might decide to trade space for quality, importing music at the highest possible quality settings and then converting copies to lower-quality, space-saving versions for iPods and other uses. Of course, you need more hard drive space to accommodate the higher-quality versions.

This chapter explains which music encoding and compression formats to use for higher quality and which to use for cramming more songs into your hard drive space.

Trading Quality for Space

The encoding format and settings that you choose for importing music when ripping a CD affect sound quality, iPod space, and hard drive space on your computer. The format and settings might also affect the music files' ability to play on other types of players and computers.

The audio compression methods that are good at reducing space have to throw away information. In technospeak, these methods are known as *lossy* (as opposed to lossless) compression algorithms. For example, the AAC and MP3 encoding formats compress the sound by using lossy methods. However, lossy compression algorithms reduce the sound quality by throwing away information to make the file smaller, so you lose information and some quality in the process. On the other hand, the Apple Lossless encoder compresses the sound without any loss in quality or information, but the resulting file is only a bit smaller than the uncompressed version — the main reason to use Apple Lossless is to maintain quality for burning CDs while also playing the songs on iPods. The AIFF and WAV encoders do not compress the sound and are the best choices for burning CDs.

With lossy compression formats such as MP3 or AAC, the amount of compression depends on the *bit rate* that you choose as well as the encoding format and other options. The bit rate determines how many bits (of digital music information) can travel during playback in a given second. Measured in kilobits per second (Kbps), a higher bit rate, such as 320K, offers higher quality than a bit rate of 192K because the sound is not compressed as much — which means the resulting sound file is larger and takes up more iPod and hard drive space.

Using more compression (a lower bit rate) means that the files are smaller, but the sound quality is poorer. Using less compression (a higher bit rate) means that the sound is higher in quality, but the files are larger. You can trade quality for space and have more music of lower quality, or trade space for quality and have less music of higher quality.

Power is also an issue with the iPod. Playing larger files takes more power because the hard drive inside the iPod has to refresh its memory buffers more frequently to process information as the song plays — you might even hear hiccups in the sound.

We prefer a higher-quality sound overall, and we typically don't use the lower-quality settings for encoders except for voice recordings and music recorded in ancient times — before 1960. (Ancient recordings are already low in quality, so you don't hear that much of a difference when they're compressed.) We can hear differences in music quality at the higher compression levels, and we prefer going out and buying another hard drive to store more music if necessary.

Choosing an iTunes Encoder

Your iPod's music software gives you a choice of encoders. This choice is perhaps the most important to make before starting to rip music CDs and build up your library. Here we leapfrog years of technospeak about digital music file formats and get right to the ones that you need to know.

If you're using Musicmatch, visit the companion Web site at www.dummies. com/go/ipod4e to choose an appropriate encoder.

Choose iTunes➪Preferences (Mac) or Edit➪Preferences (Windows), click the Advanced tab, and then click the Importing tab to see the Importing preferences. You can choose one of five encoders from the Import Using pop-up menu:

- **AAC:** All your purchased music from the iTunes Music Store comes in this format. We recommend it for all uses except when ripping your CDs to burn new audio CDs. Technically known as MPEG-4 Advanced Audio Coding, AAC is a higher-quality format than MP3 at the same bit rate — meaning that AAC at 128 Kbps is higher quality than MP3 at 128 Kbps. (*MPEG* stands for Moving Picture Experts Group, a committee that recognizes compression standards for video and audio.)

  We think the AAC encoder offers the best tradeoff of space and quality for iPod users. It's suitable for burning to an audio CD (though not as good as AIFF or Apple Lossless), and it's excellent for playing on an iPod or from a hard drive. However, as of this writing, only Apple supports AAC.

- **AIFF:** Audio Interchange File Format (AIFF) is the standard digital format for uncompressed sound on a Mac, and it provides the highest-quality digital representation of the sound. Like the WAV encoder for Windows, the AIFF encoder uses a platform-specific version of the original Pulse Code Modulation (PCM) algorithm required for compliance with audio CDs.

  Use AIFF if you plan to burn songs onto an audio CD or DVD or to edit the songs with a digital sound-editing program. Mac-based sound-editing programs import and export AIFF files, and you can edit and save in AIFF format repeatedly with absolutely no loss in quality. The downside is that AIFF files take up enormous amounts of hard drive and iPod space — 10MB per minute — because they're uncompressed. Don't use AIFF for songs that you want to play on an iPod — use the Apple Lossless encoder, AAC, or MP3 instead.

- **Apple Lossless:** The Apple Lossless encoder is a compromise between the lower-quality encoding of AAC or MP3 (which results in lower file sizes) and the large file sizes of uncompressed, high-quality AIFF or WAV audio. The Apple Lossless encoder provides CD-quality sound in a file size that's about 60 to 70 percent of the size of an AIFF or WAV encoded file. The virtue of this encoder is that you can use it for songs that you intend to burn onto audio CDs *and* for playing on iPods — the files are just small enough that they don't hiccup on playback, but they're still much larger than their MP3 or AAC counterparts.

Using the Apple Lossless encoder is the most efficient method of storing the highest-quality versions of your songs. You can burn the songs to CDs without any quality loss and still play them on your iPod. You can't store as many songs on your iPod as with AAC or MP3, but the songs that you do store have the highest-possible quality.

✔ **MP3:** The MPEG-1, Layer 3 format, also known as MP3, is supported by most computers and some CD players. Use the MP3 format for songs that you intend to use with MP3 players besides your iPod (which also plays MP3 songs, obviously), or to use with applications that support MP3, or to burn on an MP3 CD. (AIFF, WAV, or Apple Lossless formats are better for regular audio CDs.) The MP3 format offers quite a lot of different compression and quality settings, so you can fine-tune the format, sacrificing hard drive (and iPod) space as you dial up the quality. Use the MP3 format for a song that you intend to use with MP3 players, MP3 CDs, and applications that support MP3.

✔ **WAV:** Waveform Audio File Format (WAV) is a digital audio standard that Windows PCs can understand and manipulate. Like AIFF, WAV is uncompressed and provides the highest-quality digital representation of the sound. As the AIFF encoder does for the Mac, the WAV encoder uses a Windows-specific version of the original Pulse Code Modulation (PCM) algorithm required for compliance with audio CDs.

Use WAV if you plan on burning the song to an audio CD or using the song with Windows-based digital sound-editing programs, which import and export WAV files. (There is no difference between AIFF and WAV except that AIFF works with Mac applications and WAV works with Windows applications.) WAV files take up enormous amounts of hard drive and iPod space — 10MB per minute — because they're uncompressed. Don't use WAV for songs that you want to play on an iPod — use the Apple Lossless encoder, AAC, or MP3 instead.

If you want to share your music with someone who uses an MP3 player other than an iPod, you can import or convert songs with the MP3 encoder. As an iPod user, you can use the higher-quality AAC encoder to produce files that are either the same size as their MP3 counterparts but higher in quality, or the same quality but smaller in size.

To have the best possible quality that you can get for future growth and for music editing, consider not using compression at all (as with AIFF or WAV) or using Apple Lossless. You can import music at the highest possible quality, burn it to audio CDs, and then convert it to a lesser-quality format for use in the iPod or other devices. If you use Apple Lossless for songs, you can use those songs on an iPod, but they take up much more space than AAC- or MP3-encoded songs. We describe how to convert music in Chapter 19.

The past, present, and future of music

Our suggestions for encoders and importing preferences for ripping CDs are based on our listening experiences and our preference of the highest quality and the best use of compression technology. You might be quite happy with the results of using these suggestions, but listening pleasure depends entirely on you and the way the song itself was recorded. Some people can hear qualitative differences that others don't hear or don't care about. Some people can also tolerate a lower-quality sound in exchange for the convenience of carrying more music on their iPods. And sometimes the recording is so primitive-sounding that you can get away with using lower-quality settings to gain more hard drive space.

Just a century ago, people gathered at *phonography parties* to rent a headset and listen to a new invention called a phonograph, the predecessor to the record player. Before records, radio, and jukeboxes, these parties and live performances were the only sources of music, and the quality of the sound must have been crude by today's standards, but still quite enjoyable.

The choices of formats for sound have changed considerably from the fragile 78 rpm records from the phonography parties of the early 1900s and the scratchy 45 rpm and 33 rpm records of the 1940s through the 1980s to today's CDs. Consumers had to be on the alert then, as you do now, for dead-end formats that could lock up music in a cul-de-sac of technology, never to be played again. You know what we're talking about — dead-end formats, such as the ill-fated 8-track cartridge or the legendary quadraphonic LP. You want your digital music to last forever and play at high quality — not get stuck with technology that doesn't evolve with the times.

Digital music has evolved beyond the commercial audio CD, and computers haven't yet caught up to some of the latest audio formats. For example, iTunes can't yet import sound from these formats:

- **DVD-audio:** DVD-audio is a relatively new digital audio format developed from the format for DVD video. DVD-audio is based on PCM recording technology but offers improved sound quality by using a higher sampling frequency and longer word lengths. Neither iTunes nor Musicmatch Jukebox support the DVD-audio format, but you can import a digital video file containing DVD-audio sound into iMovie, extract the sound, and export the sound in AIFF or WAV format, which you can use with iTunes. You can also use Toast 7 Titanium from Roxio (www.roxio.com) to import and burn DVD-audio. You can maintain its sampling frequency of 48 kHz (which is higher than the 44.1 kHz sampling rate of audio CDs) by setting the Sample Rate pop-up menu in the custom settings for AIFF or WAV to 48.0 kHz.

- **Super Audio CD (SACD):** Super Audio CD is a new format developed from the past audio format for CDs. The SACD format is based on Direct Stream Digital (DSD) recording technology that closely reproduces the shape of the original analog waveforms to produce a more natural, higher-quality sound. Originally developed for the digital archiving of priceless analog masters tapes, DSD is based on 1-bit sigma-delta modulation and operates with a sampling frequency of 2.8224 MHz (64 times the 44.1 kHz used in audio CDs). Philips and Sony adopted DSD as the basis for SACD, and the

(continued)

(continued)

format is growing in popularity among audiophiles. However, neither iTunes nor Musicmatch Jukebox support SACD. If you buy music in the SACD format, choose the hybrid format that offers a conventional CD layer and a high-density SACD layer. You can then import the music from the conventional CD layer.

You might also want to take advantage of the compression technology that squeezes more music onto your iPod. Although the Apple-supported AAC format offers far better compression and quality than the MP3 format does (at the same bit rates), the MP3 format is more universal, supported by other players and software programs as well as iPods and iTunes. Sticking with AAC or Apple Lossless as your encoder might make you feel like your songs are stuck inside iTunes with the MP3 blues again. However, with iTunes and your iPod, you can mix and match these formats as you please.

Manic Compression Has Captured Your Song

Every person hears the effects of compression differently. You might not hear any problem with a compressed song that someone else says is tinny or lacking in depth.

Too much compression can be a bad thing. Further compressing an already-compressed music file — say, by converting a song — reduces the quality significantly. Not only that, but after your song is compressed, you can't uncompress the song back to its original quality. Your song is essentially locked into that quality, at best.

The lossy-style compression of the MP3 and AAC formats loses information each time you use it, which means that if you compress something that has already been compressed, you lose even more information. This is bad. Don't compress something that's already compressed with a lossy method.

The Apple Lossless encoder doesn't use a lossy method, which is why it's called *lossless*. This is also why it reduces sound files to only two-thirds of their AIFF or WAV counterparts — which isn't as useful for saving space as the compression to one-tenth the size that's common with MP3 or AAC.

MP3 and AAC use two basic lossy methods to compress audio:

✔ **Removing non-audible frequencies:** The compression removes what you supposedly can't hear (although this subject is up for debate). For example, if a background singer's warble is totally drowned out by the intensity of a rhythm guitar chord, the compression algorithm loses the singer's sound while maintaining the guitar's sound.

✔ **Removing less important signals:** Within the spectrum of sound frequencies, some frequencies are considered to be less important in terms of rendering fidelity, and some frequencies most people can't hear at all. Removing specific frequencies is likely to be less damaging to your music than other types of compression, depending on how you hear things. In fact, your dog might stop getting agitated at songs that contain ultra-high frequencies that only dogs can hear (such as the ending of "Day in the Life" by The Beatles).

Selecting Import Settings

The AAC and MP3 formats compress sound at different quality settings. iTunes lets you set the bit rate for importing, which determines the audio quality. You need to use a higher bit rate (such as 192 or 320 Kbps) for higher quality, which — all together now — increases the file size.

Variable Bit Rate (VBR) encoding is a technique that varies the number of bits used to store the music depending on the complexity of the sound. Although the quality of VBR is endlessly debated, it's useful when set to the highest setting because VBR can encode at up to the maximum bit rate of 320 Kbps in those rare cases where the sound requires it, but it keeps the majority of the sound at a lower bit rate.

iTunes also lets you control the *sample rate* during importing, which is the number of times per second the sound waveform is captured digitally (or *sampled*). Higher sample rates yield higher-quality sound and large file sizes. However, never use a higher sample rate than the rate used for the source. CDs use a 44.100 kHz rate, so choosing a higher rate is unnecessary unless you convert a song that was recorded from Digital Audio Tape (DAT), DVD, or directly into the computer at a high sample rate, and you want to keep that sample rate.

Another setting to consider during importing is the Channel choice. *Stereo,* which offers two channels of music for left and right speakers, is the norm for music. However, *mono* — monaural or single-channel — was the norm for pop records before the mid-1960s. (Phil Spector was known for his high-quality monaural recordings, and the early Rolling Stones records are in mono.) Monaural recordings take up half the space of stereo recordings when digitized. Most likely, you want to keep stereo recordings in stereo, and mono recordings in mono.

Chapter 19

Changing Encoders and Encoder Settings

*Y*ou might want to change your import settings before ripping CDs, depending on the type of music, the source of the recording, or other factors, such as whether you plan to copy the songs to your iPod or burn an audio or MP3 CD. The encoders offer general quality settings, but you can also customize the encoders and change those settings to your liking. Whether you use iTunes or Musicmatch Jukebox, the software remembers your custom settings until you change them again.

If you're using Musicmatch, visit the companion Web site at www.dummies. com/go/ipod4e to find out what type of encoders it offers.

This chapter provides the nuts-and-bolts details on changing your import settings to customize each type of encoder, importing sounds other than music, and converting songs from one format to another. With the choice of settings for music encoders, you can impress your audiophile friends — even ones who doubted that your computer could reproduce magnificent music.

You can also convert songs to another format, as we describe in "Converting Songs to a Different Encoder Format in iTunes" later in this chapter. However, you can't convert songs that you buy from the iTunes Music Store to another file format, because they're encoded as protected AAC files. If you could, they wouldn't be protected, would they? You also can't convert Audible audio books and spoken-word content to another format. (However, you can burn them to an audio CD and re-import them, which might cause a noticeable drop in quality.)

Customizing the Encoder Settings in iTunes

To change your encoder and quality settings and other importing preferences before ripping an audio CD or converting a file in iTunes, follow these steps:

1. **Choose iTunes⇨Preferences (Mac), or Edit⇨Preferences (Windows), click the Advanced tab, and then click the Importing tab.**

   The Importing preferences appear, allowing you to make changes to the encoding format and its settings.

2. **Choose the encoding format that you want to convert the song into and select the settings for that format.**

   The Setting pop-up menu offers different settings depending on your choice of encoder in the Import Using pop-up menu. See the sections on each encoding format later in this chapter for details on settings.

3. **Click OK to accept changes.**

   After changing your importing preferences and until you change them again, iTunes uses these preferences whenever it imports or converts songs.

The AAC, MP3, AIFF, and WAV encoders let you customize the settings for the encoders. The Apple Lossless encoder is automatic and offers no custom settings to change.

Changing AAC encoder settings

We recommend using the AAC encoder for everything except music that you intend to burn on an audio CD or an MP3 CD; AAC offers the best trade-off of space and quality for hard drives and iPods.

The Setting pop-up menu for the AAC encoder offers three choices: High Quality, Spoken Podcast, and Custom, as shown in Figure 19-1. The Spoken Podcast setting is useful for converting podcasts exported from GarageBand or a similar audio-editing application into iTunes. We recommend using the High Quality setting for most music you rip from CDs, but for very intense music (such as complex jazz or classical music, recordings with lots of instruments, or your most favorite songs), you might want to fine-tune the settings. To customize your AAC encoder settings, select the Custom option from the Setting pop-up menu to see the AAC Encoder dialog, as shown in Figure 19-2.

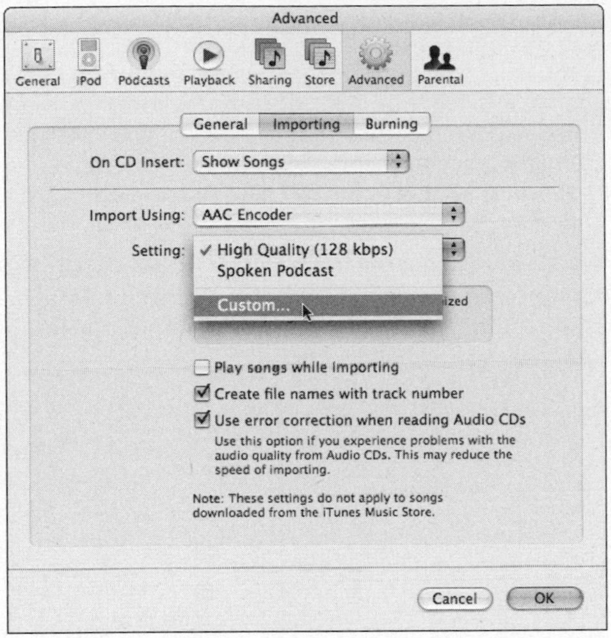

Figure 19-1:
Customize
the settings
for the AAC
encoder.

The custom settings for AAC (see Figure 19-2) allow you to change the
following:

✔ **Stereo Bit Rate:** This pop-up menu allows you to select the bit rate,
which is measured in kilobits per second (Kbps). Use a higher bit rate
for higher quality, which also increases the file size. The highest-quality
setting for this format is 320 Kbps; 128 is considered high quality.

✔ **Sample Rate:** This pop-up menu enables you to select the *sample rate*,
which is the number of times per second the sound waveform is captured digitally (or *sampled*). Higher sample rates yield higher-quality
sound and larger file sizes. However, never use a higher sample rate than
the rate used for the source. CDs use a 44.1 kHz rate.

✔ **Use Variable Bit Rate Encoding (VBR):** This option helps keep file size
down, but quality might be affected. VBR varies the number of bits used
to store the music depending on the complexity of the sound. If you
select the Highest setting from the Quality pop-up menu for VBR, iTunes
encodes up to the maximum bit rate of 320 Kbps in sections of songs
where the sound is complex enough to require a high bit rate. Meanwhile, iTunes keeps the rest of the song at a lower bit rate to save file
space. The lower limit is set by the rate that you select in the Stereo Bit
Rate pop-up menu.

✔ **Channels:** This pop-up menu enables you to choose how you want the music to play through speakers — in stereo or mono. Stereo offers two channels of music for left and right speakers, and mono offers only one channel but takes up half the space of stereo recordings when digitized. If the recording is in stereo, don't choose mono; you lose part of the sound. (You might lose vocals or guitar riffs, depending on the recording.) Select the Auto setting to have iTunes use the appropriate setting for the music.

✔ **Optimize for Voice:** This option filters the sound to favor the human voice. Podcasters can use this option, along with the AAC encoder, to convert audio recordings into a podcast format optimal for iTunes.

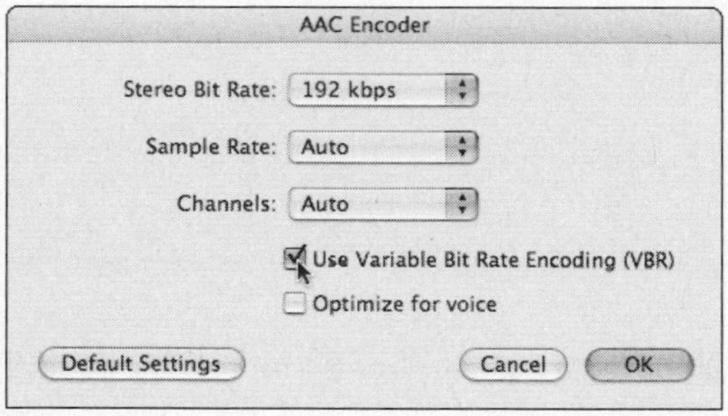

Figure 19-2:
Set the AAC encoder to import with the highest bit rate and with automatic detection of sample rate and channels.

AAC Encoder
Stereo Bit Rate: 192 kbps
Sample Rate: Auto
Channels: Auto
☑ Use Variable Bit Rate Encoding (VBR)
☐ Optimize for voice
Default Settings   Cancel   OK

We recommend selecting the highest bit rate in the Stereo Bit Rate pop-up menu and leaving the other two pop-up menus set to Auto.

Changing MP3 encoder settings

We prefer using the AAC encoder for music that we play on our iPods, but as of this writing, other MP3 players don't support AAC. The iPod supports both AAC and MP3 formats. You might want to use the MP3 encoder for other reasons, such as acquiring more control over the compression parameters and gaining compatibility with other applications and players that support MP3.

The MP3 encoder offers four choices for the Setting pop-up menu on the Importing preferences tab:

✔ **Good Quality (128 Kbps):** This is certainly fine for audio books, comedy records, and old scratchy records. You might even want to use a lower bit rate for voice recordings.

✔ **High Quality (160 Kbps):** Most people consider this high enough for most popular music, but we go higher with our music.

✔ **Higher Quality (192 Kbps):** This one's high enough for just about all types of music.

✔ **Custom:** To fine-tune the MP3 encoder settings, select the Custom setting. Customizing your MP3 settings increases the quality of the sound and keeps file size low.

The MP3 encoder offers a bunch of choices in its custom settings dialog (see Figure 19-3):

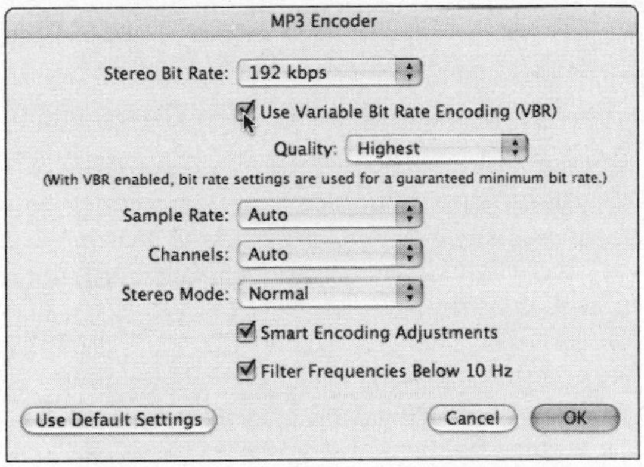

Figure 19-3:
Customize the settings for the MP3 encoder.

> MP3 Encoder
>
> Stereo Bit Rate: 192 kbps
> ☑ Use Variable Bit Rate Encoding (VBR)
> Quality: Highest
> (With VBR enabled, bit rate settings are used for a guaranteed minimum bit rate.)
> Sample Rate: Auto
> Channels: Auto
> Stereo Mode: Normal
> ☑ Smart Encoding Adjustments
> ☑ Filter Frequencies Below 10 Hz
>
> Use Default Settings   Cancel   OK

✔ **Stereo Bit Rate:** This pop-up menu's choices are measured in kilobits per second; select a higher bit rate for higher quality, which increases the file size. The most common bit rate for MP3 files you find on the Web is 128 Kbps. Lower bit rates are more appropriate for voice recordings or sound effects.

We recommend at least 192 Kbps for most music, and we use 320 Kbps, the maximum setting, for songs that we play on our iPods.

✔ **Use Variable Bit Rate Encoding (VBR):** This option helps keep file size down, but quality might be affected. VBR varies the number of bits used to store the music depending on the complexity of the sound. If you select the Highest setting from the Quality pop-up menu for VBR, iTunes encodes up to the maximum bit rate of 320 Kbps in sections of songs where the sound is complex enough to require a high bit rate.

Meanwhile, iTunes keeps the rest of the song at a lower bit rate to save file space. The lower limit is set by the rate that you select in the Stereo Bit Rate pop-up menu.

Some audiophiles swear by VBR, but others don't ever use it. We use it only when importing at low bit rates, and we set VBR to its highest-quality setting.

Although your iPod plays VBR-encoded MP3 music, other MP3 players might not support VBR.

✔ **Sample Rate:** This pop-up menu enables you to select the sample rate (the number of times per second that the sound waveform is captured digitally). Higher sample rates yield higher quality sound and larger file sizes. However, never use a higher sample rate than the rate used for the source — CDs use a 44.1 kHz rate.

✔ **Channels:** This pop-up menu enables you to choose how you want the music to play through speakers; in stereo or mono. Stereo, which offers two channels of music for left and right speakers, is the norm for music. Monaural (mono) recordings take up half the space of stereo recordings when digitized. Choose the Auto setting to have iTunes use the appropriate setting for the music.

✔ **Stereo Mode:** This pop-up menu enables you to select Normal or Joint Stereo. Normal mode is just what you think it is — normal stereo. Select the Joint Stereo setting to make the file smaller by removing information that's identical in both channels of a stereo recording, using only one channel for that information while the other channel carries unique information. At bit rates of 128 Kbps and below, this mode can actually improve the sound quality. However, we typically don't use the Joint Stereo mode when using a high-quality bit rate.

✔ **Smart Encoding Adjustments:** This option, when selected, tells iTunes to analyze your MP3 encoding settings and music source and to change your settings as needed to maximize the quality of the encoded files.

✔ **Filter Frequencies Below 10 Hz:** This option, when selected, filters out low frequency sounds. Frequencies below 10 Hz are hard to hear, and most people don't notice if they're missing. Filtering inaudible frequencies helps reduce the file size with little or no perceived loss in quality. However, we think selecting this option and removing the low-frequency sounds detracts from the overall feeling of the music, and we prefer not to filter frequencies.

Changing AIFF and WAV encoder settings

We recommend that you use the AIFF, WAV, or Apple Lossless encoders for songs from audio CDs if you intend to burn your own audio CDs with the music. You get the best possible quality with these encoders because the music isn't compressed with a lossy algorithm. The Apple Lossless encoder (which is automatic and offers no settings to change) reduces file size to about 60–70 percent of the size of AIFF or WAV versions. However, AIFF or WAV files are preferable for use with digital sound-editing programs, and they offer settings that you can change, such as the number of channels (Stereo or Mono) and the sampling rate.

The AIFF and WAV formats have technical differences, but the only major difference in storing and playing music is that AIFF is the standard for Mac applications and computers, and WAV is the standard for PC applications and computers.

You can import music with AIFF or WAV at the highest possible quality and then convert the music files to a lesser-quality format for use in your iPod.

AIFF and WAV files take up huge amounts of hard drive space (about 10MB per minute), and although you can play them on your iPod, they take up way too much space and battery power to be convenient for anyone but the most discerning audiophile who can afford multiple iPods. You can handle these large files by adding another hard drive or by backing up portions of your music library onto other media, such as a DVD-R (which can hold 4.38GB). The high quality of AIFF and WAV ensures an excellent listening experience through a home stereo. However, if multiple hard drives and backup scenarios sound like unwanted hassles, use the AAC or MP3 encoders to compress files so that they take up less space on your hard drive.

The AIFF and WAV encoders offer similar custom settings dialogs; the AIFF Encoder dialog is shown in Figure 19-4. The pop-up menus offer settings for Sample Rate, Sample Size, and Channels. You can select the Auto setting for all three pop-up menus, and iTunes automatically detects the proper sample rate, size, and channels from the source. If you select a specific setting, such as the Stereo setting in the Channels pop-up menu, iTunes imports the music in stereo, regardless of the source. Audio CDs typically sample at a rate of 44.1 kHz, with a sample size of 16 bits, and with stereo channels.

Figure 19-4:
The
Channels
pop-up
menu in the
AIFF
encoder
custom
settings
allows you
to import
regardless
of the
source.

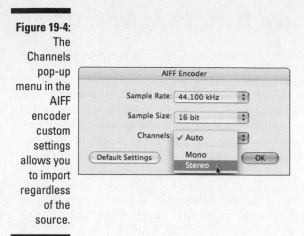

The Sample Rate pop-up menu for AIFF and WAV offers more choices than for AAC, down to a very low sample rate of 8 kHz, which is suitable only for voice recordings.

Importing Voice and Sound Effects in iTunes

Audio books are available from Audible (www.audible.com) and from the iTunes store in a special format that doesn't require any further compression, but you can also import audio books, spoken-word titles, comedy CDs, and other voice recordings in the MP3 format.

If the recording has any music at all or requires close listening to stereo channels (such as a Firesign Theatre or Monty Python CD), treat the entire recording as music and skip this section. ("Nudge-nudge, wink-wink. Sorry! Everything you know is wrong!")

By fine-tuning the import settings for voice recordings and sound effects, you can save a significant amount of space without reducing quality. We recommend the following settings, depending on your choice of encoder:

- ✔ **AAC:** AAC allows you to get away with an even lower bit rate than MP3 to achieve the same quality, thereby saving more space. We recommend a bit rate as low as 80 Kbps for sound effects and voice recordings. Use the Optimize for Voice option to filter the sound to favor the human voice.

- ✔ **MP3:** Use a low bit rate (such as 96 Kbps). You might also want to reduce the sample rate to 22.05 kHz for voice recordings. Filter frequencies below 10 Hz because voice recordings don't need such frequencies.

Converting Songs to a Different Encoder Format in iTunes

Converting a song from one format to another is useful if you want to use one format for one purpose, such as burning a CD, and a second format for another task, such as playing on your iPod. It's also useful for converting uncompressed songs or podcasts that were created in GarageBand (or a similar audio-editing application) and exported or copied to iTunes.

Converting a song from one compressed format to another is possible (say from AAC to MP3), but you might not like the results. When you convert a compressed file to another compressed format, iTunes compresses the music *twice,* reducing the quality of the sound. You get the best results by starting with an uncompressed song that was imported in the AIFF or WAV format and then converting that song to the compressed AAC or MP3 format.

You can tell what format a song is in by selecting it and then choosing File⇨ Get Info. Then click the Summary tab to see the song's format. You might want to keep track of formats by creating CD-AIFF-version and iPod-MP3-version playlists for different formats.

To convert a song to another encoding format, follow these steps:

1. **Choose iTunes⇨Preferences (Mac), or choose Edit⇨Preferences (Windows), click the Advanced tab, and then click the Importing tab.**

   The Importing preferences appear, allowing you to make changes to the encoding format and its settings.

2. **Select the encoding format that you want to convert the song into from the Import Using pop-up menu; in the Custom Settings dialog that appears, select the settings for that encoder.**

For example, if you're converting songs in the AIFF format to the MP3 format, choose MP3 Encoder from the Import Using pop-up menu and then select the settings that you want in the MP3 Encoder dialog that appears.

3. **Click OK to accept the settings for your chosen format.**

4. **In the iTunes window, select the song(s) that you want to convert, and then choose Advanced⇨Convert Selection⇨*encoder*.**

   The encoding format that you chose in Step 2 appears on the menu: Convert Selection to MP3, Convert Selection to AAC, Convert Selection to AIFF, or Convert Selection to WAV. Choose the appropriate menu operation to perform the conversion. When the conversion is complete, the newly converted version of the song appears in your iTunes library (with the same artist name and song name, so it's easy to find). iTunes doesn't delete the original version — both are stored in your music library.

If you convert songs obtained from the Internet, you might find MP3 songs with bit rates as low as 128 Kbps, and choosing a higher stereo bit rate doesn't improve the quality — it only wastes space.

The automatic copy-and-convert operation can be useful for converting an entire music library to another format — press Option (Mac) or Alt (Windows), choose Advanced⇨Convert Selection, and all the songs copy and convert automatically. If you have a library of AIFF tunes, you can quickly copy and convert them to AAC or MP3 in one step and then assign the AIFF songs to the AIFF-associated playlists for burning CDs, and MP3 or AAC songs to MP3 or AAC playlists that you intend to copy to your iPod.

Chapter 20

Enhancing Your iTunes Library

Your iTunes library is the center of your entertainment world — your control console for playing Master DJ at the party, your video player that plays the latest releases from the iTunes Music Store, your basement studio for burning CDs, and your archive of the most important content in the universe. Of course you want to enhance it in any way possible.

In this chapter, we cover ways to enhance your iTunes library. We cover downloading music from online sources other than the iTunes Music Store as well as digitizing records, tapes, and music from other analog sources. We also cover converting video from sources such as DVDs, adding songs and podcasts you create in GarageBand and other applications, and modifying the starting and stopping points within songs, audio books, podcast episodes, and videos. We also cover how to split a track into multiple tracks.

Downloading Music from Other Sources

The iTunes Music Store isn't the only place to get music online for your iPod. Other digital music services such as Napster 2.0, Rhapsody, BuyMusic.com, MusicNow, and Musicmatch also offer music you can purchase.

You can find music in the following types of places online:

✔ **From the source:** New artists and musicians and even legendary bands are increasingly offering a bit of music on their Web sites for free. This is the best source of free music because it's legal and benefits the artists directly — they want you to listen and tell your friends. Examples include The Zen Tricksters (www.zentricksters.com/home.html), Little Feat (www.littlefeat.net), and the Flying Other Brothers (www.flyingotherbros.com).

✔ **Protected music:** Online music stores and services offer protected music for sale. You can't import Windows Media–protected songs and other protected formats into iTunes; they're tied to the computer and player used for the format. However, you can burn a CD with the music (using a different player, such as Windows Media Player) and then import the CD into iTunes. You lose no quality because burning a CD doesn't reduce the music's quality, and ripping the CD in iTunes doesn't reduce the music's quality if you use the AIFF format or the Apple Lossless encoder.

✔ **Unprotected music:** Some online services and Web sites offer unprotected music for sale or for free downloading as part of a promotion for artists. These sites and services typically offer MP3 files that you can import directly into either the Mac or Windows versions of iTunes, or Windows Media (WMA) unprotected files you can import into the Windows version of iTunes. For example, Warp Records (a prominent electronic music label) hosts Bleep (www.warprecords.com/bleep), which offers downloads of ordinary MP3s from several independent labels, without copy protection, for about $1.35 a song.

✔ **Swapped music:** Free networks using peer-to-peer technology allow users to swap music for free. That is, people can trade music, but the network essentially allows them to download music from others on the network for free. Some artists use these networks to freely disseminate their works to the largest possible audience. One of the largest, if not the largest, is Usenet, which offers music-related newsgroups that accommodate nearly everyone's musical tastes, along with samples that you can download for free. In order to download music files from Usenet, you need a Usenet newsreader program such as Barca or News Rover (see www.newsreaders.com for a list), or you can use a Web Gateway such as Google Groups (http://groups.google.com).

Some networks are considered "pirate" networks because they allow copyrighted content to be traded and operate outside the legal jurisdiction of the United States copyright law and the laws of other countries. We don't recommend pirate networks for two reasons. One, we believe copyright owners deserve to have some control over distribution, even free distribution. Two, the music might not be the highest quality because of compromises (such as lower bit rates for MP3 files, which make for poorer quality music).

If you have a choice of music formats to download, choose the highest-quality format that you can download (depending on the bandwidth of your Internet connection) — typically MP3 at the highest bit rate offered. iTunes can import AIFF, WAV, AAC, Apple Lossless, and MP3 files, and the Windows version of iTunes can also import WMA (unprotected) files if you have Windows Media Player version 9 installed on your PC. You can use AIFF, WAV, AAC, Apple Lossless, or MP3 files in your iPod and convert files from other formats into these formats, as we describe in Chapter 19.

If you're using Musicmatch, visit the companion Web site at www.dummies. com/go/ipod4e to find out how to choose the appropriate formats to download music successfully to Musicmatch.

Recording Records, Tapes, and Other Analog Sources

You can find millions of songs on the Internet, and some digital recordings of songs might even be good enough to please audiophiles. With so many songs available in the iTunes Music Store, you might not want to spend a lot of time recording and digitizing the hits from your record collection, or even the B-sides and album cuts. Most likely those songs are also available from the online store in digital form, ready to play.

However, you might have sounds that were never released on CD or made available to the public. Rare record collectors and tape archivists — you know who you are — have recordings that aren't available on the Internet or on CD, and if you create your own music, how do you get that stuff into your iTunes library so that you can burn a CD or include the songs on your iPod?

You can record and digitize sounds from other sources, such as tape players and turntables, and store the digital recordings in your iTunes library. You can also set the start and stop times of songs in your iTunes library, as we describe later in this chapter — which is a trick you can use to edit the beginnings and endings of songs.

All the applications described here are commercially available for downloading from the Internet. Some are free to use, some are free for a limited time before you have to pay, and some require cash up front. Nevertheless, all are worth checking out if you have sounds you want to put into iTunes.

You can bring sound directly into your computer from a sound system or home stereo that offers a stereo audio output connection (such as tape-out) or even directly from a cassette player or microphone. If you have old vinyl records with music that can't be found anymore, on CD or otherwise, you can convert the music to digital by using a phonograph connected to a stereo system with a tape-out connection.

You can copy songs already converted to digital into iTunes directly without any recording procedure. For example, MP3 CDs are easy to import. Because they're essentially data CDs, simply insert them into your CD-ROM drive, open the CD in Windows or the Mac Finder, and drag and drop the MP3 song files into the iTunes window. Downloaded song files are even easier — just drag and drop the files into iTunes. If you drag a folder or CD icon, all the audio files that it contains are added to your iTunes library.

Before recording sound into your computer, be sure that you have enough hard drive space to record the audio in an uncompressed form (which is best for highest quality). If you're recording an hour of high-quality music, you need about 600MB of hard drive space to record it.

Connecting and setting up audio input

Most computers offer a line-in connection that accepts a cable with a stereo mini-plug. You can connect any kind of mono or stereo audio source, such as an amplifier or a preamp, a CD or DVD player, or an all-in-one stereo system that offers recording through a tape-out or similar connection.

Find the line-out or tape-out connection in your stereo system and connect a cable that uses RCA-type left and right stereo plugs or a stereo mini-plug to this connection. See Chapter 16 for more information about audio cables. Connect the stereo mini-plug to your computer's line-in connection. You can then record anything that plays on your home stereo into your computer.

If your computer doesn't offer a line-in connection, you can purchase a Universal Serial Bus (USB) audio input device, such as the Griffin iMic (www.griffintechnology.com).

When recording from a phonograph (turntable for vinyl records), the phonograph must either include an amplifier or be connected to an amplifier in order to raise the signal to line levels and apply proper equalization curves.

After connecting the audio source to your computer, set the audio input for your computer and adjust the volume for recording.

On a Mac, follow these steps:

1. **Choose System Preferences from the Apple menu or the Dock and then click the Sound icon.**

2. Click the Input tab.

The Input tab displays the sound input preferences, as shown in Figure 20-1.

3. Choose Line In from the list of input devices.

Use Line In to record into your computer. The alternative is to use the built-in microphone, which is useful for recording live performances but not for records or tapes because it also picks up any noise in the room.

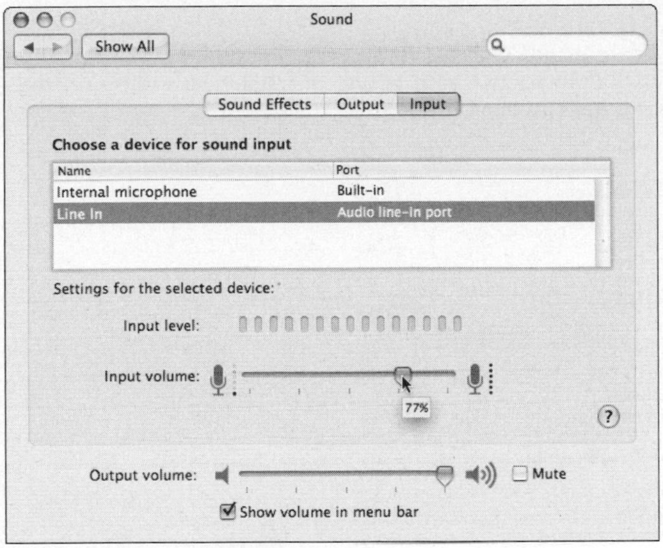

Figure 20-1:
Set audio input to Line In and adjust the input volume.

4. Play the source of the sound.

5. While playing, adjust the volume for the line-in input.

As it plays, watch the input level meter. As the volume gets louder, the oblong purple dots seem to light up with highlights, from left to right. To adjust the volume, drag the Input Volume slider. If all the dots are high-lighted all the time, you're way too *hot* (studio tech talk for being too loud). If the dots are not highlighted at all, you're way too *low*. (For some reason, the studio techs don't say *cool* or *cold* — just *low*.) You want the dots to be highlighted about three-fourths of the way across from left to right for optimal input volume.

6. Quit System Preferences by choosing System Preferences⇨Quit System Preferences (⌘-Q) or by clicking the red button in the top-left corner of the window.

On a Windows PC, you must have a line-in connection and an audio card driver that controls it. Some PCs are equipped only with microphone-controlling drivers, and some offer both line-in and microphone input. If you have the appropriate hardware, follow these steps:

1. **Open the sound properties control panel.**

   Right-click the small speaker icon in the system tray and choose Adjust Audio Properties. In the Windows Mixer dialog that appears, choose Options⇨Properties.

2. **Click the Audio tab.**

   As shown in Figure 20-2, the Sounds and Audio Devices Properties window offers sections for sound playback, sound recording, and MIDI (Musical Instrument Digital Interface) music playback.

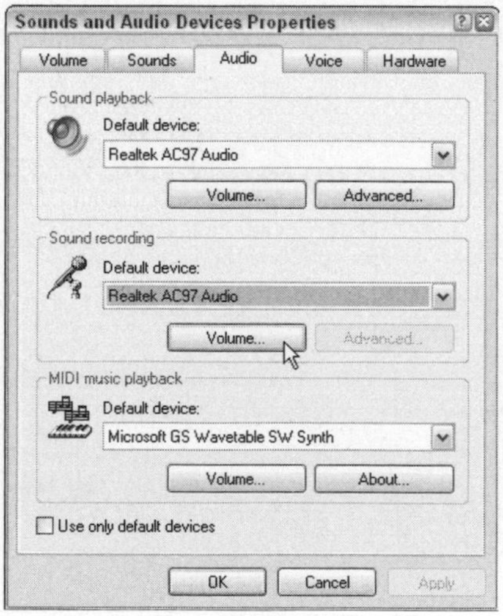

Figure 20-2:
Set audio input and adjust the volume of input for a Windows PC.

3. **Choose the input device for sound recording.**

   Use the pop-up menu in the Sound Recording section to choose the input device, which is the hardware for controlling the line-in connection or microphone. In Windows Mixer, select Recording in the Adjust Volume section and then turn on the option for Line-In or Microphone to get to the Recording Control panel.

4. **Click the Volume button in the Sound Recording section to set the input volume.**

   The Volume window offers a Volume slider.

5. **Drag the Volume slider to set the input volume.**

   The left side is low, and the right is high.

6. **Click OK to finish and save your settings.**

Choosing a sound-editing application

The Sound Studio application lets you record and digitize directly to your hard drive on a Mac running OS X. You can download a copy free from Felt Tip Software (www.felttip.com/products/soundstudio). You can then use it for two weeks before having to pay $49.99 for it.

Toast 7 Titanium from Roxio (www.roxio.com) for Mac OS X includes the CD Spin Doctor (version 3.1, at present) application for recording sounds. CD Spin Doctor offers a Noise Reducer option to select filters for noise reduction: *de-click* removes loud distortions, which occur frequently with vinyl records; *de-crackle* removes surface crackling, which happens often with well-played vinyl records; and *de-hiss* removes the hissing noise that occurs with many different analog sources, including records and tapes. Roxio also offers a Windows application, Easy Media Creator 8, which includes the LP and Tape Assistant for streamlining the process of converting classic analog recordings. You can apply similar cleaning effects as CD Spin Doctor to easily remove noise, pops, and clicks from old recordings.

Recording from Video Sources

You can find video on the Internet from sources such as YouTube (www.youtube.com) and iPod Movies Unlimited (www.ipodmoviesunlimited.com), as well as the iTunes Music Store. You may also want to bring into iTunes video from other sources, such as camcorders, as we describe in Chapter 5. However, you need to know the best methods for converting videos to work properly with your iPod. This section also describes how to bring in movies from commercial DVDs.

Converting video files to use with iPods

Although iTunes accepts a number of different video file formats (including MPEG-4 and H.264), not all of these formats, and not all of the settings for these formats, work on your iPod display. The major reason is display resolution: The iPod can display no more than 76,800 pixels for H.264 and no more than 230,400 for MPEG-4, and these pixels must be collected into square 16-pixel blocks, limiting you to certain aspect ratios.

When converting videos from other sources, such as DVDs, keep in mind the following settings and resolutions for these formats that work in an iPod:

- ✓ **H.264:** This format is best for playing on the iPod. You can set your video image size to 320 x 240 pixels with a data rate up to 768 Kbps and a frame rate up to 30 fps. Although it might not look as good as MPEG-4 on a television, most people don't know the difference, and the file size is usually smaller. Other resolutions you can use include 480 x 160, 432 x 176, 400 x 192, and 272 x 272 pixels.

- ✓ **MPEG-4:** This format is better for playing on a television connected to your iPod, but also looks fine on an iPod; it just takes up more iPod space and uses more power during playback. You can set your image size to 480 x 480 pixels with a data rate up to 2.5 Mbps and a frame rate up to 30 fps. It might not look as good as H.264 on the iPod, but it looks better than H.264 on a television. Other resolutions you can use include 784 x 288, 752 x 304, 720 x 320 (excellent for movies displayed in *letterbox,* a format that maintains the rectangular theater image on a television), and 640 x 352 pixels.

To bring a video file into iTunes, simply drag it into the iTunes window or over the iTunes icon. When the video is in iTunes, you can use it in your iPod immediately, or after you have iTunes perform a simple (but often time-consuming) conversion. You can also perform this conversion yourself by using other software (such as a DVD ripper and converter).

To convert videos in the iTunes library into a format that looks better when played on an iPod, select the video in your iTunes library, Control-click (Mac) or right-click (Windows), and choose Convert Selection for iPod. The selected videos are automatically copied, and the copies are converted to the H.264 format at a width of 320 pixels. The original versions remain unchanged.

Converting video from DVD

Commercial DVDs are typically encrypted with antipiracy software called the Content Scramble System (CSS) as well as Macrovision copy protection and region-coding. Almost all Windows PCs and Macs with DVD players can play DVDs because the systems support regional codes and are licensed by Macrovision and licensed to decrypt the CSS-protected content. Computers that offer a video output connector (such as S-video) must also support the protection technology in order to play copy-protected movies.

All Macs and most new computers equipped with DVD drives are set up to play a DVD automatically upon insertion. Some Windows PC manufacturers, such as Dell, bundle DVD player software. But the bundled player is typically "overruled" by Windows Media Player, which installs itself as the primary DVD player software, unless you've changed the file type assignment for DVD Video (files with `.vob` extension). If you've turned off this file assignment, Windows displays a dialog when you insert a DVD, giving you a choice of players on the system, so that you can pick your own DVD program — such as one of the DVD ripper or converter programs. On a Mac, you can simply quit the DVD Player application when it pops up and then run a program such as Instant HandBrake (`http://handbrake.m0k.org`) to rip the DVD into a suitable file for iTunes.

A variety of free and commercial products offer DVD ripping — if you don't believe us, just Google "DVD ripper" and try to find the right product among the 16,000,000 links. The key feature you need is the ability to save the digital file as MPEG-4 or H.264 or convert it to one of those formats without loss of quality. The following are some that we know are useful, but it certainly isn't a long list — there are just too many to review. (For reviews and comparisons, see DVD Copy Software Review at `http://dvd-copy-software-review.toptenreviews.com`.)

- ✔ **Xilisoft DVD to iPod Converter** (`www.xilisoft.com/dvd-to-ipod-converter.html`) is a powerful DVD ripper that converts DVDs directly to the iPod MP4 movie format optimized for the iPod display.

- ✔ **DVDx** (`http://sourceforge.net/projects/dvdx`) lets you convert DVDs to AVI or Windows Media formats in one step. You can then use a video conversion program such as the Xilisoft Video Converter (`www.xilisoft.com/video-converter.html`) to convert the Windows Media video file to MPEG-4 or H.264.

- ✔ **PQ DVD to iPod Video Converter Suite** (`www.pqdvd.com/dvd-to-ipod-video-converter.html`) converts DVD, TiVo, DivX Video, MPEG, WMV, AVI, RealMedia, and many more formats to iPod Video.

On a Mac, you can use Instant HandBrake (`http://handbrake.m0k.org`), an open source, freely available, DVD-to-MPEG-4 ripper/converter. Instant Hand-Brake can detect all the titles on a DVD and save each title as MPEG-4 or H.264. After ripping the DVD to a file, locate the file and drag it into your iTunes library. Other software for ripping DVDs include iSquint (`www.isquint.org`) and ffmpegX (`www.ffmpegx.com`), which offers iPod preset settings.

Modifying Content in iTunes

Although iTunes was never meant to be a media-editing application, it offers a simple control over the starting and stopping points for playing back media. You can use this feature to cut out unwanted *intros* and *outros* of a song, such as announcers and audience applause, or to skip over opening credits or commercials of movie. You can also use it in conjunction with the Convert feature to split an item into multiple items (or, in the parlance of record label executives and artists, split a track into multiple tracks).

To do more significant modifications or editing, use the applications described in the "Recording Records, Tapes, and Other Analog Sources" section, earlier in this chapter.

Setting the start and stop points

iTunes can play only a portion of a song, video, audio book, or podcast episode — if you specify start and stop times for the item. To set the start and/or stop points, select the item, choose File➪Get Info, and then click Options. You can specify the start and stop times in the Info dialog, as shown in Figure 20-3.

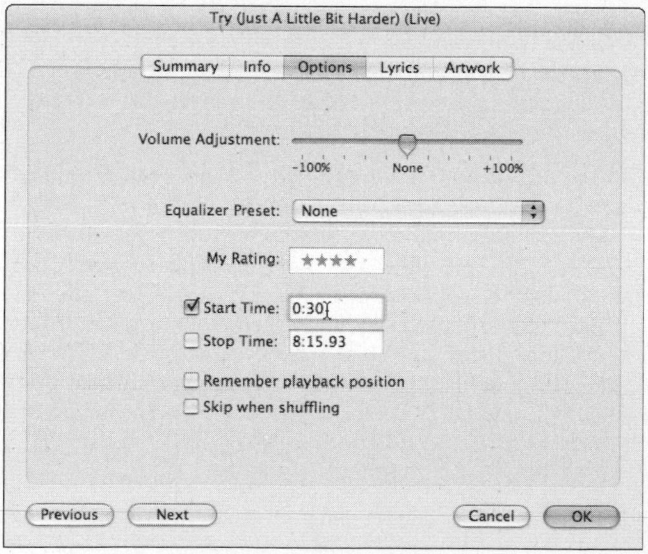

Try (Just A Little Bit Harder) (Live)

| Summary | Info | Options | Lyrics | Artwork |

Volume Adjustment: ———⬤———
-100%   None   +100%

Equalizer Preset: None

My Rating: ★★★★

☑ Start Time: 0:30

☐ Stop Time: 8:15.93

☐ Remember playback position
☐ Skip when shuffling

Previous   Next   Cancel   OK

Figure 20-3:
Set the start time.

Click inside the Start Time field to set the start time; for example, in Figure 20-3, we set the Start Time to 0:30 (30 seconds). Click inside the Stop Time field to set the stop time. The time is in minutes, seconds, and hundredths of a second (decimal) — 8:15.93 is 8 minutes and 15.93 seconds.

To determine with accuracy the time for the start and stop points, play the file and look in the Status pane at the top-center part of the iTunes window for the Elapsed Time. You can drag the slider in the Status pane to move quickly and find the exact times for the start and stop points you want to set. *Note:* If you click Elapsed Time in the Status pane, it toggles to Remaining Time; click it again for Total Time, and click it once more to see Elapsed Time again.

iTunes plays only the part of the content between the start and stop times. You can use this feature to your advantage because when you convert a song to another format (such as AIFF to MP3), iTunes converts only the part of the song between the start and stop times.

Splitting a track into multiple tracks

You might have a CD that was created with all the songs combined into one track, or you might have recorded an entire side of a vinyl record or cassette tape into one sound file. Either way, you probably want to separate the songs into separate tracks in iTunes.

The best way to split a long track into smaller tracks is to open the sound file in a sound-editing program that lets you select sections and save them separately, as we describe in "Recording Records, Tapes, and Other Analog Sources," earlier in this chapter.

However, you can also separate a track into smaller tracks in iTunes as long as you use the AIFF format at first. Follow these steps:

1. **Before ripping a CD or importing a sound file, set the encoder in your importing preferences to AIFF.**

   See Chapter 5 to find out how to import music with the AIFF encoder.

2. **Rip the CD track into iTunes or import an AIFF sound file into iTunes.**

   Because you set the importing preferences to AIFF, the CD track is imported into iTunes as AIFF at full quality. You want to do this step because you're going to convert it in iTunes later, and you need the uncompressed version to convert. Use a song name to identify this track as a long track with multiple tracks — for example, call it *side one* or something like that.

3. **Change your importing preferences to AAC or MP3. (We use AAC mostly.)**

   See Chapter 5 for more about importing.

4. **Select the song in iTunes and choose File⇨Get Info.**

   The song information dialog appears.

5. **Click Options to show the Start Time and Stop Time fields.**

   You can set the start and stop times for the song (refer to Figure 20-3).

6. **Define the Start Time and Stop Time for the first song in the long track and then click OK.**

   Play the song and look in the Status pane at the top-center part of the iTunes window for the Elapsed Time. You can drag the slider in the Status pane to move quickly through the song and find the exact times for the start and stop points you want to set. For example, if the first song were exactly 3 minutes and 12 seconds, you would define the first section to start at 0:00 and stop at 3:12. After setting the start and stop times, click OK to close the song information window.

7. **Convert the defined segment of the long track from AIFF to AAC or MP3.**

   Select the long track *(side one)* and choose Advanced⇨Convert Selection to AAC (or Advanced⇨Convert Selection to MP3 if you chose the MP3 encoder in Step 3). iTunes converts only the section of the song defined by the Start Time and Stop Time fields that you set in Step 6, and creates a new song track in the AAC or MP3 format (depending on your choice in Step 3). iTunes converts the uncompressed AIFF segment into the compressed AAC or MP3 format.

8. **Change the song name of the newly converted track to the actual song name.**

   The converted section of the long track still has the same name *(side one)*. Change its name by clicking inside the song name in the iTunes song list or by choosing File⇨Get Info, clicking the Info tab, and clicking in the Name field. You can also enter a track number in the Track field.

9. **Repeat Steps 4–8 for each song segment.**

   Repeat these steps, selecting the long track *(side one)* each time and setting a new start and stop time for each new song, converting the song to MP3 or AAC, and then changing each newly converted song's name.

10. **When you finish, delete the long track in AIFF format.**

    Delete the long track *(side one)* by selecting it and pressing Delete/Backspace. You don't need it anymore if you converted all the segments to separate songs.

Part V
Have iPod, Will Travel

The 5th Wave
By Rich Tennant

"Why can't you just bring your iPod like everyone else?"

In this part . . .

This part explains how you can use your iPod to take care of personal business the way people often use PDAs — especially on the road. It also covers how to troubleshoot problems with your iPod.

- Chapter 21 helps you listen to tunes whenever you head out on the highway or stay at the "Heartbreak Hotel."

- Chapter 22 covers managing your life on the road — setting the time and date, waking up with the alarm clock, playing games, sorting your contacts, recording voice memos, setting the combination lock, and customizing the iPod menu and display settings.

- Chapter 23 is about using your iPod as a hard drive, and it includes transferring folders and files, storing notes and text, transferring photos from a digital camera, and even saving a copy of the Mac system or a Linux system on your iPod.

- Chapter 24 shows you how to use both Apple and Microsoft applications to enter personal contact and calendar information in preparation for iPod synchronization.

- Chapter 25 describes automatically synchronizing your iPod with personal information by using iTunes. Here you can also find out about adding information manually to your iPod so that you don't miss any of your appointments or forget anybody's name, address, and phone number.

- Chapter 26 gets into the nitty-gritty of troubleshooting iPod problems, including how to use the iPod Updater to update or restore your iPod.

Chapter 21

Listening While on the Move

You can truly go anywhere with an iPod. If you can't plug it into a power source while it's playing, you can use the battery for quite a while before having to recharge. You can find all the accessories that you need to travel with an iPod in the Apple Store at www.apple.com.

Put on "Eight Miles High" by the Byrds while cruising in a plane at 40,000 feet. Watch the "Lust for Life" music video by Iggy Pop on a bus heading out of Detroit. Ride the rails listening to "All Aboard" by Muddy Waters, followed by "Peavine" by John Lee Hooker. Or cruise on the Autobahn in Germany with Kraftwerk. The iPod provides high-quality sound and excellent picture quality no matter what the environment — even in an earthquake. With skip protection, you don't have to worry about turbulence, potholes, or strenuous exercise causing the audio to skip. In addition to the hard drive, iPods use a memory cache. The cache is made up of solid-state memory, with no mechanical or moving parts, so movement doesn't affect playback. Skip protection works by preloading up to 20 minutes of sound to the cache at a time (depending on the iPod model). The iPod plays sound from the memory cache rather than the hard drive. The iPod nano is entirely solid-state memory, which completely eliminates skipping.

Connecting Headphones and Portable Speakers

Apple designed the iPod to provide excellent sound through headphones, and with the headphone/line-out connection, the iPod can also play music through portable speaker systems. The speaker systems must be self-powered or able to work with very little power (like headphones) and allow audio to be input through a 3.5 mm mini-plug stereo connection. Even the tiny iPod shuffle offers a standard headphone/line-out connection, as shown in Figure 21-1. Portable speaker systems such as the iBoom from DLO (www.dlo.com), and the Bose iPod Speaker Dock (www.bose.com), provide a dock connection for playing audio.

Figure 21-1:
A first-gen iPod shuffle with headphones connected to its headphone/line-out connection.

The iPod includes a small amplifier powerful enough to deliver audio through the headphone/line-out connection. All current models, including the iPod shuffle, have a frequency response of 20 to 20,000 Hz (hertz), which provides distortion-free music at the lowest or highest pitches. Hertz in this case has nothing to do with rental cars — a *hertz* is a unit of frequency equal to one cycle per second. At pitches that produce frequencies of 20 cycles per second or 20,000 cycles per second, the iPod responds with distortion-free sound.

Portable speaker systems typically include built-in amplifiers and a volume control, and they offer a stereo mini-plug that you can attach directly to the iPod headphone/line-out connection or to the dock headphone/line-out connection. To place the external speakers farther away from the iPod, use a stereo mini-plug extension cable — available at most consumer electronics stores — which has a stereo mini-plug on one end and a stereo mini-socket on the other.

Portable speaker systems typically have volume controls to raise or lower the volume. Set your iPod volume to half and then raise or lower the volume of your speaker system.

When you travel, take an extra pair of headphones (or earbuds) and a splitter cable, such as the one in Figure 21-2, which are available in any consumer electronics store. The Monster iSplitter is available in the Apple Store. You can plug both headphones into the iPod and share the music with someone on the road.

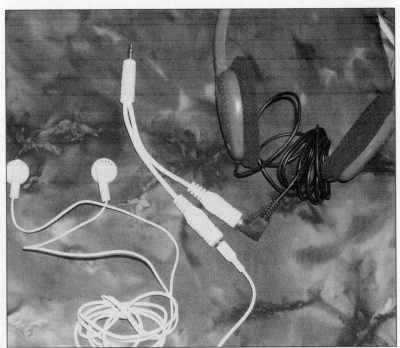

Figure 21-2:
This headphone cable splits into two, allowing two sets of headphones to connect.

For a portable stereo system that offers big sound on a rechargeable battery and is perfect for environments like the beach or a boat, check out the i-Fusion from Sonic Impact (www.si-technologies.com), which includes a docking station for the iPod. It includes universal adapters for all iPod models and an audio input connection for connecting your computer or an audio player. The case is a durable cover that acts as a speaker cabinet to give the speakers better bass response.

Playing Car Tunes

We always wanted a car that we could fill up with music just as easily as filling it up with gasoline, without having to carry dozens of cassettes or CDs. With an iPod, an auto-charger to save on battery power, and a way to connect the iPod to your car's stereo system, you're ready to pump music. (Start your engine and queue up "Getting in Tune" and then "Going Mobile" by The Who.) You can even go one step further and get a new BMW or similar car that offers an iPod installed and integrated into the car's stereo system so that you can control it from your steering wheel.

You can link your iPod to a car stereo in three ways:

✓ **Use a cassette player:** Use a standard cassette adapter and an iPod power adapter for your car's lighter socket. This method works even with rental cars (as long as they're supplied with cassette players). For a semi-permanent installation, you can add a car mount to keep your iPod secure. Cassette adapters offer medium quality that is usually better than wireless adapters.

✓ **Use your radio and a wireless adapter:** Use a wireless adapter that plays your iPod as if it were a station on your FM radio dial. Some car mounts offer built-in wireless adapters. This might be your only inexpensive choice if you don't have a cassette deck. *Note:* Wireless adapters might not work well in cities where FM stations crowd the radio dial.

✓ **Install an iPod interface:** Install an iPod interface for your car stereo that offers high-quality, line-in audio input and power. After you install this interface, you simply plug your iPod into a cable, hide it in the glove box, and control the iPod from your car stereo's head unit. This method offers the best sound quality.

Unfortunately, not many car stereos offer a mini-socket for audio input, and as of this writing, the few accessories that integrate directly with car stereos require custom car installations. So far, no standard dock connectors for car stereos exist, which would be totally cool because the iPod is clearly designed for plugging in to a "car dock" that offers both power and a connection to the car's stereo system. (Stay iTuned, because car docks are on the horizon.)

Getting in tune with cassette and power adapters

Until you can get a car with a mini-socket for stereo audio input (also called *stereo-in connection*) or an iPod connection — or get one installed — you can use a cassette-player adapter to connect with your car stereo or a wireless device that we describe later in this chapter, in the section "Connecting by Wireless Radio." These solutions provide lower sound quality than iPod interface installations or stereo-in connections but are inexpensive and work with most cars.

Many car stereos have a cassette player, and you can buy a cassette adapter from most consumer electronics stores or from the Apple Store (such as the Sony CPA-9C Car Cassette Adapter). The cassette-player adapter, shown in Figure 21-3, looks like a tape cassette with a mini-plug cable (which sticks out through the slot when you're using the adapter).

Power adapter

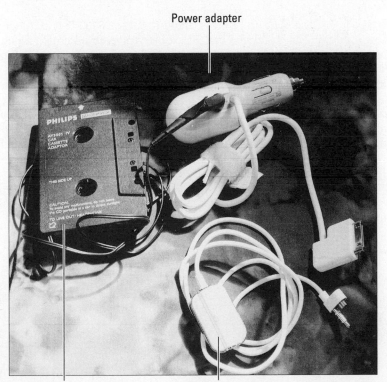

Figure 21-3:
Inexpensive
car acces-
sories.

Cassette-player adapter   Apple Remote

You can connect the mini-plug cable directly to the iPod, to the auto-charger if a mini-socket is offered, or to the Apple Remote that in turn is connected to the iPod. Then insert the adapter into the cassette player, being careful not to get the cable tangled up inside the player.

One inherent problem with this approach is that the cable that dangles from your cassette player looks unsightly. You also might have some trouble ejecting the adapter if the cable gets wedged in the door, but overall, this method is the best for most cars because it provides the best sound quality.

Although some new vehicles (particularly SUVs and cars such as the Toyota Matrix mini-station wagon) offer 110-volt power outlets you can use with your Apple-supplied battery charger, most cars offer only a lighter/power socket that requires a power adapter to use with your iPod. Be careful to pick the right type of power adapter for your car's lighter/power socket. The automobile power adapters for first- and second-generation iPods provide a FireWire connector, but the adapters for the new dockable iPods use a dock connector cable. Some adapters, such as the Kensington Cassette Adapter/Charger for iPod (`www.kensington.com`), include a retractable power cord that doesn't dangle in front of the dashboard or tangle with other cords and cables.

Belkin (`www.belkin.com`) offers the Auto Kit for $49.95, and it includes a car power adapter with a convenient socket for a stereo mini-plug cable (which can connect directly to a car stereo if the stereo has a mini-socket for audio input). The adapter includes a volume-adjustable amplifier to boost the sound coming from the iPod before it goes into the cassette adapter or car stereo.

Even with a cassette adapter and power adapter, you have at best a clumsy solution that uses one cable (power) from a power adapter to the iPod and another cable (audio) to your car stereo cassette adapter. Attached to these wires, your iPod needs a secure place to sit while your car moves — you don't want it bouncing around on the passenger seat.

You can fit your iPod securely in position in a car without getting a custom installation. The TuneDok ($29.95) from Belkin (`www.belkin.com`) holds your iPod securely and fits into your car's cup-holder; see Figure 21-4. The TuneDok's ratcheting neck and height-adjustment feature lets you reposition the iPod to your liking. The cable-management clip eliminates loose and tangled cables, and the large and small rubber base and cup fits most cup holders.

MARWARE (`www.marware.com`) offers an inexpensive solution for both car use and personal use. The $5.95 Car Holder, available when you select a MARWARE SportSuit case, attaches to the dashboard of your car, as shown in Figure 21-5, and lets you attach an iPod that's wearing one of the MARWARE SportSuit covering cases (see "Dressing Up Your iPod for Travel," later in this chapter). The clip on the back attaches to the Car Holder.

ProClip (`www.proclipusa.com`) offers mounting brackets for clip-on devices. The brackets attach to the dashboard and can be installed in seconds. After you install the bracket, you can use different custom holders for the iPod models or for cell phones and other portable devices.

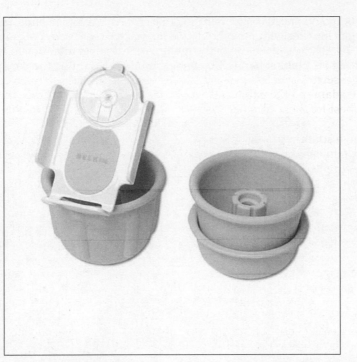

Figure 21-4:
The TuneDok mount for a car cup holder.

Figure 21-5:
Mounting the MARWARE iPod holder that works with the SportSuit carrying case.

Going mobile . . . with car stereo integration

Premium car manufacturers are introducing new cars that are iPod-ready — they include an iPod interface for the car stereo system. For example, BMW offers an iPod-ready model with audio controls on the steering wheel. Mercedes-Benz, Volvo, Mini-Cooper, Nissan, Alfa Romeo, and Ferrari all offer iPod-ready models. In addition, car stereo manufacturers such as Alpine and Clarion offer car audio systems with integrated iPod interfaces; see Figure 21-6. Many of these installations make use of the multiple CD changer interface to the car stereo for attaching separate CD changer units, substituting the iPod for the CD changer unit.

Figure 21-6:
An iPod-
integrated
car stereo
installation.

Unless you can afford a new car that's iPod-ready, you can opt for a custom installation of an iPod interface for your existing car stereo and car power (such as using a custom cable interface for a CD changer, which a skilled car audio specialist can install into your dashboard). For example, you can order a professional installation with the Dension ICE-Link ($149 to $239, depending on your car), which adds line-level audio output and recharging capability to almost any vehicle. It uses the CD-changer connections in car CD players to directly connect your iPod into the car's audio system. Dension (www.densionusa.com) assumes that the buyer is a professional installer, and although it's possible to install it yourself (especially if you already have a CD changer unit in your trunk), most installations require taking apart the dashboard and installing the ICE-Link behind your CD stereo. ICE-Link can be combined with almost any iPod mount. Dension also offers the DICE Integration Kit from DICE Electronics (www.diceelectronics.com) to connect your iPod to factory-made vehicle entertainment systems.

If your car stereo doesn't offer a CD changer interface, you might want to have a new car stereo professionally installed that offers a CD changer interface, such as the Alpine CDA-9835, which can be installed with the Alpine KCA-420i Interface Adapter for iPod (www.alpine-usa.com/driveyouripod). Using this integrated iPod setup, you can control the iPod from the Alpine head unit, which can be any Alpine head unit that is compatible with Ai-NET, Alpine's car network. The car stereo provides power to the iPod to keep it fully charged — in fact, the iPod is always charged up with power while the vehicle's ignition is on or in ACC mode (the car stereo itself does not have to be powered on). You can hide your iPod in the glove box while it's connected to the Alpine, and you can control the iPod as if it were the Alpine's CD changer, selecting songs by playlist, artist, or album.

Connecting by Wireless Radio

A wireless music adapter lets you play music from your iPod on an FM radio with no connection or cable, although the sound quality might suffer a bit due to interference. We always take a wireless adapter with us whenever we rent a car because even if a rental car has no cassette player (ruling out the use of our cassette adapter), it probably has an FM radio.

You can use a wireless adapter in a car, on a boat, on the beach with a portable radio, or even in your home with a stereo system and tuner. We even use it in hotel rooms with a clock radio.

To use a wireless adapter, follow these steps:

1. **Set the wireless adapter to an unused FM radio frequency.**

   Some adapters offer only one frequency (typically 87.9 MHz). Others offer you a choice of several frequencies — typically 88.1, 88.3, 88.5, and 88.7 MHz — and some even let you pick any FM frequency. If given a choice, you can choose the frequency and set the adapter according to its instructions. Avoid FM stations at specific frequencies that would interfere with your iPod signal.

2. **Connect the wireless adapter to the iPod headphone/line-out connector or to the line-out connector on the iPod dock.**

   The wireless adapter acts like a miniature radio station, broadcasting to a nearby FM radio. (Sorry, you can't go much farther than a few feet, so no one else can hear your Wolfman Jack impersonation.)

3. **Tune to the appropriate frequency on the FM dial.**

   Tune any nearby radio to the same FM frequency that you chose in Step 1.

You need to set the adapter close enough to the radio's antenna to work, making it impractical for home stereos — you can get better quality sound by connecting to a home stereo with a cable.

Don't be surprised if the wireless adapter doesn't work as well in cities — other radio stations might cause too much interference.

Here are just a few wireless adapters that we recommend:

- For the budget-minded or casual user (such as when renting a car), the **RoadTrip!** ($14.99) from Newer Technology (www.newertech.com) is both a charger and a transmitter (one frequency, 87.9).

- For $19.99, the **irock! 410 FM** (www.myirock.com) is a bargain. It requires standard replaceable batteries but also includes a car power adapter. You can select frequencies of 88.1, 88.3, 88.5, 88.7, 88.9, 107.1, 107.3, 107.5, 107.7, or 107.9 Mhz. It works with any portable audio device and connects to the headphone/line-out connection on your iPod.

- The **TuneCast II Mobile FM Transmitter** ($39.99) from Belkin (www.belkin.com) is particularly convenient in a car because it includes a 14-inch cable that delivers power when used with the Belkin Mobile Power Cord for iPod, so you can preserve your batteries for times when you're away from an alternate source. It offers four programmable memory slots for saving the clearest radio frequency wherever you go.

- The **Monster iCarPlay Wireless** ($69.95) from Monster Cable (www.monstercable.com) offers a power adapter as well as excellent quality playback for a wireless radio unit. You can select radio frequencies of 88.1, 88.3, 88.5, 88.7, 88.9, 89.1, 89.3, or 89.5 MHz. Although it is a bit more expensive, we prefer it for its sound quality.

- The **DLO TransPod FM** ($49.99) from Digital Lifestyle Outfitters, available from Everything iPod (www.everythingipod.com), is an excellent all-in-one wireless FM transmitter, mounting system, and power adapter for using your iPod in a car, and it costs less than purchasing all three items separately.

Dressing Up Your iPod for Travel

The simple protective carrying case supplied with some iPod models is just not as stylin' as the myriad accessories that you can get for dressing up your iPod for travel. You can find different types of protective gear, from leather jackets to aluminum cases, in many different styles and colors. Apple offers access to hundreds of products from other suppliers on its accessories pages (www.apple.com/ipod/accessories.html). Some are designed primarily for protecting your iPod from harm; others are designed to provide some measure of protection while also providing access to controls.

On the extreme end of the spectrum are hardened cases that are ready for battlefields in deserts or jungles — the Humvees of iPod protective gear. The Matias Armor ($39.95) by Matias Corporation (www.ipodarmor.com) is a sturdy case that fits all iPod models and offers possibly the best protection against physical trauma on the market. Your iPod rests within a hard, resilient metal exoskeleton that can withstand the abuse of bouncing down a flight of metal stairs without letting your iPod pop out. Of course, the very same feature that prevents your iPod from popping out also makes the iPod Armor difficult to open to get access to your iPod — this is not a case to use while listening to music.

Business travelers can combine personal items into one carrying case. The iPod Leather Organizer (about $15) from Belkin (www.belkin.com) is made from fine-grain leather that even Ricardo Montalban would rave about. The case holds personal essentials, such as business and credit cards, in four convenient slots. A handy mesh pocket keeps earphones easily accessible, and a billfold holds money and receipts.

On the sporty side, MARWARE (www.marware.com) offers the Sportsuit Convertible case ($34.95) with a patented belt clip system offering inter-changeable clip options for use with the MARWARE Car Holder or with an armband or belt for jogging or working out. The neoprene case has vulcan-ized rubber grips on each side and bottom for a no-slip grip and plastic inserts for impact protection, offering full access to all iPod controls and con-nections while the iPod is in the case. There's even space inside the lid to store earbud headphones.

If you like to carry a backpack with everything in it, consider the very first backpack ever designed to control an iPod within it: The Burton Amp Pack (http://lonelyplanet.altrec.com/shop/detail/24004), priced at $199.95, lets you switch songs on your iPod by pressing a button on the shoulder strap. Constructed from ballistic nylon, the Amp Pack offers a secure iPod storage pocket, a headphone port located on a shoulder strap, an easy-access side entry laptop compartment, and padded ergonomic shoul-der straps with a soft, flexible control pad built in to a strap. It's perfect for listening to Lou Reed while hanging on to a pole in a subway car, or the Hollies while navigating your way to the back of the bus.

Using Power Accessories

If you want to charge your iPod battery when you travel abroad, you can't count on finding the same voltage as in your home country. However, you still need to plug your Apple power adapter into something to recharge your iPod. Fortunately, power adapters are available in most airports, but the worldly traveler might want to consider saving time and money by getting a travel kit of power accessories.

We found several varieties of power kits for world travel in our local international airport. Most kits include a set of AC plugs with prongs that fit different electrical outlets around the world. You can connect your iPod power adapter to these adapters. The AC plugs typically support outlets in North America, Japan, China, the United Kingdom, Continental Europe, Korea, Australia, and Hong Kong. You should also include at least one power accessory for use with a standard car lighter, such as car chargers from Belkin (www.belkin.com), Kensington (www.kensington.com), or Newer Technology (www.newertech.com).

One way to mitigate the battery blues is to get an accessory that lets you use replaceable alkaline batteries — the kind that you can find in any convenience store. The Battery Pack for iPod ($49.95) from Belkin (www.belkin.com) lets you power your iPod with four standard AA alkaline replaceable batteries — even when your internal iPod battery is drained. Discreet suction cups secure the unit to the back of your iPod without marring your iPod's finish. A charge-level indicator tells you when your batteries are running low.

Another way to supply power to your iPod on the road is to use your FireWire-equipped or USB 2.0–equipped laptop to supply the power (make sure that you use FireWire or USB 2.0 hardware that provides power; see Chapter 1) and then use a power adapter with your laptop. You can use, for example, the Kensington Universal Car/Air Adapter from Apple to plug a Mac PowerBook or iBook into any car cigarette lighter or EmPower-equipped airline seat (the EmPower in-seat power system can provide either 110 volt AC or 15 volt DC power in an aircraft seat for passenger use). Then connect the iPod to the laptop with a FireWire cable.

Chapter 22

Sleeping with Your iPod

*Y*ou might have purchased an iPod simply to listen to music or watch videos, but those thoughtful engineers at Apple who get to travel often with their iPods put a lot more into this device.

Your iPod also keeps time.

Time is a useful measure. In the 18th Century, the earliest forms of the modern pocket watch — a marine chronometer that could keep accurate time on a rolling ship — offered the means of determining longitude on long sea voyages, presenting a new, revolutionary way of navigating the world. The iPod provides you with a timekeeper that enables you to navigate your personal life to some extent while on the road — checking your calendar and To-Do list, setting alarms to wake up to music, and with current fifth-generation iPod and iPod nano, using a stopwatch for timing tasks such as jogging or commuting. You can also alleviate the boredom of travel by playing games. You can look up contact names, addresses, and phone numbers. You can even speak into full-size iPods and record dictation, conversations, or notes. This chapter also shows you how to make your iPod more convenient to use while traveling by customizing the iPod menu.

Using the Clock

Whereas older iPods (updated to use iPod software 2.0) include a clock and the ability to set the time and date, alarm, and sleep timer, the fifth-generation iPod and iPod nano let you set multiple clocks for different time zones as well as alarms for each clock, and they include a stopwatch along with the sleep timer.

To look at the clock, choose Extras➪Clock from the main menu.

To set the date and time, follow these steps:

1. **Press the Menu button until you see the iPod main menu.**

2. **Choose Settings➪Date & Time.**

   A menu appears with selections for setting the time zone, setting the date and time, setting the time format, and setting the time in the title.

3. **Select the Set Time Zone option.**

   A list of time zones (actually geographical regions) appears in time zone order starting with Eniwetok and Midway Island (near the international date line) and heading east toward Hawaii, Alaska, the Pacific coast of the United States, and so on around the world to Auckland, just west of the international date line. Each region offers a daylight saving time (DST) setting.

4. **Scroll the Time Zone list and select a time zone.**

   Press the Select button to choose the time zone (DST or standard time) that's right for you. After selecting it, the Date & Time menu appears again.

5. **Select the Set Date & Time option.**

   The Date & Time display appears with up and down arrow indicators over the hour field, which is now highlighted.

   To show the military time, select the Time option and press the Select button. The option changes from *12-hour* to *24-hour* (military style). With 24-hour display, 11 p.m. is displayed as 23:00:00 rather than 11:00:00. To switch back to *12-hour,* press the Select button again with the Time option highlighted.

6. **Change the hour field setting by using the scroll wheel.**

   Scroll clockwise to go forward and counterclockwise to go backward.

7. **Press the Select button after scrolling to the appropriate setting.**

   The up and down arrow indicators move over to the minutes field, which is now highlighted.

8. **Repeat Steps 6 and 7 for each field of the date and time: minutes, AM/PM, the calendar date, calendar month, and year.**

9. **Press the Select button after setting the year.**

   The Date & Time menu appears again.

TIP

To display the time in the menu title, scroll to the Time in Title option in the Date & Time menu and press the Select button to turn this option On. Press the Select button again to switch it back to Off to stop showing the time in the menu title.

Displaying multiple clocks

With fifth-generation iPods and the iPod nano, you can display clocks with different time zones — useful If you travel across time zones quickly or simply want to keep track of time in another time zone (so that you know the right time in Paris if you're calling from New York). The initial clock and any clocks you add show a clock face with a white background and black hands during the daytime (from 6 a.m. to 5:59 p.m.) and a black background with white hands at night (from 6 p.m. to 5:59 a.m.).

To create more clocks with fifth-generation iPods and the iPod nano, follow these steps:

1. **Press the Menu button until you see the iPod main menu.**

2. **Choose Extras➪Clock from the main menu.**

   A clock appears, showing the present time and location. Underneath is a clock that says New Clock, as shown in Figure 22-1.

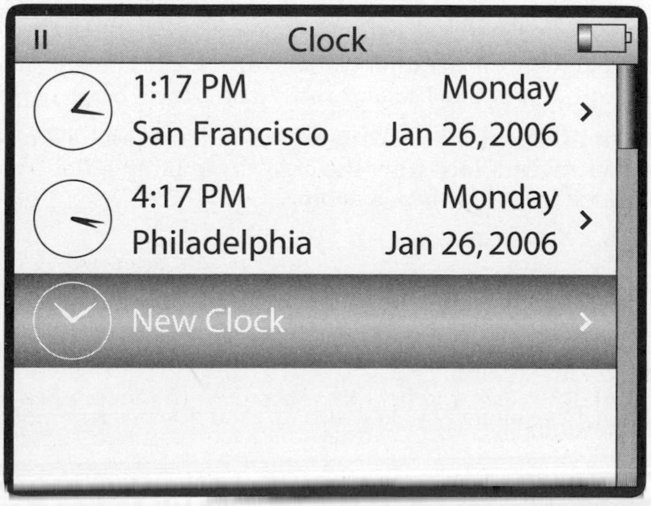

‖	Clock	▭
🕐	1:17 PM San Francisco	Monday Jan 26, 2006 ›
🕑	4:17 PM Philadelphia	Monday Jan 26, 2006 ›
◡	New Clock	›

Figure 22-1:
The iPod offers multiple clock faces for different time zones.

3. **Select the New Clock.**

   A list of geographical regions appears in alphabetical order, from Africa to South America.

4. **Scroll the Region list, choose a region, and press the Select button.**

   After selecting it, the City menu appears with a list of cities in the region in alphabetical order.

5. **Scroll the City list, choose a city, and press the Select button.**

   After selecting it, you return to the list of clocks. You now have a new clock with the city name, time, and date underneath the first clock.

6. **Repeat Steps 3–5 to create more clocks.**

To change a clock's settings, select the clock. You can set the clock's alarm, or change its region and city. You can also change whether the city observes daylight saving time by selecting that option to turn it off or on. You can also delete a clock by first selecting the clock and then selecting Delete This Clock.

Setting the alarm clock

Time is on your side with your iPod. You can set an alarm in third-, fourth-, and fifth-generation models that plays an audible beep, or you can connect your iPod to speakers and wake up to music. With fifth-generation models and the iPod nano, you can set an alarm for each clock (see "Displaying multiple clocks" earlier in this chapter). To set an alarm, follow these steps:

1. **Choose Extras⇨Clock from the main menu.**

   A clock appears, showing the present time and location.

   In current fifth-generation iPods and iPod nano, the clock has a face with hands, you see any multiple clocks you've created and a New Clock.

   In third- and fourth-generation models, the clock is digital, and a menu appears with Alarm Clock, Sleep Timer, and Date & Time options.

2. **In current fifth-generation iPods and iPod nano, select a clock and then select Alarm Clock from the clock's menu; in older iPods, select Alarm Clock from the clock's menu.**

   The Alarm Clock menu appears.

3. **Highlight the Alarm option and press the Select button.**

   Off changes to On.

4. **Select the Time option.**

   The Alarm Time menu appears with up- and down-arrow indicators.

5. **Change the time by using the scroll wheel.**

   Scroll clockwise to go forward and counterclockwise to go backward. See the description on how to set the time in "Using the Clock," earlier in this chapter.

6. **Press the Select button after scrolling to the appropriate alarm time.**

   The Alarm Clock menu appears again.

7. **Select the Sound option in the Alarm Clock menu.**

   A list appears. The Beep option is at the top of the list, followed by playlists on your iPod in alphabetical order.

8. **Choose an option as the alarm sound and then press the Select button.**

   If you choose Beep, the alarm beeps without the need for any head-phones or speakers. If you choose a playlist, the playlist plays when the alarm goes off. Of course, you need speakers or headphones to hear the music.

9. **You can return to the main menu by pressing Menu until you see the main menu.**

A bell icon appears next to any clock that has its alarm set. You can turn off an alarm by performing Steps 1–3; when you select the Alarm option, On turns to Off.

When the alarm goes off, the playlist (or beep tone) plays until you stop the alarm by pressing the Play/Pause button.

If you set an alarm for a new clock you created (see "Displaying multiple clocks" earlier in this chapter), the alarm goes off at the proper time for that time zone (based on the actual time kept by your iPod).

For example, you can keep your iPod set to Eastern U.S. time while in Los Angeles but use the Los Angeles clock to set your morning alarm.

Setting the sleep timer

Just like a clock radio, you can set your iPod to play music or a slideshow for a while before going to sleep. Although you can display multiple clocks in current fifth-generation iPods and iPod nano, you can set only one sleep timer.

To set the sleep timer, select a clock and then select the Sleep Timer option from the clock's menu. A list of intervals appears from 0 (Off) up to 120 minutes (2 hours). You can select a time amount or the Off setting (at the top of the list) to turn off the sleep timer. After the iPod shuts itself off or you turn it off, the preference for the Sleep Timer is reset to the default status, Off.

To turn off the iPod, press the Pause button; if you don't press Pause, it remains idle for a few minutes and shuts itself off.

Using the stopwatch

With fifth-generation iPods and iPod nano, you can display a stopwatch with a lap timer — useful for timing exercises, jogging, track racing, timing how long it takes the bus to travel across town, or finding out how long it takes your friend to recognize the song you're playing. Whatever you want to measure with time, the stopwatch is ready for you.

You can use the iPod's menus, and also play music, audio books, and podcasts, while running the stopwatch. When you return to the stopwatch while something is playing, the stopwatch display shows an icon in the upper-left corner, indicating whether the iPod is playing or pausing. When you play video, the stopwatch continues to count as usual, but when you press Menu to switch to the stopwatch display, the video automatically pauses.

To use the stopwatch, follow these steps:

1. **Choose Extras⇨Stopwatch⇨Timer from the main menu.**

   A stopwatch appears, as shown in Figure 22-2, with Start and Clear buttons and 00:00:00.00 as the stopwatch counter (hours, minutes, seconds, and fractions of second). Underneath is a lap counter with its own time in smaller digits.

2. **Scroll to highlight the Start button and press the Select button to push the Start button.**

   The stopwatch starts counting immediately with both the main and lap counters. After these counters begin, the left button changes to Pause, and the right button changes to Lap.

   The stopwatch stops if the counter reaches 24 hours, if you connect your iPod to your computer, or if you allow it to lapse into hibernation.

3. **(Optional) Select the Lap button to mark each lap.**

   Scroll to highlight the Lap button and then press the Select button. The current lap time is recorded, the lap time is reset to zero, and counting resumes accurately. However, your iPod displays the total lap time for about five seconds so that you can quickly view it before it changes to reflect the actual count. Repeat this step for each lap.

4. Select Pause to pause.

Scroll to highlight the Pause button and press Select to push the Pause button. Both the main counter and the lap counter stop counting. The left button changes to Resume, and the right button changes to Done.

5. Click Resume to resume counting where you left off. Click Done to finish counting.

The iPod saves the main counter and lap counter results in a session log for convenience, so you don't have to write them down.

After clicking Done, the stopwatch display still shows the final results. The buttons change back to Start and Clear.

6. To reset the stopwatch counters, select the Clear button.

Scroll to highlight the Clear button and then press the Select button.

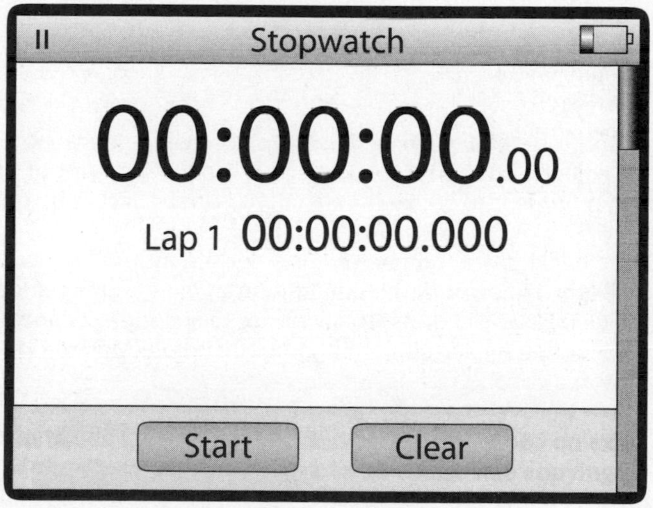

Figure 22-2:
The iPod stopwatch with lap counter.

Each time you select the Done button, the stopwatch saves the results of the counters in a session log. Your iPod can store up to five session logs, but it deletes the oldest log when it records a sixth session. To view your session logs, follow these steps:

1. Choose Extras➪Stopwatch to see the list of session logs under the Timer option.

2. Scroll to highlight the session log you want to see and then press the Select button to see it.

The session log includes the date and time of the session, the total time, the shortest and longest lap times, the average lap time, and a list of each individual lap time. You can scroll the session log to see all of it.

To delete a session log, select it and choose Delete.

Choosing Display Settings

Your future might be so bright that you got to wear shades, but your iPod display might not be bright enough without its backlight on. With the iPod Settings menu, you can change the timer for the backlight and also set the contrast of black-and-white displays for better visibility. (The contrast setting for color-display iPod models is not adjustable.) Choose the Settings menu from the iPod main menu.

Backlight timer

Ordinarily, your iPod display's backlight turns on when you press a button or use the scroll wheel, and then it turns off after a short amount of time. On third-generation iPods, the backlight also lights up the iPod buttons.

You can set the backlight to remain on for a certain interval of time. Choose Settings➪Backlight Timer from the main menu. A menu appears, giving you the options 2 seconds, 5 seconds, 10 seconds, 15 seconds, 20 seconds, and Always On. Select one by scrolling to highlight the selection and then press the Select button.

The backlight drains the iPod battery; the longer you set the interval, the more frequently you need to recharge the battery.

To set the backlight to *always* be on, choose Always On. If you want the backlight to *always* be off, choose Always Off. If you set it to always be off, the backlight doesn't turn on automatically when you press any button or use the scroll wheel.

Don't be alarmed if your backlight turns itself on at midnight for a brief flash. The iPod is just setting its internal clock. If you find this annoying, turn off the Backlight Timer.

Contrast for better visibility

You can set the contrast of black-and-white iPod displays to make the black characters appear sharper against the display background. (This feature isn't provided in color-display iPod models.) You might need to adjust the contrast after a sharp temperature difference freezes or bakes your iPod. If you keep your iPod in your car overnight in the cold or even in direct sunlight for a time, the contrast can change so much that you can't see your iPod display. Allow the iPod to warm up (slowly — don't use the oven or microwave) if it's cold or cool down if the display is hot. Then adjust the contrast.

To adjust the contrast, choose Settings⇨Contrast from the main menu. The Contrast screen appears with a slider that shows the contrast setting, which ranges from low contrast (a black-and-white dot) to high contrast (a full black dot). Scroll clockwise to increase the contrast (toward the black dot) and counterclockwise to decrease the contrast (toward the black-and-white dot).

If you accidentally set the contrast too dark or too light, you can reset it to the halfway point between too dark and too light by pressing and holding the Menu button for at least four seconds.

Playing Games

The games that come with the iPod — Brick, Parachute, and Solitaire — are a bit dorky for the information age, but hey, they're extras. Music Quiz, on the other hand, is a cool way to test your knowledge of your music library.

To find the games, choose Extras⇨Games. (On older iPods, choose Extras⇨Game.) And of course you can listen to music while you play — in fact, with Music Quiz, you have to.

Brick and Parachute

Brick is like the original version of Breakout for the Atari. To access this game, choose Brick from the Games menu (or Game on older iPods) and press the Select button to start the game. Move the paddle from side to side along the bottom of the display by scrolling with the scroll wheel. You get a point for each brick you knock out. If you break out — knock out all the bricks — you move up a level in the game, and the game starts again.

Parachute is a crude shoot-'em-up game where you play the role of an anti-aircraft gunner. Choose Parachute from the Games menu (or Game menu on older iPods) and press the Select button to start the game. You pivot the gun at the bottom with the scroll wheel. Press the Select button to fire on helicopters and paratroopers. Don't let the paratroopers reach the ground, or else they'll heave grenades at you. War is hell.

Solitaire

Rather than playing the card game *'til one, with a deck of 51,* try the iPod version of Solitaire (also known as Klondike). Choose Solitaire from the Games menu (or Game menu on older iPods) and press the Select button to start the game. To move cards, place the hand pointer over a card by scrolling and then pressing the Select button to select the card. Then scroll again to move the hand pointer to the new location for the card and press Select to place the card at that position. To deal another round of three cards, move the hand pointer over the card deck in the top-left corner of the display and press the Select button. After going through an entire deck, the game places the remaining cards into a new deck so that you can continue dealing cards. The game improves considerably in a smoke-filled room with take-out pizza nearby; gangsters are optional.

Music Quiz

Music Quiz tests your knowledge of your music library and is probably the greatest time-waster of them all. The game plays the first few seconds of a song picked at random from your iPod. Choose Music Quiz from the Games menu (or Game menu on older iPods), put on your headphones or connect your iPod to speakers, and press the Select button to start the game. As the song plays, you have ten seconds to pick the song title from a list of five titles. If you choose the wrong title, the game displays Incorrect! and moves on to the next one. If you choose the right title, you gain points and move on to the next one. ("Life's a Long Song" by Jethro Tull would be appropriate.)

Checking Your Calendar

Imagine a musician going backstage after a performance and meeting a promoter who says he can get him ten more gigs if he can confirm the dates *right now.* This musician happens to carry around an iPod, and amid the backstage craziness, he scrolls through his calendar for the entire year, finding all the details he needs about gigs and recording sessions, right down to the minute, including travel directions to each gig. "No problem," the musician says.

Your iPod accepts calendars from calendar applications, such as iCal on a Mac or Outlook in Windows. You can view these calendars (or a blank calendar if you haven't updated your iPod with your calendar files) by choosing Extras⇨Calendars and then selecting a specific calendar by name or selecting All for a merged view of all your calendars. Select a calendar and then use the scroll wheel to go through the days of the calendar. Select an event to see its details. Press the Next and Previous buttons to skip to the next or previous month. To see your To-Do list, choose Extras⇨Calendars⇨To Do.

If your calendar events use alarms, you can turn on the iPod's calendar alarms. Choose Extras⇨Calendars⇨Alarms. Select Alarms once to set the alarm to Beep, select Alarms twice to set it to Silent (so that only the message for the alarm appears), or select it a third time to set it to Off. (The Alarms choices cycle from Beep to Silent to Off and then back to Beep.)

Calendars are far more useful if you enter your personal information; turn to Chapter 24 to do so.

Sorting Your Contacts

The bits of information that you're most likely to need on the road are phone numbers and addresses. The iPod stores up to 4,000 contacts right alongside your music. To see how to put your personal contacts into your iPod, check out Chapter 25.

The iPod contact list is sorted automatically, and the iPod displays contact names in alphabetical order when you choose Extras⇨Contacts. You can display contacts by last or first name. Choose Settings⇨Contacts⇨Display and then press the Select button in the scrolling pad for each option:

- ✔ **First Last:** Displays the contacts list by first name and the last name, as in *Ringo Starr*.
- ✔ **Last, First:** Displays the contacts list by last name followed by a comma and the first name, as in *McCartney, Paul*.

You can also change how the contacts sort so that you don't have to look up people by their first names (which can be time-consuming with so many friends named Elvis). The sort operation uses the entire name, but you decide whether to use the first name or the surname first. Choose

Settings⇨Contacts⇨Sort. Press the Select button in the scrolling pad for each option:

- ✔ **First Last:** Sorts the contact list by first name, followed by the last name, so that *Mick Jagger* sorts under *Mick* (after *Mick Abrahams* but before *Mick Taylor*).

- ✔ **Last, First:** Sorts the contacts by last name, followed by the first name, so that *Brian Jones* sorts under *Jones*. (*Jones, Brian* appears after *Jones, Alice* but before *Jones, Norah*.)

Setting the Combination Lock

If you think your iPod might fall into the wrong hands, consider setting the Screen Lock feature, which is available in current fifth-generation iPods and the iPod nano. You can set a four-digit combination that locks your iPod's navigation controls, preventing anyone else from selecting content on your iPod. It works only when your iPod is not attached to a computer.

If you're playing music when you lock your iPod, the music continues playing — and you can even use the Play/Pause button to pause and resume playback — but you can't navigate the iPod until you provide the combination. You also can't change the volume.

To conserve power, you can force your iPod to go to sleep by pressing the Play/Pause button, but it won't unlock. When it awakes, it remembers everything — including its combination.

To use Screen Lock, you must first set a combination by following these steps:

1. **Choose Extras⇨Screen Lock.**

   The Screen Lock menu appears.

2. **Choose Set Combination.**

   The Enter New Code display appears, as shown in Figure 22-3.

3. **Select the first number of the combination by scrolling.**

   As you scroll with your iPod, the first digit of the combination changes in the Enter New Code display. You can also press the Previous/Rewind or Next/Fast-Forward button to scroll through numbers.

4. **Press the Select button to confirm.**

By pressing the Select button, you confirm your choice for the first number and move on to the next number of the combination.

5. **Scroll to select each number of the combination and then press the Select button to confirm.**

Repeat this step for each number of the combination. When you confirm the last digit, the iPod displays the Screen Lock menu.

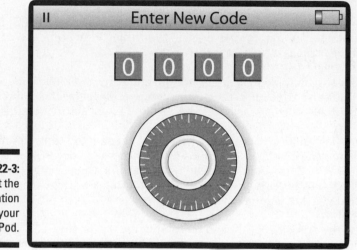

Figure 22-3:
Set the combination to lock your iPod.

Don't forget this combination! Use a four-digit number that is easy to commit to memory.

To lock your iPod with this combination, follow these steps:

1. **(Optional) Start playing music before locking the iPod.**

2. **Choose Extras➪Screen Lock➪Turn Screen Lock On.**

The iPod displays a `If you forget the code, connect iPod to your computer to unlock it` message. Underneath the message are the Lock and Cancel choices.

3. **Choose Lock.**

When it's locked, an Enter Code display appears on your iPod even while music is playing. A key in the upper-right corner indicates that your iPod is locked.

To unlock a locked iPod, you must do one of the following:

- Enter the same combination Enter Code display (choose Extras⇨Screen Lock⇨Set Combination. (If the numbers flash red, it means you didn't enter it correctly.) After correctly entering the combination, the iPod unlocks and returns to the last viewed screen.

- Attach the iPod to the computer you used to update the iPod with iTunes; when you disconnect it after iTunes updating, the iPod is no longer locked.

- Restore your iPod to its original factory settings by using iPod Updater (as described in Chapter 26), erasing everything in the process. This is, of course, a measure of last resort.

Don't bother to call Apple to see whether the company can unlock your iPod for you. If you can't attach it to the proper computer or enter the correct combination, your only recourse is to restore the iPod to its factory conditions.

You can lock and unlock your iPod as you wish, keeping the same combination. To change the combination, choose Extras⇨Screen Lock⇨Change Combination. The Enter Old Code display appears for you to enter the original combination. After entering it correctly, the Enter New Code display appears, and you can enter a new combination.

If you turn your Screen Lock on and off frequently, you might want to add it to your iPod main menu for fast access — see "Customizing the Menu and Settings" in this chapter.

Speaking into Your iPod

Do you record conversations and interviews on the road? Throw out that tape recorder. Your iPod can record hundreds of hours of voice-quality memos, meetings, notes, and interviews with a touch of a button. All you need is an accessory for your iPod model designed for voice recording, such as the MicroMemo from XtremeMac (www.xtrememac.com) for fifth-generation iPods (also known as iPods with video) for about $60. For third- and fourth-generation iPod models, check out the tiny Belkin iPod Voice Recorder (www.belkin.com), about $30, or the Griffin iTalk Voice Recorder (www.griffintechnology.com), about $40.

The voice memos are stored on your iPod, where you can review them immediately by using the built-in speaker of the accessory or your headphones or speakers. Even better, the voice memos are automatically transferred to your iTunes library for archiving or reviewing on your computer.

The MicroMemo plugs in to the dock connector on your fifth-generation iPod and includes a flexible, detachable microphone (you can also use any other input device with a 3.5 mm connector) and a built-in speaker.

The Belkin iPod Voice Recorder and the Griffin iTalk Voice Recorder attach to the remote connector on the top of full-size third- and fourth-generation iPods (updated by version 2.1 of the iPod software or newer). Sorry, you can't use voice recorders with the iPod nano, iPod mini, or iPod shuffle.

Recording voice memos

To record voice memos, connect the voice recorder to the iPod and choose Extras⇨Voice Memos⇨Record Now. The iPod displays the Record screen. Press the Play/Pause button to begin recording and then point the voice recorder's microphone at the sound source, such as your mouth for your voice. (With the Belkin iPod Voice Recorder, a green LED turns on when recording.) You can pause the recording by pressing the Play/Pause button again.

When you finish recording, press the Menu button. The audio files for voice memos are stored on your iPod in the Recordings folder, using the date and time of the recording as the filename.

Playing back voice memos

To play back a voice memo, choose Extras⇨Voice Memos and choose the voice memo from the list. (The Voice Memos menu doesn't appear unless you have already connected the voice recorder at least once.) Then select Play or press the Play/Pause button.

The voice memo plays just like any other song on your iPod — you can press Play/Pause to pause playback and press it again to resume. You can hear the playback in the voice recorder's tiny speaker; attach headphones to your iPod; or connect your iPod to a home stereo, car stereo, or self-powered speakers.

You can play music through the speaker of the voice recorder by connecting the accessory to your iPod and playing. This trick comes in handy if you set your iPod as an alarm clock to play a music playlist; you can hear music when you wake up without having to connect the iPod to speakers. See the earlier section, "Setting the alarm clock."

Managing voice memos in iTunes

Just like your music, your voice memos synchronize automatically with your iTunes library if you set your iPod to update automatically. (See Chapter 12 to find out how to set your iPod to update automatically.) iTunes stores the voice memos in the library and creates a Voice Memos playlist, as shown in Figure 22-4, so that you can find them easily.

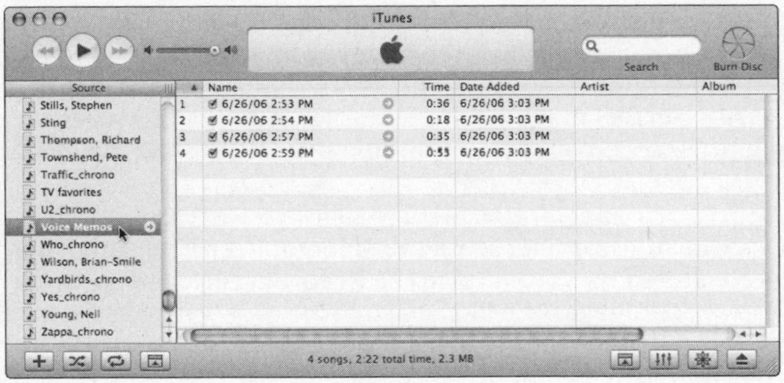

Figure 22-4:
The Voice
Memos
playlist in
iTunes.

If you update your iPod manually, you can drag voice memo files directly from the Recordings folder to your hard drive or drag and drop them over the iTunes window. *Note:* The iPod must already be enabled as a hard drive. (Check out Chapter 23 to see how to enable your iPod as a hard drive.)

Voice memos are stored as WAV files. If you want to archive them in a format that takes up less hard drive space, convert them by using the AAC or MP3 encoder, as we describe in Chapter 19.

Customizing the Menu and Settings

When traveling or using your iPod in situations or environments where portability is important, you might want to customize your iPod menu and display to make doing things easier, such as selecting certain albums, displaying the time, setting the screen lock, displaying menus with backlighting turned on longer than usual, and so on.

The Settings menu in the iPod main menu offers ways to customize your iPod experience by changing the main menu to have more choices. Choose Settings⇨ Main Menu from the main menu. The iPod displays a list of menus; each menu is set to either On or Off. On means the menu appears in the iPod main menu; Off means the menu doesn't appear in the main menu.

Don't worry; the menus are still where they are supposed to be. Turning one to On simply adds it to the main menu as well.

For example, to put the Screen Lock option on the iPod's main menu, choose Settings⇨Main Menu, scroll to the Screen Lock option, and select it to add it to the main menu. Select it again to remove it from the main menu.

Other ways to customize your experience include setting the clicker sound and setting the language to use for the menus. The options in the Settings menu are

- **About:** This displays information about the iPod, including number of songs, videos, and photos, how much space is used, how much space is available, the software version in use, and the serial number and model number.

- **Main Menu:** This allows you to customize the main menu on iPods that use iPod software 2.0 or newer. For example, you can add items from other menus, such as Artists or Songs from the Music menu (Browse menu in older iPods), to the main menu.

- **Backlight Timer:** You can set the backlight to remain on for a certain amount of time by pressing a button or using the scroll wheel. Specify 2 seconds, 5 seconds, and so on. You can also set it to always be on.

  The backlight drains the iPod battery; the longer you set the interval, the more you need to recharge the battery.

- **Audiobooks:** You can set audio books to play back at normal speed, or slower, or faster.

- **Compilations:** This option, available in the color-display models, works with the Group Compilations When Browsing setting in iTunes. It removes from the Artists (but not Albums) menu the artists and songs designated as compilation albums in iTunes. It groups them into a new entry in the Music menu called Compilations. Using this option, you can reduce the number of artists in the Artists menu to just those artists with songs that aren't part of compilations.

- ✔ **Contrast:** With black-and-white iPod displays, you can set the contrast by using the scroll wheel to increase or decrease the slider in the Contrast screen. If you accidentally set the contrast too dark, you can reset it by pressing the Menu button for at least four seconds. This option isn't offered in the color-display iPod.

- ✔ **Clicker:** When this setting is on, you hear a click when you press a button; when it's off, you don't hear a click. With color-display, fourth-generation iPod models, the Clicker can be set to Speaker (the iPod speaker), Headphones, Both, or Off.

- ✔ **Language:** This sets the language used in all the menus. See Chapter 1 for how to set the language.

- ✔ **Legal:** This displays the legal message that accompanies Apple products.

- ✔ **Reset All Settings:** This resets all the items on the Settings menu in your iPod, returning them to the state they were in originally. However, your music and data files on the iPod are not disturbed. This is not the same as resetting (and restarting) the iPod software itself; Reset All Settings simply returns all settings to their defaults. See Chapter 26 for how to reset the iPod itself.

Chapter 23

Using the iPod as a Hard Drive

You have a device in your pocket that can play music and videos, sort your contacts, remind you of events, wake you up in the morning, and tuck you in at night. Did you also know that you can use your iPod to keep a safe backup of your most important files?

You read that right. Windows and Mac users can put their most important files on an iPod and use it just like a hard drive. You can also copy applications and utility programs that you might need on the road or even copy your entire User folder to the iPod if you have room after putting music on it. Although the iPod is the road warrior's dream weapon for combating fatigue and boredom, if you update and maintain its hard drive contents wisely, it can also be invaluable as a tool for providing quick information and for saving your files from disaster. Don't let hard drive space go to waste: Fill up your iPod and let it be your road manager. You can put your most important applications, utilities, and files on the iPod hard drive as a backup.

Mac users can even put a version of the Mac system on FireWire-based second-, third-, and fourth-generation iPods in case of emergencies, and they can start the system from the iPod. (Unfortunately, you can't do this with Windows.) Apple doesn't recommend putting the Mac system on these older iPods because using the iPod as a startup hard drive might make your iPod too hot from overuse.

But that's not all. You can use software, such as Pod2Go, that offers synchronized feeds that supply your iPod with news, weather forecasts, and even sections of Web pages for reading on the iPod screen. The handy iPod shuffle, which plugs directly into a USB connection, can double as a USB flash memory drive for portable file storage.

If you format an iPod for Windows first, you can transfer files to and from Mac and Windows computers. An iPod shuffle, which fits in the palm of your hand and draws its power from the computer, is especially useful for transferring files back and forth.

The key to these capabilities is the fact that the iPod serves as an external hard drive. After you mount the iPod on your Mac or Windows desktop, you can use it as a hard drive, but do so sparingly.

We don't recommend using the iPod regularly as a hard drive to launch applications. The iPod is designed more for sustained playback of music and video, and you can eventually burn out the device by using it to launch applications all the time. Instead, use it as an external hard drive for backing up and copying files, and copy the applications to a hard drive before launching them.

Enabling the iPod as a Hard Drive

You can use any iPod, including an iPod shuffle, as an external hard drive (or in the case of iPod shuffle or iPod nano, a flash memory drive). And like any hard drive, you can transfer files and applications from your computer to your iPod and take them with you wherever you go. The iPod is smart enough to keep your files separate from your content libraries so that you don't accidentally erase them when you update your iTunes library and photo library. And because your iPod is *with you,* it's as safe as you are.

The iPod, as shipped, is formatted as a Macintosh hard drive and can be connected to any Mac. When you connect it to Windows, the iPod is reformatted as a Windows hard drive. You can then connect it to any Windows PC or any Mac. (This is because Macs can use hard drives formatted for Windows PCs; however, you can't boot a Mac from a Windows-formatted hard drive or iPod.)

Setting up the iPod hard drive on a Mac

To use your iPod as an external hard drive on a Mac, follow these steps:

1. **Connect your iPod to your Mac.**

2. **Select the iPod name in the iTunes Source pane.**

3. **Click the iPod Options button in the bottom-right corner of the iTunes window.**

   The iPod Options button appears only when an iPod is connected and selected in the Source pane. You can also choose iTunes➪Preferences and click the iPod tab — whether or not the iPod is selected in the Source pane (although it has to be connected).

   The iPod preferences appear.

4. **Click the Music tab.**

   The iPod music updating preferences display, as shown in Figure 23-1.

5. **Select the Enable Disk Use option and click OK.**

   The Enable Disk Use option is available if your iPod is set to automatically update. If you already set your iPod to manual updating (see Chapter 12), this option is grayed out because it isn't needed — setting the iPod to update manually automatically enables you to use it as a hard drive.

6. **Open the iPod icon in the Finder to see its contents.**

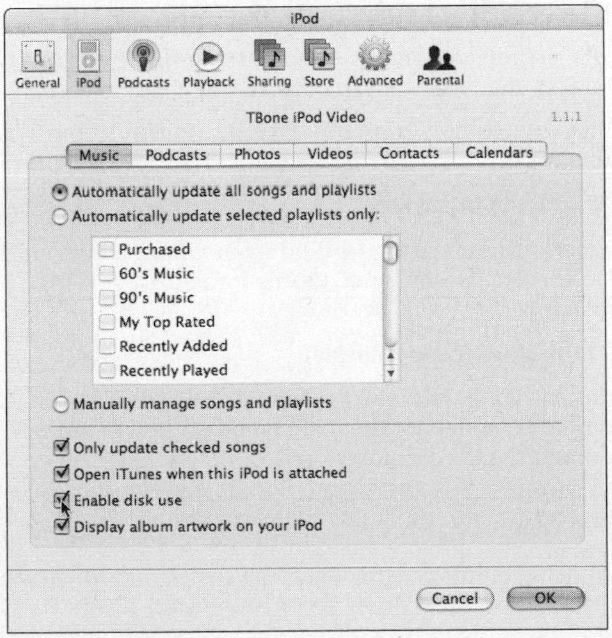

Figure 23-1:
Enable the
iPod as a
Mac hard
drive.

The iPod hard drive opens up to show several folders — including Calendars, Contacts, and Notes (see Figure 23-2). You might also have other folders, depending on the iPod model; for example, a fifth-generation video iPod includes a Photos folder. You can add new folders, rename your new folders, and generally use the iPod as a hard drive.

Don't rename the folders already provided on the iPod. They link directly to functions on the iPod — for example, the Calendars folder links directly to the Calendar menu on the iPod.

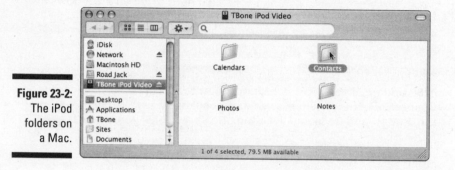

Figure 23-2:
The iPod folders on a Mac.

7. **(Optional) Drag files or folders to the iPod window.**

   To keep data organized, create new folders on the iPod and then drag files and folders that you want to copy to the newly created folders.

   To delete files and folders from the iPod, drag them to the Trash just like an external hard drive.

8. **Eject the iPod from the system.**

   Click the Eject button next to the iPod name in the Finder or drag the iPod icon to the Trash icon, which turns into an Eject button as you drag the iPod icon into it.

9. **Disconnect the iPod from your Mac.**

   After ejecting the iPod, wait until its display shows the `OK to disconnect` message on older models or the main menu on newer models. You can then disconnect the iPod from its dock or disconnect the dock from the computer. Don't ever disconnect an iPod before ejecting it. You might have to reset your iPod. (If you do, head to Chapter 26.)

Don't use a hard drive utility program, such as Disk Utility or Drive Setup, to erase or format the iPod's hard drive. If you erase your iPod's hard drive in this way, it might be unable to play music and videos.

To see how much free space is left on the iPod, you can use the Finder. Select the iPod icon on the desktop and then choose File⇨Show Info. You can also choose Settings⇨About from the iPod's main menu.

Setting up the iPod hard drive on a Windows PC

You can set up your iPod to use as an external hard drive on a Windows PC by following these steps:

1. **Connect your iPod to your computer.**

2. **Select the iPod name in the iTunes Source pane.**

3. **Click the iPod Options button on the bottom-right side of the iTunes window.**

   The iPod Options button appears only when an iPod is connected and selected in the Source pane. You can also choose Edit⇨Preferences and click the iPod tab — whether or not the iPod is selected In the Source pane (although it has to be connected).

   The iPod preferences appear.

4. **Click the Music tab.**

   The iPod music updating preferences display, as shown in Figure 23-3.

5. **Select the Enable Disk Use option and click OK.**

   The Enable Disk Use option is available if your iPod is set to automatically update. You must select this option to use your iPod as a hard drive. If you already set your iPod to manual updating (as we describe in Chapter 12), this option is grayed out because it isn't needed — setting the iPod to update manually automatically enables you to use it as a hard drive.

6. **Double-click the iPod icon in the My Computer or Windows Explorer window to see its contents.**

   If you open the My Computer window, the iPod appears as an external hard drive, as shown in Figure 23-4. Windows automatically assigns the iPod hard drive to a Windows drive letter. (The iPod in the figure is named *Journeyman* and assigned to drive E.)

   The iPod hard drive opens to show several folders, including Calendars, Contacts, and Notes. You might also have other folders, depending on the iPod model. You can add new folders, rename your new folders, and generally use the iPod as a hard drive.

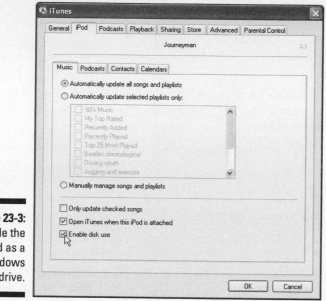

Figure 23-3:
Enable the
iPod as a
Windows
hard drive.

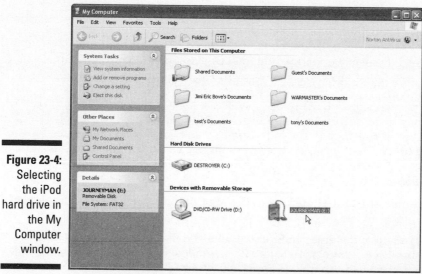

Figure 23-4:
Selecting
the iPod
hard drive in
the My
Computer
window.

Don't rename the folders already provided on the iPod. They link
directly to functions on the iPod — for example, the Calendars folder
links directly to the Calendar menu on the iPod.

7. **(Optional) Copy files or folders to the iPod.**

   To keep data organized, create new folders on the iPod and then copy files and folders to the newly created folders by using the drag-and-drop method in the My Computer window or Windows Explorer, or by copying and pasting.

   To delete files and folders from the iPod, select the filename and press Backspace or choose File⇨Delete from the Windows Explorer menu, just like you do on your internal hard drive.

8. **Eject the iPod from Windows.**

   Right-click the iPod name or icon and choose Eject from the shortcut menu. You can do this from within iTunes by clicking the Eject button next to the iPod's name in the Source pane.

9. **Disconnect your iPod from the computer.**

   Wait until the iPod displays the `OK to disconnect` message on older models, or the main menu on newer models. You can then disconnect the iPod from its dock or disconnect the dock from the computer. Don't ever disconnect an iPod before ejecting it. You might have to reset your iPod. (If you do, head to Chapter 26.)

Don't use the Windows formatting utility or another company's hard drive utility program to erase or format the iPod's hard drive. If you erase the hard drive in your iPod in this way, it might be unable to play music and videos.

To see how much free space is left on the iPod, select the iPod icon in My Computer and choose File⇨Properties. You can also choose Settings⇨About from the iPod's main menu.

Setting up iPod shuffle as a flash memory drive

iPod shuffle makes a really convenient flash memory drive, which is like a hard drive except that it uses flash memory rather than a hard drive. *Flash memory* is a rewritable memory chip that holds its content without power. The name "flash memory" was coined by Toshiba to express how much faster it could be erased (in a flash, you see). Flash memory is widely used for external storage devices such as USB keychain-sized drives and digital camera memory cards. The iPod software makes the flash memory look like a hard drive to the operating system.

To enable your iPod shuffle to act as a flash memory drive to transfer folders and data files, follow these steps:

1. **Connect the iPod shuffle and select it in the Source pane.**

2. **Click the iPod Options button.**

   The iPod Options button appears only when an iPod is connected and selected in the Source pane. You can also choose iTunes⇨Preferences on a Mac or Edit⇨Preferences on a Windows PC, and click the iPod tab.

3. **Click the Music tab.**

   The iPod music updating preferences display, as shown in Figure 23-5.

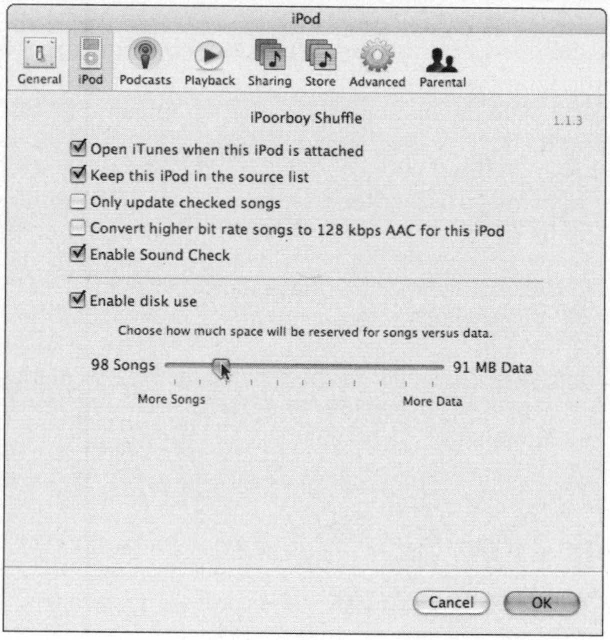

Figure 23-5:
Enable your iPod shuffle as a flash memory drive that looks like a hard drive.

iPod

General iPod Podcasts Playback Sharing Store Advanced Parental

iPoorboy Shuffle   1.1.3

☑ Open iTunes when this iPod is attached
☑ Keep this iPod in the source list
☐ Only update checked songs
☐ Convert higher bit rate songs to 128 kbps AAC for this iPod
☑ Enable Sound Check

☑ Enable disk use

   Choose how much space will be reserved for songs versus data.

98 Songs ———————————————————— 91 MB Data
        More Songs   More Data

Cancel   OK

4. **Select the Enable Disk Use option.**

   The Enable Disk Use option in the iPod preferences pane enables the iPod shuffle to act as a hard drive.

5. **Drag the storage allocation slider to the right to enable more space for data.**

   The iPod preferences for the iPod shuffle (refer to Figure 23-5) include a storage allocation slider with More Songs on the left side and More Data on the right side. Drag the slider to the right to open up more space for data.

6. **Click OK to close the iTunes Preferences dialog.**

   If you set the storage allocation slider to allocate more space for data, and you have music stored on the iPod shuffle that takes up more space than what you've just allocated, iTunes asks if you want to delete music from the iPod shuffle to make room for data. You can click Yes to delete music or No to leave the music alone — in which case you have less room for data.

7. **Open the iPod shuffle icon in the Finder (Mac) or My Computer (Windows) to see its contents.**

   The iPod shuffle window opens up appearing as an empty folder — the music is stored in a hidden folder. You can add your own folders to the iPod shuffle window and generally use the iPod shuffle as a hard drive. Windows automatically assigns the iPod hard drive to a Windows drive letter, such as drive E.

8. **Drag files or folders to the iPod shuffle window.**

   To keep data organized, create new folders on the iPod shuffle and then drag files and folders that you want to copy to the newly created folders.

   To delete files and folders from the iPod shuffle, drag them to the Trash just like an external hard drive.

9. **Eject the iPod shuffle and then disconnect it.**

   Click the iPod Eject button, which appears in the bottom-right corner of the iTunes window, or click the Eject icon next to the iPod shuffle name in the Source pane. When the iPod shuffle's status light stops blinking and stays on, you can disconnect the iPod shuffle.

On a Mac, you can also eject the iPod shuffle by dragging the iPod shuffle icon to the Trash. On a Windows PC, you can eject the iPod shuffle by clicking the Safely Remove Hardware icon in the Windows system tray and selecting the iPod shuffle.

The Mac can use Windows-formatted hard drives, but Windows can't use Mac-formatted hard drives. If you want to transfer data files to and from Mac and Windows computers, set up the iPod shuffle on a Windows computer to format as a Windows hard drive.

Adding Notes and Text

You can add text notes to your iPod so that you can view them on the iPod display — all sorts of notes, such as driving directions, weather information, or even news items. If you just use your iPod for music, you might want notes about the music. This feature works with iPods that run iPod software 2.0 or newer (including iPod mini and all iPods that use the dock connector).

Using the Notes folder

In a perfect world, you could rip audio CDs and also capture all the information in the liner notes — the descriptions of who played which instruments, where the CD was produced, and other minute detail. Then, while sharing your iPod music with others, you could view the liner notes on the iPod screen whenever a question arises about the music.

You can almost achieve the same result by typing some of the liner notes or any text you want into a word-processing program, such as TextEdit on a Mac or Notepad in Windows. You can then save the document as a text-only file (with the `.txt` filename extension) and drag it to the Notes folder of the iPod.

You must save documents as text-only files to view them on the iPod display. If you use a word processor, such as Microsoft Word, choose File⇨Save As and select the Text Only option (or the Text Only with Line Breaks option) from the Save As Type pop-up menu in Windows or the Format pop-up menu on a Mac. Notes text files can be up to 4K in size — that's roughly 2 or 3 printed pages of information. You can transfer up to 1,000 notes.

Text files in the Notes folder are organized by filename. You can view these notes files by choosing Extras⇨Notes. Make sure that your notes have descriptive filenames so that you can easily scroll the list of notes files to find the notes you want.

Your iPod can also display a folder hierarchy in the Notes folder, allowing you to organize your notes by creating folders (using the Finder with your iPod mounted as a hard drive) and putting notes files within the folders in the Notes folder.

Notes can include basic HTML tags (used on Web pages) such as paragraph markers (`<P>` and `</P>`) and line breaks (`<BR>`). The HTML tags can define links to other notes text files and to audio files. Software companies such as Talking Panda (`http://talkingpanda.com`) have created textual guides you can install in the iPod Notes folder that use these tags and links to present text on the iPod screen and play audio files. You can find out how to develop your own HTML tags by downloading Using iPod as a Tour Guide from the following site:

```
http://developer.apple.com/hardwaredrivers/ipod/iPodNoteReaderGuide.pdf
```

To navigate the Notes section of your iPod, use the iPod controls as follows:

- ✔ Press the Select button to open a Note from its folder, just like playing a song in an album.

- ✔ Use the scroll wheel to scroll up and down the list of notes in a folder, and up and down the text in a Note.

- ✔ As you scroll through text, iPod jumps from link to link, highlighting each link. When a link is already highlighted, press the Select button to follow the link. To go back to the previous link, press the Menu button.

- ✔ To go up to the folder that contains the Note text file, press the Menu button to back up through the links until the iPod displays the folder.

Adding guides, books, and news feeds

Do you want the latest news, weather, sports scores, or driving directions available at the touch of a button of your iPod? How about lessons on speaking French, German, Italian, Spanish, or other languages? Enterprising software entrepreneurs have moved in to fill the vacuum left by Apple with accessories that provide displayable text on your iPod screen, such as the following:

- ✔ **Life2Go** (www.kainjow.com/life2go) for Mac OS X offers synchronized feeds for news, weather forecasts, movie listings, stock quotes, horoscopes, sections of Web pages, and driving directions.

- ✔ **NewsMac Pro** (www.thinkmac.co.uk/newsmacpro), also for Mac OS X, lets you keep tabs on world news Web sites and lets you transfer entire Web pages.

- ✔ **iLingo** (http://talkingpanda.com/ilingo.php) offers language lessons, with over 400 essential words and phrases of your chosen language, organized as Notes folders and files. It also includes audio files created by native speakers that provide proper pronunciation for all included phrases.

- ✔ **iBar** (http://talkingpanda.com/ibar.php) offers drink recipes with ingredients, instructions for mixing and proper garnishing, and

advice on which glass to use. Many recipes are linked to audio anec-
dotes about the origin of the cocktail as well as instructions on how to
mix it.

- ✔ **EphPod 2** for Windows (`www.ephpod.com`) lets you update your iPod
  with news, weather, and other information updates.

- ✔ **Book2Pod** (`www.tomsci.com/book2pod`) is a shareware program for
  the Mac that allows you to read entire books on your iPod display.
  There's also a similar shareware program for Windows called
  iPodLibrary (`www.sturm.net.nz`).

- ✔ You can also take advantage of the Notes folder and other iPod features
  by using some of the handy AppleScripts provided for iTunes and the
  iPod, which you can download from the Apple site (`www.apple.com/
  applescript/ipod`).

Transferring Photos from a Camera

You can use your iPod as a portable hard drive that doubles as a storage
repository for your photos — even an older iPod that doesn't display photos.
With full-size iPods that have a dock connector, you can use an accessory to
temporarily store photos from digital camera memory cards at full resolution, so that you can later import the photos into your computer.

If you're traveling with just your digital camera and your iPod, you can shoot
all the pictures you want without worrying about filling up your camera's
memory card. Shoot the pictures you want and then connect the camera
to your iPod with an accessory such as the Belkin Media Reader for iPod or
the Digital Camera Link for iPod w/ Dock Connector (`http://catalog.
belkin.com`), and transfer the photos to your iPod hard drive. Then delete
the pictures from your camera's memory card and go snap some more. You
could travel for weeks on end, shooting thousands of photos in locations
around the world without running out of space in your iPod.

The key to these capabilities is the fact that the iPod serves as an external
hard drive. After you mount the iPod on your Mac or Windows desktop, you
can use it as a hard drive.

Both the Belkin Media Reader for iPod and the Digital Camera Link for iPod
connect to the iPod's dock connection to transfer photos quickly to the
Photos folder on your iPod hard drive. Your iPod can hold hundreds or even
thousands of photos (depending on how much music is already stored on it).
Available from the Apple Store, the Belkin accessory works only with full-
sized iPod models with dock connectors.

To transfer the photos to the iPhoto library on a Mac, mount the iPod as a hard drive. Then import the photos by dragging the files directly from the iPod hard drive and dropping them over the iPhoto window. To transfer the photos to a Windows photo application such as Adobe Photo Album or Photoshop Elements, drag the files or the entire Photos folder directly from the iPod hard drive into a folder on your hard drive and then open them with the photo application.

Apple's iPod Camera Connector, available from the Apple Store, is a compact storage solution that lets you shoot your photos, dump them into a color-display iPod for storage, preview them on the iPod, and continue shooting. Depending how much space you have on your iPod, you could continue shooting photos indefinitely without having to visit your computer or use more memory cards.

The iPod Camera Connector is a convenient adapter — about the size of a flash memory card and about twice as thick — that connects to a color-display iPod's dock connection and lets you plug in a USB cable connected to your digital camera. You can then temporarily store photos from digital camera memory cards at full resolution on the iPod, and later you can import them into your computer.

To transfer photos using the iPod Camera Connector, follow these steps:

1. **Connect your digital camera to the iPod Camera Connector.**

   Use the USB cable supplied with your camera.

2. **Connect the iPod Camera Connector to the dock connection of your color-display iPod.**

3. **Turn on your digital camera.**

   The Import menu appears on the iPod color display, showing the number of photos in the camera and the space occupied, along with the Import and Cancel menu functions.

4. **To import photos, highlight Import and press the Select button.**

   The Photo Import menu appears, showing the progress of the download to your iPod. During this process, you can choose the Stop and Save function to save the pictures you've downloaded or Cancel to cancel the download. When the download finishes, your color-display iPod gives you the option to erase the camera's memory card.

Transferring full-resolution photos and images

Picture quality with a digital camera is measured by the number of pixels — specific points of information in a picture, also known as the image *resolution.* Digital cameras are often described by the image resolution in millions of pixels, or *megapixels.* Higher megapixel counts usually result in better images. A 2-megapixel camera produces good 4-x-6-inch prints and acceptable 8-x-10-inch prints. A 3-megapixel camera produces very good 4-x-6-inch prints and magazine-quality 8-x-10-inch prints. A 5-megapixel camera produces good quality 10-x-14-inch prints. And so on.

A color-display iPod, by default, doesn't need the full resolution of photos to display them well on televisions and use them with video projectors, which are far lower in resolution than prints; certainly the tiny iPod display doesn't need high resolution in the photos it displays. The more resolution you have, the more space the photo takes up, so during the transfer, the color-display iPod software optimizes photos for video display to save space.

If you intend to use your color-display iPod to transfer images to another computer or to make a backup of your photos in their original resolution, you can set an option to include full-resolution versions of the photos when updating your iPod with photos (see Chapter 12). You would preserve the full quality of the photo so that you can use the version on the iPod for making prints.

Taking Your System on the Road

Life on the road can be hazardous to your laptop's hard drive, and if any portion of the hard drive containing system files is damaged, your system might not start up. When this happens, you ordinarily use the installation CDs to start the computer, scan and fix the hard drive trouble spots, and reinstall the operating system. The installation CDs let you load and start, or *boot,* the system onto your computer regardless of the status of the hard drive. With a Mac, you can accomplish the same thing with another hard drive set up with a system to boot your computer.

Well, your iPod *is* another hard drive. The older iPod models that use FireWire for updating — the first through fourth generations — can also boot a Mac with an operating system. This feature could be handy for saving your Mac in a system crisis, because you'd have a spare system on your iPod. It's even more useful for people who want to boot another operating system, such as Linux. Unfortunately it doesn't work with the current fifth-generation models that rely on USB 2.0 for updating, but does work with the Intel-based Mac models that can boot from a USB 2.0 drive. Although Apple doesn't officially support system booting from an iPod, you can load the iPod with a minimally configured Mac or Linux system and then use the iPod to start up your Mac. Depending on the size of your iPod, you should be able to fit both a minimal system and a considerable amount of music on the iPod. (Mac models introduced after January 2003 can't start up with Mac OS 9, so you need to save Mac OS X to your iPod unless you use an older Mac.)

Although it is safe to copy files and folders to and from your iPod (using it as a hard drive), booting a system from an iPod severely strains the hard drive and shortens the life of your iPod — it should be done only in an emergency. The iPod's drive just wasn't designed to support that kind of activity over a long period of time, and the heat alone could eventually fry your iPod.

To get the most functionality from your iPod, make sure that you have the latest version of iPod software. To update your iPod software to the latest version, see Chapter 26.

To copy files and applications to your iPod, first enable the iPod as a hard drive, as we describe earlier in this chapter.

Installing Mac OS X

To install a custom version of OS X 10.1 on your iPod, connect your FireWire-updating iPod (first through fourth generation models) as a hard drive, as we describe earlier in this chapter, and then follow these steps:

1. **Insert your Mac OS X installation CD into your Mac and follow the directions to start the installation process.**

   You have to restart the Mac with the installation CD while holding down C to start the computer from the CD.

2. **When the installer asks you to select a destination, choose the iPod hard drive.**

   Don't use the option to erase and format the hard drive, because the hard drive of your iPod is specially formatted for playing music, and formatting it in this manner prevents it from playing music again. So *don't* format it! If you format or erase the iPod's hard drive by mistake, you must restore it to its factory condition; see Chapter 26.

3. **Specify a custom installation rather than a standard installation.**

   To make sure that you don't use too much hard drive space on your iPod, choose a custom installation of OS X. In the custom installation section, choose only the languages that you need. These language options take up a lot of space, and you probably don't need them.

4. **After installation finishes and the Mac restarts from the iPod, continue through the setup procedure and then use Software Update in System Preferences to update the Mac system on your iPod.**

   Most likely, a lot of system updates are waiting for you — updates released after the date of your installation CDs. Take the time to update your system because these updates might make a difference in how your computer performs with certain applications.

To install a custom version of OS X version 10.2 (Jaguar) through version 10.4.7 (Tiger) on your iPod, you can use Carbon Copy Cloner from Bombich Software (www.bombich.com/software/ccc.html). Although you could clone your system by using the UNIX ditto command in the Terminal window of Mac OS X, this process is tedious, and you could easily make a mistake. Carbon Copy Cloner lets you specify what parts of the system you don't need cloned, and you can use its Preferences dialog to make the "target disk" (your iPod) bootable. You can also install OS X on your iPod using SuperDuper! (www.shirt-pocket.com/SuperDuper/SuperDuperDescription.html).

You can also install a custom version of OS X version 10.3 (Panther) or version 10.4 (Tiger) on your iPod by connecting your iPod as a hard drive and then using the Disk Utility program supplied with OS X. (It's in the Utilities folder inside your Applications folder.) Using Disk Utility, drag the icon for a source hard drive with a version of OS X to the Source text box in the Disk Utility dialog, and then drag your iPod hard drive icon into the Destination text box. Then click Restore, and the program does everything for you.

To start a Mac in an emergency situation from an iPod that runs Mac OS X, connect the iPod, hold down Option, and choose Restart from the Apple menu (or if your system is already hosed, use the Power button to reboot while holding down Option). Eventually, as the Mac resets itself and scans itself for any startup drives, all the startup drives appear as icons in a row, with a right-pointing arrow underneath the icons. Click the icon representing the iPod hard drive and then click the right-pointing arrow to start the system from that drive.

While you're at it, copy the Disk Utility program to your iPod so that you can repair any Mac's hard drive by using your iPod as the startup drive.

Installing Mac OS 9

Macs sold since 2003 no longer use OS 9, and some older models can't use a FireWire drive (such as an iPod) as a startup drive. However, you can still install OS 9 on an iPod to use as a startup drive for a Mac that can run OS 9.

To install a custom version of OS 9 on your iPod, connect your iPod as a hard drive and then follow these steps:

1. **Insert your Mac OS 9 installation CD into your Mac and follow the directions to start the installation process.**

   You have to restart the Mac with the installation CD while holding down C to start the computer from the CD.

2. **When the installer asks you to select a destination, select the iPod hard drive.**

3. **After the installation finishes, quit the installation program.**

   That's all you have to do — the installer does everything for you.

To start a Mac from an iPod that holds Mac OS 9, connect the iPod, hold down Option, and choose Restart from the Apple menu (or if your system is already hosed, use the Power button to reboot while holding down Option). Eventually, as the Mac resets and scans itself for any startup drives, all the startup drives appear as Icons in a row, with a right-pointing arrow underneath the icons. Click the icon representing the iPod hard drive and then click the right-pointing arrow to start the system from that drive.

Removing the Mac OS from your iPod

Removing Mac OS 9 from an iPod is easy: Drag the System Folder from the iPod hard drive to the Trash when your iPod is connected as a hard drive.

Removing Mac OS X isn't as easy because OS X installs hidden files and directories, and there is no easy way to drag them to the Trash. (Perhaps that's why Apple doesn't support this feature.) The quickest and easiest way to remove OS X from an iPod is to restore the iPod, as we describe in Chapter 26. Restore erases and reformats the iPod to its original factory condition. Be sure to copy any important files stored on your iPod before restoring it. Although all your music and files are erased in this one step, it's much easier to add your music from iTunes, your calendars and contacts, and your files than it is to try to delete files associated with OS X. Restore and then copy everything back to your iPod as needed.

Installing Linux

Linux, first conceived and implemented by Linus Torvalds when he was a student programmer in Finland, has been enhanced and refined by an enormous community of volunteer programmers to become the flagship work of the open-source software movement. One of Linux's many virtues is that it can run on just about any computing platform. Linux already runs well on a variety of processors from Intel, Motorola, IBM, and others and behaves similarly on all of them.

People who use Linux on their desktop or laptop PCs or Macs can also put Linux on their iPods. Although versions of Linux can be downloaded for free, commercial companies also package Linux in a *distribution* — either on CD-ROM or DVD or for downloading — and often include automatic installation programs or wizards that help you through the process of configuring the system for different hardware configurations. Yellow Dog Linux, in a distribution from Terra Soft Solutions Corp. (www.yellowdoglinux.com), can be set up to boot a computer on any model iPod that uses FireWire for updating. You can then use the iPod to boot Linux on your Mac and experiment with Linux without ever installing Linux on your Mac's hard drive. You can fit a minimal 1GB configuration onto any FireWire-model iPod and still have room for music.

To enable use of an iPod with computers running Linux, the iPodLinux Project (http://ipodlinux.org) provides a customized uClinux (www.uclinux.org) kernel to run on the iPod, and a simple user interface for it dubbed podzilla — which offers familiar navigational menus for accessing various functions in iPodLinux, such as playing music, file browsing, and image viewing. As of this writing, iPodLinux is safe to install on first-, second-, and third-generation iPods.

Chapter 24

Getting Personal

Your iPod is capable of helping you manage your activities on the road to the point where it competes in some respects with personal digital assistants (PDAs). Although you still add to and edit your address book, calendar, and To-Do list on your computer, you can update or synchronize your iPod to have all the information that you need for viewing and playback. As a result, you might not ever need an additional PDA — especially if you *prefer* using your computer to manage your data and your iPod to view it. Your iPod is a *player* — not just in the world of music and video, but also in the world of personal productivity.

Your iPod can store your personal information right alongside your music, podcasts, audio books, and videos so that the information is available at your fingertips. After entering and managing your personal information on your computer, you can then copy the information to your iPod or synchronize with information already on your iPod.

The iPod accepts industry-standard iCalendar and vCalendar files for calendars and To-Do lists, which you can export from most applications that offer calendars and To-Do lists. It also accepts industry-standard *vCards,* or *virtual business cards,* which are records containing contact information for people, including physical addresses, e-mail addresses, phone numbers, and so on.

If you're a Mac user, you have it easy: You can use the free iCal and Address Book applications that come with Mac OS X. If you're a Windows user, you can choose between Microsoft Outlook (and its accompanying Address Book,) and Outlook Express. In either case, you can automatically synchronize the information with your iPod calendar and contact list with iTunes (as we describe in Chapter 25).

If you don't mind updating your iPod manually with contacts and calendar information, you have even more choices in applications as long as you use standard formats that work with the iPod. You also have choices of third-party utilities for putting the information on an iPod, as well as the tried-and-true technique of exporting (or dragging) information to the iPod.

This chapter shows you how to enter your personal information into the computer by using Address Book and iCal (Mac) or Microsoft Outlook and Microsoft Address Book (Windows PC).

Keeping Appointments with iCal

iCal is a free desktop calendar application supplied with Mac OS X; if for some reason you don't have it, you can download it from Apple's software download page (www.info.apple.com/support/downloads.html). iCal creates calendars that you can automatically update to your iPod using iTunes or directly copy to your iPod. iCal requires Mac OS X version 10.2.3 or newer. You can create custom calendars for different activities, such as home, office, road tours, exercise and diet schedules, mileage logs, and so on. You can view them separately or all together. After editing your calendars on the Mac, you can synchronize your iPod to have the same calendars. See Chapter 25 when you're ready to sync your calendar to your iPod.

If you use another application to manage your personal calendar, you might still want to use iCal just to transfer your calendar information to the iPod painlessly. You can import calendars from other applications that support the iCal or vCal format, such as Microsoft Entourage, Microsoft Outlook, and Palm Desktop.

Launch iCal by double-clicking the iCal application or clicking its icon in the Mac OS X Dock. iCal displays a calendar, as shown in Figure 24-1, and you can switch the view from an entire month to just one week or one day by clicking the Day or Week buttons at the bottom of the window.

iCal starts you off with two calendars: Home and Work. Their names have check marks next to them in the upper-left corner of the iCal window, indicating that both are visible, and they're merged into the calendar view. To see only your Home calendar, deselect the Work option in the Calendars pane on the left, and vice versa. It's easy to set up appointments and events for either calendar.

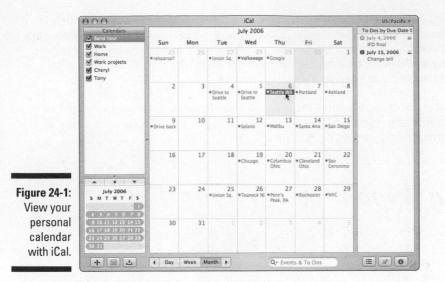

Figure 24-1:
View your
personal
calendar
with iCal.

Setting up an appointment or event

Some appointments and events are a drag, and some are fun, but either way you can drag your mouse to create one. Click the Week button at the bottom of the window to see just a week and then click and drag over a period of time to create an appointment. You can choose File⇨New Event to do the same thing.

To see the details of an event or appointment, do one of these things:

✔ Double-click the event or appointment.

✔ Click the event or appointment to select it and then click the *i* icon in the lower-right corner.

✔ Click the event or appointment to select it and then choose Window⇨ Show Info.

The detail for the event or appointment appears in the info drawer that sticks out on the right or left side (depending on display room) of the iCal window, as shown in Figure 24-2.

In the info drawer, you can type over the filler "New Event" and "location" text, change the date and time, add attendees, specify the status and whether the event or appointment should be repeated, and so on. You can type a note in the Notes section at the bottom and assign the event to a specific calendar (in this case, the Home calendar). If you have created custom calendars within iCal (as we describe in "Creating a custom calendar"), select the calendar that you want to add the event to from the Calendar pop-up menu. You can set the event to automatically repeat every day, week, month, or year by using the Repeat pop-up menu.

Figure 24-2: View the details of a new iCal event or appointment in the info drawer.

Adding a To-Do item

iCal can keep track of your To-Do list. Click the thumbtack icon to view the To Do items pane of the iCal window (or choose Window⇨Show To Dos). Choose File⇨New To Do to add an item to the list.

You can set the priority of the To-Do item so that it sorts to the top (highest priority) or bottom (no priority) of the To-Do list. You can also set its due date in the Due Date pop-up menu — if you set a due date, the alarm pop-up appears so that you can also set an alarm for the To-Do item. (The alarm works in your iPod when you synchronize your calendar with your iPod.) iCal lets you assign the To-Do item to a specific calendar and even add a Web address to the URL field to link the To-Do item to a Web page. To mark a To-Do item as finished, select the Completed option for the item.

Creating a custom calendar

You can create custom calendars in iCal that show only the events that are assigned to the custom calendar. For example, you might create one custom calendar for work events, another for family events, another for an exercise plan, and so on. Your custom calendars are maintained by iCal so that you can see them all at once or individually in the calendar view. The list of custom calendars appears in the top-left corner of the iCal window, with a check box next to each calendar. When you select the check box, the custom calendar's events show up in the calendar view.

To create a custom calendar, follow these steps:

1. **Choose File⇨New Calendar or click the plus (+) button in the bottom-left corner of the iCal window.**

   An Untitled item appears in the list of calendars in the top-left corner.

2. **Type a new name for the Untitled item.**

   Click inside the Name text box and type a new name.

3. **Turn the custom calendar on or off.**

   Deselect the custom calendar if you don't want its events to be displayed. Select it to display the custom calendar along with other selected custom calendars (merged with the other custom calendar events).

Keeping Appointments with Outlook

Microsoft Outlook is offered as part of Microsoft Office (Windows version), and Microsoft Outlook Express is offered free with Windows. You can use any of these applications to create calendars and export the calendar information to your iPod.

With your calendar and To-Do tasks set up in Outlook, you can export the information to your iPod, as we describe in Chapter 25.

Setting up an appointment or event

To set up an appointment or event in Microsoft Outlook, launch Outlook and then follow these steps:

1. **Click the Calendar icon and click any time slot to select it in the Outlook calendar.**

   The time slots in the Outlook calendar, as shown in Figure 24-3, appear when you click the Calendar icon.

Figure 24-3:
Select a
time slot in
the Outlook
calendar
for an
appoint-
ment.

2. **Choose File⇨New⇨Appointment to create an appointment or event, and then fill in the information.**

   Alternatively, you can right-click the selected time slot and choose New Appointment (or choose New Recurring Appointment for appointments that repeat often). Specify start and end times and a location.

3. **Click the Save and Close button to save the appointment or event.**

Adding a To-Do task

The outlook for your future plans might be bright, but you need more than a crystal ball to keep them that way. If you already use Outlook for your e-mail and calendar functions, you might also want to use it to keep track of your To-Do list.

To create a To-Do task in Outlook, choose New⇨Task and type a subject name for the task. To make the task a recurring task, select the Recurrence option and choose a frequency (Daily, Weekly, Monthly, or Yearly) for the recurring task. Click the Save and Close button to save the task.

Storing Contacts in the Mac OS X Address Book

Address Book, a free application that's provided with OS X for the Mac, has just about all the features you could ever want for storing names, addresses, phone numbers, e-mail addresses, and physical addresses. You can drag and drop addresses and phone numbers from incoming e-mails to avoid having to type the information, and you can wirelessly copy cards from your address book to cell phones, PDAs, and other Bluetooth-enabled devices. Keeping your iPod synchronized with your addresses and phone numbers is simple and automatic. You can then have your friends' addresses and phone numbers with you at all times, right on your iPod.

If you use some other application for storing contact information, you might want to use Address Book in addition to your other application so you can import contact information from other applications that support vCards or the LDIF format. (LDIF is the file format for *LDAP*, which stands for *Lightweight Directory Access Protocol*.) To do so, launch Address Book and choose File➪ Import, select the format that you used from the submenu, and select the file that contains the exported information. When your information is in Address Book, you can synchronize the information with your iPod, eliminating the hassle of dragging vCards to the iPod individually.

Adding and editing contact information

Launch Address Book by double-clicking the Address Book application or by clicking its icon in the Mac OS X Dock. To add a new card, follow these steps:

1. **Choose File➪New Card or click the plus (+) button at the bottom of the Name pane.**

   A new blank card appears, ready for you to add information.

2. **Type the person's first and last name over the placeholders in the first and last name text boxes and then add contact information to the other text boxes.**

   You can type addresses, phone numbers, e-mail addresses, and so on, as shown in Figure 24-4. To add multiple addresses, phone numbers, or other text boxes, click the tiny plus (+) icon next to each type of information to add more. If some of the text boxes don't apply, skip them, and they won't show up in the edited card. You can even enter a two-line address by pressing Return to continue to the second line.

3. **Save your changes by clicking the Edit button.**

   Address Book saves the edits.

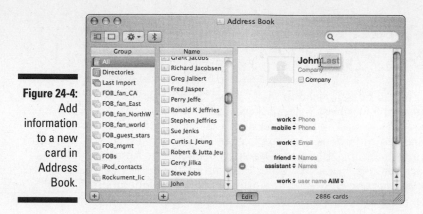

Figure 24-4:
Add
information
to a new
card in
Address
Book.

To edit a card, select the person in the Name pane and click the Edit button. To save your changes, click the Edit button again, and Address Book saves the edits.

You can also add new people to your address book from the Mail program by selecting an e-mail message and choosing Message⇨Add Sender to Address Book. Then open Address Book, click the name in the Name pane, and click the Edit button to edit the person's card. Choosing Add to Address Book in the Mail program From field's contextual menu adds the address and opens the card for editing in Address Book. iChat also works directly with Address Book to store and use addresses.

If you receive a vCard as an e-mail attachment (with the .vcf extension), you can simply drag the attachment to your Address Book window to add the vCard to your address book. Wouldn't it be nice if all your friends sent you vCards to keep you up to date, and you never had to retype the information?

Be wary of vCards from unknown persons — vCards can carry viruses.

Merging cards

One of the coolest features of Address Book is its ability to merge cards. You might occasionally end up with multiple cards for the same person in Address Book, typically by saving the sender's e-mail address from the Mail application while also dragging a vCard from the same person. To fix that, select the cards in the Name pane and choose Card⇨Merge Cards. Address Book creates a new card that combines all the unique information. You can then delete the excess cards.

Searching in Address Book

Address Book lets you search for any text in any of the text boxes of any card. If you're searching for a person and all you have is part of a phone number or even just part of the person's name, type the text in the Search text box at the top-right corner of the Address Book window. As you type, Address Book displays the names of the people who have the text fragment anywhere in their cards. Address Book searches all the information on the cards, including the Notes text box, and it searches *fast,* displaying names immediately. If more than one matching card is found, click the arrow buttons at the bottom of the window to switch between the cards. Or, choose View⇨ Card And Columns to see a list of all the cards.

Managing contacts in groups

You can combine address cards in Address Book into a *group* to make it easy to select all the addresses at once. For example, you might want to group together all your local friends or all your co-workers. You can then send an e-mail to all of them at once by choosing the group as the e-mail recipient.

You can also use a group to keep track of a subset of contacts. For example, you might want only a subset of your contact list on your iPod rather than the entire list. To do this, create a group for the subset of contacts and export the group as a single vCard file that you can then use on your iPod.

To create a group of contacts in Address Book

1. **Click the plus (+) sign at the bottom of the Group pane.**

   Address Book creates a new entry in the Group column with a high-lighted text box so that you can type a new name for the group.

2. **Type a name for the group.**

3. **Select the All item in the Group pane to see your entire list of names.**

4. **Drag and drop names over the group name to add them to your new group.**

After creating a new group, you can see the names in the group by clicking the group name in the Group pane. Select the All item in the Group pane to see all the names in the address book.

To put your addresses on the iPod, you can export a vCard file to the iPod Contacts folder or use iTunes, as we describe in Chapter 25.

Storing Contacts in Microsoft Address Book or Outlook

Microsoft Outlook, included with the Windows version of Microsoft Office, provides extensive features for managing contacts with e-mail and address information. You can also import address books and contact information into Outlook from programs such as Eudora, Lotus Organizer, Netscape Messenger, Microsoft Mail, or Microsoft Schedule+.

Outlook actually uses another application, Microsoft Address Book, to store the contact information. Microsoft Address Book lets you gather address books from other sources, including Microsoft Exchange Server and Internet directory services (depending on how you've set up Outlook). It also includes all the contacts in your Outlook Contacts folder. When you update the information in your Outlook Contacts folder, the Microsoft Address Book is updated as well, so you can make all your changes in the Outlook Contacts folder.

To create a contact in Outlook, which saves the contact information in Microsoft Address Book, launch Outlook and then follow these steps:

1. **Click the Contacts icon to open the Contacts folder.**

   The Contacts icon appears in the Outlook Shortcuts pane on the left of the Outlook display; refer to Figure 24-3.

2. **Choose New⇨Contact and then type a name for the contact.**

   To enter multiple entries for a text box, such as more than one physical address or e-mail address, click the down-arrow next to the text box to display more lines for that text box. Enter all the information you want (or as little as you want).

3. **Click Save and Close to save the contact.**

   Your contacts are displayed in the Contact window of Outlook.

You can also create a new contact automatically for the sender of an e-mail message that you receive. Open the e-mail message, and in the From text box, right-click the name that you want to add to your Contacts folder and then choose Add to Contacts.

You can export the contact information from Microsoft Outlook (and Microsoft Address Book) to your iPod, and for more on that, flip to Chapter 25.

Chapter 25

Synchronizing Information with Your iPod

*W*e chose the iPod for music and videos, but we also find it useful while traveling for viewing the personal information — contacts, appointments, events, and To-Do tasks — that we manage on our computers.

If you've already read Chapter 24, you know how to manage your calendar activities and your contacts on your computer. In fact, you're probably knee-deep in *vCards* (virtual business cards) for your Address Book, and the calendars in your vCalendar files look like they were drawn up in the West Wing. Information changes often, and new information accumulates quickly, but you're well armed with an iPod that you can keep up to date. This chapter shows you how to *synchronize* your iPod to have all the information that you need for viewing and playback. We also show you how to simply copy the information to your iPod to update it.

Chances are good that you make a lot of changes to addresses, phone numbers, calendar events, and To-Do lists on your Mac. Even though you can update your iPod with this information manually, remembering to copy each file you need is difficult. iTunes (version 4.8 and newer versions) can perform this function automatically and keep all your information updated on your iPod.

Synchronizing with Mac Calendars and Contacts

To synchronize your iPod with calendars in iCal on a Mac, follow these steps:

1. **Connect your iPod to the Mac.**

   iTunes launches automatically.

2. **Select the iPod name in the iTunes Source pane.**

3. **Click the iPod Options button in the bottom-right corner of the iTunes window.**

   The iPod Options button appears only when an iPod is connected and selected in the Source pane. You can also choose iTunes➪Preferences and click the iPod tab — whether or not the iPod is selected in the Source pane (although it has to be connected).

   The iPod preferences appear.

4. **Click the Calendars tab to view the iPod Calendars preferences.**

   The iPod Calendars preferences appear, as shown in Figure 25-1.

5. **Select the Synchronize iCal calendars option.**

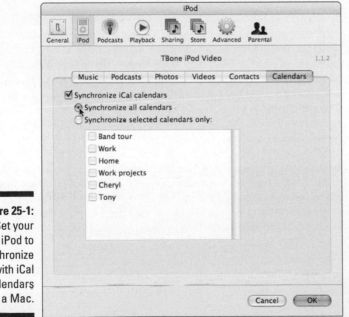

Figure 25-1:
Set your iPod to synchronize with iCal calendars on a Mac.

6. **Select the Synchronize All Calendars option. Alternatively, select the Synchronize Selected Calendars Only option and pick calendars to synchronize.**

   You can synchronize all calendars in iCal or just those you select.

7. **Set other iPod preferences or click OK to finish.**

8. **Eject the iPod by clicking the Eject button and then disconnect your iPod.**

   Remember to wait for the OK to disconnect message before disconnecting your iPod.

After setting the iPod Calendars preferences, every time you connect your iPod, iTunes goes to work synchronizing your iPod with your calendars automatically.

To synchronize your iPod with contacts in Address Book on a Mac, follow these steps:

1. **Connect your iPod to the Mac.**

   iTunes launches automatically.

2. **Select the iPod name in the iTunes Source pane.**

3. **Click the iPod Options button in the bottom-right corner of the iTunes window or click the iPod tab in the iTunes Preferences window.**

4. **Click the Contacts tab to view the iPod Contacts preferences.**

   The iPod Contacts preferences appear, as shown in Figure 25-2.

5. **Select the Synchronize Address Book Contacts option.**

6. **Select the Synchronize All Contacts option. Alternatively, select the Synchronize Selected Groups Only option and pick groups to synchronize.**

   You can synchronize all contacts in Address Book or just selected groups of contacts.

7. **Set other iPod preferences or click OK to finish.**

8. **Wait for the updating to finish and then click the Eject button to eject the iPod.**

   Wait until the iTunes status pane (up at the top) reads iPod update is complete before ejecting your iPod.

After setting the iPod Contacts preferences, every time you connect your iPod, iTunes synchronizes your iPod with your Address Book contacts automatically.

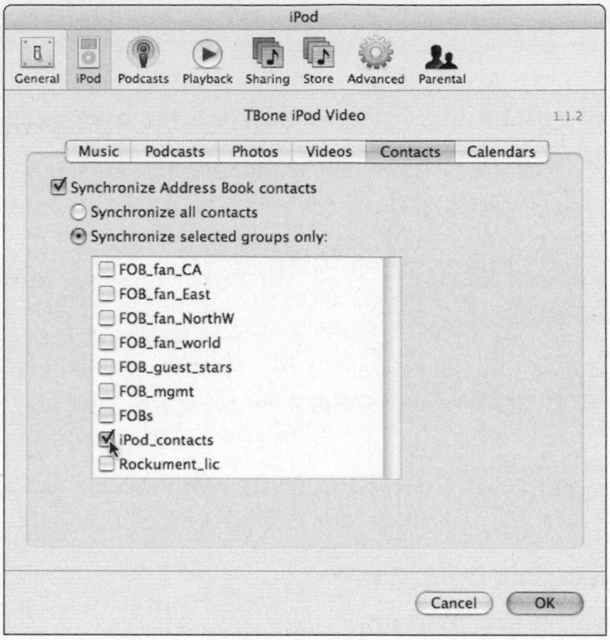

Figure 25-2:
Set your
iPod to
synchronize
with a group
of contacts
in Address
Book on
a Mac.

After you finish synchronizing and otherwise using your iPod with your Mac, be sure to eject the iPod. If you forget this, your iPod's hard drive might freeze up, and you might need to reset your iPod — find out how in Chapter 26.

Synchronizing with Windows Calendars and Contacts

To synchronize your iPod with calendars in Outlook in Windows, follow these steps:

1. **Connect your iPod to the Windows PC.**

   iTunes launches automatically.

2. **Select the iPod name in the iTunes Source pane.**

3. **Click the iPod Options button in the bottom-right corner of the iTunes window.**

   The iPod Options button appears only when an iPod is connected and selected in the Source pane. You can also choose Edit⇨Preferences and click the iPod tab — whether or not the iPod is selected in the Source pane (although it has to be connected).

The iPod preferences appear.

4. **Click the Calendars tab to view the iPod Calendars preferences.**

The iPod Calendars preferences pane appears, as shown in Figure 25-3.

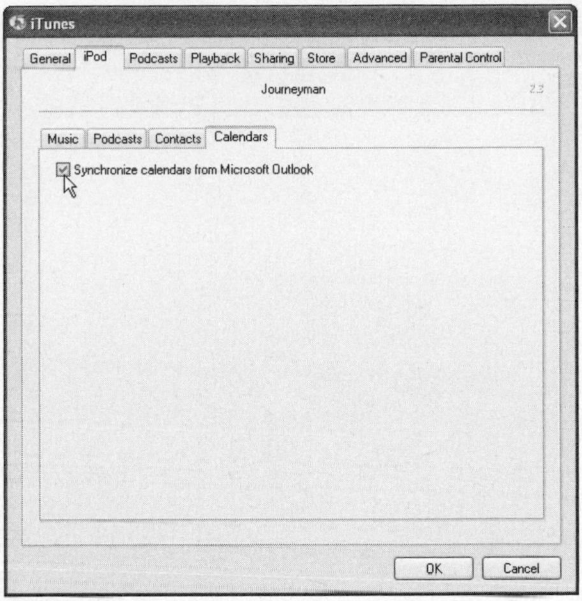

Figure 25-3:
Set your
iPod to
synchronize
with Outlook
calendars on
a Windows
PC.

iTunes

General | iPod | Podcasts | Playback | Sharing | Store | Advanced | Parental Control

Journeyman   2.3

Music | Podcasts | Contacts | Calendars

☑ Synchronize calendars from Microsoft Outlook

OK   Cancel

5. **Select the Synchronize Calendars from Microsoft Outlook option.**

6. **Set other iPod preferences or click OK to finish.**

7. **Eject the iPod and then disconnect it.**

After setting the iPod Calendars preferences, every time you connect your iPod, iTunes goes to work synchronizing your iPod with your Outlook calendars automatically.

To synchronize your iPod with contacts in Outlook or Outlook Express, follow these steps:

1. **Connect your iPod to the Windows PC.**

iTunes launches automatically.

2. **Select the iPod name in the iTunes Source pane.**

3. **Click the iPod Options button in the bottom-right corner of the iTunes window or click the iPod tab in the iTunes Preferences dialog.**

4. **Click the Contacts tab to view the iPod Contacts preferences.**

   The iPod Contacts preferences pane appears, as shown in Figure 25-4.

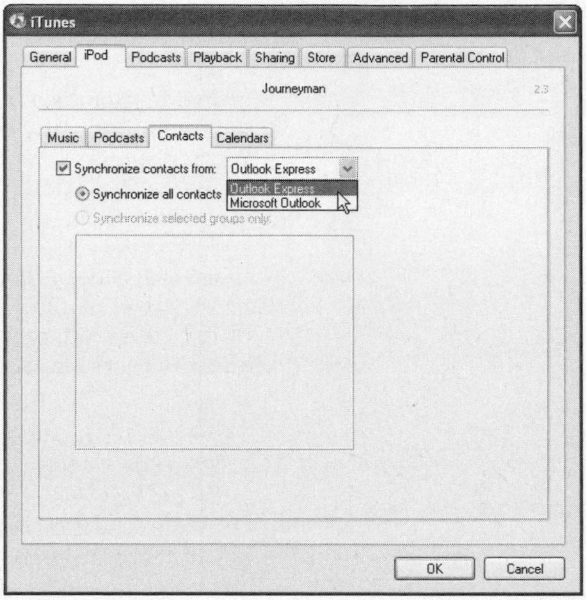

Figure 25-4:
Set your
iPod to
synchronize
with
contacts in
Outlook or
Outlook
Express.

5. **Choose Microsoft Outlook or Outlook Express for the Synchronize Contacts From pop-up menu.**

6. **(Optional) Select the Synchronize Selected Groups Only option and pick groups to synchronize.**

   You can synchronize all contacts or just selected groups of contacts.

7. **Set other iPod preferences or click OK to finish.**

8. **Wait for the updating to finish and then click the Eject button to eject the iPod.**

   Wait until the iTunes status pane (up at the top) reads `iPod update is complete` before ejecting your iPod.

After setting the iPod Contacts preferences, every time you connect your iPod, iTunes synchronizes your iPod with your Outlook or Outlook Express contacts automatically.

After you finish synchronizing and otherwise using your iPod with your PC, be sure to eject the iPod before disconnecting it. If you forget this, your iPod's hard drive might freeze up, and you might need to reset your iPod — find out how in Chapter 26.

Besides iTunes, other applications for Windows iPod users can automatically synchronize your iPod with contacts and calendar info from Microsoft Outlook. For example, iPodSync (available at `www.ipod-sync.com`) is a utility for Windows that lets you keep your Outlook calendar, contacts, and To-Do tasks synchronized between your PC and your iPod.

Outlook can export contacts and calendar information, but It's a tedious process of exporting each contact and appointment individually. This failing of Outlook opens a window of opportunity for entrepreneurs, and several utilities and applications provide ways to export contacts and calendar data all at once. The following are enterprising shareware utilities:

- ✔ **Outpod** at `http://outpod.stoer.de`. This utility lets you export contact and calendar information in bulk from Microsoft Outlook to vCard and vCalendar files, which you can then drag to the iPod, as we describe in "Adding Calendars Manually" and "Adding Contacts Manually" in this chapter.

- ✔ **EphPod** at `www.ephpod.com`. This utility lets you update your iPod with contacts from Outlook. EphPod is a full-featured Windows application that you can use in place of Musicmatch Jukebox. It supports standard Winamp (`.m3u`) playlists and can synchronize the iPod with a library of music files. It imports Microsoft Outlook contacts and lets you create and edit your own contacts. EphPod can also download the latest news, weather, eBooks, and movie listings to an iPod.

Adding Calendars Manually

If you use your iPod as a hard drive, you can copy calendar files directly to the Calendars folder on your iPod. You can copy industry-standard iCalendar or vCalendar files, which many applications, including Microsoft Entourage, Microsoft Outlook, and Palm Desktop, can export.

In most cases, you can drag an iCalendar file (with the filename extension `.ics`) or a vCalendar file (with the filename extension `.vcs`) to your iPod Calendars folder. To save calendar information in the iCalendar format from Microsoft Outlook, you must save each appointment separately as an ICS (iCalendar) file. Follow these steps:

1. **Select the appointment in the calendar view or open the appointment by double-clicking it.**

2. **Choose File⇨Save As.**

3. **Select iCalendar from the Save As Type pop-up menu and then select a destination for the ICS file.**

   The destination can be a folder on your hard drive, or the iPod's Calendars folder. If you select a folder on your hard drive, be sure to copy the files to the iPod's Calendars folder.

4. **Click Save.**

iCal can import Entourage calendars, so you can import into iCal (choose File⇨Import) and then use iTunes to synchronize your iPod, as we describe earlier in this chapter.

You can look at your calendars on the iPod by choosing Extras⇨Calendars⇨All. Select a calendar and then use the scroll wheel to scroll through the days of the calendar, or select an event to see the event's details. Press the Next and Previous buttons to skip to the next or previous month. To see your To-Do list, choose Extras⇨Calendars⇨To Do.

To remove a calendar from your iPod, connect the iPod to your computer and enable the iPod as a hard drive (see Chapter 23). You can then open the Calendars folder on the iPod and delete the calendar file. You can also copy calendar files from the iPod to your hard drive.

Adding Contacts Manually

If you use your iPod as a hard drive, you can copy contacts in vCard files directly to the Contacts folder on your iPod.

A vCard, or *virtual business card,* is a standard format for exchanging personal information. The iPod sorts and displays contacts in the vCard format — you can use separate vCard files for each person or use a group vCard file that contains records for many people.

After enabling the iPod as a hard drive, simply export your contacts as vCards directly into the Contacts folder of your iPod. In most cases, you can drag vCard-formatted contacts from the application's address book to the iPod Contacts folder.

You can copy one card, a group of cards, or even the entire list as a vCard file (with a .vcf extension) by dragging the vCard file into the Contacts folder. Contacts must be in the vCard format to use with the iPod.

You can use applications to export vCard files directly to your iPod. For example, in Microsoft Outlook, you can export a vCard file for a contact directly into your iPod's Contacts folder by following these steps:

1. **Choose File⇨Export to vCard.**

2. **Select the iPod as the destination drive from the Save In pop-up menu.**

3. **Select the Contacts folder to save the contacts file.**

Using Utilities to Copy Files and Music

The iPod has spawned a thriving industry of third-party accessories and products. Some of the most useful products are utility programs that expand the capabilities of the iPod or your ability to update the iPod. Full-featured programs have even been designed as replacements for iTunes. With so many programs to check out, you might be overwhelmed. We've selected three of the best programs for the Mac and Windows (as of this writing).

If you're using Musicmatch Jukebox, see this book's companion Web site at www.dummies.com/go/ipod4e to find out what utilities you can use.

Keep in mind, with programs that allow music copying functions, that copying copyrighted material to other computers without permission is illegal. Don't steal music — or anything else, for that matter.

Mac utilities

On the Mac, third-party offerings have focused on extending the capabilities of the iPod and its software to do things like copying music from the iPod to the computer and updating the iPod with contacts and calendar information. Take a glance at the following examples:

✔ **iPDA (www.zapptek.com/ipda):** With this software, you can transfer personal information to your iPod from Entourage, Stickies, Mail, Address Book, and iCal. You can even download weather forecasts and news headlines directly to your iPod.

✔ **iPod Access (www.findleydesigns.com/ipodaccess):** This utility lets you transfer songs from an iPod to a Mac. iPod Access is available from Findley Designs, Inc.

✔ **Senuti (www.fadingred.org/senuti):** This program lets you copy songs back to your computer from your iPod. You can search for songs and even play songs directly off of your iPod using the program. Senuti reads the playlists you made on your iPod and lets you to transfer them back to your computer. You can also automatically add songs to your iTunes library.

✔ **iPodRip (`www.thelittleappfactory.com/application.php?app=iPodRip`):** This third-party utility, available from The Little App Factory, lets you transfer music from your iPod back to your iTunes library and listen to music on your iPod through your computer (saving hard drive space). It supports all iPod song formats including MP3, AAC, Protected AAC, and Audible.com books.

Windows utilities

Many third-party programs exist for Windows, and they do everything from extending the capabilities of the iPod and updating contacts and calendar information to replacing the need for Musicmatch Jukebox and iTunes.

✔ **iPodSync (`www.ipod-sync.com`):** Keep Outlook calendars, contacts, tasks, and notes synchronized between Windows and an iPod. iPodSync exports industry standard vCards for contacts and uses the iCalendar format for appointment information. iPodSync can even synchronize Outlook notes and tasks.

✔ **EphPod 2 (`www.ephpod.com`):** This utility lets you update your iPod with contacts from Outlook. It's a full-featured Windows application that you can use in place of Musicmatch Jukebox or iTunes. It supports standard Winamp (m3u) playlists and can synchronize the iPod with a library of music files. It imports Outlook contacts and also lets you create and edit your own contacts. EphPod can also download the latest news, weather, eBooks, and movie listings to an iPod.

✔ **XPlay 2 (`www.mediafour.com/products/xplay`):** This utility, from Mediafour Corp., provides read and write access to your iPod hard drive for documents and data files, plus the ability to organize your music from the Explorer-based XPlay interface or from Windows Media Player. It's an alternative to Musicmatch Jukebox or iTunes. XPlay makes your iPod appear as a normal drive under Windows for the sharing of data files, and it makes your songs, playlists, artists, and albums appear in custom folders in Explorer, so they're easy to access and manipulate and organized similarly to how the iPod organizes them.

Chapter 26

Updating and Troubleshooting

*T*his chapter describes some of the problems that you might encounter with your iPod and computer and how to fix them. If your iPod fails to turn on or your computer fails to recognize it, you can most likely find a solution here.

This chapter also covers updating the firmware and software on your iPod and restoring your iPod to its factory default condition. (*Firmware* is software encoded in hardware.) That last option is a drastic measure that erases any music or information on the iPod, but it usually solves the problem if nothing else does.

Taking Your First Troubleshooting Steps

Problems can arise with electronics and software that can prevent the iPod from turning on at all or from turning on properly with all its content and playlists. You can also have problems in the connection between your iPod and your computer.

Checking the Hold switch

If your iPod refuses to turn on, check the position of the Hold switch on top of the iPod. The Hold switch locks the iPod buttons so that you don't accidentally activate them. Slide the Hold switch away from the headphone connection, hiding the orange layer, to unlock the buttons. (If you see the orange layer underneath one end of the Hold switch, the switch is still in the locked position.)

Checking the power

Got power? The battery might not be charged enough. If the battery is too low for normal operation, the iPod doesn't turn on. Instead, a low battery screen appears for about three seconds and then disappears. At that point, your only choice is to connect the iPod to an AC power source, wait for a moment, and then turn the power on by pushing any button on the iPod. If your source of AC power is your computer, make sure that the computer is on and not set to go to sleep. The battery icon in the upper-right corner of the display indicates whether the iPod battery is full or recharging. For more information about maintaining a healthy battery, see Chapter 1.

If your iPod shuffle doesn't turn on or respond, recharge its battery by connecting it to the USB connection on your computer.

Resetting the iPod

This operation resets the operating system of the iPod and restarts the system. Sometimes when your iPod gets confused or refuses to turn on, you can fix it by resetting it.

For current fifth-generation iPod video, iPod nano, fourth-generation iPods, iPod mini, iPod U2 Special Edition, and color-display iPods, follow these steps:

1. **(Optional) Connect the iPod to a power outlet by using the AC power adapter.**

   You can reset your iPod without connecting it to power if it has enough juice in its battery. However, if you have access to power, it makes sense to use it because the reset operation uses up power.

2. **Toggle the Hold switch.**

   Push the Hold switch to hold (lock) and then set it back to unlock.

3. **Press the Menu and Select buttons simultaneously and hold for at least six seconds or until the Apple logo appears; then release the buttons when you see the Apple logo.**

The appearance of the Apple logo signals that your iPod is resetting itself, so you no longer have to hold down the buttons.

It's important to release the Menu and Select buttons as soon as you see the Apple logo. If you continue to press the buttons after the logo appears, the iPod displays the low battery icon, and you must connect it to a power source before using it again.

For first-, second-, and third-generation iPod models, follow these steps:

1. **(Optional) Connect the iPod to a power outlet by using the AC power adapter.**

2. **Toggle the Hold switch.**

   Push the Hold switch to hold (lock) and then set it back to unlock.

3. **Press the Menu and Play/Pause buttons simultaneously and hold for at least five seconds until the Apple logo appears; then release the buttons when you see the Apple logo.**

   The appearance of the Apple logo signals that your iPod is resetting itself, so you no longer have to hold down the buttons.

To reset your iPod shuffle, disconnect it from a computer, switch the slider on the back to the Off position — the green stripe under the switch should not be visible. Wait five seconds and then switch the slider back to the Shuffle Songs or Play in Order position.

After resetting, everything should be back to normal, including your music and data files.

Draining the iPod battery

Certain types of battery-powered devices sometimes run into problems if the battery hasn't drained in a while. In rare cases, the iPod might go dark. Try resetting the iPod first, and if your iPod still doesn't work, disconnect the iPod from any power source and leave it disconnected for approximately 24 hours. After this period, connect it to power and reset.

Try to keep the iPod at room temperature — generally near 68 degrees Fahrenheit (20 degrees Celsius). However, you can use the iPod anywhere between 50 to 95 degrees Fahrenheit (10 and 35 degrees Celsius). If you've left the iPod in the cold, let it warm up to room temperature before waking it from sleep. Otherwise, a low-battery icon might appear, and the iPod won't wake up properly. If the iPod doesn't wake from sleep after warming up, connect the power adapter and reset the iPod, as we describe in the preceding section.

Hitting the panic button (Disk Mode)

Actually it's never a good idea to hit the panic button, even if there is one. However, if all you see on the iPod display is the Apple logo and iPod name and the device seems to be restarting over and over, try force-enabling your iPod as a hard drive. (This is also known as "putting your iPod into Disk Mode.")

For current fifth-generation video iPods, iPod nano, fourth-generation iPods, iPod mini, iPod U2 Special Edition, and color-display iPod, follow these steps:

1. **Be sure your iPod is charged with power.**

   If your iPod needs to be recharged, connect it to a power source as described in Chapter 1.

2. **Reset the iPod.**

   If you don't know how to reset your iPod, see the "Resetting the iPod" section, earlier in this chapter.

3. **When the Apple icon appears on the display, immediately press and hold the Select and Play/Pause buttons until OK to disconnect and Disk Mode appears on the iPod display.**

4. **If your iPod isn't connected to your computer, disconnect the iPod from the power adapter and connect it to your computer.**

   You can now use the iPod Updater to update or restore the iPod — see "Using iPod Updater" later in this chapter.

If the OK to disconnect and Disk Mode messages don't appear, repeat Steps 2 and 3. (You might need to press the buttons more quickly.) If, after repeating these steps, the message still doesn't appear, the iPod might need to be repaired.

For first-, second-, and third-generation iPod models, follow these steps:

1. **Connect the iPod to your computer's FireWire or powered USB connection, or to an AC power adapter.**

   This procedure doesn't work with older USB connections that don't provide power. Make sure the computer is on and isn't set to go to sleep.

2. **Reset the iPod.**

If you're not sure how to reset your iPod, see the "Resetting the iPod" section earlier in this chapter.

3. **When the Apple icon appears on the display, immediately press and hold the Previous and Next buttons until the Do not disconnect message or FireWire icon appears.**

4. **If your iPod isn't connected to your computer, disconnect the iPod from the power adapter and connect it to your computer.**

   Some iPods show the message OK to Disconnect before you connect it to the computer. This changes to the Do not disconnect message after you connect it.

   You can now use the iPod Updater to update or restore the iPod — see "Using iPod Updater" later in this chapter.

If the Do not disconnect message or FireWire icon doesn't appear, repeat Steps 2 and 3. (You might need to press the buttons more quickly.) If the message or FireWire icon still doesn't appear, the iPod might need to be repaired.

After using the iPod in Disk Mode, you need to reset the iPod (as described in "Resetting the iPod" earlier in this chapter) to return your iPod to normal operation.

You can get more information, updated troubleshooting instructions, and links to the iPod repair site by visiting the Apple support site for the iPod (www.apple.com/support/ipod).

Using iPod Updater

When you turn on your iPod, built-in startup diagnostic software checks the iPod hard drive for damage and attempts to repair it if necessary. If the iPod finds an issue while it's on, it automatically uses internal diagnostics to repair any damage. You might see a disk scan icon on your iPod screen after turning it on, indicating that a problem was fixed. If see this indicator, update your iPod firmware and software with the iPod Updater.

The iPod Updater can update the system software that controls the iPod and can also update the firmware for the iPod's hard drive, if necessary. The update doesn't affect the music or data stored on iPod's drive. iPod Updater is provided on the CD-ROM that comes with your iPod, and updates are automatically downloaded along with Mac system updates for Mac users. To check for the availability of an updated version for Windows, choose Help⇨ Check for iTunes Updates. You can also find out whether a new version is available by visiting the Apple download page for the iPod Updater (`www.apple.com/ipod/download`).

If you use Musicmatch Jukebox rather than iTunes on your Windows PC, skip this section and see this book's companion Web site at www.dummies.com/go/ipod4e to use iPod Updater with Musicmatch.

If you use a Mac and you've turned on the Software Update option in your System Preferences, Apple automatically informs you of updates to your Apple software for the Mac, including iTunes, iCal, Address Book, and the iPod system software. All you need to do is select which updates to download and click the Install button to download them.

Before downloading the iPod Updater from the Apple download page, make sure that you pick the appropriate version — Mac or Windows. The iPod Updater includes updates for all generations of iPods and can detect which iPod you have.

Checking for the iPod Updater version

To determine which version of the iPod software is installed on your iPod, choose Settings⇨About from the iPod main menu. (With first- and second-generation iPods, choose Settings⇨Info.) You see information, next to the word Version, that describes the software version installed on the iPod.

You can also determine the software version on your iPod by using iPod Updater. Connect the iPod to your computer and launch iPod Updater. The iPod Updater window appears. The software version appears next to the Software Version heading. If this version of the iPod Updater application has a newer software version that it can install on the iPod, you see (`needs update`) next to the version number; if not, you see (`up to date`).

Updating the iPod Updater

To update the iPod's firmware and software, download the newest version of the iPod Updater and then connect your iPod to your computer. If the newly downloaded iPod Updater contains newer software for your iPod, the program launches automatically, and you see a message to update your iPod software. In Windows, click Run Updater to start the iPod Updater program and then click Update to start the process. On a Mac, click OK to install the software update.

You can also launch iPod Updater manually. Follow these steps for both the Mac and Windows versions:

1. **Connect the iPod to your computer.**

   iTunes opens (unless you have set your iTunes preferences for the IPod not to open iTunes automatically; see Chapter 12 for details about iPod preferences in iTunes).

2. **Prevent the automatic update by pressing ⌘-Option (Mac) or Ctrl-Alt (Windows).**

3. **Quit iTunes.**

   On a Mac, choose iTunes⇨Quit iTunes. In Windows, choose File⇨Exit.

4. **Launch the iPod Updater application.**

   On a Mac, this application is located in the Utilities folder, which is in your Applications folder. On a Windows PC, choose Start⇨iPod.

   The Updater dialog appears, as shown in Figure 26-1 (Mac version) and Figure 26-2 (Windows version).

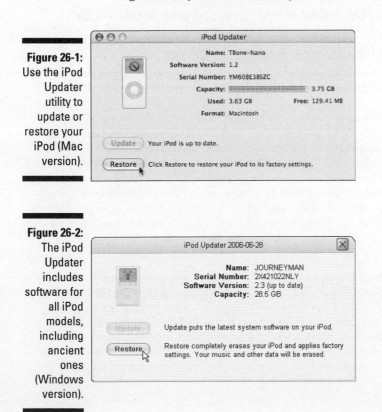

Figure 26-1: Use the iPod Updater utility to update or restore your iPod (Mac version).

Figure 26-2: The iPod Updater includes software for all iPod models, including ancient ones (Windows version).

5. **Click the Update button.**

In Mac OS X, you might need to click the padlock and type an administrator account name and password first.

If the Update button is grayed out, the software on the iPod is the same version or a newer version than the iPod Updater application.

Note: The Update button is grayed out if the iPod isn't properly formatted for Windows. It might be formatted for a Mac. You must use the Restore button and restore the iPod to its original factory condition, erasing all music and data, to reformat it for Windows.

6. **Follow the instructions to disconnect your iPod and connect it to an AC power adapter, if required.**

You need to disconnect some older iPod models temporarily and connect the iPod to an AC power adapter during the process of updating the software. If you see a message asking you to disconnect the iPod, follow the instructions displayed with the message. You might also need to reconnect some iPod models to the computer after this process.

The iPod Updater notifies you when the update is finished, and the Update button is grayed-out, indicating that your iPod no longer needs an update.

7. **When the update is finished, quit iPod Updater.**

On a Mac, choose iPod Updater⇨Quit iPod Updater. In Windows, quit by clicking the dialog's Close button.

8. **Eject the iPod.**

When you quit iPod Updater, iTunes might launch again because your iPod is still connected. You can eject the iPod by clicking the iPod Eject button in iTunes.

After ejecting the iPod, wait for its display to show the main menu or the OK to disconnect message. You can then disconnect the iPod from its dock or disconnect the dock from the computer. Don't ever disconnect an iPod before ejecting it, because you might have to reset your iPod.

Restoring an iPod with iPod Updater

Restoring the iPod erases the iPod's hard drive and returns the device to its original factory settings, so make sure that you back up any important data that you keep stored on your iPod. To replace music that was erased by the restore operation, synchronize or update your iPod from your computer's music library, as we describe in Chapter 12.

To restore an iPod, follow these steps for both the Mac and Windows versions:

1. **Connect the iPod to your computer.**

   iTunes opens (unless you have set your iTunes preferences for the iPod not to open iTunes automatically; see Chapter 12 for details about iPod preferences in iTunes).

2. **Prevent the automatic update by pressing ⌘-Option (Mac), or Ctrl-Alt (Windows).**

3. **Quit iTunes.**

   On a Mac, choose iTunes➪Quit iTunes. In Windows, choose File➪Exit.

4. **Launch the iPod Updater application.**

   On a Mac, this application is located in the Utilities folder, which is in your Applications folder. In Windows, choose Start➪iPod.

   The Updater dialog appears; refer to Figure 26-1 and Figure 26-2.

5. **Click the Restore button.**

   In Mac OS X, you might need to click the padlock and type an administrator account name and password first.

   An alert dialog appears to confirm that you want to restore iPod.

6. **Click the Restore button again to confirm the restore operation.**

   A progress bar appears, indicating the progress of the restore operation.

7. **Follow the instructions to disconnect your iPod and connect it to an AC power adapter, if required.**

   You might need to disconnect your iPod temporarily and connect it to an AC power adapter after the restore operation and during the process of updating the software. If you see a message asking you to disconnect the iPod, follow the instructions displayed with the message. You might also need to reconnect your iPod to the computer after this process.

   The iPod Updater notifies you when the restore is finished, and the Update button is grayed out, indicating that your iPod no longer needs an update.

8. **When the restore operation is finished, quit iPod Updater.**

   On a Mac, choose iPod Updater➪Quit iPod Updater. In Windows, click the dialog's Close button.

9. **Synchronize your iPod with content from your iTunes library.**

   Update your iPod with the content in your library, as we describe in Chapter 12. You can also copy data to the iPod while it's mounted as a hard drive; see Chapter 23.

 10. **When you finish synchronizing the iPod with content and data, eject the iPod by clicking the Eject button.**

Part VI
The Part of Tens

The 5th Wave   By Rich Tennant

@RICHTENNANT

iPod Knockoff ...

THE HANDPOD

"I understand how the thumb is the navigator, but why does this finger have to be the antenna?"

In this part . . .

In this part, you find two chapters chock full of information.

- Chapter 27 offers 10 common iPod problems and their solutions.
- Chapter 28 provides 11 tips on using the equalizer.

Chapter 27

Ten iPod Problems and Solutions

*U*nfortunately, humans and the machines they make are not perfect. Even though we think the iPod comes as close to perfection as possible, at some point your iPod isn't going to work as you expect it to. When that happens, turn to this chapter. Here we show you how to fix the most common problems.

How Do I Get My iPod to Wake Up?

If your iPod doesn't turn on, don't panic — at least not yet. Try the following suggestions to get your iPod to respond:

- **Check the Hold switch's position on top of the iPod.** The Hold switch locks the iPod buttons so you don't accidentally activate them. Slide the Hold switch away from the headphone connection, hiding the orange layer, to unlock the buttons.

- **See whether the iPod has enough juice.** Is the battery charged? Connect the iPod to a power source and see whether it works.

- **Reset your iPod if the iPod still doesn't turn on.** See Chapter 26 for resetting instructions.

If your iPod shuffle doesn't turn on or respond, recharge its battery by connecting it to the USB connection on your computer. If the iPod shuffle status light blinks orange when you press a button, it means the buttons are disabled. Press and hold the Play/Pause button for at least three seconds or until the status light blinks green.

How Do I Get My Battery to Last Longer?

You can do a lot to keep your battery going longer (much to the envy of your friends), including the following:

- ✔ **Press the Play/Pause button to pause (stop) playback.** Don't just turn off your car or home stereo or remove your headphones — if you don't also pause playback, your iPod continues playing until the playlist or album ends. When playback is paused, the power-save feature turns off the iPod after two minutes of inactivity.

- ✔ **Press and hold the Play/Pause button to turn off the iPod when you're not using it.** Rather than wait for two minutes of inactivity for the power-save feature to turn off the iPod, you can turn it off yourself and save battery time.

- ✔ **Turn off the backlighting.** If you don't need to use backlighting, turn it off. It can drain the power.

- ✔ **Set the Hold switch to lock when you're not using the iPod.** Keep your iPod controls locked so that they don't accidentally turn on your iPod when you're not using it.

- ✔ **Avoid changing tracks by pressing the Previous/Rewind or Next/Fast-Forward buttons.** The iPod uses a memory cache to load and play songs. If you frequently change tracks by pressing the Previous or Next buttons, the cache has to turn on the hard drive to load and play the songs, which drains the battery.

- ✔ **Use compressed AAC or MP3 files.** Playing larger uncompressed AIFF or WAV files takes more power because the hard drive inside the iPod has to refresh its memory buffers more frequently to process more information as the song plays. Apple Lossless files, though compressed, also deplete battery power a bit more than AAC or MP3 files.

How Do I Keep My Scroll Wheel from Going Crazy?

Occasionally an iPod's scroll wheel stops working properly. If the scroll wheel doesn't scroll, try resetting the iPod as described in Chapter 26. *Remember:* Resetting the iPod doesn't change the iPod's contents. After resetting, the iPod should work properly.

Second- and third-generation iPods use a nonmoving scroll wheel that works like the *trackpad* (also sometimes called a *touchpad*) of a laptop computer. Although the trackpad-style scroll wheel is far better than the first-generation moving wheel (which could be hampered by sand or dirt and had moving parts that could be damaged), it has problems of its own: It goes crazy sometimes, and it can be very sensitive — not sensitive to criticism but to the touch of your finger.

The trackpad-style scroll wheel translates the electrical charge from your finger into movement on the iPod display. If you use more than one finger or have another finger nearby, the scroll wheel might detect the signal and skip over selections or go backward while scrolling forward, and so on. If the scroll wheel has excessive moisture on it from humidity or a wet hand, wipe the wheel with a soft, dry cloth.

Don't use lotion or moisturizer on your hand right before touching the scroll wheel. Don't use pencil erasers, pen caps, or other types of pointers to scroll the scroll wheel. (They won't work with trackpad-style scroll wheels and might damage other types of scroll wheels.) Don't use your ring finger or the hand that sports a heavy bracelet or similar jewelry — these can throw off the sensors in the scroll wheel.

How Do I Get My Computer to Recognize My iPod?

Follow the first troubleshooting steps outlined in Chapter 26. If these steps don't fix the problem, make sure that the iPod is securely connected to your computer's USB connection (or FireWire connection in older models), and that it is the *only* device using that connection. (If you use a hub to share devices, try not using the hub for a change, to see whether it works without the hub.)

If iTunes or Musicmatch Jukebox still does not recognize the iPod, you can use the iPod Updater to restore the iPod.

If you're using Musicmatch, go to this book's companion Web site at www. dummies.com/go/ipod for more troubleshooting tips.

Also, make sure that your USB or FireWire cable is in good condition for connecting to your computer. For iPods that work with either FireWire or USB, try one type of connection or the other; if one connection type works but not the other, the problem is probably not in your iPod. Try connecting your iPod to another computer by using the same type of connection to see whether the same problem occurs. (Your computer might be to blame.) If the same type of connection (FireWire or USB) to the other computer works, the problem is most likely your computer's connection or software. If it doesn't work, the problem is most likely your cable or connection. You can try a new cable to see whether that works, or try the same type of connection with a different computer. While these suggestions seem obvious, doing them in the right order can help you diagnose the problem.

What Do I Do If a Strange Icon Appears on My iPod?

If you see a circle with a diagonal line across it, you should also see the words Do not disconnect. Don't do anything until it finishes its update and displays the main menu or the OK to disconnect message. If this symbol stays on for a very, very long time (like, 20 minutes), try resetting the iPod as described in Chapter 26.

Other strange icons are possible. When you turn on your iPod, built-in diagnostic software checks the iPod hard drive. If the iPod finds a problem when it's turned on, it automatically uses internal diagnostics to check for and repair any damage. You might see a disk scan icon on your iPod screen after turning it on, indicating that a problem was fixed. If this happens, restore your iPod to its original factory condition (see Chapter 26), and reload content into it.

If the iPod displays any other strange icon, such as a backwards Apple logo, a disk icon with a flashing question mark, or the dreaded disk-with-magnifying glass icon, it might need to be repaired. If you get the "sad iPod" icon (with a frown and asterisks for eyes) or the folder icon with an exclamation point, try the troubleshooting steps in Chapter 26, including setting your iPod in Disk Mode if necessary (which is equivalent to pressing the panic button before resorting to restoring). If nothing seems to work, the iPod probably needs to be repaired. You can arrange for repair by visiting the Apple support site for the iPod (www.apple.com/support/ipod).

How Do I Restore My iPod to Its Original Condition from the Factory?

Restoring the iPod erases its hard drive and returns the device to its original factory condition. Restoring erases all the data on the hard drive, so make sure that you back up any important data that you have stored on your iPod. You can use the iPod Updater utility to restore your iPod, as we describe in Chapter 26. When finished, add music back to your iPod from the iTunes library or from your Musicmatch Jukebox library and then resynchronize your iPod with calendar and contact information.

If you're using Musicmatch, check out the companion Web site available at www.dummies.com/go/ipod4e to find out how to fill your iPod with music.

How Do I Update My iPod's Software?

To determine which version of the iPod software is installed on your iPod, press the Menu button until you see the iPod main menu, and then choose Settings➪About (in earlier versions, choose Settings➪Info). Look at the version number that describes the software version installed on your iPod. You can use the iPod Updater application to check which software version you're using and to update or restore your iPod (see Chapter 26).

How Do I Update My iPod Content When My Library Is Larger Than My iPod's Capacity?

If you have less space on your iPod than content in your iTunes library, you can update manually, update automatically by selected content only, or update automatically by playlist. You can also change the iPod preferences in iTunes for each iPod to be more discriminating about how you update each iPod automatically. You can, for example, limit the photos to specific photo albums or limit the videos to certain playlists.

When you update by playlist automatically, you can create playlists exclusively for your iPod. You can also limit a smart playlist to, for example, 18GB (for a 20GB iPod).

By combining the features of smart playlists (Chapter 10) and updating automatically by playlist (Chapter 12), you can control the updating process while also automatically limiting the amount of content you copy to your iPod.

You can also update automatically and keep your iPod synchronized to a subset of your library. iTunes creates a new playlist specially designed for updating your iPod automatically — a smart playlist named "*your iPod name* Selection." iTunes decides which songs and albums to include in this playlist by using the ratings that you can set for each song in the iTunes song information, as we describe in Chapter 9.

How Do I Cross-Fade Music Playback with My iPod?

You can fade the ending of one song into the beginning of the next one to slightly overlap songs, just like a radio DJ, when you use iTunes. The *cross-fade setting* is the amount of time between the end of the fade-out from the first song and the start of the fade-in to the second song.

To cross-fade songs on your iPod, you have to play your iPod songs through iTunes on your computer. Connect your iPod to your computer and connect your computer to a stereo or connect speakers (or headphones) to your computer. Press ⌘-Option (Mac) or Ctrl-Alt (Windows) as you launch iTunes and then select iPod in the iTunes Source pane.

By default, iTunes is set to have a short cross-fade of one second.

If you're playing songs on an iPod that's connected to your computer and also playing songs from your iTunes library (or even on a second iPod, both connected to your computer), your songs cross-fade automatically.

You can change this cross-fade setting by choosing iTunes⇨Preferences (Mac) or Edit⇨Preferences (Windows) and then clicking the Playback tab. You can then increase or decrease the amount of the cross-fade with the Crossfade Playback option.

How Do I Decrease Distortion or Set a Lower Volume?

iPod models designed for the Unites States have a powerful 60-milliwatt amplifier to deliver audio signals through the headphone connection. It has a frequency response of 20 Hz to 20 kHz, which provides distortion-free music at the lowest or highest pitches, but it might cause distortion at maximum volume depending on the recorded material — not to mention ear damage.

For optimal sound quality, set the iPod volume at no more than three-quarters of the maximum volume and adjust your listening volume by using the volume control or equivalent on your car stereo or portable speaker system. (If no volume control exists, you have no choice but to control the volume from the iPod.) By lowering the iPod from maximum volume, you give your ears a break and also prevent over-amplification, which can cause distortion and reduce audio quality. See Chapter 15 for details on how to set the iPod's volume limit and adjust the iPod volume.

Chapter 28

Eleven Tips for the Equalizer

. . . .

In This Chapter

▶ Adjusting the equalizer on your home stereo

▶ Taking advantage of the iPod's equalizer preset

▶ Getting rid of unwanted noise

. . . .

You play your iPod in many environments. The same song that sounds like music to your ears in your car might sound like screeching hyenas on a plane. In this chapter, we show you how to fix most sound problems that occur with iPods. Soon you'll be cruising to the beat all the time — no matter where you are.

Setting the Volume to the Right Level

Before using the iPod equalizer (EQ) to refine the sound, make sure the volume of the iPod is set to about half or three-quarters (not more) so that you don't introduce distortion — see Chapter 15 for details on how to set the iPod's volume limit and adjust the volume. Then set your speaker system or home stereo volume before trying to refine the sound with equalizers.

Adjusting Another Equalizer

When you have the iPod connected to another system with an equalizer, try adjusting that equalizer:

✔ **Home stereo system:** Refine the sound with your home stereo's equalizer because it might offer more flexibility and can be set precisely for the listening environment.

✔ **Car stereos:** The same rule applies as your home stereo: Adjust the car stereo's equalizer as you begin to listen to music on your iPod, before adjusting the iPod's equalizer.

Setting Booster Presets

When playing music with your iPod through a home stereo or speakers (without a built-in equalizer) in a heavily draped and furnished room, try the iPod's Treble Booster EQ preset or create your own EQ preset (see Chapter 17) that raises the frequencies above 1 kHz. Boosting these higher frequencies makes the music sound naturally alive.

Reducing High Frequencies

When using your iPod to play music through a home stereo (without a built-in equalizer) in a basement with smooth, hard walls and concrete floors, you might want to use the iPod's Treble Reducer EQ preset, which reduces the high frequencies to make the sound less brittle.

Increasing Low Frequencies

If you use high-quality, acoustic-suspension compact speakers, you might need to add a boost to the low frequencies (bass) with the Bass Booster EQ preset so that you can boogie with the beat a little better. The Small Speakers EQ preset also boosts the low frequencies and lowers the high frequencies to give you a fuller sound.

Setting Presets for Trucks and SUVs

We use our iPods in different types of cars — one is a sedan; the other a 4-wheel drive truck. Trucks need more bass and treble, and the Rock EQ preset sounds good for most of the music that we listen to. We also recommend the Bass Booster EQ preset when using your iPod in a truck if the Rock preset doesn't boost the bass enough. In the sedan, the iPod sounds fine without any equalizer adjustment.

Setting Presets When You're Eight Miles High

When using your iPod on an airplane where jet noise is a factor, try using the Bass Booster EQ preset to hear the lower frequencies in your headphones and compensate for the deficiencies of headphones in loud environments. You might want to use the Classical EQ preset, which boosts both the high and low frequencies for extra treble and bass. Try the Bose QuietComfort 3 Acoustic Noise Canceling headphones (www.bose.com) for plane travel — they work great!

If you're in an unpressurized environment at or above 10,000 feet — such as a mountain peak — don't try to use a full-size iPod. Leave it turned off. Like many laptops, iPods that use hard drives can fail if operated at altitudes above 10,000 feet. The drive heads float above the recording surface on a small cushion of air produced by the spinning platters, and if the air is too thin to create this cushion, the heads may contact the surface, possibly even damaging it.

Reducing Tape Noise and Scratch Sounds

To reduce the hiss of an old tape recording or the scratchy sound of songs recorded from an old vinyl record, reduce the highest frequencies with the Treble Reducer EQ preset.

Reducing Turntable Rumble and Hum

To reduce the low-frequency rumble in songs recorded from a turntable (for vinyl records) or recorded with a hum pickup, choose the Bass Reducer EQ preset.

Reducing Off-Frequency Harshness and Nasal Vocals

To reduce a particularly nasal vocal sound reminiscent of Donald Duck (caused by off-frequency recording of the song source, making the song more harsh-sounding), try the R&B EQ preset, which reduces the midrange frequencies while boosting all the other frequencies.

Cranking Up the Volume to Eleven

If you want that larger-than-life sound, use the Loudness preset and then jack up the Preamp slider to the max, turn up your stereo all the way, and put your fingers in your ears to protect them. Then consult the DVD *This Is Spinal Tap* or the Spinal Tap fan site at `http://spinaltapfan.com`.

Index